Lecture Notes in Computer Science 9873

Commenced Publication in 1973
Founding and Former Series Editors:
Gerhard Goos, Juris Hartmanis, and Jan van Leeuwen

More information about this series at http://www.springer.com/series/7407

Bijaya Ketan Panigrahi
Ponnuthurai Nagaratnam Suganthan
Swagatam Das · Suresh Chandra Satapathy (Eds.)

Swarm, Evolutionary, and Memetic Computing

6th International Conference, SEMCCO 2015
Hyderabad, India, December 18–19, 2015
Revised Selected Papers

 Springer

Editors
Bijaya Ketan Panigrahi
IIT
New Dehli
India

Ponnuthurai Nagaratnam Suganthan
Nanyang Technological University
Singapore
Singapore

Swagatam Das
Indian Statistical Institute
Kolkata
India

Suresh Chandra Satapathy
Department of Computer Science
  Engineering
Anil Neerukonda Institute of Technology
  and Sciences
Visakhapatnam
India

ISSN 0302-9743   ISSN 1611-3349 (electronic)
Lecture Notes in Computer Science
ISBN 978-3-319-48958-2   ISBN 978-3-319-48959-9 (eBook)
DOI 10.1007/978-3-319-48959-9

Library of Congress Control Number: 2016956619

LNCS Sublibrary: SL1 – Theoretical Computer Science and General Issues

Printed on acid-free paper

This Springer imprint is published by Springer Nature
The registered company is Springer International Publishing AG
The registered company address is: Gewerbestrasse 11, 6330 Cham, Switzerland

Preface

This LNCS volume contains the papers presented at the 6th Swarm, Evolutionary and Memetic Computing Conference (SEMCCO 2015) held during December 18–19, 2015, at CMR Technical Campus, Hyderabad, India. SEMCCO is regarded as one of the prestigious international conference series that aims at bringing together researchers from academia and industry to report and review the latest progress in cutting-edge research on swarm, evolutionary, memetic computing, and other novel computing techniques like neural and fuzzy computing, to explore new application areas, to design new bio-inspired algorithms for solving specific hard optimization problems, and finally to raise awareness of these domains in a wider audience of practitioners.

SEMCCO 2015 received 150 paper submissions from 12 countries across the globe. After a rigorous peer-review process involving 400 reviews in total, 40 full-length articles were accepted for oral presentation at the conference. This corresponds to an acceptance rate of 27 % and is intended for maintaining the high standards of the conference proceedings. The papers included in this LNCS volume cover a wide range of topics in swarm, evolutionary, memetic, and other intelligent computing algorithms and their real-world applications in problems selected from diverse domains of science and engineering.

The conference featured the following distinguished keynote speakers: Dr. P.N. Suganthan, NTU, Singapore, and Dr. Rammohan Mallipeddi, Kyungpook National University, South Korea.

We take this opportunity to thank the authors of all submitted papers for their hard work, adherence to the deadlines, and patience with the review process. The quality of a refereed volume depends mainly on the expertise and dedication of the reviewers. We are indebted to the Program Committee/Technical Committee members who not only produced excellent reviews but also did so in the short time frames that they were given.

We would also like to thank our sponsors for providing all the logistic support and financial assistance. First, we are indebted to Management and Administrations (faculty colleagues and administrative personnel) of CMR Technical Campus, Hyderabad. We thank Prof. Carlos A. Coello Coello, and Prof Nikhil R. Pal, the General Chairs, for providing valuable guidelines and inspiration to overcome various difficulties in the process of organizing this conference. We would also like to thank the participants of this conference. Finally, we would like to thank all the volunteers for their tireless efforts in meeting the deadlines and arranging every detail to make sure that the conference could run smoothly. We hope the readers of these proceedings and the participants of the conference found the papers and conference inspiring and enjoyable.

December 2015

Bijaya Ketan Panigrahi
P.N. Suganthan
Swagatam Das
S.C. Satpathy

Organization

General Chairs

Nikhil R. Pal   Indian Statistical Institute, Kolkata, India
Carlos A. Coello   Instituto Politécnico Nacional, México
  Coello

General Co-chairs

Swagatam Das   Indian Statistical Institute, Kolkata, India
B.K. Panigrahi   IIT Delhi, New Delhi, India

Program Chair

S.C. Satapathy   Anil Neerukonda Institute of Technology and Sciences, Visakhapatnam, India

Finance Chair

Srujan Raju   CMR Technical Campus, Hyderabad, India

Steering Committee Chair

P.N. Suganthan   NTU, Singapore

Special Session Chairs

Sanjoy Das   Kansas State University, Kansas, USA
Zhihua Cui   Taiyuan University of Science and Technology, China
Samuelson Hong   Oriental Institute of Technology, Taiwan

International Advisory Committee/Technical Review Committee

Almoataz Youssef Abdelaziz, Egypt
Athanasios V. Vasilakos, Athens, Greece
Alex K. Qin, France
Amit Konar, India
Anupam Shukla, India
Ashish Anand, India
Boyang Qu, China

Carlos A. Coello Coello, Mexico
Chilukuri K. Mohan, USA
Delin Luo, China
Dipankar Dasgupta, USA
D.K. Chaturvedi, India
Dipti Srinivasan, Singapore
Fatih M. Tasgetiren, Turkey

Frank Neumann, Australia
Fayzur Rahman, Portugal
G.K. Venayagamoorthy, USA
Gerardo Beni, USA
Hai Bin Duan, China
Heitor Silvério Lopes, Brazil
Halina Kwasnicka, Poland
Hong Yan, Hong Kong, SAR China
Javier Del Ser, Spain
Jane J. Liang, China
Janez Brest, Slovenia
Jeng-Shyang Pan, Taiwan
Juan Luis Fernández Martínez, Spain
Jeng-Shyang Pan, Taiwan
Kalyanmoy Deb, India
K. Parsopoulos, Greece
Kay Chen Tan, Singapore
Ke Tang, China
K. Shanti Swarup, India
Lakhmi Jain, Australia
Leandro Dos Santos Coelho, Brazil
Ling Wang, China
Lingfeng Wang, China
M.A. Abido, Saudi Arabia
M.K. Tiwari, India
Maurice Clerc, France
Meng Joo Er, Singapore
Meng-Hiot Lim, Singapore
M.F. Tasgetiren, Turkey

Namrata Khemka, USA
N. Puhan, India
Oscar Castillo, Mexico
Pei-Chann Chang, Taiwan
Peng Shi, UK
Qingfu Zhang, UK
Quanke Pan, China
Rafael Stubs Parpinelli, Brazil
Rammohan Mallipeddi, Singapore
Roderich Gross, UK
Ruhul Sarker, Australia
Richa Sing, India
Robert Kozma, USA
Suresh Sundaram, Singapore
S. Baskar, India
S.K. Udgata, India
S.S. Dash, India
S.S. Pattanaik, India
S.G. Ponnambalam, Malaysia
Saeid Nahavandi, Australia
Saman Halgamuge, Australia
Shizheng Zhao, Singapore
Sachidananda Dehuri, Korea
Samuelson W. Hong, Taiwan
Vincenzo Piuri, Italy
X.Z. Gao, Finland
Yew Soon Ong, Singapore
Ying Tan, China
Yucheng Dong, China

Contents

Self-adaptive Ensemble Differential Evolution with Sampled Parameter Values for Unit Commitment

Nandar Lynn[1], Rammohan Mallipeddi[2],
and Ponnuthurai Nagaratnam Suganthan[1(✉)]

[1] School of Electrical and Electronics Engineering,
Nanyang Technological University, Singapore, Singapore
{nandar001, epnsugan}@ntu.edu.sg
[2] School of Electronics Engineering, Kyungpook National University,
Daegu, South Korea
mallipeddi.ram@gmail.com

Abstract. In literature, empirically and theoretically, it has been well-demonstrated that the performance of differential evolution (DE) is sensitive to the choice of the mutation and crossover strategies and their associated control parameters. According to the No Free Lunch theorem, a single set of well-tuned combination of strategies and their associated parameter combination is not suitable for optimization problems having different characteristics. In addition, different mutation and crossover strategies with different parameter settings can be appropriate during different stages of the evolution. Based on this observation, DE with an ensemble of mutation and crossover strategies and their associated control parameters referred to as EPSDE was proposed. However, it has been observed that the fixed discrete parameter values as in EPSDE may not yield optimal performance. In this paper, we propose self-adaptive DE algorithm (Sa-EPSDE) with a set of mutation strategies while their associated parameter values F and CR are sampled using mean and standard deviation values. In addition, the probability of selecting a combination to produce an offspring at a particular generation during the evolution process depends on the success of the combination. The performance of the proposed Sa-EPSDE algorithm is evaluated on a set of 14 bound-constrained problems designed for Conference on Evolutionary Computation (CEC) 2005. In order to validate the performance of proposed Sa-EPSDE algorithm on real-world applications, the algorithm is hybridized with a simple priority listing method and applied to solve unit commitment problem by considering 10-, 20-, 40-, 60-, 80- and 100-bus systems for one day scheduling period. The results showed that the proposed method obtained superior performance against other compared algorithms.

Keywords: Differential evolution · Global optimization · Parameter adaptation · Ensemble · Mutation strategy adaptation · Unit commitment · Scheduling

© Springer International Publishing AG 2016
B.K. Panigrahi et al. (Eds.): SEMCCO 2015, LNCS 9873, pp. 1–16, 2016.
DOI: 10.1007/978-3-319-48959-9_1

1 Introduction

Differential Evolution (DE) [1] is a simple and efficient population based stochastic search technique that is inherently parallel. Due to its ability to handle a variety of optimization problems, DE is being employed in diverse fields of science and engineering [2–5]. During the last decade, significant research has been done to improve the search performance of DE. However, to face the challenges posed by the modern application areas, the performance of DE needs to be enhanced further.

Experimentally [6, 7] and theoretically [8], it has been verified that the performance of DE is sensitive to the mutation strategy, crossover strategy and intrinsic control parameters such as population size (NP), crossover rate (CR) and scale factor (F). In other words, the best combination of strategies and their associated control parameters can be different for different optimization problems. In addition, for the same optimization problem the best combination can vary depending on the available computational resources and accuracy requirements [9]. Therefore, to successfully solve a specific optimization problem, it is necessary to perform trial-and-error search for the most appropriate combination of strategies and their associated parameter values. However, the trial-and-error search process is time-consuming and incurs high computational costs. Therefore, to overcome the time consuming trial-and-error procedure, DE algorithm with different adaptation schemes [10–13] have been proposed in the literature. In addition, motivated by the observation that during the evolution process the population of DE may traverse through different regions in the search space, within which different strategies with different parameter settings may be more effective than others, in [9, 14] the authors proposed a DE algorithm (EPSDE) based on the idea of ensemble strategies and parameters. In EPSDE [14], pools of distinct mutation and crossover strategies along with pools of distinct parameters values for each control parameter (F and CR) coexist throughout the evolution process and compete to produce offspring population.

From the literature, it is observed that ensemble of parameters and strategies with their associated parameters shows significant impact on the performance of the DE algorithms. However, it has been observed that the performance of the DE algorithm can be improved by using parameter values sampled from distributions whose mean values are distributed with the range of the parameters [15, 16]. In addition, during every generation the number offspring members produced by a combination in the ensemble depend on its performance during the previous few generations of the evolution. In other words, the probability of a combination producing an offspring in the current generation depends on its performance during the previous generations of the evolution. The reminder of this paper is organized as follows: Sect. 2 presents a brief overview of the differential evolution algorithm and a literature survey on the variants of DE algorithms. Section 3 presents the proposed Sa-EPSDE algorithm. The performance of proposed Sa-EPSDE is evaluated using numerical benchmark problems in Sect. 4 and unit commitment problem in Sect. 5. Finally, the paper is concluded in Sect. 6.

2   Literature Review

2.1   Differential Evolution

Differential Evolution (DE) being a parallel direct search method utilizes NP D-dimensional parameter vectors, so-called individuals, which encode the candidate solutions, i.e. $X_{i,G} = \left\{ x_{i,G}^1, \ldots, x_{i,G}^D \right\}, i = 1, \ldots, NP$. G represents the generation count. The uniform randomization of the initial population tries to cover the search space constrained by the prescribed minimum and maximum parameter bounds, $X_{min} = \{x_{min}^1, \ldots, x_{min}^D\}$ and $X_{max} = \{x_{max}^1, \ldots, x_{max}^D\}$, as much as possible. For example, the initial value of the jth parameter of the ith individual at generation $G = 0$ is generated by:

$$x_{i,0}^j = x_{min}^j + rand^j(0,1).\left(x_{max}^j - x_{min}^j\right) j = 1, 2, \ldots, D \qquad (1)$$

where $rand^j(0,1)$ is a uniformly distributed random variable in the range [0,1) [19].

After initialization, DE employs mutation operation to produce mutant vector $V_{i,G}$ corresponding to each individual $X_{i,G}$, so-called target vector, in the current population. For each target vector $X_{i,G}$ in generation G, its associated mutant vector can be generated via mutation strategy. The most frequently used mutation strategies are [9]:
"DE/best/1":

$$V_{i,G} = X_{best,G} + F.(X_{r_1^i,G} - X_{r_2^i,G}) \qquad (2)$$

"DE/best/2":

$$V_{i,G} = X_{best,G} + F.(X_{r_1^i,G} - X_{r_2^i,G}) + F.(X_{r_3^i,G} - X_{r_4^i,G}) \qquad (3)$$

"DE/rand/1":

$$V_{i,G} = X_{r_1^i,G} + F.(X_{r_2^i,G} - X_{r_3^i,G}) \qquad (4)$$

"DE/rand/2":

$$V_{i,G} = X_{r_1^i,G} + F.(X_{r_2^i,G} - X_{r_3^i,G}) + F.(X_{r_4^i,G} - X_{r_5^i,G}) \qquad (5)$$

"DE/current-to-rand/1":

$$U_{i,G} = X_{i,G} + K.(X_{r_1^i,G} - X_{i,G}) + F.(X_{r_2^i,G} - X_{r_3^i,G}) \qquad (6)$$

The indices $r_1^i, r_2^i, r_3^i, r_4^i, r_5^i$ are mutually exclusive integers randomly generated anew for each mutant vector within the range [1, NP], which are also different from the index i. $X_{best,G}$ is the best individual vector with the best fitness value in the population at generation G. K is randomly chosen within the range [0, 1]. In the above equations, the scale factor $F \in (0, 1+)$ [17] is a positive real number that controls the rate of population evolution. There are various claims and counter-claims regarding the suitable range of the F values [17]. However, F must be above a certain critical value to avoid premature convergence [6]. In addition, a larger F increases the probability of escaping from a local optimum [6]. But if F becomes too large, the number of function evaluations to find the optimum grows very quickly. In [18], it was theoretically proved that DE could converge to global optimum in the long time limit if F can be transformed into a Gaussian random variable. However, it was later demonstrated [17] that unless the variance of the randomizing distribution is very small, DE will suffer a significant performance loss on highly conditioned non-separable functions.

After the mutation, crossover operation is applied to each pair of the target vector $X_{i,G}$ and its corresponding mutant vector $V_{i,G}$ to generate a trial vector: $U_{i,G} = \{u^1_{i,G}, \ldots, u^D_{i,G}\}$. The crossover operation speeds the convergence by a constant factor [17]. In the basic version, DE employs the binomial crossover defined as follows:

$$u^j_{i,G} = \begin{cases} v^j_{i,G} & \text{if } (rand^j\,(0,1) \leq CR) \text{ or } (j=j_{rand}) \quad j=1,2,\ldots,D \\ x^j_{i,G} & \text{otherwise} \end{cases} \tag{7}$$

In Eq. (7), the crossover probability, $CR \in [0, 1]$ is a user-specified constant that controls the fraction of parameter values that are copied to the trail vector from the mutant vector. j_{rand} is a randomly chosen integer in the range $[1, D]$. The crossover rate (CR) is a probability ($0 \leq CR \leq 1$) of mixing between trial and target vectors and controls how many components are mutated in each element of the current population. In [6], various guidelines to select the appropriate values for a problem-at-hand were put forward. However, a simple guideline which states that small values are suitable for separable problems while larger values of CR are suitable for multi-modal, parameter dependent problems [17] is commonly used.

If generated trial vector exceeds the corresponding upper and lower bounds, it is randomly and uniformly reinitialized in the range of lower and upper bound. The objective function values of all trial vectors are evaluated. After crossover operation, a selection operation is performed. The fitness function value of each trial vector $f\,(U_{i,G})$ is compared to that of its corresponding target vector $f(X_{i,G})$. If the trial vector has less or equal fitness function value (in a minimization problem), the trial vector will replace the target vector and enter the population of the next generation. Otherwise, the target vector will remain in the population for the next generation. The selection operation can be expressed as follows:

$$X_{i,G+1} = \begin{cases} U_{i,G}, & \text{if } f(U_{i,G}) \leq f(X_{i,G}) \\ X_{i,G}, & \text{otherwise} \end{cases} \tag{8}$$

The 3 steps (mutation, crossover and selection) are repeated generation after generation until a termination criterion (reaching the maximum number of function evaluations set) is satisfied.

2.2   Literature Review

As DE is sensitive to parameter settings [7], to avoid manual tuning of parameter settings and to get an optimal performance, several variants of DE based on the adaptation and self-adaptation of mutation strategies and control parameters have been proposed. DE may suffer from stagnation and premature convergence due to improper selection of control parameters, parameters being kept fixed through the whole search process [19]. To overcome these problems FADE was proposed which adapts the control parameters F and CR based on fuzzy logic controllers whose inputs are the relative function values and individuals of successive generations to adapt the parameters for the mutation and crossover operation [19]. FADE enables to choose the initial control parameters freely and adjust the control parameters on-line to dynamically adapt to changing situations. A parameter adaptation of DE (ADE) based on controlling the population diversity and a multi-population approach was proposed [20]. In [10], a self-adaptation scheme (SDE) in which CR is generated randomly for each individual using a normal distribution $N(0.5, 0.15)$, while F is adapted analogous to the adaptation of crossover rate CR in [21].

DE can encompass a number of trial vector generation strategies, each of which may be effective over certain problems but poorly perform over the others. In [12], a self-adaptive DE algorithm (SaDE) was proposed in which the mutation strategies and the respective control parameter are self-adapted based on their previous experiences of generating promising solutions. F was randomly generated with a mean and standard deviation of 0.5 and 0.3 respectively. In SaDE, four effective trial vector generation strategies namely the DE/rand/1/bin, DE/rand-to-best/2/bin, DE/rand/2/bin and finally DE/current-to-rand/1 were chosen to constitute a strategy candidate pool. In SaDE algorithm, for each target vector in the current population, one trial vector generation strategy is selected from the candidate pool according to the probability learned from its success rate in generating improved solutions within a certain number of previous generations, called the Learning Period (LP). The selected strategy is subsequently applied to the corresponding target vector to generate a trial vector. More specifically, at each generation, the probabilities of choosing each strategy in the candidate pool are summed to 1. These probabilities are initially equal ($1/K$ for K strategies in the pool) and are then gradually adapted during evolution, based on the *Success and Failure Memories* ($ns_{k,g}$ and $nf_{k,g}$) over the previous LP generations. The adaptation of the probabilities take place in such a fashion that, the larger the success rate for the kth strategy in the pool within the previous LP generations, the larger is the probability of applying it to generate trial vectors at the current generation. The probability of selecting the strategies ($k = 1, 2... K$) in the pool is updated at the generation G using the following equation:

$$p_{k,G} = \frac{S_{k,G}}{\sum_{k=1}^{K} S_{k,G}} \qquad (9)$$

where,

$$S_{k,G} = \frac{\sum_{g=G-LP}^{G-1} nS_{k,g}}{\sum_{g=G-LP}^{G-1} nS_{k,g} + \sum_{g=G-LP}^{G-1} nf_{k,g}} + \varepsilon \qquad (10)$$

($k = 1, 2, .., K; G > LP$)

In Eq. (10), $S_{k,G}$ is the success rate of trail vectors generated by the kth strategy that can successfully enter the next generation within learning period LP. In order to avoid the null success rate, $\varepsilon = 0.01$ is used.

In JADE [22], a new mutation strategy "DE/current-to-pbest", a generalization of the classic "DE/current-to-best" was proposed. The reliability of the algorithm is further improved by the adaptive parameter control. "DE/current-to-pbest" utilizes not only the best solution information but also the information of other good solutions.

$$V_{i,G} = X_{i,G} + F_{i,G}.(X_{best,G}^{p} - X_{i,G}) + F_{i,G}.(X_{r_1^i,G} - X_{r_2^i,G}) \qquad (11)$$

$X_{best,G}^{p}$ is randomly chosen as one of the top $100p$ % individuals in the population with $p \in (0, 1]$. $F_{i,G}$ is the mutation factor of $X_{i,G}$, generated independently at each generation G, according to a Cauchy distribution as follows:

$$F_{i,G} = randc_i(\mu_F, 0.1) \qquad (12)$$

S_F denotes the set of all successful mutation factors in generation G. The location parameter μ_F is initialized to be 0.5 and then updated at the end of each generation as:

$$\mu_F = (1 - c).\mu_F + c.mean_L(S_F) \qquad (13)$$

$$mean_L = \frac{\sum_{F \in S_F} F^2}{\sum_{F \in S_F} F} \qquad (14)$$

where, $mean_L(.)$ is the Leher mean. $CR_{i,G}$ is the crossover probability of $X_{i,G}$, generated independently at each generation G, according to a normal distribution as follows:

$$CR_{i,G} = randn_i(\mu_{CR}, 0.1) \qquad (15)$$

S_{CR} denotes the set of all successful crossover probabilities in generation G. The mean μ_{CR} is initialized to be 0.5 and then updated at the end of each generation as:

$$\mu_{CR} = (1 - c).\mu_{CR} + c.mean_A(S_{CR}) \qquad (16)$$

where, $mean_A(.)$ is the usual arithmetic mean. JADE usually performs better with $1/c \in$ [5, 20] and $p \in$ [5 %, 20 %]; i.e., life span of μ_{CR} and μ_F values ranges from 5 to 20 generations and top 5–20 % high quality solutions are considered for mutation. In [15], an improved version of JADE called success history based adaptive DE (SHADE) algorithm was proposed in which history-based parameter adaptation scheme is used. In SHADE, F and CR values are generated using Eqs. (12) and (15) and mean values of successful F and CR are stored in historical memory. Linear population size reduction was introduced to improve the search performance of SHADE in [16].

3   Self-adaptive DE with Ensemble of Mutation Strategies and Sampled Parameter Values (Sa-EPSDE)

An ensemble of mutation strategies and parameter values for DE (EPSDE) in which a pool of mutation strategies, along with a pool of values corresponding to each associated parameter competes to produce successful offspring population was proposed. Moreover, EPSDE is incorporated with a self-adaptive framework [23] in which the mutation and crossover strategies and parameters in the pool are gradually self-adapted by learning from their previous recorded performance [12]. In Sa-EPSDE, the parameter values are fixed discrete values. However, the performance of the Sa-EPSDE algorithm can be further enhanced if the parameter values used during evolution process are sampled from the distribution with different mean values [15, 16]. Therefore, Sa-EPSDE is modified with the values of F and CR which are sampled from fixed mean values using Eqs. 12 and 15, respectively. In order to balance the speed and efficiency while solving problems with different characteristics, the pool of CR values is taken in the range 0.1 to 0.9 in steps of 0.1. Based on the literature, the pool of F values is taken in the range 0.4 to 0.9 in steps of 0.1. The mutation strategies are used as same as in EPSDE [9]. The proposed Sa-EPSDE algorithm is demonstrated below:

STEP 1: Set $G=0$, and randomly initialize NP individuals $P_G = \{X_{1,G},...,X_{NP,G}\}$ with $X_{i,G} = \{x_{i,G}^1,...,x_{i,G}^D\}, i=1,...,NP$ uniformly distributed in the range $[X_{min}, X_{max}]$, where $X_{min} = \{x_{min}^1,...,x_{min}^D\}$ and $X_{max} = \{x_{max}^1,...,x_{max}^D\}$. Initialize strategy probability ($p_{k,G}$, $k=1,..., K$; K is number of available strategies in the pool) and learning period LP.

STEP 2: Select a pool of mutation strategies and a pool of values for each associated parameters corresponding to each mutation strategy.

STEP 3: Each population member is randomly assigned with one of the mutation strategy from the pool and the associated parameter values are chosen randomly from the corresponding pool of values.

STEP 4: WHILE stopping criterion is not satisfied

    DO

    FOR $i = 1$ to NP

    STEP 4.1 Calculate strategy probability $p_{k,G}$ and update *Success and Failure Memory* ($ns_{k,g}$ and $nf_{k,g}$)

        IF $G > LP$

          FOR $k=1: K$

            update $p_{k,G}$ by equation (9)

            remove $ns_{k,G-LP}$ and $nf_{k,G-LP}$ out of *Success and Failure Memory* respectively

          END FOR

        END IF

    STEP 4.2 *Mutation:*

        Generate a mutated vector corresponding to the target vector $X_{i,G}$. Sample the F value to be used during the mutation using equation 12, where mean value to be used in equation 12 is the discrete value selected from the pool.

    STEP 4.3 *Crossover*

        Generate a trial vector for each target vector $X_{i,G}$. Sample the CR value to be used during the mutation using equation 15, where mean value to be used in equation 15 is the discrete value selected from the pool.

    STEP 4.4 *Selection*

        Evaluate the trial vector $U_{i,G}$

    IF $f(U_{i,G}) \leq f(X_{i,G})$, THEN $X_{i,G+1} = U_{i,G}$, $f(X_{i,G+1}) \leq f(U_{i,G})$, $ns_{k,G} = ns_{k,G+1}$

        IF $f(U_{i,G}) < f(X_{best,G})$, THEN $X_{best,G} = U_{i,G}$, $f(X_{best,G}) \leq f(U_{i,G})$

        /* $X_{best,G}$ is the best individual in generation G */

        END IF

    ELSE

        $X_{i,G+1} = X_{i,G}$, $f(X_{i,G+1}) \leq f(X_{i,G})$, $nf_{k,G} = nf_{k,G+1}$

    END IF

    STEP 4.5 *Updating*

        IF $f(U_{i,G}) > f(X_{i,G})$, THEN randomly select a new mutation strategy and parameter values from the pools or from the stored successful combinations.

        END IF

    END FOR

    Store $ns_{k,G}$ & $nf_{k,G}$, $k=1,..., K$, into *Success and Failure Memory* respectively.

    STEP 4.6 *Increment the generation count $G = G + 1$*

    END WHILE

4   Experimental Study on Numerical Benchmark Problems

In this paper, CEC 2005 benchmark functions featuring different properties (uni-modal/multi-modal, shifted, rotated, scalable, separable/non-separable) are used to evaluate the performance of the proposed Sa-EPSDE with F and CR sampled from the distribution with fixed mean values using Eqs. 12 and 15. The proposed Sa-EPSDE algorithm is compared with SaDE and EPSDE and the experiments are conducted on the first 14 benchmark problems described in [24]. In the experiments, the population NP is set to 30 and three different dimension D sizes (10D, 30D and 50D) are tested. The number of function evaluation (FES) is set up 100,000 for 10D problems, 300, 000 for 30D problems and 500,000 for 50D problems. For all the algorithms, the experiment is run 25 times for each problem. The experiment results for 10D, 30D and 50D are shown in Tables 1, 2 and 3 respectively and the best experimental results are highlighted in bold in each table.

For 10 dimensional uni-modal problems, all the algorithms perform approximately equal on function $F1$. The proposed Sa-EPSDE algorithm outperforms best on functions $F2$, $F4$ and $F5$ and EPSDE offers best performance on function $F3$. For multi-modal problems, SaDE performance is best on $F7$, $F11$ and $F14$, EPSDE on $F9$ and $F10$ and Sa-EPSDE on all other problems. Overall, compared to SaDE and EPSDE algorithms, proposed Sa-EPSDE algorithm provides best performance on 8 out of 14 10 dimensional problems.

For 30 dimensional problems in Table 2, compared to SaDE, the proposed Sa-EPSDE algorithm outperforms on 9 out of 14 functions and performs approximately equal on test function $F8$. Compared to EPSDE algorithm, Sa-EPSDE algorithm offers

Table 1. Comparison between Sa-EPSDE, SaDE and EPSDE for 10D problems

Type	F	Error means $(F(x) - F(x^*)) \pm$ Standard Deviation for 10D problems					
		SaDE		EPSDE		Sa-EPSDE	
		mean	$\pm std$	mean	$\pm std$	mean	$\pm std$
Uni-modal	F1	**0.00E+00**	**0.00E+00**	**0.00E+00**	**0.00E+00**	**0.00E+00**	**0.00E+00**
	F2	1.48E–27	4.22E–27	1.92E–28	1.59E–28	**8.94E–29**	**1.25E–28**
	F3	2.56E+04	3.44E+04	**3.45E+01**	**1.24E+02**	1.12E+03	3.09E+03
	F4	1.37E–28	1.82E–28	4.06E–28	4.95E–28	**1.11E–28**	**1.08E–28**
	F5	3.01E–08	1.36E–07	3.60E+01	4.28E+01	**0.00E+00**	**0.00E+00**
Multi-modal	F6	5.57E+00	1.45E+01	3.19E–01	1.10E+00	**6.78E–26**	**1.63E–25**
	F7	**5.96E–02**	**4.57E–02**	2.13E–01	2.04E–02	6.84E–02	4.42E–02
	F8	2.04E+01	6.72E–02	2.04E+01	8.00E–02	2.02E+01	1.07E–01
	F9	3.98E–02	1.99E–01	**0.00E+00**	**0.00E+00**	**0.00E+00**	**0.00E+00**
	F10	7.08E+00	2.74E+00	**6.02E+00**	**2.08E+00**	1.24E+01	6.00E+00
	F11	**2.21E+00**	**1.09E+00**	6.08E+00	9.79E–01	3.94E+00	1.66E+00
	F12	1.96E+02	5.13E+02	2.22E+02	1.23E+02	**2.27E+01**	**5.80E+01**
	F13	4.04E–01	1.25E–01	2.49E–01	3.81E–02	**2.15E–01**	**8.25E–02**
	F14	**2.47E+00**	**4.66E–01**	3.51E+00	3.21E–01	3.06E+00	3.59E–01

Table 2. Comparison between Sa-EPSDE, SaDE and EPSDE for 30D problems

Type	Error means $(F(x) - F(x^*)) \pm$ Standard Deviation for 30D problems					
	F	SaDE		EPSDE		Sa-EPSDE	
		mean	±std	mean	±std	mean	±std
Uni-modal	F1	3.43E–29	1.03E–28	1.57E–29	4.22E–29	**0.00E+00**	**0.00E+00**
	F2	9.60E–05	2.85E–04	1.78E–24	4.81E–24	**1.27E–25**	**4.26E–25**
	F3	6.25E+05	2.12E+05	**5.24E+04**	**3.91E+04**	1.19E+05	6.46E+04
	F4	6.77E+02	6.21E+02	1.47E+03	2.35E+03	**1.15E+00**	**3.48E+00**
	F5	4.40E+03	6.74E+02	1.99E+03	7.75E+02	**1.89E+03**	**8.34E+02**
Multi-modal	F6	4.84E+01	3.96E+01	1.12E+00	1.83E+00	**2.69E–23**	**4.77E–23**
	F7	2.03E–02	1.52E–02	6.20E+00	4.40E+00	**1.78E–02**	**1.84E–02**
	F8	2.09E+01	4.78E–02	2.10E+01	4.91E–02	2.07E+01	2.06E–01
	F9	1.83E+00	1.74E+00	1.19E–01	3.30E–01	**0.00E+00**	**0.00E+00**
	F10	5.76E+01	1.39E+01	**5.38E+01**	**1.54E+01**	5.97E+01	2.12E+01
	F11	**2.02E+01**	**3.17E+00**	3.33E+01	4.25E+00	2.42E+01	3.52E+00
	F12	3.23E+03	3.03E+03	3.58E+04	2.76E+04	**2.80E+03**	**2.58E+03**
	F13	2.46E+00	8.81E–01	1.71E+00	4.85E–01	**8.78E–01**	**1.70E–01**
	F14	**1.23E+01**	**4.81E–01**	1.35E+01	4.33E–01	1.25E+01	4.49E–01

Table 3. Comparison between Sa-EPSDE, SaDE and EPSDE for 50D problems

Type	Error means $(F(x) - F(x^*)) \pm$ Standard Deviation for 50D problems					
	F	SaDE		EPSDE		Sa-EPSDE	
		mean	±std	mean	±std	mean	±std
Uni-modal	F1	1.89E–28	3.78E–28	2.82E–28	2.57E–28	**0.00E+00**	**0.00E+00**
	F2	7.16E–01	1.60E+00	**3.01E–19**	**1.43E–18**	2.40E–13	5.97E–13
	F3	1.19E+06	3.79E+05	1.44E+07	3.99E+07	**3.81E+05**	**1.27E+05**
	F4	1.23E+04	5.24E+03	1.70E+04	1.56E+04	**1.36E+03**	**1.88E+03**
	F5	1.16E+04	1.62E+03	**6.43E+03**	**1.85E+03**	7.37E+03	1.81E+03
Multi-modal	F6	1.24E+02	1.10E+02	2.40E+00	2.00E+00	**1.60E–19**	**7.45E–19**
	F7	**4.14E–03**	**8.14E–03**	1.05E+00	1.12E–01	5.31E–03	1.21E–02
	F8	2.11E+01	3.23E–02	2.11E+01	4.07E–02	2.11E+01	6.83E–02
	F9	1.05E+01	4.77E+00	9.15E–01	2.20E+00	**2.39E–01**	**4.34E–01**
	F10	1.72E+02	3.21E+01	1.60E+02	3.65E+01	**1.15E+02**	**2.77E+01**
	F11	**4.33E+01**	**3.34E+00**	7.16E+01	3.72E+00	4.89E+01	4.56E+00
	F12	**1.04E+04**	**6.20E+03**	2.41E+05	4.07E+04	1.67E+04	1.16E+04
	F13	4.04E+00	1.48E+00	5.29E+00	4.05E–01	**1.50E+00**	**2.74E–01**
	F14	**2.16E+01**	**6.68E–01**	2.34E+01	3.72E–01	2.22E+01	5.78E–01

better performance 10 out 14 test functions and performs approximately equal on function *F2* and *F8*. SaDE performs better on function *F10*, *F11* and *F14* and EPSDE does on *F3* and *F10*.

For 50 dimensional problems in Table 3, compared to SaDE, the proposed Sa-EPSDE algorithm performs better on 9 out of 14 problems. SaDE performs best on function *F7*, *F11*, *F12* and *F14*. Compared to EPSDE algorithm, Sa-EPSDE algorithm provides better performance on 11 out 14 problems. EPSDE outperforms Sa-EPSDE on functions, *F2* and *F5*. The three algorithms perform approximately equal on function *F8*. Overall, Sa-EPSDE algorithm outperforms best on 7 out of 14 uni-modal and multi-modal 50D problems.

In all three dimensions, Sa-EPSDE algorithm outperforms SaDE and EPSDE algorithms by a large margin such as in function *F6* and *F9*. The algorithm performs only slightly worse than the other two algorithms on few problems such as in function *F11* and *F12*. Therefore, proposed Sa-EPSDE algorithm offers best performance on all 10D, 30D and 50D shifted rotated benchmark problems.

5   Experimental Study on Unit Commitment Problem

Unit commitment (UC) problem is one of the important optimization problems in the electrical power system. UC problem deals with producing the optimal schedule of available power generating units over a scheduling period while satisfying load demand and spinning reserve requirements at the minimum production cost. UC can be divided into two subproblems: unit scheduled subproblem and economic dispatch subproblem. Unit scheduled subproblem determines on/off schedule of generating units while meeting the system and generating unit constraints. Economic dispatch subproblem deals with allocating load demand and spinning reserve requirements among the committed units during each scheduling hour.

Therefore, mathematically, UC has been commonly formulated as a nonlinear, large scale, mixed-integer combinatorial optimization problem with constraints and the two subproblems can be solved separately. A large number of deterministic and metaheuristic optimization methods have been applied to solve the UC problem in the literature. Deterministic methods are fast yet may miss the optimal solution and meta-heuristic methods are flexible yet computationally expensive. However, by combining these two methods, they can benefit from each other and enable us to solve the large scale UC problems. Thus, in this paper, we hybridized our proposed Sa-EPSDE with simple priority listing method to solve the UC problem. In the proposed hybrid solution, simple priority listing method is used as a deterministic method to solve the unit scheduled subproblem and our proposed Sa-EPSDE is used as a metaheuristic method to handle the economic dispatch subproblem.

5.1   Problem Formulation

Objective Function: Mathematically, overall UC objective function can be described as follows:

Minimize Production Cost *(PC):*

$$PC = \sum_{i=1}^{N} \sum_{t=1}^{T} F_{it}(P_{it}) + ST_{it} \tag{16}$$

where, $F_{it}(P_{it})$ is fuel cost of unit i at time t which is a quardic function of output power generation of a unit.

$$F_{it}(P_{it}) = a_i + b_i P_{it} + c_i P_{it}^2 \tag{17}$$

a_i, b_i and c_i are cost coefficients.

ST_{it} is start up cost unit i at time t. The start up cost depends on the time the unit has been off before start up. The start up cost will be cold start up cost (SC_{ic}) when down time duration (T_i^{off}) of unit i exceedes cold start hour $(c\text{-}s\text{-}hour_i)$ in excess of minimum down time (T_{idown}) and will be hot start up cost (SC_{ih}) when down time duration is less than $c\text{-}s\text{-}hour_i$ in excess of T_{idown}.

$$SC_{it} = \begin{cases} SC_{ih} \text{ if } T_i^{off} \leq T_{idown} + c - s - hour_i \\ SC_{ic} \text{ if } T_i^{off} > T_{idown} + c - s - hour_i \end{cases} \tag{18}$$

Constraints: The constraints to be satisfied during the optimization are as follows:

(a) System power balance: Generated power from the committed units must be balanced with the system power load demand D_t at time t.

$$\sum_{i=1}^{N} P_{it} = D_t \tag{19}$$

(b) System spinning reserve requirement: Spinning reserve R_t is required in the operation of a power system in order to prevent load interruption from certain equipment outages. The reserve is usually considered to be 5 % or 10 % of the forecasted load demand.

$$\sum_{i=1}^{N} I_{it} P_i^{max} \geq D_t + R_t \tag{20}$$

(c) Generation power limits: each unit has generation range limited by the minimum P_i^{min} and maximum P_i^{max} power values as follows:

$$P_i^{min} \leq P_{it} \leq P_i^{max} \tag{21}$$

(d) Unit minimum up T_i^{up} and down T_i^{down} time: Once each unit is turn on/shut down, it must be committed/decommitted for a certain predefined time before it is shut down/brought online.

$$T_i^{up} \leq T_i^{on} \tag{22}$$

$$T_i^{down} \leq T_i^{off} \tag{23}$$

(e) Unit initial status: At the start of the scheduling period, initial status of each unit must be taken into account.

5.2   Simple Priority Listing Method

Priority listing method is the simple solution which is based on maximum power generation capacity of each unit. The units with higher maximum power generation capacity will have higher priority to commit. Thus, a unit with the highest maximum generation power capacity will be located on the top of the priority list and the other units will be located in the ascending order of their maximum output power towards the bottom of the list. For the units of equal maximum power generation capacity, the one with lower heat rate will have higher priority. The heat rate is calculated according to the following formula:

$$HR_i = \frac{F_{it}(P_{it})}{P_{it}} \tag{24}$$

Based on the priority list, the units are committed until the load demand and the spinning reserve constraints are satisfied at each time interval.

5.3   Experimental Results

A benchmark system of 10 generators from [25] is used as a power system testbed in this paper. The experiment is conducted for 10-, 20-, 40-, 60-, 80-, and 100-bus systems. For the 20-bus system and above, the base 10 units are replicated and the load demand is multiplied accordingly. The spinning reserve is considered to be 10 % of the load demand in this experiment. The scheduling period is for one day (24 h) and the load demand for 24 h is presented in Table 4 [26]. The performance of proposed hybrid model is evaluated with other hybrid model combined basic DE and PL method. The results are compared in terms of average production cost averaged over 30 runs

Table 4. Load demand [26]

hr	D_t	hr	D_t	hr	D_t	hr	D_t	hr	D_t	hr	D_t
1	700	5	1000	9	1300	13	1400	17	1000	21	1300
2	750	6	1100	10	1400	14	1300	18	1100	22	1100
3	850	7	1150	11	1450	15	1200	19	1200	23	900
4	950	8	1200	12	1500	16	1050	20	1400	24	800

Table 5. Performance comparison in terms of production cost ($)

Unit systems	Sa-EPSDE with PL	DE with PL	Cost difference
10	624774.92	624807.60	3.27E+01
20	1349484.31	1349520.18	3.59E+01
40	2752714.27	2753588.75	8.74E+02
60	4152472.31	4153835.67	1.36E+03
80	5545851.90	5548220.52	2.37E+03
100	6291795.18	6293104.69	1.31E+03

and shown in Table 5. As seen in Table 5, the hybrid model of SaEPSDE and PL performs better than DE+PL hybrid model in all the power systems. Especially SaEPSDE with PL obtains lower production cost of $1000 \sim 2400$ per day on the large power system of 60-, 80- and 100- bus systems.

6 Conclusion

In this paper, self-adaptive DE algorithm with ensemble of strategies and sampled parameter values (Sa-EPSDE) with F and CR sampled from the distribution of different fixed mean values is proposed to determine suitable strategy with associated parameter settings for different stages of the search process. The performance of Sa-EPSDE algorithm is tested on shifted rotated uni-modal and multi-modal CEC 2005 benchmark functions and compared with SaDE and EPSDE algorithms on 10D, 30D and 50D problems. According to mean and standard deviation criteria, the proposed Sa-EPSDE algorithm performs better than other two DE algorithms on all three dimensions. In order to evaluate the performance of Sa-EPSDE on real-world applications, Sa-EPSDE is combined with priority listing method and applied to solve unit commitment power problem. The performance is compared with basic DE algorithm in terms of mean production cost averaged over 30 trial runs. The experimental results showed that proposed Sa-EPSDE offered lower production cost than compared DE algorithm.

Acknowledgement. This work was supported by the Singapore National Research Foundation (NRF) under its Campus for Research Excellence and Technological Enterprise (CREATE) programme, and Cambridge Advanced Research Centre in Energy Efficiency in Singapore (CARES), C4T project.

References

1. Das, S., Suganthan, P.N.: Differential evolution: a survey of the state-of-the-art. IEEE Trans. Evol. Comput. **15**, 4–31 (2011)
2. Das, S., Konar, A.: Automatic image pixel clustering with an improved differential evolution. Appl. Soft Comput. **9**(1), 226–236 (2009)
3. Mallipeddi, R., et al.: Efficient constraint handling for optimal reactive power dispatch problems. Swarm Evol. Comput. **5**, 28–36 (2012)

4. Mallipeddi, R., et al.: Robust adaptive beamforming based on covariance matrix reconstruction for look direction mismatch. Prog. Electromagn. Res. Lett. **25**, 37–46 (2011)

5. Venu, M.K., Mallipeddi, R., Suganthan, P.N.: Fiber Bragg grating sensor array interrogation using differential evolution. Optoelectron. Adv. Mater. Rapid Commun. **2**, 682–685 (2008)

6. Gämperle, R., Müller, S.D., Koumoutsakos, P.: A parameter study for differential evolution. In: Advances in Intelligent Systems, Fuzzy Systems, Evolutionary Computation, pp. 293–298. WSEAS Press, Interlaken, Switzerland (2002)

7. Liu, J., Lampinen. J.: On setting the control parameter of the differential evolution method. In: Proceedings of MENDEL 2002 8th International Conference on Soft Computing (2002)

8. Jingqiao, Z., Sanderson. A.C.: An approximate gaussian model of differential evolution with spherical fitness functions. In: IEEE Congress on Evolutionary Computation (2007)

9. Mallipeddi, R., Mallipeddi, S., Suganthan, P.N., Tasgetiren, M.F.: Differential evolution algorithm with ensemble of parameters and mutation strategies. Appl. Soft Comput. **11**, 1679–1696 (2011)

10. Omran, Mahamed, G.,H., Salman, A., Engelbrecht, Andries, P.: Self-adaptive differential evolution. In: Hao, Y., Liu, J., Wang, Y., Cheung, Y.-m., Yin, H., Jiao, L., Ma, J., Jiao, Y.-C. (eds.) CIS 2005. LNCS (LNAI), vol. 3801, pp. 192–199. Springer, Heidelberg (2005). doi:10.1007/11596448_28

11. Brest, J., et al.: Self-adapting control parameters in differential evolution: a comparative study on numerical benchmark problems. IEEE Trans. Evol. Comput. **10**, 646–657 (2006)

12. Qin, A.K., Huang, V.L., Suganthan, P.N.: Differential evolution algorithm with strategy adaptation for global numerical optimization. IEEE Trans. Evol. Comput. **13**, 398–417 (2009)

13. Tvrdik, J.: Adaptation in differential evolution: a numerical comparison. Appl. Soft Compu. **9**, 1149–1155 (2009)

14. Mallipeddi, R., Suganthan, P.N.: Differential evolution algorithm with ensemble of parameters and mutation and crossover strategies. In: Panigrahi, B.K., Das, S., Suganthan, P.N., Dash, S.S. (eds.) SEMCCO 2010. LNCS, vol. 6466, pp. 71–78. Springer, Heidelberg (2010). doi:10.1007/978-3-642-17563-3_9

15. Tanabe, R., Fukunaga. A.: Evaluating the performance of SHADE on CEC 2013 benchmark problems. In: IEEE Congress on Evolutionary Computation (2013)

16. Tanabe, R., Fukunaga. A.S.: Improving the search performance of SHADE using linear population size reduction. In: IEEE Congress on Evolutionary Computation (2014)

17. Price, K.V., Storn, R.M., Lampinen, J.A.: Differential Evolution: A Practical Approach to Global Optimization. Natural Computing Series. Springer, Berlin (2005)

18. Zaharie, D.: Critical values for the control parameters of differential evolution. In: Proceedings of 8th International Conference on Soft Computing, MENDEL 2002, Brno, Czech Republic (2002)

19. Liu, J., Lampinen, J.: A fuzzy adaptive differential evolution algorithm. Soft. Comput. **9**, 448–462 (2005)

20. Zaharie, D.: Control of population diversity and adaptation in differential evolution algorithms. In: Proceedings of the 9th International Conference on Soft Computing, Brno, pp. 41–46 (2003)

21. Abbass, H.A.: The self-adaptive pareto differential evolution algorithm. In: IEEE Congress on Evolutionary Computation, pp. 831–836 (2002)

22. Zhang, J.: JADE: adaptive differential evolution with optional external archive. IEEE Trans. Evol. Comput. **13**, 945–958 (2009)

23. Shi-Zheng, Z., Suganthan. P.N.: Comprehensive comparison of convergence performance of optimization algorithms based on nonparametric statistical tests. In: IEEE Congress on Evolutionary Computation (2012)

24. Suganthan, P.N., Hansen, N., Liang, J.J., Deb, K., Chen, Y.-P., Auger, A., Tiwari, S.: Problem definitions and evaluation criteria for the CEC 2005 special session on real-parameter optimization. In: Proceedings of Congress on Evolutionary Computation, pp. 1–50 (2005)
25. Kazarlis, S.A., Bakirtzis, A.G., Petridis, V.: A genetic algorithm solution to the unit commitment problem. IEEE Trans. Power Syst. 11, 83–92 (1996)
26. Juste, K.A., Kita, H., Tanaka, E., Hasegawa, J.: An evolutionary programming solution to the unit commitment problem. IEEE Trans. Power Syst. 14, 1452–1459 (1999)

Empirical Assessment of Human Learning Principles Inspired PSO Algorithms on Continuous Black-Box Optimization Testbed

M.R. Tanweer[✉], Abdullah Al-Dujaili, and S. Suresh

School of Computer Engineering, Nanyang Technological University,
Singapore, Singapore
{muhammad170,aldujail001}@e.ntu.edu.sg, ssundaram@ntu.edu.sg

Abstract. This paper benchmarks the performance of one of the recent research directions in the performance improvement of particle swarm optimization algorithm; human learning principles inspired PSO variants. This article discusses and provides performance comparison of nine different PSO variants. The Comparing Continuous Optimizers (COCO) methodology has been adopted in comparing these variants on the noiseless BBOB testbed, providing useful insight regarding their relative efficiency and effectiveness. This study provides the research community a comprehensive account of suitability of a PSO variant in solving selective class of problems under different budget settings. Further, certain rectifications/extensions have also been suggested for the selected PSO variants for possible performance enhancement. Overall, it has been observed that SL-PSO and MePSO are most suited for expensive and moderate budget settings respectively. Further, iSRPSO and TPLPSO have provided better solutions under cheap budget settings where iSRPSO has shown robust behaviour (better solutions over dimensions). We hope this paper would mark a milestone in assessing the human learning principles inspired PSO algorithms and used as a baseline for performance comparison.

Keywords: PSO · Human learning principles inspired PSO variants · COCO methodology · Black-box optimization

1 Introduction

Particle Swarm Optimization (PSO) [10] is a population-based search optimization algorithm, inspired from the social behavior a swarm of bird. It has been widely used for solving numerous optimization problem [4,11,22] and has successfully provided solutions to the complex real-world optimization problems [15,19,21]. In the past two decades, its simplicity and computational efficiency has attracted the researchers. As a result, several research directions have been studied including parameter tuning, neighbourhood topology, learning strategies etc. [5,13,27]. The current state-of-the-art research in PSO includes a diverse

© Springer International Publishing AG 2016
B.K. Panigrahi et al. (Eds.): SEMCCO 2015, LNCS 9873, pp. 17–28, 2016.
DOI: 10.1007/978-3-319-48959-9_2

collection of modified PSO variants, with one variant performing better than other on a class of optimization problems. It has been shown in human learning psychology that human beings are better planners and possess intelligent information processing skills. This helps one to perform better self-regulation of the cognitive strategies and hence enhance the decision making abilities [14]. Therefore, algorithms developed using human learning principles have shown promising characteristics [17,20]. Inspired from these findings, researchers have tried to design such PSO variants that can provide better solutions on various classes of problems by introducing human-like learning principles [18,22,24,25]. This research direction has provided robust and efficient PSO variants capable of solving more classes of optimization problems. Recently, researchers have developed several human learning principles inspired PSO variants which has significantly enhanced the algorithms' performance. Therefore, it is required to benchmark the performance of these algorithms to come up with a baseline for performance comparison in assessing the human learning principles inspired PSO algorithms.

This paper aims towards comparing eight different human learning principles inspired PSO variants carefully selected to reflect different self and social principles applied to the PSO algorithm against the standard PSO algorithm. Through experimental evaluation, this paper marks the differences among them and investigates the suitability of the algorithms for solving optimization problems with different characteristics for different computational requirements. Furthermore, it draws several concluding points that can help the future development in the PSO research. To achieve the paper's goals, the experimental evaluation must be able to discover and distinguish the good features of the variants over others, and show their differences over different stages of the search for various goals and situations. In this paper, the Comparing Continuous Optimizer (COCO) methodology [7] has been adopted as it meets the requirements. It comes with a testbed of 24 scalable noiseless functions [8] addressing such real-world difficulties as ill-conditioning, multi-modality, and dimensionality. The selected PSO variants have diverse behaviour in terms of solution accuracy, convergence rate and robustness. Some require more time to converge [9,23] whereas others are computationally efficient [12,21,24]. Therefore, the performance has been assessed over different settings of function evaluations to investigate the capability of the algorithms in solving computationally expensive, moderate and cheap budget optimization problems. This evaluation provide the researchers an insight of selection of an appropriate algorithm depending on what is known about the optimization problem in terms of evaluation budget, dimensionality and function structure.

The rest of the paper is organized as follows: Sect. 2 provides a brief description of the selected human learning principles inspired PSO variants. In Sect. 3, the numerical assessment of the algorithms is presented, including experimental setup, procedure for evaluating the algorithms' performance and discussion of the results. Section 4 summarizes the main conclusions from this study, and suggests possible extensions for further performance improvements.

2   Selected Human Learning Principles Inspired PSO Algorithms

Human learning principles inspired PSO variants broadly fall into three different categories: Self-learning principles based PSO, Social-learning principles based PSO and Combined self and social learning principles based PSO. In this paper, the following PSO variants carefully selected to represent different categories have been chosen for performance evaluation.

Self Learning Principles based PSO: The Self Regulating PSO (SRPSO) algorithm [21] and the Globally Adaptive Inertia Weight PSO (GAIWPSO) algorithm [1] are the two selected human self-learning inspired PSO variants. In SRPSO, human self-cognition in the form of regulation and perception has been incorporated in the basic PSO algorithm for enhanced exploration and intelligent exploitation of the search space. In GAIWPSO, a greedy approach for inertia weight has been adopted where a human-like adaptation strategy (increasing and decreasing according to fitness) has been incorporated which has successfully accelerated the convergence towards better solutions.

Social Learning Principles based PSO: The two selected algorithms inspired from human social learning principles are the Social Learning PSO (SL-PSO) algorithm [2] and the Competitive Swarm Optimizer (CSO) [3]. The SL-PSO algorithm introduced a new concept where a particle is allowed to learn from any particle that has a better performance instead of just the best particle whereas in CSO, a pairwise competition mechanism is introduced for the particles where all the losing particles learn from the winner particles.

Combined Self and Social Learning Principles based PSO: This category includes those PSO variants where the particles have a self-learning mechanism together with a guidance mechanism for better performance. These PSO variants have shown faster convergence characteristics with efficiency and robustness over a wide range of optimization problems. The four selected algorithms from this category are: the Mentoring based PSO (MePSO) algorithm [24], the Teaching and Peer-Learning PSO (TPLPSO) algorithm [12], the Example-based Learning PSO (ELPSO) algorithm [9] and the improved SRPSO (iSRPSO) algorithm [23]. In MePSO, the particles are divided into mentors, mentees and independent learners where the mentees are socially guided by the mentors and other particles perform independent search. Two phases of learning, the teaching and the peer learning phase are introduced in TPLPSO where the under performing particles from the teaching phase are guided through the exemplar in the peer-learning phase. Similarly, in ELPSO, multiple exemplars are selected forming a group of elite particles to guide other particles. A new directional update strategy for guidance of poorly performing particles has been introduced in the iSRPSO algorithm.

Furthermore, the basic PSO algorithm [10] has been selected as a baseline of performance. The detailed experimental procedures are given in the next section.

3   Numerical Assessment

3.1   Setup

The selected PSO variants are benchmarked on 24 functions (15 instances per function) of the BBOB testbed using $10^4 \times D$ function evaluations for different dimensions. The algorithms are implemented in MATLAB R2013b on Dell Precision T3600 machine having 16 Gb RAM and 64-bit operating system using 50 particles. The parameters of all the PSO variants are set to their standard values provided in the respective literature. A termination criteria has been used where the execution will stop if the target function value is achieved.

3.2   Performance Evaluation Procedure

The experiments are setup following the guidelines from [7], where each algorithm is evaluated on the functions [6,8] multiple trials per function with specific target values. The algorithms are evaluated based on the number of function evaluations required to reach the target. The Expected Running Time (ERT) used in the figures and tables in this paper is dependent on a given target function value, $f_t = f_{\text{opt}} + \Delta f$. This ERT is computed over all relevant trials as the summation over all trails of the total number of executed function evaluations during each trail when the best function value has not achieved f_t, divided by the number of trials that actually reached f_t [7,16]. For a given target Δf_t the rank-sum test has been used for providing the **Statistical significance**. For each trial, the test has been conducted using either the number of needed function evaluations to reach Δf_t (inverted and multiplied by -1), or, if the target was not reached, the best Δf-value achieved, measured only up to the smallest number of overall function evaluations for any unsuccessful trial under consideration.

3.3   Performance Evaluation Discussion

The experimental evaluations are reported in Figs. 1, 2, 3, 4 and 5; and in Tables 1 and 2. Overall, Fig. 1 shows that the ERT of all variants grows on a super-linear order with respect to the problem dimensionality. Furthermore, the Linear Slope function and the Griewank-Rosenbrock function appear to be the most challenging functions. From the rest of figures and tables, it has been observed that the performance gap between the algorithms varies over different budget settings of the function evaluations. Therefore, the discussion is based on three different budget settings of function evaluations, viz., expensive ($10^2 * D$ FEs), moderate ($10^3 * D$ FEs) and Cheap ($10^4 * D$ FEs). Under the three different budget settings, the following can be stated about the selected PSO variants.

Expensive Budget Settings ($10^2 * D$ **FEs**): It has been stated in the respective literature that the MePSO [24], SL-PSO [2] and SRPSO [21] algorithms have faster convergence characteristics which is evident from the experimental results where these algorithms are performing better than others on expensive budget settings. The performance of all the algorithms are coupled in the lower dimensions where SL-PSO has a marginally better performance. In higher dimensions, there is a significant performance gap where MePSO has a remarkable performance on the separable functions whereas TPLPSO and CSO are leading the moderate and ill-conditioned functions categories. Further, the SRPSO, SL-PSO and ELPSO algorithms are providing better solutions to the multi-modal and weakly structured multi-modal functions. Overall, SL-PSO is performing better on the expensive budget setting followed closely by CSO and GAIWPSO on lower dimensions and by MePSO, SRPSO and ELPSO on the higher dimensions. In limited budget, more participants are required to simultaneously contribute towards convergence i.e. perform more exploitation. Human strategies applied in SL-PSO favours exploitation over exploration, therefore, SL-PSO is performing better.

Moderate Budget Settings ($10^3 * D$ **FEs**)**:** The maximum gap among the performances of the algorithms has been observed under moderate budget settings. Here, MePSO and TPLPSO have a coupled performance in all the dimensions and are successfully providing better performance on most of the functions from each category with a remarkable performance gap. PSO, being the baseline of performance has the worst performance with a significant gap compared to the other algorithms. Both the MePSO and TPLPSO algorithms belongs to the same category of human learning principles where there is intelligent exploration and balanced exploitation of the search space. The peer learning strategy is present in both algorithms that has significantly contributed towards convergence by diverging the particles towards better search areas in the solution space.

Cheap Budget Settings ($10^4 * D$ **FEs**)**:** In cheap budget setting, the particles are given fair amount of time for exploration of the search space. As a results, the performance of all the algorithms are coupled on lower dimensions. However, there is a slight gap observed in the higher dimensions where the performance of iSRPSO, TPLPSO and SRPSO are better than the others. This suggest that the concept of guidance present in iSRPSO and TPLPSO that first allows the particles to explore the search space and then guide the lesser performing particles towards optimum solution has a better convergence characteristic under the cheap budget settings.

To summarize, it can be stated that none of the PSO variants is capable enough of solving all the functions and it is also evident from the "No free lunch theorems" [26]. But it has been observed that an algorithm is exceptionally better than another on a class of problem (MePSO-separable functions, ELPSO-moderate functions and TPLPSO-weakly structured multi-modal functions). Also, different algorithms have varying performance on different budget settings. MePSO, SL-PSO and TPLPSO have performed better under limited and moderate budget settings whereas iSRPSO and TPLPSO have better performances under expensive budget settings. Further, robust solutions have also been observed by ELPSO (separable and moderate functions) and iSRPSO algorithms. Overall, SL-PSO can be termed as better performer under expensive budget settings followed by MePSO. Next, MePSO can be termed as better per-

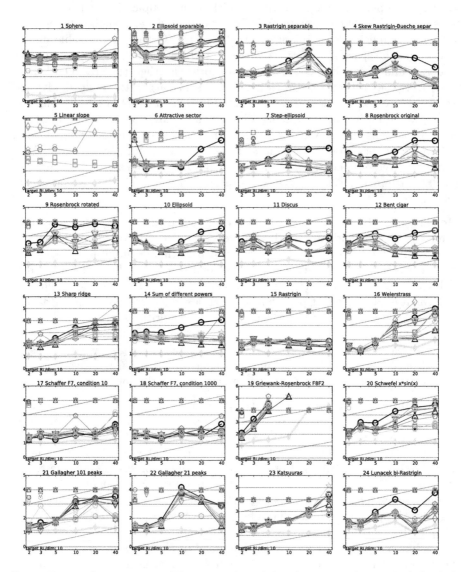

Fig. 1. Expected running time (ERT in number of f-evaluations as $\log_{10}$ value) divided by dimension versus dimension. The target function value is chosen such that the best-GECCO2009 artificial algorithm just failed to achieve an ERT of $10 \times$ DIM. Different symbols correspond to different algorithms given in the legend of f_1 and f_{24}. Light symbols give the maximum number of function evaluations from the longest trial divided by dimension. Black stars indicate a statistically better result compared to all other algorithms with $p < 0.01$ and Bonferroni correction number of dimensions (six). Legend: ○:PSO, ▽:SRPSO, ⋆:iSRPSO, □:MePSO, △:SL − PSO, ◇:ELPSO, ◔:TPLPSO, ⬠:CSO, ◯:GAIWPSO

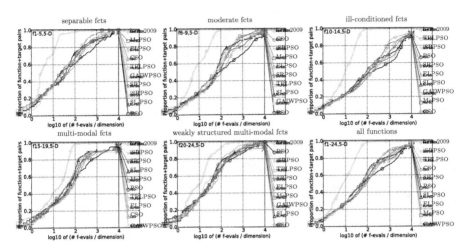

Fig. 2. Bootstrapped empirical cumulative distribution of the number of objective function evaluations divided by dimension (FEvals/DIM) for all functions and subgroups in 5-D. The targets are chosen from $10^{[-8..2]}$ such that the bestGECCO2009 artificial algorithm just not reached them within a given budget of $k \times$ DIM, with $k \in \{0.5, 1.2, 3, 10, 50\}$. The "best 2009" line corresponds to the best ERT observed during BBOB 2009 for each selected target

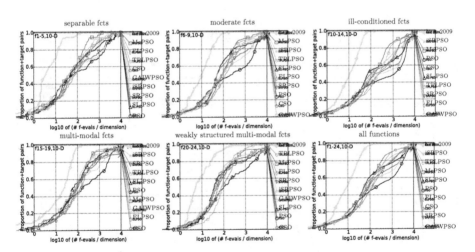

Fig. 3. Bootstrapped empirical cumulative distribution of the number of objective function evaluations divided by dimension (FEvals/DIM) for all functions and subgroups in 10-D. The targets are chosen from $10^{[-8..2]}$ such that the bestGECCO2009 artificial algorithm just not reached them within a given budget of $k \times$ DIM, with $k \in \{0.5, 1.2, 3, 10, 50\}$. The "best 2009" line corresponds to the best ERT observed during BBOB 2009 for each selected target

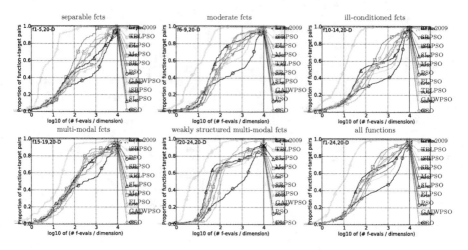

Fig. 4. Bootstrapped empirical cumulative distribution of the number of objective function evaluations divided by dimension (FEvals/DIM) for all functions and sub-groups in 20-D. The targets are chosen from $10^{[-8..2]}$ such that the bestGECCO2009 artificial algorithm just not reached them within a given budget of $k \times$ DIM, with $k \in \{0.5, 1.2, 3, 10, 50\}$. The "best 2009" line corresponds to the best ERT observed during BBOB 2009 for each selected target

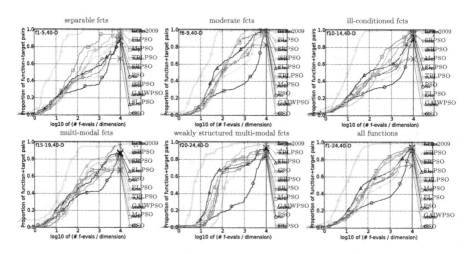

Fig. 5. Bootstrapped empirical cumulative distribution of the number of objective function evaluations divided by dimension (FEvals/DIM) for all functions and sub-groups in 40-D. The targets are chosen from $10^{[-8..2]}$ such that the bestGECCO2009 artificial algorithm just not reached them within a given budget of $k \times$ DIM, with $k \in \{0.5, 1.2, 3, 10, 50\}$. The "best 2009" line corresponds to the best ERT observed during BBOB 2009 for each selected target

Table 1. Expected running time (ERT in number of function evaluations) divided by the respective best ERT measured during BBOB-2009 in dimension 5. The ERT and in braces, as dispersion measure, the half difference between 90 and 10%-tile of bootstrapped run lengths appear for each algorithm and run-length based target, the corresponding best ERT (preceded by the target Δf-value in *italics*) in the first row. #succ is the number of trials that reached the target value of the last column. The median number of conducted function evaluations is additionally given in *italics*, if the target in the last column was never reached. Entries, succeeded by a star, are statistically significantly better (according to the rank-sum test) when compared to all other algorithms of the table, with $p = 0.05$ or $p = 10^{-k}$ when the number k following the star is larger than 1, with Bonferroni correction by the number of instances.

Table 2. Expected running time (ERT in number of function evaluations) divided by the respective best ERT measured during BBOB-2009 in dimension 20. The ERT and in braces, as dispersion measure, the half difference between 90 and 10 %-tile of bootstrapped run lengths appear for each algorithm and run-length based target, the corresponding best ERT (preceded by the target Δf-value in *italics*) in the first row. #succ is the number of trials that reached the target value of the last column. The median number of conducted function evaluations is additionally given in *italics*, if the target in the last column was never reached. Entries, succeeded by a star, are statistically significantly better (according to the rank-sum test) when compared to all other algorithms of the table, with $p = 0.05$ or $p = 10^{-k}$ when the number k following the star is larger than 1, with Bonferroni correction by the number of instances.

The statistical table on this page is reproduced in the source as a dense two-panel grid of numerical ERT values for functions f1–f24 across algorithms (PSO, SRPSO, iSRPSO, MePSO, SL-PSO, ELPSO, TPLPSO, CSO, GAIWPSO) at run-length based targets (#FEs/D = 0.5, 1.2, 3, 10, 50) with #succ columns. The individual cell values are not legibly resolvable at this reproduction quality.

former under moderate budget settings followed by TPLPSO. Finally, iSRPSO can be termed as the better performing algorithm on the functions followed by TPLPSO under cheap budget settings.

4   Conclusion

This paper provides an extensive comparison of eight human learning principles inspired PSO variants on the noiseless BBOB testbed. Based on the results, SL-PSO and MePSO are performing better on expensive budget settings, MePSO and TPLPSO are performing better on moderate budget settings and iSRPSO and TPLPSO are performing better under cheap budget settings. Further, iSRPSO has shown the most promising performance with robustness. From the results, it can be inferred that MePSO and ELPSO are the most suited algorithms for separable functions, TPLPSO and SRPSO are most suited for low dimensional ill-conditioned and high dimensional ill-conditioned functions respectively. TPLPSO and iSRPSO are most suited for multi-modal and weakly structured multi-modal functions. Further, SRPSO and SL-PSO can also be chosen for multi-modal functions.

It has been observed that the top performing algorithm, iSRPSO has not been able to locate the optimum solutions on the separable functions. The algorithm can be further investigated for providing better solutions on the separable functions. Similarly, TPLPSO can be further investigated for performance enhancement on moderate and multi-modal functions. The performance of ELPSO and MePSO can be further enhanced by considering modifications in the algorithm to tackle with ill-conditioned and multi-modal functions.

Acknowledgement. The authors wish to extend their thanks to the ATMRI:2014-R8, Singapore, for providing financial support to conduct this study.

References

1. Arya, M., Deep, K., Bansal, J.C.: A nature inspired adaptive inertia weight in particle swarm optimisation. Int. J. AI Soft Comput. **4**(2–3), 228–248 (2014)
2. Cheng, R., Jin, Y.: A social learning particle swarm optimization algorithm for scalable optimization. Inf. Sci. **291**, 43–60 (2015)
3. Cheng, R., Jin, Y.: A competitive swarm optimizer for large scale optimization. IEEE Trans. Cybern. **45**(2), 191–204 (2015)
4. Epitropakis, M., Plagianakos, V., Vrahatis, M.: Evolving cognitive and social experience in particle swarm optimization through differential evolution: a hybrid approach. Inf. Sci. **216**(1), 50–92 (2012)
5. Eslami, M., Shareef, H., Khajehzadeh, M., Mohamed, A.: A survey of the state of the art in particle swarm optimization. Res. J. Appl. Sci. Eng. Technol. **4**(9), 1181–1197 (2012)
6. Finck, S., Hansen, N., Ros, R., Auger, A.: Real-parameter black-box optimization benchmarking 2009: presentation of the noiseless functions. Technical Report 2009/20, Research Center PPE (2009). Updated, February 2010

7. Hansen, N., Auger, A., Finck, S., Ros, R.: Real-parameter black-box optimization benchmarking 2012: experimental setup. Technical report, INRIA (2012)
8. Hansen, N., Finck, S., Ros, R., Auger, A.: Real-parameter black-box optimization benchmarking 2009: noiseless functions definitions. Technical report RR-6829, INRIA (2009). Updated February 2010
9. Huang, H., Qin, H., Hao, Z., Lim, A.: Example-based learning particle swarm optimization for continuous optimization. Inf. Sci. **182**(1), 125–138 (2012)
10. Kennedy, J., Eberhart, R.: Particle swarm optimization. In: Proceedings of IEEE International Conference on Neural Networks, pp. 1942–1948 (1995)
11. Liang, J., Qin, A., Suganthan, P., Baskar, S.: Comprehensive learning particle swarm optimizer for global optimization of multimodal functions. IEEE Trans. Evol. Comput. **10**(3), 281–295 (2006)
12. Lim, W., Isa, N.: Teaching and peer-learning particle swarm optimization. Appl. Soft Comput. **18**, 39–58 (2014)
13. Lynn, N., Suganthan, P.: Heterogeneous comprehensive learning particle swarm optimization with enhanced exploration and exploitation. Swarm Evol. Comput. **24**, 11–24 (2015)
14. Nelson, T., Narens, L.: Metamemory: a theoretical framework and new findings. Psychol. Learn. Motiv. **26**, 125–141 (1990)
15. Poli, R.: Analysis of the publications on the applications of particle swarm optimization. Artif. Evol. Appl. **28**, 1–10 (2008)
16. Price, K.: Differential evolution vs. the functions of the second ICEO. In: Proceedings of the IEEE International CEC, pp. 153–157 (1997)
17. Shi, Y.: Brain storm optimization algorithm. In: Tan, Y., Shi, Y., Chai, Y., Wang, G. (eds.) ICSI 2011. LNCS, vol. 6728, pp. 303–309. Springer, Heidelberg (2011). doi:10.1007/978-3-642-21515-5_36
18. Sun, S., Li, J.: A two-swarm cooperative particle swarms optimization. Swarm Evol. Comput. **15**, 1–18 (2014)
19. Suresh, S., Sujit, P., Rao, A.: Particle swarm optimization approach for multi-objective composite box-beam design. Compos. Struct. **81**(4), 598–605 (2007)
20. Tanweer, M.R., Suresh, S., Sundararajan, N.: Human meta-cognition inspired collaborative search algorithm for optimization. In: IEEE MFI, pp. 1–6 (2014)
21. Tanweer, M.R., Suresh, S., Sundararajan, N.: Self regulating particle swarm optimization algorithm. Inf. Sci. **294**, 182–202 (2014)
22. Tanweer, M.R., Suresh, S., Sundararajan, N.: Dynamic mentoring and self-regulation based particle swarm optimization algorithm for solving complex real-world optimization problems. Inf. Sci. **326**, 1–24 (2015)
23. Tanweer, M.R., Suresh, S., Sundararajan, N.: Improved SRPSO algorithm for solving CEC 2015 computationally expensive numerical optimization problems. In: IEEE CEC, pp. 1943–1949 (2015)
24. Tanweer, M.R., Suresh, S., Sundararajan, N.: Mentoring based particle swarm optimization algorithm for faster convergence. In: IEEE CEC, pp. 196–203 (2015)
25. Wang, H., Qiao, Z., Xia, C., Li, L.: Self-regulating and self-evolving particle swarm optimizer. Eng. Opt. **47**(1), 129–147 (2015)
26. Wolpert, D.H., Macready, W.G.: No free lunch theorems for optimization. IEEE Trans. Evol. Comput. **1**(1), 67–82 (1997)
27. Zhang, Y., Wang, S., Ji, G.: A comprehensive survey on particle swarm optimization algorithm and its applications. Math. Prob. Eng. **501** (2015) 931256

Visual Cryptography Based Lossless Watermarking for Sensitive Images

Surekha Borra[1]([⊠]), Viswanadha Raju S.[2], and Lakshmi H.R.[1]

[1] Department of ECE, K.S. Institute of Technology, Bangalore, India
borrasurekha@gmail.com, hrl.lakshmi@gmail.com
[2] Department of CSE, JNTUHCEJ, JNT University, Hyderabad, India
svraju.jntu@gmail.com

Abstract. Digital technology has resulted in a cost effective and easy means for storage and communication of the multimedia data, which can also be easily downloadable and reproducible. Hence, there is a growing need for techniques that identify the right owner of Intellectual Property (IP). Visual Cryptography based Lossless Watermarking (VCLW) techniques are hybrid schemes that are now being developed as a potential replacement for conventional watermarking systems as they are effective in resolving existing tradeoff among the requirements. This paper presents theoretical analysis of spatial domain VCLW techniques and performs practical performance analysis, to identify gaps. These hybrid techniques offer promising quality of target image after watermarking; there are still a number of challenges associated such as security, robustness, pixel expansion, complexity, image formats etc. Among multiple requirements, achieving fewer rates of false positives is identified as fundamental requirement in order to discourage malicious owners and to protect Intellectual Property. The analysis of comparative results shows that with the existing techniques, the false positive rate could not reach 10^{-6}, which is the maximum limit suggested by Cox et al. for watermarking. This is due to the unique security challenge called C^3 rule that involves the design of code tables, selection of features, thresholds and combination functions. It is concluded that in the applications where the images to be protected are very sensitive such as military, medical and satellite images, VCLW techniques can be a potential replacement for conventional watermarking systems, given that the algorithms fills the important gaps.

1 Introduction

Today, a variety of E-Commerce web sites have grown up with an intention of exhibiting, advertising, distributing, and transacting the digital versions of artworks, photographs, product models, manuscripts, newspapers etc. The owners or distributors of this digital content are very much concerned about the negative growth of the technology, which simply allows copying and duplicating the Intellectual Property (IP) without proper rights. Hence, they are in need of techniques that are able to detect right ownership. Watermarking is a popular technique to perform this action. The term watermark corresponds to the copyright information, which is in the form of an image. Since the time, Cox et al. [1] developed robust invisible watermarking technique; hundreds of watermarking methodologies are suggested in the literature, both in

© Springer International Publishing AG 2016
B.K. Panigrahi et al. (Eds.): SEMCCO 2015, LNCS 9873, pp. 29–39, 2016.
DOI: 10.1007/978-3-319-48959-9_3

transform and spatial domains. Though there are numerous ways of watermarking available, copyright protection is still a challenging task as the pixels of the target image are always scaled while embedding the watermark into it. Hence these schemes always results in a loss of target image quality and a clash among the performance issues such as capacity, complexity, security, robustness and imperceptibility. Minimizing this tradeoff [2] is an important goal in copyright protection of highly sensitive and expensive images.

Many lossless Copyright protection techniques such as CBCD (Content Based Copy Detection) [3], zero-watermarking [4] and VCLW (Visual Cryptography based Lossless Watermarking) are developed to address the above concerns. After the registration of valuable images, the CBCD methods utilize the services of web crawlers to search the duplicates of the original image, by approaches similar to the Content Based Image Retrieval (CBIR). However, these methods result in high false positive rates and high computational complexity. In zero-watermarking methods, the owner makes his own verification key by applying logical XOR on watermark and from some data extracted from unique characteristics of the target image. During disputes, the watermark is extracted upon applying same logical XOR on the extracted features and verification key. The security of such systems is further improved by VCLW schemes. They construct large and well balanced verification key image, called owner share using (2, 2) visual cryptography coding tables. In this manner, the VCLW methods provide more security when compared to zero-watermarking methods.

Following are the major application scenarios of VCLW techniques:

- Telemedicine and Health insurance companies often watermark the radiology images before storing and transmitting them.
- Satellite and military map images contain important location information, such as borders, position, density and distribution of interested quantities.

Section 2 gives the basic VC concept, and its adaptability to lossless watermarking. Section 3 focuses on existing spatial domain Visual Cryptography based Lossless Watermarking (VCLW) techniques. Section 4 gives the comparison of VCLW schemes with respect to various parameters and their practical considerations along with the recommendations for future development. Section 5 concludes the paper.

2 Visual Cryptography Based Lossless Watermarking (VCLW)

Naor et al. [5, 18] developed VC as a gentle approach to hide one image in two other random images. The attracting feature is that even illiterates can decode the secret without using any complex devices. In this section, theory on visual cryptography is recalled along with the associated requirements for using it with watermarking applications. The working principle, the merits and the requirements of VCLW are then briefed.

Theory of (2, 2)-VC. A simple (2, 2) - VC converts a binary image into pair of binary shares which are random in nature. To create these random images, individual pixels of secret image are coded with m pixels (code blocks) for each random image. Table 1 shows a sample code table that is used to associate the code blocks corresponding to the secret pixels. Note that, in contrast to black pixels, white pixels are coded identically in both shares. Careful stacking (logical OR operation) of random images reveals the secret image. Sample VC results are shown in Fig. 1.

Table 1. Sample code table

Pixel	White		Black	
Bits of secret key	'0'	'1'	'0'	'1'
First Share				
Second Share				
Stacked code blocks				

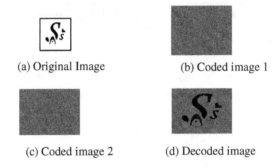

(a) Original Image   (b) Coded image 1

(c) Coded image 2   (d) Decoded image

Fig. 1. Visual cryptography

Requirements of VC. The security of the *(2, 2)* VC is ensured by the design of code table and in the manner code blocks are selected. Following are the three basic requirements (C^3 rule) [2] to be met in order to discourage the cryptanalysts by gaining information from any of the shares.

(i) Column rule: Table 1 shows multiple ways to code a secret binary pixel. Note that, to confuse attackers, all the ways must be equally selected. To achieve this requirement, a secret binary matrix, called master key matrix is utilized. Assuming that the element zero in the key matrix selects the first option (first sub-column) and the element one in the key matrix selects the second option (second sub-column), for coding either pixel color, the security of VC increases as the number of ones and zeros in the master key matrix are equally distributed.

(ii) Code rule: Table 1 reveals that the code block patterns adapted for coding B/W pixel color are similar. If different patterns are used in coding, then the cryptanalysts

can easily decrypt the secret by observing the individual blocks of any available share. The security of VC increases, if all the code patterns available for coding a white color pixel are also used to code the black pixels.

(iii) Color rule: Domination of any one color in any of the code pattern attracts the attacker's attention. For example, if code patterns consist of dominant black pixels, then an approximation of secret image can be obtained, if one share is overlaid on an empty transparency. This means the scheme becomes independent of the secret key. Therefore, to improve the security of VC, each code pattern should be comprised of equal number of B/W pixels.

Visual Cryptography Based Lossless Watermarking (VCLW). These techniques do not hide the watermarks into the target image, but conceals it in a separate image called an owner share using Owner Share Generation (OSG) algorithm. Figure 2 shows the block diagrams of OSG process along with the Watermark Extraction (WE) process.

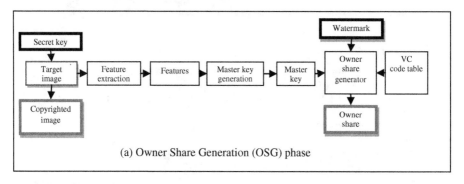

(a) Owner Share Generation (OSG) phase

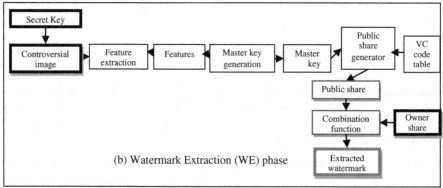

(b) Watermark Extraction (WE) phase

Fig. 2. Block diagram of typical VCLW system

A feature vector is first constructed from a secret key and a target image that is to be protected. In the master key generation process, feature vector is converted to binary matrix using some thresholds. Basic VC code table along with master key are used in constructing owner shares according to pixels in binary watermark. An arbitrator registers time stamped owner images. In case of controversies, a public share is created in a similar manner using Watermark Extraction (WE) algorithm. A combination function combines the public and owner images to extract secret watermark. In this total process, no pixel of target image is modified, and hence its quality is unaffected. Hence in VCLW scheme robustness is independent of imperceptibility and watermark image size is independent of target image. Further, multiple watermarks belonging to multiple owners can be hidden from the same target image, without any overlap.

Security Requirements of VCLW. The efficiency of VCLW is based on several factors such as thresholds, features, combination functions and code tables. The security requirements of VCLW are:

- *Satisfaction of C^3 Rule.*
- *Less False Positive Rate.* If an illegal owner is capable of detecting his own registered watermark by using his own secret key from any other images that are not belonging to him, the result is a false positive. A VCLW scheme should result in less false positive rate.
- *Robustness.* During storage or publication of copyrighted image over the internet, it has to undergo some types of processing's like coding, compression etc., for improving the bandwidth, speed and security. A VCLW scheme should be designed to provide good robustness to multiple attacks.

3   Spatial Domain VCLW Techniques

The spatial domain VCLW schemes are simple and are the focus of this paper. This section gives an overview of existing spatial domain VCLW techniques. In the year 2000, Hwang [6] proposed a method that uses target image's random MSBs as features. Feature extraction block constructs a binary feature matrix with MSB's of all the randomly selected pixels. Though the Hwang's method is simple and robust to many common attacks, the security is not always assured. It is because; the count of ones and zeros in the generated master key is not always balanced. Hence, these owner shares when combined with other public shares results in a high false positive rate. Another drawback of Hwang's method is pixel expansion that leads to expanded shares and low quality extracted watermarks. Two variations of Hwang's method are proposed by Huo [7] and Nag et al. [8]. Huo's method extracts every MSB of the target image and constructs a bit plane. The bits in the bit plane are then randomized to remove traces of the image.

Zaghloul et al. [9] presented VCLW for protection of color target images. The target image is first converted into its corresponding HSV planes. The histograms of the three planes are calculated and a set of histogram values that are all greater than some threshold value are chosen as features. Further, Hwang's [6] MSB scheme is enforced on these feature values in generating required shares. This method is resistant to many common attacks like JPEG compression, blurring, and geometrical attacks such as rotations and flipping, but is not robust to noise attacks and contrast changes. While this method is better than Hwang's scheme in many ways, the problems like pixel expansion and high false positive rate remain unsolved.

Huo et al. [10] proposed a VCLW scheme with an aim of reducing the memory requirements. This method adapted the code table of probability based VC technique [11], where there is no pixel expansion. Huo et al. performed comparison of two randomly selected pixels of the target image, in constructing master key. The law of large numbers ensures Column rule but results noisy owner share. Singh et al. [12] constructed the master key by comparing the global mean of the target image with randomly selected pixels of the target image. In this method, pixel expansion of four is used. This method shows good robustness to JPEG compression, blurring, sharpening, contrast changes and resizing, but shows poor resistance to noise and geometric attacks. A true reduction in the false positive rate is achieved with Hsu et al.'s scheme [13], in which global mean is compared with a random sample mean of the target to construct master key bit for each bit of the watermark. Hsu's method applied SDM theory to ensure satisfaction of VC's column rule.

Surekha et al. [14] proposed a VCLW method to minimize false positives and memory requirements. Random pixels' MSBs of target image are chosen and are bitwise XORed with the bits that represent spatial information in order to create a master matrix balanced in logical 1's and 0's. To cut down storage requirements of existing VCLW methods with respect to share size, and to retrieve good quality extracted watermarks, the concept of Block Visual Cryptography (BVC) is employed in generating shares. Usage of BVC code tables also meet VC's code rule and color rule. Surekha et al. [15] also proposed another spatial domain method to resist flipping attacks by building a balanced master key by applying Central Limit Theorem (CLT) on Spatial Co-occurrence of Colors (SCC) matrix, obtained from the target image. SCC is a feature that represents both intensity and spatial information. Wang et al. [16] proposed robust scheme by applying SVD on random windows of target. The bits of the master key matrix are obtained by doing a series of comparisons between a set of largest Eigen values with the median of such set. This method satisfies the VC's column rule to a maximum extent, and offer higher robustness but can't survive over geometric attacks.

Some authors proposed spatial domain VCLW schemes with restricted watermark size. Chang et al. [17] combined the concepts of visual cryptography with torus automorphism. Though Chang's scheme has an advantage of generating meaningful owner share, the size of shares generated is 9 times larger than the original along with poor quality detected watermark. Further, watermark size must be much less than the target image. Tu and Hassan [19] proposed VCLW schemes that are based on the Probability based Visual Secret Sharing (PBVSS) [20] to generate unexpanded shares. Hassan et al. [21] proposed a VCLW scheme, where the owner share is obtained by taking XOR of the watermark, extended secret key, and a master key. The watermark size cannot be greater than 1/8th of size of target. Sliet et al. [22] extended the work of Hassan et al. so as to watermark group of images as a whole. Another multiparty VCLW scheme proposed by Ying et al. [23] generates share images that look innocent with a trace of watermark being used. The drawback with this method is that the watermark size cannot exceed the target image size and the pixel expansion is four.

It is to be noted that VCLW techniques hide watermarks in a random images that are maintained by the arbitrators. Though this virtual integration avoids altering and detecting of watermark by the attackers, the issue of high false positive rate attracts attention. Another parameter that needs to be focused is share size. When trying to hide multiple and large sized watermarks, the situation becomes even challenging, as the decrease in share size has a direct impact on the security of the system. Further, with such pixel expansion all the above-mentioned methods results in low contrast extracted watermarks. Nevertheless, some of the existing schemes make use of additional resizing operation after the combination function to improve the quality. Most of the VCLW schemes cannot resist geometric attacks. Further, they are limited to binary watermarks.

4 Results and Discussion

The performance of existing VCLW methods is carried out by implementing OSG and WE algorithms on multiple targets and binary watermarks of various image sizes and details. The similarity of detected and original watermarks is carried out by Normalized Correlation (NC) and is given by:

$$NC = \frac{\sum_{k=1}^{c} \sum_{l=1}^{d} \overline{(X_{k,l} \oplus X'_{k,l})}}{c \times d}. \tag{1}$$

Where $X_{k,l}$ and $X'_{k,l}$ correspond to gray values of original and detected watermarks, with $c \times d$ as its size.

Similarly, the similarity of attacked and original targets is carried out by PSNR and is given by:

$$MSE = \frac{1}{a \times b} \sum_{k=1}^{a} \sum_{l=1}^{b} (P_{k,l} - P'_{k,l})^2. \tag{2}$$

$$PSNR = 10 \times \log \frac{255^2}{MSE}. \tag{3}$$

Where $P_{k,l}$, $P'_{k,l}$ are gray values of original and attacked target image with $a \times b$ as size.

Further, VCLW methods are judged for their effectiveness under three kinds of tests: quality test, robustness test and false positive test.

Quality Test. The owner share generation algorithm is implemented on the given target images and the watermark image. The corresponding owner shares are then extracted. The watermark extraction algorithm is implemented without subjecting copyrighted with any attack. Higher extracted watermark quality means closer value of *NC* to 1.

Robustness Test. The attack survival capability of VCLW methods is verified by performing various attacks with Matlab version 7.3 on test target images. The OSG algorithm is implemented on the test target images using test watermark images and the corresponding owner shares are generated. The WE algorithm is then implemented on the attacked copyrighted images to test the qualities of extracted watermarks. Higher the quality of extracted watermark, closer is the value of *NC* to 1, and more robust the method is.

False Positive Test. Procedure for conducting false positive test in VCLW scheme is as follows: Given a watermark and multiple target images, the public and owner shares are generated by executing Watermark Extraction and Owner Share Generation algorithms. The wrong combinations of public and owner shares of multiple target images are done arbitrarily to test if a visible trace of watermark can be seen. Numerically, it is given in [24] that a false positive results if NC value exceeds 0.7. It is to be observed that results of subjective analysis always vary with objective analysis. It is also noted that, selecting a watermark with more details improves successful subjective tracing and results poor performance.

Comparative Analysis. To compare the practical performances of spatial domain VCLW schemes seven methods are implemented on 200 target images [25]. Figure 3 shows three different watermarks which are used in the implementations. Note that, for schemes with nonzero pixel expansion, NC values were calculated after resizing the extracted watermark to original size. The results of all the three tests are given in Table 2.

Table 2 gives average objective results of robustness test, when applied on 200 target images and for three different watermarks. The objective results indicate that the spatial VCLW methods offers good resistance to variety of noise attacks, median filtering JPEG compression, sharpening, blurring, scaling, resizing and histogram equalizations. While the schemes survive to contrast adjustments and speckle noise to some extent, they offer poor resistance to cropping, rotations, and flipping attacks. It is observed as a whole that the spatial domain methods are simple and can resist common image processing attacks. However, for a VCLW scheme, the security claiming robustness is meaningful if it meets Kerckhoffs's principle. Further, if the rate of false positive [26] doesn't exceed limit. Among all the seven schemes, Hwang's and Huo's schemes resulted in high false positive rates, indicating that these schemes are insecure as they result in high false positives. Hence, these two schemes are ruled out for further comparison. Wang's method found best in providing robustness, but cannot be a best method due to its complexity.

Among other four schemes, the VCLW methods proposed by Surekha et al. resulted in high quality extracted watermark without any contrast loss or stretching,

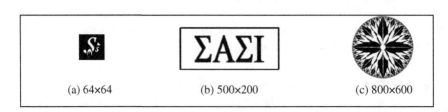

(a) 64×64   (b) 500×200   (c) 800×600

Fig. 3. Test watermark images

Table 2. Results of quality, robustness and false positive tests

Sl. No.	Parameter	Hwang et al. [6]	Huo et al. [7]	Singh et al. [12]	Hsu et al. [13]	Wang et al. [16]	Surekha et al. [14]	Surekha et al. [15]
1	Quality of extracted watermark	ZKU	ZKU	ZKU	ZKU	ZKU	ZKU	ZKU
2	Pixel expansion	2	No	4	4	4	No	No
3	JPEG (Q = 50 %)	0.9892	0.5311	0.9740	0.9713	0.9967	0.9799	0.9617
4	Blur (mask = 3 × 3)	0.9681	0.5108	0.9300	0.9249	0.9878	0.9519	0.9330
5	Sharpening (α = 0.5)	0.9643	0.4981	0.9314	0.9018	0.9657	0.9212	0.8618
6	Noise_salt & pepper_density = .1	0.9746	0.5009	0.9373	0.7869	0.9805	0.9465	0.8397
7	Noise_speckle_var = .1)	0.9081	0.4529	0.8071	0.8121	0.9726	0.9107	0.7582
8	Noise_gaussian_ _var = .01	0.9498	0.4778	0.8890	0.8769	0.9906	0.9204	0.8327
9	Median filtering (mask = 3 × 3)	0.9756	0.5147	0.9447	0.9270	0.9876	0.9606	0.9384
10	Resize (1/2)	0.9700	0.5147	0.9320	0.9267	0.9878	0.9539	0.9374
11	Crop (10 lines)	0.9329	0.5474	0.9355	0.9263	0.9590	0.9274	0.7697
12	Histogram equalization	0.8750	0.5468	0.9983	0.9977	0.9994	0.8758	0.9755
13	Contrast (175 colors)	0.9709	0.4722	0.8385	0.7713	0.8827	0.8706	0.9742
14	Rotation (30 anti clockwise)	0.8803	0.3962	0.7194	0.6742	0.8532	0.7832	0.7923
15	Rotation (1800 anti clockwise)	0.5067	0.2883	0.4890	0.4861	0.5061	0.6622	0.9495
16	Flip upside-down	0.5519	0.3090	0.5307	0.5232	0.5720	0.58655	0.9614
17	False positive rate	0.1280	0.3899	0.0150	0.007	0.0058	0.0027	0.003
18	Encryption time (s)	0.5734	1.2263	1.2766	1.4276	1952.9	0.5962	1.67

indicating low memory requirements for storage of owner shares. Further, these methods resulted in lowest false positive rate (0.0027 and 0.003) and hence can be recommended for use in VCLW applications.

5 Conclusions

Visual Cryptography based Lossless Watermarking (VCLW) techniques are hybrid schemes that are now being developed as a potential replacement for conventional watermarking systems in such applications. However, there are many issues that crop up in the process of VCLW, due to the type of features, thresholds, code tables and the combination functions employed. The concept, requirements, performance measures of VCLW techniques, its state of art and the practical issues of implementation are presented. The minimum false positive rate achieved with the existing spatial domain techniques is 0.0027. The analysis of comparative results shows that with the existing techniques, the false positive rate could not reach 10^{-6}, which is the maximum limit suggested by Cox et al. for watermarking. This is due to the unique security challenge called C^3 rule that involves the design of code tables, selection of features, thresholds and combination functions. It is concluded that in the applications where the images to be protected are very sensitive such as military, medical and satellite images, VCLW techniques can be a potential replacement for conventional watermarking systems, given that the algorithms fills the important gaps. Further, research can be focused on improvement of VCLW algorithms in terms of performance, robustness, compatibility to a variety of image formats. Other drawbacks of VCLW are that they fall under the category of semi-blind techniques and needs a Trusted Third Party to avoid multiple claiming problems. Further, Most of the proposed VCLW schemes use basic (2, 2) VC coding rules while generating the shares. However, to recover the watermark, stacking of shares can be done only after performing little computations on the controversial image. Resolving one or all of the above limitations can be carried out as future research.

References

1. Cox, I.J., Mille, M.L., Bloom, J.A.: Watermarking applications and their properties. In: Proceedings of International Conference Information Technology: Coding and Computing, Las Vegas, NV, USA, pp. 6–10 (2000)
2. Surekha, B., Swamy, G.N.: Digital image ownership verification based on spatial correlation of colors. In: Proceedings of IET Conference on Image Processing, pp. 1–5. University of Westminster, London (2012)
3. Wan, Y.H., Yuan, Q.L., Ji, S.M., He, L.M., Wang, Y.L.: A survey of the image copy detection. In: Proceedings of IEEE Conference on Cybernetics and Intelligent Systems, Chengdu, pp. 738–743 (2008)
4. Tsai, H.H., Tseng, H.C., Lai, Y.S.: Robust lossless image watermarking based on a-trimmed mean algorithm and support vector machine. J. Syst. Softw. **83**, 1015–1028 (2010)
5. Naor, M., Shamir, A.: Visual cryptography. In: Proceedings of Workshop on the Theory and Application of Cryptographic Techniques-Advances in Cryptology, Perugia, Italy, pp. 1–12 (1994)

6. Hwang, R.: Digital image copyright protection scheme based on visual cryptography. Tamkang J. Sci. Eng. **3**(2), 96–106 (2000)
7. Hou, Y.C.: Copyright protection based on visual cryptography. In: Proceedings of 6th World Multi Conference on Systemics, Cybernetics and Informatics, Orlando, FL, USA, vol. 13, pp. 104–109 (2002)
8. Nag, A., Singh, J.P., Biswas, S., Sarkar, D., Sarkar, P.P.: A novel copyright protection scheme using visual cryptography. In: Abraham, A., Mauri, J.L., Buford, J.F., Suzuki, J., Thampi, S.M. (eds.) Advances in Computing and Communications. CCIS, vol. 191, pp. 612–619. Springer, Heidelberg (2011)
9. Zaghloul, R.I., Al-Rawashdeh, E.F.: HSV image watermarking scheme based on visual cryptography. World Acad. Sci. Eng. Technol. J. **44**, 482–485 (2008)
10. Hou, Y.C., Huang, P.H.: Image protection based on visual cryptography and statistical property. In: Proceedings of IEEE Statistical Signal Processing Workshop, Nice, France, pp. 481–484 (2011)
11. Yang, C.N.: New visual secret sharing schemes using probabilistic method. Pattern Recogn. Lett. **25**(4), 481–494 (2004)
12. Singh, K.M.: Dual watermarking scheme for copyright protection. Int. J. Comput. Sci. Eng. Syst. **3**(2), 99–106 (2009)
13. Hsu, C.S.: A study of visual cryptography and its applications to copyright protection based on goal programming and statistics. Ph.D. Dissertation, National Central University, Department of Information Management, Taiwan (2004)
14. Surekha, B., Swamy, G.N.: A spatial domain public image watermarking. Int. J. Secur. Appl. **5**(1), 1–11 (2011)
15. Surekha, B., Swamy, G.N.: Lossless watermarking technique for copyright protection of high resolution images. In: Proceedings of IEEE TENSYMP 2014, Kaula Lumpur, Malaysia, pp. 73–78 (2014)
16. Wang, M.S., Chen, W.C.: Digital image copyright protection scheme based on visual cryptography and singular value decomposition. Opt. Eng. **46**(6), 1–8 (2007)
17. Chang, C.C., Chuang, J.C.: An image intellectual property protection scheme for gray-level images using visual secret sharing strategy. Pattern Recogn. Lett. **23**, 931–941 (2002)
18. Hwang, R.J., Chang, C.C.: Hiding a picture in two pictures. Opt. Eng. **40**, 342–351 (2001)
19. Tu, S.F., Hsu, C.S.: A BTC-based watermarking scheme for digital images. Int. J. Inf. Secur. **15**(2), 214–226 (2004)
20. Yang, C.N.: New visual secret sharing schemes using probabilistic method. Pattern Recogn. Lett. **25**(4), 481–494 (2004)
21. Mahmoud Hassan, A., Mohammed Khalili, A.: Self watermarking based on visual cryptography. World Acad. Sci. Eng. Technol. J. **8**, 159–162 (2005)
22. Sliet, A., Abusitta, A.: A visual cryptography based watermark technology for individual and group images. Systemics Cybern. Inf. **5**(2), 24–32 (2008)
23. Ying, S., Yinlan, Y.: Visual cryptography based multiparty copyright protect scheme. In: Proceedings of 2nd International Conference on Advanced Computer Control, Shenyang, Liaoning, China, vol. 2, pp. 223–226 (2010)
24. Gavini, N.S., Surekha, B.: Lossless watermarking technique for copyright protection of high resolution images. In: IEEE Region 10 Symposium, Malaysia, pp. 77–82 (2014)
25. http://www.imageprocessingplace.com/DIP3E/dip3e_book_images_downloads.htm
26. Surekha, B., Ravi Babu, P., Swamy, G.N.: Security analysis of a novel copyright protection scheme using visual cryptography. In: IEEE International Conference on Computing and Communication Technologies, Osmania University, Hyderabad, pp. 1–5 (2014)

Cohort Intelligence and Genetic Algorithm Along with AHP to Recommend an Ice Cream to a Diabetic Patient

Suhas Machhindra Gaikwad[1], Rahul Raghvendra Joshi[1(✉)],
and Anand Jayant Kulkarni[1,2(✉)]

[1] Symbiosis Institute of Technology (SIT),
Symbiosis International University (SIU), Pune, India
{Suhas.gaikwad,rahulj,anand.kulkarni}@Sitpune.edu.in
[2] Odette School of Business, University of Windsor,
401 Sunset Avenue, Windsor, ON N9B 3P4, Canada
kulk0003@uwindsor.ca

Abstract. A genetic algorithm (GA) is heuristic search that replicate the process of natural selection. It is inspired by natural evolution techniques such as selection, crossover and mutation strategies. The analytical hierarchy process (AHP) is used to conceptualize complex problems. The recently developed Cohort Intelligence (CI) algorithm models behavior of individuals within the group. The research for recommending an ice cream to a diabetic patient with respect to GA, CI and with AHP is carried out. The set of equations for GA, CI with respect to AHP are proposed. AHP-GA and AHP-CI will not only verify the previous obtained results for AHP but also shows improvement in results to recommend an ice cream to a diabetic patient.

Keywords: Genetic Algorithm (GA) · Cohort Intelligence (CI) · AHP-GA · AHP-CI

1 Introduction

A well known AI optimization technique such as Genetic Algorithm (GA) is inspired from the Darwin's theory of natural selection and evolution. The algorithm is driven by three phases, mainly selection, crossover and mutation. The solution is generally robust and close to the global optimum solution [2].

There are different methodologies like clustering [12], Analytical Network Process [13] that are used to recommend to an ice cream to a diabetic patient. Also, like AHP, GA can be used for ranking purpose [11]. Analytical hierarchy process is a mathematical modeling tool [1] which deals with complex problems related to mathematics by taking into account subjective human judgments [3–10]. AHP exploits Eigen values and Eigen vectors to evaluate weights and ratios. In order to assign different weights to each criterion and alternatives AHP combines each performance indictor with one of the key performance indicator [12–14]. In this paper, a mathematical model is developed for AHP to recommend an ice cream to diabetic patients. The considered criterion

B.K. Panigrahi et al. (Eds.): SEMCCO 2015, LNCS 9873, pp. 40–49, 2016.
DOI: 10.1007/978-3-319-48959-9_4

for AHP are three different types of ice cream viz., Breyers Homemade vanilla, Breyers vanilla and Ben and jerry butter pecan. The attributes of AHP are three different diabetic patient having different blood sugar levels.

An emerging AI based optimization method referred to as Cohort Intelligence (CI) has recently been developed by Kulkarni et al. in 2013. It attempts to replicate the behavior often observed in a self-organizing scheme in which candidates in a cohort compete and interact with one another in order to achieve goals which is common to every candidate [19]. So far, the CI methodology has been used to solve several unconstrained optimization problems. These tests show that CI is computationally effective and performs comparatively well with respect to the existing algorithms. The CI is applied to solve clustering [20], 0–1 Knapsack problems [21] and recently it has been applied to three combinatorial problems from health care and inventory management, sea cargo mix and a cross border shipper selection domain [22]. In this paper, CI is applied to validate and compare with results of proposed AHP-GA. The outline of this paper is Sect. 1 gives introductory details, Sect. 2 details out methodology considered for AHP matrix, Sect. 3 discusses AHP-GA and Sect. 4 discusses AHP-CI, in Sect. 5 conclusions and future direction and references are listed at the end of the chapter.

2 AHP Matrix Methodology

In order to develop an AHP mathematical model first step is to arrange the considered problem in hierarchical levels. The level 0 is goal of AHP model. The goal is to recommend an ice cream to a diabetic patient. In next level i.e. in level 1, three different types of ice creams are considered based on their sugar content. The ice cream that has low sugar content has to be given top priority followed by ice cream's that has more sugar content than the first one. This means that ice creams are to be arranged in increasing level of their sugar content. The level 2 consists of attribute which are three different types of diabetic patients [15–18]. They are to be arranged in decreasing level of their blood sugar level. The diabetic patient that has higher blood sugar level is considered to be first followed by diabetic patient that have low sugar content.

The calculation of weights for different types of ice cream for criterion are as follows, consider the ice cream as '1'and 'A' as Breyers Homemade vanilla, '2' and 'B' as Breyers vanilla and 3 and 'C' as Ben and jerry butter pecan which are used in the Table 1.

The calculated the weights for the different types of ice cream with the help of Eigen vector are 63.33 %, 26.04 % and 10.61 % respectively. So, top priority is for Ice cream "A" followed by "B" and "C" at last. The similar kinds of calculations are done

Table 1. Matrix showing weights for criterion's of ice cream

Criterion	A	B	C
A	1	3	5
B	1/3	1	3
C	1/5	1/5	1

for diabetic patients. The Eigen vector values obtained are as 65 %, 25 % and 9 % for the same. The patient 1 has given first priority followed by patient 2 and patient 3 at the last.

3   Proposed AHP-GA Algorithm

The proposed Genetic Algorithm (GA) along with AHP consists of phases like firstly, there is collection of datasets. The datasets are ice cream and diabetic patients. The pre clustering is done on both of these datasets by removing of zero values and replacing zeros with random number values. The next phase is to assign the AHP matrix values for ice cream and diabetic patient datasets. Then, check for Eigen vector and values of the AHP matrix is applied and then GA is considered. The important step is proposing set of equation for AHP with respect to GA. For seven variables, seven unknowns and similarly, for three variables, equations having three unknown details regarding considered AHP methodology are explained in latter part of this paper. This set of proposed equations needs to be applied on the AHP matrix values, which are considered earlier in Table 1.

The parameter selection process of the GA is taken into account, as previous values of AHP matrix are considered [1]. Diabetic patient having high blood sugar content is given top propriety in the AHP matrix as well as proposed set of GA equation. Patient have lower blood sugar content is given lower priority in the AHP matrix and as well as in GA proposed set of equations. Now in the three different ice cream low sugar content is given top priority in GA parameter. Ice cream having high sugar content is given lower priority in the GA parameter. In crossover, one point cross over method along with Elitism strategy is considered. The mutation process will change the value of chromosome in random manner. The fifty to two hundred generations are considered. After, mutation the results are obtained. The obtained results are verified with AHP values and it increases its average which is nothing but end point for GA. If results are not verified with AHP values then again new values for AHP matrix are considered and this process continues till the values are verified.

3.1   Proposed Set of Equations for Different Variables

In AHP matrix, numbers of pair wise comparisons are limited. The pair wise comparison is done as criterion-to-criterion or attribute-to-attribute. In practice, these comparisons are limited to only n (number) = 7. This is indicated by n(n − 1)/2. Also, AHP is a positive number type matrix. The number of paired comparison is limited to 7 only. So, at the start equation with seven variables is considered. The criterion value or alternatives limited to seven can use this equation. The proposed sets of equations are as follows:

$$7a + 6b + 5c + 4d + 3e + 2f + g = 0 \tag{1}$$

$$6b + 5c + 4d + 3e + 2f + g = 0 \tag{2}$$

$$5c + 4d + 3e + 2f + g = 0 \tag{3}$$

$$4d + 3e + 2f + g = 0 \tag{4}$$

$$3e + 2f + g = 0 \tag{5}$$

Consider the simple pair wise comparison for 3 variables and 3 equations for Eq. 5 are as given below.

$$3e_{11} + 2f_{12} + g_{13} = 0 \tag{6}$$

$$3e_{21} + 2f_{22} + g_{23} = 0 \tag{7}$$

$$3e_{31} + 2f_{32} + g_{33} = 0 \tag{8}$$

3.2   Selection Criteria for AHP-GA

Now, consider the AHP matrix values for ice cream from the Table 1 and substitute the values for ice cream matrix in proposed Eqs. 6–8. So, equations becomes are as given below:

$$3 \times 1 + 2 \times 3 + 5 = 0 \tag{9}$$

$$3 \times 0.333 + 2 \times 1 + 3 = 0 \tag{10}$$

$$3 \times 0.2 + 2 \times 0.2 + 1 = 0 \tag{11}$$

The values of the Eq. (9) is 14, Eq. (10) is 6 and for Eq. (11) is 2. The use of elitism strategy adds an advantage in this process. The elitism strategy is simple one as the first chromosome which is Eq. (9) has higher value as compared to other two Eqs. (10) and (11) then the chromosome value of (9) is kept as it is. The crossover and mutation is done for the Eqs. (10) and (11) and that is taken into consideration (Table 2).

Table 2. AHP values of proposed equations for ice cream

AHP values of ice cream	$3 \times 1 + 2 \times 3 + 5 = 0$	$3 \times 0.333 + 2 \times 1 + 3 = 0$	$3 \times 0.2 + 2 \times 0.2 + 1 = 0$
1st generation without use of GA	=14	=6	=2

3.3 Fitness Function and Recommending an Ice Cream to Diabetic Patients

The chromosomes that are having higher fittest probability value are to be considered for next generation. The obtained fitness probability value shows fitness for respective chromosome. The fitness value for each chromosome can be calculated as follows:

$$\text{Fitness}[1] = 1/(1 + 3e_{11} + 2f_{12} + g_{13}) \tag{12}$$

$$\text{Fitness}[n] = 1/\left(1 + 3e_{n*(n)} + 2f_{n*(n+1)} + g_{n*(n+2)}\right) \tag{13}$$

$$T = F[1] + \ldots F[n] \tag{14}$$

$$p[n] = p[n]/T \tag{15}$$

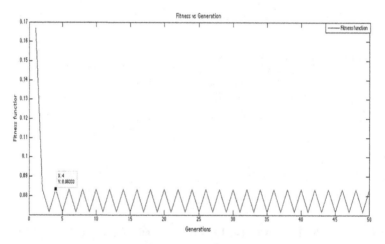

Fig. 1. Plot of fitness function values against number of generations

The above-mentioned formulas (9–15) obtain the said results. In the Fig. 1, fifty generations are considered; initially value of the fitness function is at 0.17 but finally remains between 0.07 to 0.08 which is almost equal to the zero so, obtained fitness function is good enough.

The proposed algorithm is applied on ice cream dataset of AHP for the 50 generation. The obtained results are shown in Fig. 2. It starts with value of 5.6 which conforms with the obtained values of AHP and gradually it increases up to 14.

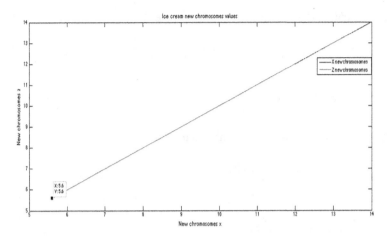

Fig. 2. Plot for new values of ice cream chromosomes

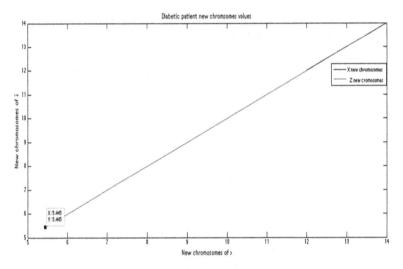

Fig. 3. Plot for new values of diabetic patient's chromosomes

4 AHP-CI Algorithm

Coherent intelligence is a group of candidates competing with one another for common goal, inherently common to all candidates. The following steps for CI are considered with respect to AHP.

Step1: Calculate Probability for each Candidate

$$\text{Fitness}[1] = 1/(1 + 3e_{11} + 2f_{12} + g_{13}) \tag{16}$$

$$\text{Fitness}[n] = 1/\left(1 + 3e_{n*(n)} + 2f_{n*(n+1)} + g_{n*(n+2)}\right) \tag{17}$$

$$T = F[1] + \ldots F[n] \tag{18}$$

$$p[n] = p[n]/T \tag{19}$$

Step 2: Roulette wheel approach

$$R[t] = p(1) + p(2) + p(3) \tag{20}$$

Step 3: Replacement of candidates

$$C_1 = C_2, \ C_2 = C_3, \ C_3 = C_1;$$

Here, candidate C_1 is represented by the Eq. (6), candidate C_2 by Eq. (7) and candidate C_3 by Eq. (8) mentioned earlier in this paper (Fig. 4).

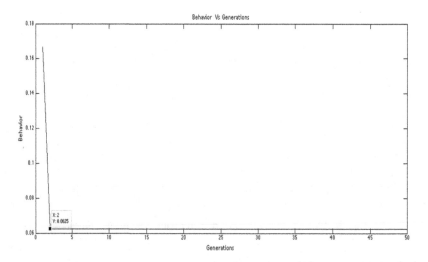

Fig. 4. Plot for behavior of candidates versus their generations

The CI gives the value or behavior of candidates within the range of 0.0625 for 50 generations. The values obtained from the GA are in the range of 0.07 to 0.08 and value of CI is 0.06, so values in case of both of these algorithms are nearly same. In this way, CI also satisfies the values obtained through GA for the concept under consideration.

As mentioned in the above Table 3, proposed algorithm is applied on ice cream dataset of AHP for the 50 generations. The obtained results are shown in Fig. 2. It starts with the value of 5.6 and shows equivalence with the obtained values of AHP and

Table 3. Time complexity details and values obtained through GA and CI for AHP matrix

AHP values of ice cream	$3 \times 1 + 2 \times 3 + 5 = 0$	$3 \times 0.33 + 2 \times 1 + 3 = 0$	$3 \times 0.2 + 2 \times 0.2 + 1 = 0$
1st Generation without use of GA	=14	=6	=2
50th generations values using AHP-GA	=14	=13.999	=13.660
200th generations value using AHP-GA	=14	=13.999	=13.600
Time complexity for 50th and 200th generations for ice cream	=1.065 s and =1.595 s	=1.065 s and =1.595 s	=1.065 s and =1.595 s
AHP values of diabetic patient	$3 \times 1 + 2 \times 3 + 7 = 0$	$3 \times 0.33 + 2 \times 1 + 3 = 0$	$3 \times 0.1482 + 2 \times 0.2 + 1 = 0$
1st generation without use of GA	=16	=6	=1.8446
50th generations value using AHP-GA	=16	=13.999	=13.428
200th generations value using AHP-GA	=16	=13.999	=13.428
Time complexity for 50th and 200th generations for diabetic patient	=0.605 s and =1.408 s	=0.605 s and =1.408 s	=0.605 s and =1.408 s
50th generations value using AHP-CI for ice cream	=14	=14	=14
200th generations value AHP-CI for ice cream	=14	=14	=14
Time complexity for 50th and 200th generations for ice cream	=0.408 s and =1.367 s	=0.408 s and = 1.367 s	=0.408 s and =1.367 s
50th generations value using proposed AHP-CI for diabetic patient	=16	=16	=16
200th generations value using proposed AHP-CI for diabetic patient	=16	=16	=16
Time complexity for 50th and 200th generations for diabetic patient	=0.507 s =1.542 s	=0.507 s =1.542 s	=0.507 s =1.542 s

gradually it increases up to 14. The time complexity of 1.065 s and 1.595 s are obtained for 50 and 200 generations of the chromosomes. The diabetic patient dataset of AHP for 50 generations is taken into account. The obtained results are shown in Fig. 3 which starts with values of 5.45 and shows equivalence with the obtained values of AHP and gradually it increases up to 14. The time complexity in this case is 0.605 s and 1.408 for 50 and 200 generations of the chromosomes.

The AHP-CI for the ice cream gives the value of 14 for the 50th generations and 200th generations. These values are is approximately equal to value obtained through AHP-GA which is having values of 14 and 13.99 for 50 and 200 generations respectively.

Similarly, for diabetic patient the value of 16 for the 50th generations and 200th generations is obtained. These values are approximately equal to values obtained from AHP-GA which has values of 16 and 13.99 for 50 and 200 generations respectively.

The results shows that proposed AHP-GA proves that recommending an ice cream to diabetic patient is possible from Figs. 2 and 3 as Breyers Homemade vanilla has first rank that can be recommended to diabetic patient1 and last rank ice cream Ben and jerry butter pecan can be recommended to the diabetic patient 3.

5   Conclusions and Future Direction

The obtained results show that AHP can be used to rank ice cream as per their sugar content like 13 mg/dl which is Breyers Homemade vanilla to 18 mg/dl which is Ben and jerry butter pecan. The ranking for diabetic patients can be done by AHP as patient 1 that has highest sugar level which is 220 mg/dl and that on go on decreasing to 190 mg/dl of sugar level of the last patient. The Breyers Homemade vanilla has the first rank that can be suggested to diabetic patient 1 and the last rank is for Ben and jerry butter pecan which can be suggested to diabetic patient 3. So, in this way recommendation of ice cream to diabetic patient can be done.

However, proposed AHP-GA gives the same results as that are obtained from AHP. So, AHP results for recommending an ice cream to diabetic patient are verified through AHP-GA. It also shows that new chromosomes produced in the upcoming generation will increase the average of AHP results. However, with this increased average of ice cream and diabetic patient, the same kind of recommendation can also be achieved. Similar kinds of results are also obtained through AHP-CI. So, proposed AHP-GA results are validated and verified with respect to AHP-CI also. Moreover the diabetic patient have high blood sugar is recommended for ice cream have low sugar content in it and vice versa.

Moreover the technique of AHP-GA, AHP-CI can also be used to validate the results of criterion to alternative matrix like criterion to criterion or alternative to alternative validation which is discussed in this paper.

References

1. Gaikwad, S.M., Mulay, P., Joshi, R.R.: Analytical hierarchy process to recommend an ice cream to a diabetic patient based on sugar content in it. Procedia Comput. Sci. **50**, 64–72 (2015)
2. Babu, P.H., Gopi, E.S.: Medical data classifications using genetic algorithm based generalized kernel linear discriminant analysis. Procedia Comput. Sci. **57**, 868–875 (2015)
3. Chen, J., Zhang, C.: Efficient clustering method based on rough set and genetic algorithm. Procedia Eng. **15**, 1498–1503 (2011)
4. Haikal, A., El-Hosseni, M.: Modified cultural-based genetic algorithm for process optimization. Ain Shams Eng. J. **2**, 173–182 (2011)
5. Ji, Z., Li, Z., Ji, Z.: Research on genetic algorithm and data information based on combined framework for nonlinear functions optimization. Procedia Eng. **23**, 155–160 (2011)
6. Khamrui, A., Mandal, J.K.: A genetic algorithm based steganography using discrete cosine transformation (GASDCT). Procedia Technol. **10**, 105–111 (2013)
7. Kiyoumarsi, F.: Mathematics programming based on genetic algorithms education. Procedia Soc. Behav. Sci. **192**, 70–76 (2015)
8. López-Espín, J.J., Giménez, D.: Obtaining simultaneous equation models from a set of variables through genetic algorithms. Procedia Comput. Sci. **1**, 427–435 (2010)
9. Sharma, P., Saroj: Discovery of classification rules using distributed genetic algorithm. Procedia Comput. Sci. **46**, 276–284 (2015)

10. Yan, L., Gui, Z., Du, W., Guo, Q.: An improved PageRank method based on genetic algorithm for web search. Procedia Eng. **15**, 2983–2987 (2011)
11. Gaikwad, S.M.: Cluster mapping with the help of new proposed algorithm and MCF algorithm to recommend an ice cream to the diabetic Patient. Int. J. Appl. Eng. Res. **10**, 21259–21266 (2015)
12. Gaikwad, S.M., Joshi, R.R., Mulay, P.: Analytical Network Process (ANP) to recommend an ice cream to a diabetic patient. IJCA **121**(12), 49–52 (2015)
13. Gaikwad, S.M., Joshi, R.R., Mulay, P.: System dynamics modeling for analyzing recovery rate of diabetic patients by mapping sugar content in ice cream and sugar intake for the day. In: Satapathy, S.C., Raju, K.S., Mandal, J.K., Bhateja, V. (eds.) IC3T 2015. AISC, vol. 379, pp. 743–749. Springer, Heidelberg (2016). doi:10.1007/978-81-322-2517-1_71
14. Gaikwad, S.M., Mulay, P., Joshi, R.R.: Mapping with the help of new proposed algorithm and modified cluster formation algorithm to recommend an ice cream to the diabetic patient based on sugar conatin in it. Int. J. Students Res. Technol. Manage. **3**, 410–412 (2015)
15. Gaikwad, S.M., Joshi, R.R., Mulay, P.: Attribute visualization and cluster mapping with the help of new proposed algorithm and modified cluster formation algorithm to recommend an ice cream to the diabetic patient based on sugar contain in it. Int. J. Appl. Eng. Res. **10**, 1–6 (2015)
16. Gaikwad, S.M.: Cluster mapping with the help of new proposed algorithm and MCF algorithm to recommend an ice cream to the diabetic patient. Int. J. Appl. Eng. Res. **10**, 21259–21266 (2015)
17. Gaikwad, S.M., Joshi, R.R., Mulay, P.: Modified analytical hierarchy process to recommend an ice cream to a diabetic patient, pp. 1–6 (2015)
18. Kulkarni, A.J., Durugkar, I.P., Kumar, M.: Cohort intelligence: a self supervised learning behavior. In: Proceedings of IEEE International Conference on Systems, Man and Cybernetics, pp. 1396–1400 (2013)
19. Krishnasamy, G., Kulkarni, A.J., Paramesaran, R.: A hybrid approach for dataclustering based on modified cohort intelligence and K-means. Expert Syst. Appl. **41**(13), 6009–6016 (2014)
20. Kulkarni, A.J., Shabir, H.: Solving 0–1 Knapsack problem using cohort intelligence algorithm. Int. J. Mach. Learn. Cybern. **7**, 427–441 (2014). doi:10.1007/s13042-014-0272-y
21. Kulkarni, A.J.: Application of the cohort-intelligence optimization method to three selected combinatorial optimization problems. Eur. J. Oper. Res. (2015). doi:10.1016/j.ejor.2015.10.008

Design, Construction and Analysis of Model Dataset for Indian Road Network and Performing Classification to Estimate Accuracy of Different Classifier with Its Comparison Summary Evaluation

Suwarna Gothane[1(✉)], M.V. Sarode[2], and K. Srujan Raju[1]

[1] CMR Technical Campus, Hyderabad, India
gothane.suvarna@gmail.com, ksrujanraju@gmail.com
[2] Jagadambha College of Engineering and Technology, Yavatmal, India
mvsarode2013@gmail.com

Abstract. Road network consist of various problems. Pothole, crack and patches are the common problems of road network. Various manual and automated solutions have been proposed by the expertise in the previous work. To overcome the problem we have came here with a novel solution approach to identify road quality. Identification of maintenance severity level and providing repair solution is done using WEKA tool 3.7. This paper presents comparison summary of classification approach and estimated which algorithm gives efficient accuracy for classification. In this paper we have obtained highest accuracy of classification 98.84 % by Support Vector Machine (SMO Function).

Keywords: Pothole · Patches · Road · Cracks · Classification algorithm · Accuracy

Paper Work: The entire paper work is summarized as follows:

Section 1 includes Introduction, Sect. 2 includes Related Work, Sect. 3 Performing Analysis of Data and Setting Threshold Levels, Sect. 4 includes Database Creation, *and* Sect. 5 *Testing Data with different Algorithm and Estimating Accuracy,* Sect. 6 includes Conclusion and Future Work.

1 Introduction

A pothole is a type of stoppage in an asphalt pavement, caused by the presence of water in the underlying soil structure and by traffic passing over the affected area. Increase in population year by year leads to growing number of means of transportation users, which increases traffic on road gradually. Among all the ways of transports, via road transport is preferable for shorter distance connectivity. Most common problems with road network are associated with climatic conditions such as according to Indian weather in summer more temperature and in rainy season heavy rainfall and floods makes traveler in ghastly circumstances as well ruin the road.

© Springer International Publishing AG 2016
B.K. Panigrahi et al. (Eds.): SEMCCO 2015, LNCS 9873, pp. 50–59, 2016.
DOI: 10.1007/978-3-319-48959-9_5

Roads in worst conditions reduce speed of vehicle transfer because of cracks and potholes appear in the road. Furthermore this problems can also causes accidents. So identification of road network problem and quick renovate solution is current need.

2 Related Work

In the literature, many methods have been introduced for detecting cracks and potholes. Taehyeong Kim and Seung-Ki Ryu [1] proposed data driven method by capturing image from optical device, and applied decision method for pothole classification. S. Varadharajan et al., [2] used Combination of Data Driven and computer vision approach based on over-segmentation algorithm to concentrate on lighting and weather condition. Lokeshwor Huidrom, Lalit Kumar Sud, [3] applied heuristically derived decision logic for potholes, cracks and patches detection.

Sylvie Chambon and Jean-Marc Moliard [4] applied a multi-scale extraction and a Markovian segmentation approach. Used sensing technique for crack detection and crack are analyzed with morphological tool. Using MATLAB Christian Koch and Ioannis Brilakis [5] identified pothole shape on the basic of geometric properties by technique of morphological thinning and elliptic regression. Yijie Su and MeiQuing Wang [6] performed experiment and shows that the inhomogeneous objects could be segmented effectively and achieve good results. Fanfan Liu et al., [7] performed automatic crack detection by segment extending for complex pavement images using Visual Studio C++ 6.0. Zhaoyun Sun et al., [8] applied image smoothing technology for pre-processing image and used algorithm of image threshold segmentation for cracks identification.

M. Mahmood et al., [9] suggested Fuzzy Logic Technique on data such as cracking, patching, bleeding using fuzzy if-then rules and examines good accuracy. A fuzzy logic inference system used for planning of maintenance treatment selection for the black topped pavement surface discussed by S.K. Suman and S. Sinha [10]. Author proved that technique works with lesser development expenses, gives better-quality features and end product performance. A.K. Sandra et al., [11] developed a framework for Fuzzy Multi Criteria Decision Making system over a number of stretches. An expert opinion inspection considered out to measure the importance of parameters on the functional condition of the pavement. T.F. Fwa and R. Shanmugam [12] examines the State-of-art Fuzzy mathematics technology provides a suitable tool to incorporate subjective analysis and uncertainty in pavement condition rating and maintenance-needs assessment.

Oliveira H. and Correia P.L [13] proposed Neural Network approach where a fully incorporated system for the automatic detection and characterization of cracks has developed using unsupervised training algorithm on Portuguese road. Saar T and Talvik O. [14] also proposed a system based on Neural Networks approach for iden-tification and classification of defects in regions of images into separate types. Guoai Xu et al. [15] implemented approach for cracking trend calculation by artificial neural network for pavement crack recognition in the area of image processing.

Ravi Bhoraskar et al. [16] developed efficient Sensor Based Model for monitoring road and traffic conditions and breaking events using sensors present on smart phones,

accelerometer, GPS and magnetometer sensor readings. Prashanth Mohan [17] investigated system that performs rich sensing by piggybacking on smart phones which
focused specifically on the sensing component accelerometer, microphone, GSM radio,
and/or GPS sensors in the phones to detect potholes, bumps, braking, and honking in
an energy efficient manner. Salman M et al., [18] proposed a highly potential technique
for multidirectional crack detection by Gabor function. Gabor filter has reported 95 %
precision in crack detection.

3   Performing Analysis of Data and Setting Threshold Levels

In this paper with expert opinion heuristically parameters has been considered and set
the limits onto the parameters for obtaining sound decision on road quality. Parameters
considered here are represented as ARFF relation name pavement and header information. WEKA ARFF Relation and Header Information is as follows:

```
@relation pavement
@attribute pothole_width{'0mm','1<=X<30 mm','30<=X<80 mm','80<=X<130mm','>130
mm'}
@attribute texture {smooth,microtexture,macrotexture,megatexture}
@attribute shape {'no shape',circular,elongated,elliptical}
@attribute speed {'<20','20<=X<40','40<X<80','80above'}
@attribute breaking_event {yes,no}
@attribute speed_bump {'big size','medium size','small size','smaller size'}
@attribute bleeding {no,low,medium,high}
@attribute single_crack {'<3mm','3<=X<6mm','>=6mm','no crack'}
@attribute multiple_crack {'<1mm','1<=X<3mm','>=3mm','no crack'}
@attribute alligator_crack{'no crack','hairlinecrack not
interconnected','inter connected crack','edge sapling and rocking pieces'}
@attribute raveling {no,'lightly rough','loose particles','pitted surface'}
@attribute patch {'no patch','large area','small area','medium area'}
@attribute shoving {'no shoving','<15mm','15<=X<30mm','>= 30mm'}
@attribute rutting {no,'<6mm','6<=X< 25mm','>= 25mm'}
@attribute corrugation {no,low,medium,high}
@attribute pothole_depth {'no pothole','<6mm','6<=X< 25mm','>= 25mm'}
@attribute edge_failure {no,low,medium,high}
@attribute age {'<1','1<=X<2','2<X<3','>3'}
@attribute no_of_potholes {'no pothole','<=1','2<=X<=3', '4<=X<=5','>5'}
@attribute no_of_cracks {'no crack','<=1','2<=X<=3', '4<=X<=5','>5'}
@attribute quality {excellent,good,poor,fail}
```

4   Database Creation

Model Data base is created first in Microsoft excel. We have created total 86 instances
for the above mentioned attributes. Data is considered for 1 km area of road network.
After data base creation it is saved as .csv file. Finally header and data is combined and
saved as arff. Sample of few instances are shown as follows:

```
'0 mm',smooth, 'noshape','80above',no, 'big size', no, 'nocrack', 'nocrack',
'nocrack', no, 'nopatch', 'noshoving', no, no, 'no pothole',no,'<1','no
pothole', 'no crack', excellent
'1<=X<30 mm',microtexture, elliptical ,'40<X<80' , yes,'medium size' ,low,
'<3mm','<1mm','hairline crack not interconnected', 'lightly rough' ,'small
area','<15mm', '<6mm', low,'<6mm',low, '1<=X<2','<=1','<=1',good
'30<=X<80mm',macrotexture,circular,'20<=X<40',yes,'smallsize',medium,'3<=X<6m
m' ,'1<=X<3mm','inter connected crack', 'looseparticles', 'medium
area','15<=X<30mm','6<=X<25mm',medium,'6<=X<25mm',
medium,'2<X<3','2<=X<=3','4<=X<=5',poor
'80<=X<130mm',megatexture,elongated,'<20',yes,'smallersize',high,'>=6mm','>=3
mm','edge sapling and rocking pieces', 'pittedsurface', 'large area','>=
30mm', '>= 25mm',high,'>= 25mm',high,'>3','4<=X<=5','>5',fail
```

5 Testing Data with Different Algorithm and Accuracy Estimation

5.1 System Architecture

Project architecture describes here about how to create dataset and the step by step procedure for obtaining accuracy by different classifier. The detailed architecture for evaluating performance of classifier is as below (Fig. 1).

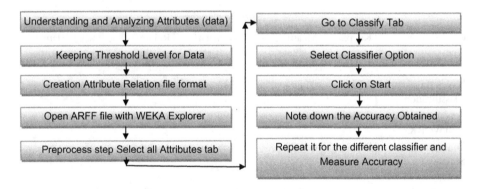

Fig. 1. System architecture

Here, we have noted accuracy and time required to build model for different classification algorithm. Accuracy of classification algorithm is shown by correctly classified instances. Result obtained after applying classifier is summarized in the Table 1.

Error for different classifier is summarized in the following Table 2.

Table 1. Accuracy of classifier (i.e. correctly classified instances) and time (in seconds).

Sr. no.	Classification types	Total instances	Correctly classified instances	In correctly classified instances	Time to build model
1	Naves Bayesian Classification	86	82.5581 %	17.4419 %	0 s
2	Function RBF NETWORK	86	94.186 %	5.814 %	0.26 s
3	Function Simple Logistics	86	96.5116 %	3.4884 %	0.55 s
4	Function SMO	86	98.8372 %	1.1628 %	0.09 s
5	Lazy LBR	86	82.5581 %	17.4419 %	0 s
6	Lazy LWL	86	95.3488 %	4.6512 %	0 s
7	MISC Hyper pipes	86	81.3953 %	18.6047 %	0 s
8	MISC VFI	86	95.3488 %	4.6512 %	0 s
9	Rules: PART	86	94.186 %	5.814 %	0.03 s
10	Rules: One R	86	89.5349 %	10.4651 %	0 s
11	Rules: Conjuctive Rule	86	61.6279 %	38.3721 %	0.02 s
12	Trees J48	86	94.186 %	5.814 %	0 s

Table 2. Error of classifier

Classification type	Kappa statistic	Mean absolute error	Root mean squares error	Relative absolute error	Root relative squared error
Naves Bayesian Classification	0.756	0.0894	0.2942	24.915 %	69.5335 %
Function RBF NETWORK	0.9187	0.045	0.1509	12.5384 %	35.6695 %
Function Simple Logistics	0.9511	0.0423	0.1155	11.7916 %	27.3114 %
Function SMO	0.9837	0.251	0.3134	69.9748 %	74.0717 %
Lazy LBR	0.756	0.0894	0.2942	24.915 %	69.5335 %
Lazy LWL	0.9344	0.0602	0.1559	16.7984 %	36.8548 %
MISC Hyper pipes	0.7499	0.3204	0.3872	89.3212 %	91.5378 %
MISC VFI	0.9348	0.0468	0.1334	13.0396 %	31.5241 %
Rules: PART	0.9178	0.0507	0.1592	14.1321 %	37.6308 %
Rules: One R	0.8528	0.0523	0.2287	14.5893 %	54.0721 %
Rules: Conjuctive Rule	0.4518	0.233	0.3392	64.9558 %	80.1852 %
Trees J48	0.9178	0.0507	0.1592	14.1321 %	37.6308 %

5.2   Final Evaluation Summary

Evaluation Summary measures are defined as:

1. TP: Positive tuples correctly labeled by classifier.
2. TN: Negative tuples correctly labeled by classifier.
3. FP: Negative tuples incorrectly labeled by classifier (example: quality = poor for which classifier predicted quality = excellent).
4. FN: Positive tuples incorrectly labeled by classifier (example: quality = excellent for which classifier predicted quality = poor).
5. TP Rate = TP/P is also called as recall or Sensitivity.
6. TN Rate = TN/P.
7. Precision $= (TP)/(TP + FP)$.
8. F - Measure $= (2 * precision * recall)/(precision + recall)$.
9. ROC Area = Receiver operating characteristics curve. It shows tradeoff between TPR and FPR.
10. Error rate $= (FP + FN)/P + N$.

Based on above measure we can able to perform classification and we can categorize road in excellent, good, poor, and as fail (Table 3).

Table 3. Detailed accuracy of classifier

Classification	TP rate/Recall	FP rate	Precision	F-Measure	ROC area	Class
Naves Bayesian Classification	1	0.054	0.75	0.857	1	excellent
	0.737	0.045	0.824	0.778	0.984	good
	0.667	0.031	0.875	0.757	0.966	poor
	0.912	0.115	0.838	0.873	0.98	fail
Function RBF NETWORK	1	0.014	0.923	0.96	1	excellent
	0.895	0	1	0.944	1	good
	0.905	0.031	0.905	0.905	0.969	poor
	0.971	0.038	0.943	0.957	0.978	fail
Function Simple Logistics	1	0	1	1	1	excellent
	1	0	1	1	1	good
	0.905	0.015	0.95	0.927	0.985	poor
	0.971	0.038	0.943	0.957	0.992	fail
Function SMO	1	0	1	1	1	excellent
	1	0	1	1	1	good
	0.952	0	1	0.976	0.982	poor
	1	0.019	0.971	0.986	0.99	fail
Lazy LBR	1	0.054	0.75	0.857	1	excellent
	0.737	0.045	0.824	0.778	0.984	good

(continued)

Table 3. (*continued*)

Classification	TP rate/Recall	FP rate	Precision	F-Measure	ROC area	Class
	0.667		0.875	0.757	0.966	poor
	0.912	0.115	0.838	0.912	0.873	fail
Lazy LWL	1	0	1	1	1	excellent
	1	0	1	1	1	good
	0.81	0	1	0.895	0.979	poor
	1	0.077	0.895	1	0.944	fail
MISC Hyper pipes	1	0	1	1	1	excellent
	1	0	1	1	0.998	good
	1	0.246	0.568	0.724	0.902	poor
	0.529	0	1	0.692	0.962	fail
MISC VFI	1	0.014	0.923	0.96	1	excellent
	1	0.015	0.95	0.974	1	good
	0.81	0	1	0.895	0.994	poor
	1	0.038	0.944	1	0.971	fail
Rules: PART	1	0	1	1	1	excellent
	1	0	1	1	1	good
	0.762	0	1	0.865	0.938	poor
	1	0.096	0.872	0.932	0.952	fail
Rules: One R	1	0.054	0.75	0.857	0.973	excellent
	0.789	0	1	0.882	0.895	good
	0.762	0	1	0.865	0.881	poor
	1	0.096	0.872	0.932	0.952	fail
Rules: Conjuctive Rule	0	0	0	0	0.764	excellent
	1	0.418	0.404	0.576	0.791	good
	0	0	0	0	0.642	poor
	1	0.096	0.872	0.932	0.952	fail
Rules: J48	1	0	1	1	1	excellent
	1	0	1	1	1	good
	0.762	0	1	0.865	0.938	poor
	1	0.096	0.872	0.932	0.952	fail

Time require to build classification model, accuracy of the classification is shown with the time and accuracy curve for different classifier. With this curves we can visualize Function SMO for support vector machine is best classifier (Figs. 2 and 3).

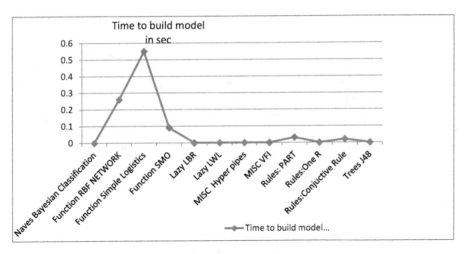

Fig. 2. Time curve (time in seconds)

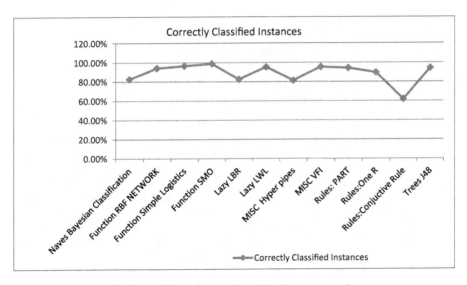

Fig. 3. Accuracy curve (accuracy in percentage)

6 Conclusion and Future Work

The WEKA Experiment Environment enables the user to create, run, modify, and analyze experiments in a more convenient manner. For example, the user can create an experiment that runs on several schemes against a series of datasets and then analyze the results to determine if one of the schemes is statistically better than the other schemes.

In this paper, using automated WEKA tool Version 3.6.9 we have obtained very convenient way to critically perform correct identification and classification of roads condition based on severity of potholes, patches, and cracks etc. measures as well as to provide qualitative solution for maintenance. With the obtained curve, we come to the conclusion highest classification accuracy 98.84 % can be achieved with the Support Vector Machine Algorithm (SMO function).

Further we can extend the model SMO function classification obtained to take up necessary action for maintenance according by observing criticality of road network. In future proposed method can be applicable for variety of the domain applications.

References

1. Kim, Taehyeong, Ryu, Seung-Ki: System and method for detecting potholes based on video data. Proc. Emerg. Trends Comput. Inf. Sci. 5(9), 703–709 (2014)
2. Varadharajan, S., Jose, S., Sharma, K., Wander, L., Mertz, C.: Vision for road inspection. In: Proceedings of IEEE International Conference on Applications of Computer Vision, Steamboat Springs, Colorado, USA, pp. 115–122 (2014)
3. Lokeshwor, H., Lalit Kumar, S.: Method for automated assessment of potholes, cracks and patches from road surface video clips. In: Proceedings of 2nd Conference on Transportation Research Group of India, vol. 104, pp. 312–321. Elsevier (2013)
4. Chambon, S., Moliard, J.-M.: Automatic road pavement assessment with image processing review and comparison. In: Proceedings of International Journal of Geophysics, Hindawi Publishing Corporation, vol. 2011, pp. 1–20, June 2011
5. Koch, C., Brilakis, I.: Pothole detection in asphalt pavement images. In: Proceeding on Advanced Engineering Informatics, vol. 25, pp. 507–515. Elsevier Ltd., August 2011
6. Su, Y., Wang, M.: Improved C-V segmentation model based on local information for pavement distress images. In: Proceedings of 3rd International Congress, IEEE Conference on Image and Signal Processing, Yantai, vol. 3, pp. 1415–1418, October 2010
7. Liu, F., Xu, G., Yang, Y., Niu, X.: Novel approach to pavement cracking automatic detection based on segment extending. In: Proceedings of IEEE International Symposium on Knowledge Acquisition and Modeling, Wuhan, pp. 610–614. IEEE, December 2008
8. Sun, Z., Li, W., Sha, A.: Automatic pavement cracks detection system based on Visual Studio C++ 6.0. In: Proceedings of IEEE Sixth International Conference Natural Computation, Yantai, Shandong, vol. 4, pp. 2016–2019, August 2010
9. Mahmood, M., Rahman, M., Nolle, L.: A fuzzy logic approach for pavement section classification. Proc. Int. J. Pavement Res. Technol. 6, 620–626 (2013)
10. Suman, S.K., Sinha, S.: Pavement maintenance treatment selection using fuzzy logic inference system. Proc. Int. J. Eng. Innovative Technol. 2, 172–175 (2012)
11. Sandra, A.K., Vinayaka Rao, V.R., Raju, K.S., Sarkar, A.K.: Prioritization of pavement stretches using fuzzy MCDM approach fuzzy logic. In: Saad, A., Dahal, K., Sarfraz, M., Roy, R. (eds.) Soft Computing Using Industrial Applications, vol. 39, pp. 265–276. Springer, Heidelberg (2007)
12. Fwa, T.F., Shanmugam, R.: Fuzzy logic technique for pavement condition rating and maintenance. In: Proceedings of 4th International Conference on Managing Pavements, Center for Transportation Research, pp. 465–476. National University of Singapore (1998)

13. Oliveira, H., Correia, P.L.: Automatic road crack detection and characterization. Proc. IEEE Trans. Intell. Transp. Syst. **14**, 155–168 (2013). http://ieeeexplore.us/xpl/RecentIssue.jsp? punumber=6979vol
14. Saar, T., Talvik, O.: Automatic Asphalt pavement crack detection and classification using neural networks. In: Proceedings of IEEE Electronics Conference, 12th Biennial Baltic, Tallinn, pp. 345–348, October 2010
15. Xu, G., Ma, J., Liu, F., Niu, X.: Automatic recognition of pavement surface crack based on BP neural network. In: Proceedings of IEEE International Conference Computer and Electrical Engineering, Phuket, pp. 19–22, December 2008
16. Bhoraskar, R., Vankadhara, N., Raman, B., Kulkarni, P.: Traffic and road condition estimation using smartphone sensors. In: Proceedings of IEEE COMSNETS, pp. 1–6, 2012
17. Mohan, P., Padmanabhan, V.N., Ramjee, R.: Rich monitoring of road and traffic conditions using mobile smartphones. In: Proceedings of 6th ACM Conference on Embedded Network Sensor Systems, pp. 357–358, November 2008
18. Salman, M., Mathavan, S., Kamal, K., Rahman, M.: Pavement crack detection using the Gabor filter. In: Proceedings of IEEE 16th International Conference Intelligent Transportation Systems, vol. 93, pp. 2039–2044, October 2013

A Hybrid EMD-ANN Model for Stock Price Prediction

Dhanya Jothimani$^{(\boxtimes)}$, Ravi Shankar, and Surendra S. Yadav

Department of Management Studies, Indian Institute of Technology Delhi,
New Delhi, India
dhanyajothimani@gmail.com

Abstract. Financial time series such as foreign exchange rate and stock index, in general, exhibit non-linear and non-stationary behavior. Statistical models and machine learning models, often, fail to predict time series with such behavior. Former models are prone to large statistical errors. While machine learning models such as Support Vector Machines (SVM) and Artificial Neural Network (ANN) suffer from the limitations of overfitting and getting stuck in local minima, etc. In this paper, a hybrid model integrating the advantages of Empirical Mode Decomposition (EMD) and ANN is used to predict the short-term forecasts of Nifty stock index. In first stage, EMD is used to decompose the time series into a set of sub-series, namely, intrinsic mode function (IMF) and residue component. In the next stage, ANN is used to predict each IMF independently along with residue component. The results show that the hybrid EMD-ANN model outperformed both SVR and ANN models without decomposition.

Keywords: Hybrid EMD-ANN model · EMD · ANN · SVR · Nifty · Time series

1 Introduction

The non-linear and non-stationary behavior of financial time series makes them difficult to predict. Several statistical and computational intelligent techniques have been proposed. [1] and [2] have compared and analyzed the role of these techniques for stock prices prediction. Statistical models such as AutoRegressive (AR) models, Moving Average (MA), Autoregressive Moving Average (ARMA) and AutoRegressive Integrated Moving Average (ARIMA) assume that financial time series is stationary and follows normal distribution, which is not the case in real world. In order to overcome this, non-linear models like Autoregressive Conditional Heteroskedastic (ARCH) model, Generalized Autoregressive Conditional Heteroskedastic (GARCH) and their extensions have been proposed. Though they try to model the stock return data series exhibiting low and high variability and handle non-linearities but they do not completely capture highly irregular phenomena in financial markets [16].

The original version of this chapter was revised: Two references have been added. The erratum to this chapter is available at DOI: 10.1007/978-3-319-48959-9_25

© Springer International Publishing AG 2016
B.K. Panigrahi et al. (Eds.): SEMCCO 2015, LNCS 9873, pp. 60–70, 2016.
DOI: 10.1007/978-3-319-48959-9_6

In the past decade, artificial intelligence techniques have captured the attention of researchers from various domains such as Computer Science, Operations Research, Statistics and Finance. The ability to model non-stationary and non-linear data has led to wide adoption of techniques including Artificial Neural Network (ANN) and Support Vector Regression (SVR). These models are not without their limitations. SVR and ANN suffer from the problem of overfitting and getting trapped in local optima.

There are broadly two ways of improving the accuracy of forecasts: (1) data preprocessing, and (2) improvement in algorithm. Data preprocessing is part of data mining where the data is transformed into a format that reveals certain characteristics of data. Decomposition of time series is one such technique, where the time series is deconstructed into several components. There are two types of decomposition models: (i) classical decomposition, and (ii) non-classical decomposition models.

In classical decomposition model, the time series is separated into trend, seasonal and error components. This model works best with linear data. Moreover, while predicting the future values, error components are ignored leading to information loss, thus, affecting the forecast accuracy [21].

Empirical Mode Decomposition (EMD) and Discrete Wavelet Transform (DWT) fall under the category of non-classical decomposition. Both EMD and DWT are signal processing techniques that decompose time series in time domain and time-frequency domain, respectively [11,12,14,15].

Proposed by [10], EMD uses Huang-Hilbert Transform (HHT) to decompose non-linear and non-stationary time series into a set of adaptive basis function called Intrinsic Mode Functions (IMFs). Unlike DWT, it is a non-parametric technique which does not require prior information on scale or levels of decomposition. Further, it does not suffer from leakage between levels [6].

Feature selection is considered to be one of the important components of any model building process. Here, IMFs obtained using EMD are considered as the feature to the machine learning models adopted. There are two approaches to feature selection: (i) scale-based approach, and (ii) feature vector based approach. In scale-based approach, the obtained IMFs are predicted independently and then reconstructed to obtain the final forecast. While the latter treats IMFs at a particular time point to be a feature vector to obtain the predicted value [17].

The paper focuses on scale-based approach to integrate the advantages of both ANN and EMD to obtain 1-period ahead predicted values for weekly Nifty stock price.

Organization of this paper is as follows: Sect. 2 presents the hybrid EMD-ANN framework. Section 3 discusses prediction of stock index followed by results and discussion in Sect. 4. Section 5 concludes the paper.

2   Hybrid EMD-ANN Framework

The steps of hybrid EMD-ANN model are listed below:

1. Decompose the original series using EMD into a set of various sub-series.

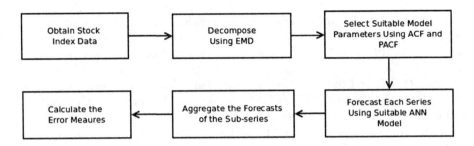

Fig. 1. Flow chart of the hybrid approach

2. Using ANN predict each sub-series independently.
3. Recombine the predicted subseries to obtain aggregated time series.
4. Calculate the error measures using the obtained aggregated series and the original series.

Figure 1 shows the flow chart of the above described procedure.

2.1   Steps of EMD

The original time series of stock index $F(t)$ is decomposed as follows [10,19]:

1. *Formation of Lower and Upper Envelopes:* Identify all local minima in $F(t)$ and interpolate using cubic spline method to generate a lower envelope $F_l(t)$. Similarly, identify all local maxima and interpolate to obtain a upper envelope $F_u(t)$
2. *Calculation of Mean Envelope:* Calculate the mean envelope using $M(t) = (F_l(t) + F_u(t))/2$.
3. *Local Detail:* Obtain local detail $Z(t)$ by subtracting $M(t)$ from the original series $F(t)$ i.e., $G(t) = F(t) - M(t)$.
4. *Sifting:* Repeat the above two steps on $G(t)$ until one of the following stopping criteria is reached: (a) the value of mean envelope approaches zero, (b) the difference between the number of zero crossings and number of local extrema is at most 1, or (c) the number of user-defined iteration is reached. This process is called *Sifting*. $G(t)$ represents the first intrinsic mode function $IMF_1(t)$ and the residue $R_1(t)$ is obtained using $R_1(t) = F(t) - G(t)$.
5. *Repeat the process:* Repeat steps 1–4 to obtain subsequent IMFs and residual component.

The original series $F(t)$ and its decomposed series are represented as

$$F(t) = \sum_{i=1}^{N} IMF_i(t) + R_N(t) \tag{1}$$

2.2   Steps of ANN

Artificial Neural Network (ANN) is a most commonly used machine learning technique which is inspired by structure and functioning of human brain. The ability to model non-linear dataset and robust performance have led to its wide acceptability and adaptability. Following factors affect the performance of the neural network:

Input data format: Since each sub-series will be predicted independently, the number of neural network will be equal to the number of sub-series obtained after decomposition. The input layer of the neural network would consist of each sub-series and its lags. Lags are determined using AR and ARIMA models with Partial Auto-correlation Function (PACF) and Auto-correlation Function (ACF) as the criteria.

Network Structure: A three-layer resilient feed forward neural network consisting of input layer, hidden layer and output layer is considered for this study. In previous studies, three layered network structure was found to be efficient for predicting non-linear time series [4, 14, 15].

Training Algorithm: Resilient Back Propagation (RBP) [20] is adopted for training the model due to its superior performance as compared to the most commonly used Back Propagation algorithm [15]. Further, the training of the model using RBP is faster and does not require specifying parameters during the training phase.

The final forecasted value is obtained by aggregating the predicted sub-series.

3   Analysis

3.1   Data Description

The original time series comprised of weekly closing prices of Nifty ranging from September 2007 to July 2015 covering a period of 8 years. The data was collected from Yahoo! Finance. Nifty is the stock index of National Stock Exchange, India comprising of 50 stocks covering 22 sectors. It is the benchmark index for Indian equity market.

3.2   EMD

The weekly closing prices of Nifty were decomposed using EMD resulting in a total of 7 components comprising of six IMFs and a residual component. It can be observed from Fig. 2 that IMFs produced are relatively stationary. These sub-series produced are predicted independently using ANN. The Box-Jenkins methodology is adopted to determine the model parameters of the ANN model [23].

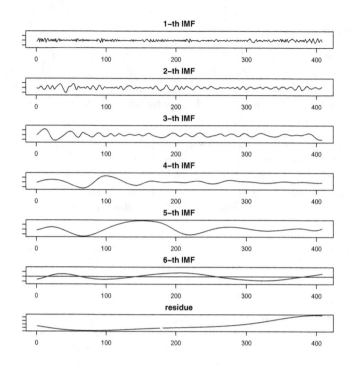

Fig. 2. Decomposition of $F(t)$ using EMD

3.3 Box-Jenkins Methodology

Figure 3 represents the Box-Jenkins methodology ([3,18]) adopted to identify the model parameters of ANN. The steps are detailed as below:

1. *Stationarity Check:* In this step, the commonly adopted Augmented Dickey-Fuller (ADF) test ([7,8]) is used to check the stationarity of each IMF independently and the residual component obtained using EMD. For instance, IMF_1 was found to be stationary. If a series is identified to be non-stationary, then first difference of the series is obtained which is again tested for stationarity using ADF test. The process is continued until the series becomes stationary or reaching maximum number of iterations. In case of IMF_5, the series and its first difference were found to be non-stationary, hence second difference[1] of the series was determined. Since the second difference series was found to be stationary, the iteration process for this series terminates.

2. *Identification of Lag Parameter:* The lag parameter of series obtained from previous step is determined using ACF and PACF. The lag parameter of IMF_1 is found to be 4 while that of second difference of IMF_5 as 5.

The steps 1 and 2 are repeated for each sub-series.

---

[1] Difference of the first difference of the series. Suppose $F(t) = y(t), y(t-1)...y(t-n)$, then the first difference is $d1 = y(t-1) - y(t), y(t-2) - y(t-1), ...$ and the second difference $d2 = y(t-2) - 2y(t-1) + y(t), ...$

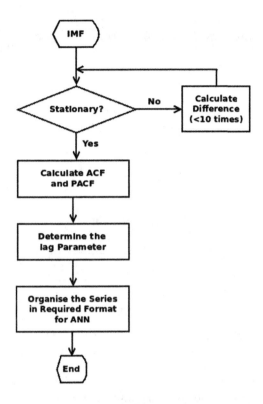

Fig. 3. The Box-Jenkins methodology for ANN input data format

Table 1. Performance of ANN for different IMFs and residue

IMFs	Number of neurons		
	Input neurons	Hidden neurons	Output neurons
IMF_1	4	10	1
IMF_2	5	10	1
IMF_3	4	10	1
IMF_4	4	10	1
IMF_5	5	10	1
IMF_6	5	10	1
Residue	4	10	1

3.4 ANN

ANN model was used to predict 1-period ahead forecast for each IMF and residue component. 70 % of the data was used for training the model and remaining 30 % for testing the model.

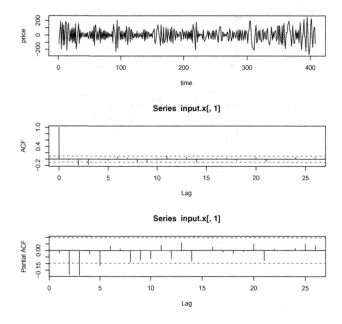

Fig. 4. ACF and PACF plot for IMF_1

The lag parameter, which estimates the interrelationship of a time series with its past values, is considered as the input for the neural network. ACF and PACF are used to identify the lag parameter for each sub-series (as explained in previous section). For instance, the lag parameter of first sub-series IMF_1 is 4 (Fig. 4) since it cuts off at lag 4 and also exhibits autoregressive process. This indicates that the sub-series IMF_1 at point t is dependent on its past 4 values, hence, the number of neurons in the input layer is four. This can be expressed mathematically as:

$$X(t) = f[X(t-1), X(t-2), X(t-3), X(t-4)] \tag{2}$$

Since it is a prediction problem, the number of neurons in the output layer is 1. The number of neurons in the hidden layer is selected on the basis of best performances of the model. Table 1 represents the number of neurons in various layers of the neural network.

Neural networks have the limitation of getting trapped in local minima. In order to overcome this, data is normalized using z-scores, normalization between $[-1, 1]$ and $[0, 1]$ [5]. The model using z-score normalization seemed to show better performance compared to other two processes. In addition, data normalization process quickens the training of the neural network [22]. The predicted values are later denormalized before calculating the error measures. In the similar way, the first and second differences applied to sub-series are transformed back. In case of sub-series IMF_5, the second difference and its past 5 values are used as output and input neurons, respectively in the neural network training model. Hence, the predicted values of this sub-series are transformed back to the original form.

1-period ahead predicted values are obtained using SVR and ANN to compare and analyze the effectiveness of the hybrid EMD-ANN model.

4   Results and Discussion

4.1   Error Measures

The predicted values obtained using SVR, ANN and EMD-ANN models are compared using two error measures: (a) directional accuracy, and (b) Root Mean Square Error (RMSE). Test data is used to calculate these error measures. Directional Accuracy (DA) measures number of times the predicted value matched the direction of the original series. It is represented as percentage. Higher the value better is the predictive model.

Error $(E_i(t))$ is defined as the difference between the original series $(F_i(t))$ and the predicted value $(P_i(t))$. Root Mean Square Error is calculated as the square root of mean of error values. RMSE is expressed mathematically as:

$$E_i(t) = F_i(t) - P_i(t) \tag{3}$$

$$RMSE = \sqrt{\sum_{i=1}^{n} E_i(t)^2/n} \tag{4}$$

Lower is the value of RMSE, better the predictive model.

The error measures of the models under consideration are shown in Table 2. Here, it can be seen that hybrid EMD-ANN model has shown superior performance. RMSE value of the hybrid model is less compared to the remaining two models. DA is clearly better than that of ANN model and is relatively better than SVR model. The 1-period ahead predicted values obtained using these three models are shown in Fig. 5.

Table 2. Error measures

	RMSE	DA (%)
ANN	184.28	51.02
SVR	169.45	58.16
EMD-ANN	102.50	65.30

4.2   Significance Test

One of the most commonly used techniques, Wilcoxon Signed-Rank Test (WSRT) is a non-parametric and distribution-free technique to evaluate the predictive capabilities of two different models [9,13]. In this test, the signs and the ranks are compared to identify whether two predictive models are different.

Here, WSRT is used to analyze whether the presented hybrid model outperformed both SVR and ANN models without decomposition.

Two-tailed WSRT was carried out on RMSE values and results of which are shown in Table 3. From the table, it can be seen that z statistics value is beyond $(-1.96, 1.96)$, hence the null hypothesis of two models being same is not accepted. The results are significant at 99 % confidence level ($\alpha = 0.01$). The sign "+" in the table represents that predictive capability of hybrid EMD-ANN model is superior than two traditional computational intelligence techniques, namely, SVR and ANN. Signs "−" and "=" (not shown in table) refer to underperformance and similar performance of the hybrid model compared to other two models, respectively. The WSRT results confirm that the hybrid EMD-ANN model outperformed the traditional SVR and ANN models.

Table 3. Wilcoxon signed rank test On RMSE of hybrid EMD-ANN with SVR and ANN

	z	WSRT
SVR	−4.771	+
ANN	−4.188	+

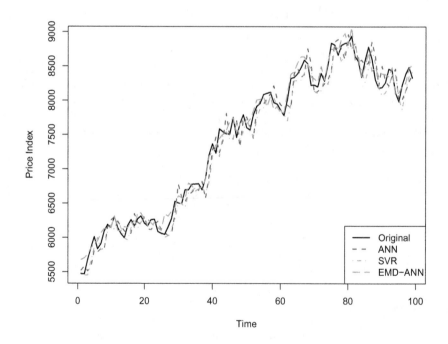

Fig. 5. Forecasts obtained using ANN, SVR and EMD-ANN

5   Conclusion

The paper presented a hybrid Empirical Mode Decomposition - Artificial Neural Network model to predict the Nifty stock index. The model incorporates the advantages of above-mentioned methods. In the first stage, EMD was used to decompose the stock index into various sets of series. In the second stage, ANN was used to predict each sub-series independently. These predicted sub-series are then recombined to obtain the final predictions. The presented hybrid model exhibited better performance compared to SVR and ANN models. It can be concluded that EMD enhanced the performance of machine learning model, namely, ANN. Further, this hybrid model can be used for predicting non-stationary and non-linear time series.

The paper also analyzed the effect of data normalization procedure on ANN model. The performance of ANN model based on z-score normalization was consistently better than the model based on $[0, 1]$ and $[-1, 1]$ normalization.

The paper dealt with scale-based decomposition approach for predicting Nifty. A comparative analysis of both feature-based and scale-based approach on Nifty can be carried out.

References

1. Atsalakis, G., Valavanis, K.: Surveying stock market forecasting techniques- Part II: soft computing methods. Expert Syst. Appl. **36**(3, Part 2), 5932–5941 (2009). http://www.sciencedirect.com/science/article/pii/S0957417408004417
2. Atsalakis, G., Valavanis, K.: Surveying stock market forecasting techniques- Part I: conventional methods. In: Zopounidis, C. (ed.) Computation Optimization in Economics and Finance Research Compendium, pp. 49–104. Nova Science Publishers Inc., New York (2013)
3. Box, G.E.P., Jenkins, G.: Time Series Analysis, Forecasting and Control. Holden-Day, Incorporated, San Francisco (1990)
4. Cadenas, E., Rivera, W.: Wind speed forecasting in three different regions of Mexico, using a hybrid ARIMA-ANN model. Renew. Energy **35**(12), 2732–2738 (2010). http://www.sciencedirect.com/science/article/pii/S0960148110001898
5. Crone, S., Guajardo, J., Weber, R.: The impact of preprocessing on support vector regression and neural networks in time series prediction. In: Proceedings of the International Conference on Data Mining (DMIN 2006), pp. 37–42. CSREA, Las Vegas (2006)
6. Crowley, P.: Long cycles in growth: explorations using new frequency domain techniques with US data. Bank of Finland Research Discussion Paper No. 6/2010, February 2010
7. Dickey, D.A., Fuller, W.A.: Distribution of the estimators for autoregressive time series with a unit root. J. Am. Stat. Assoc. **74**(366), 427–431 (1979). http://www.jstor.org/stable/2286348
8. Dickey, D.A., Fuller, W.A.: Likelihood ratio statistics for autoregressive time series with a unit root. Econometrica **49**(4), 1057–1072 (1981). http://www.jstor.org/stable/1912517
9. Diebold, F.X., Mariano, R.S.: Comparing predictive accuracy. J. Bus. Econ. Stat. **13**, 253–265 (1995)

10. Huang, N., Shen, Z., Long, S., Wu, M., Shih, H., Zheng, Q., Yen, N., Tung, C., Liu, H.: The empirical mode decomposition and the Hilbert spectrum for nonlinear and non-stationary time series analysis. Proc. R. Soc. Lond. A Math. Phys. Eng. Sci. **454**(1971), 903–995 (1998)

11. Jothimani, D., Shankar, R., Yadav, S.S.: Discrete wavelet transform-based prediction of stock index: a study on National Stock Exchange Fifty index. J. Financ. Manage. Anal. **28**(2), 35–49 (2015)

12. Jothimani, D., Shankar, R., Yadav, S.S.: A comparative study of ensemble-based forecasting models for stock index prediction. In: Proceedings of MWAIS 2016, paper 5 (2016). http://aisel.aisnet.org/mwais2016/5

13. Kao, L.J., Chiu, C.C., Lu, C.J., Chang, C.H.: A hybrid approach by integrating wavelet-based feature extraction with MARS and SVR for stock index forecasting. Decis. Support Syst. **54**(3), 1228–1244 (2013). http://dx.doi.org/10.1016/j.dss.2012.11.012

14. Lahmiri, S.: Wavelet low- and high-frequency components as features for predicting stock prices with backpropagation neural networks. J. King Saud Univ. Comput. Inf. Sci. **26**(2), 218–227 (2014). http://dx.doi.org/10.1016/j.jksuci.2013.12.001

15. Liu, H., Chen, C., Tian, H., Li, Y.: A hybrid model for wind speed prediction using empirical mode decomposition and artificial neural networks. Renew. Energy **48**, 545–556 (2012). http://www.sciencedirect.com/science/article/pii/S096014811200362X

16. Matei, M.: Assessing volatility forecasting models: why GARCH models take the lead. J. Econ. Forecast. **4**, 42–65 (2009)

17. Murtagh, F., Starck, J., Renaud, O.: On neuro-wavelet modeling. Decis. Support Syst. **37**(4), 475–484 (2004). http://www.sciencedirect.com/science/article/http://pii/S0167923603000927. datamining for financial decision making

18. Pankratz, A.: Introduction to Box - Jenkins Analysis of a Single Data Series, pp. 24–44. Wiley, Hoboken (2008). http://dx.doi.org/10.1002/9780470316566.ch2

19. Ren, Y., Suganthan, P., Srikanth, N.: A comparative study of empirical mode decomposition-based short-term wind speed forecasting methods. IEEE Trans. Sustain. Ener. **6**(1), 236–244 (2015)

20. Riedmiller, M., Braun, H.: A direct adaptive method for faster backpropagation learning: the RPROP algorithm. In: 1993 IEEE International Conference on Neural Networks, vol. 1, pp. 586–591 (1993)

21. Theodosiou, M.: Forecasting monthly and quarterly time series using STL decomposition. Int. J. Forecast. **27**(4), 1178–1195 (2011). http://www.sciencedirect.com/science/article/pii/S0169207011000070

22. Wu, G., Lo, S.: Effects of data normalization and inherent-factor on decision of optimal coagulant dosage in water treatment by artificial neural network. Expert Syst. Appl. **37**(7), 4974–4983 (2010). http://www.sciencedirect.com/science/article/pii/S0957417409010628

23. Zhang, G.: Time series forecasting using a hybrid ARIMA and neural network model. Neurocomputing **50**, 159–175 (2003). http://www.sciencedirect.com/science/article/pii/S0925231201007020

Development of Back Propagation Neural Network (BPNN) Model to Predict Combustion Parameters of Diesel Engine

M. Shailaja$^{(\boxtimes)}$ and A.V. Sita Rama Raju

Department of Mechanical Engineering,
Jawaharlal Nehru Technological University, Hyderabad, India
Shailaja324@rediffmail.com

Abstract. Effective utilization of fuel in diesel engines is the major challenge posed to the engine designers today, due to large demand of fuel. In this context, control of design, as well as operating parameters for better performance are focused in the present work. Experiments are done on a 4-s, variable compression ratio (VCR) diesel engine and the required data is collected by varying fuel injection timing (IJT), compression ratio (CR), load and fuel injection pressure (IP). The combustion parameters, viz. combustion duration (CD), ignition delay (ID), peak pressure (PP) and heat release (HR) are determined at various operating conditions, as these parameters could influence fuel consumption and performance. For the investigation purpose, an artificial neural network (ANN) with back propagation algorithm is adopted. ANN is trained with the experimental data. The number of nodes in the hidden layer is varied from 3 to 22, to architect a suitable network for the prediction of combustion parameters with good accuracy. Test results show that network with 4-19-4 architecture with trainlm algorithm can predict the four parameters (ID, CD, PP and HR) with correlation coefficients as 0.9892, 09892, 0.9944 and 0.9909 taken in the order.

Keywords: Diesel engine · Compression ratio · Combustion parameters · Injection timing · Back propagation neural network · Injection pressure

1 Introduction

Diesel engines are considered to be superior to the gasoline engines owing to their fuel economy, ruggedness, low CO_2 emissions, flexibility to operate at higher compression ratios and so forth. Their high fuel economy and thermal efficiency credited the diesel engines for wide applications in the fields of transportation, automotive, agriculture and industrial sectors. However, two major challenges of present day energy sector are demand-supply mismatch of fuel and the environmental pollution. Majority of the researches for solving these problems are focused toward feasibility of biodiesel usage in diesel engines. Hardly, any margin of energy demand could be met by the application of biodiesels. In fact, in the very first attempt, Rudolf Diesel was successful with peanut oil as a fuel but not for the fuel efficiency. Thence, another better possible solution could be thought of with controlling design and operating variables of the

© Springer International Publishing AG 2016
B.K. Panigrahi et al. (Eds.): SEMCCO 2015, LNCS 9873, pp. 71–83, 2016.
DOI: 10.1007/978-3-319-48959-9_7

engine so as to reduce fuel consumption, and enhance efficiency and performance. Parameters like compression ratio (CR), fuel injection timing (IJT), and injection pressure (IP) significantly influence combustion, performance and emissions. Broad explorations have been carried out to discern the influence of compression ratio, injection pressure and injection timing (advance/retard) [1–7] on combustion parameters and reports are quite encouraging. The inferences from the research can motivate to design a new engine to achieving the best performance from the favorable values of combustion parameters. In fact, the combustion process in diesel engines is non linear, dynamic and highly complex phenomenon and very difficult to model mathematically. Several researchers in the field of internal combustion (IC) engines proved that artificial neural networks (ANN) can extensively be for prediction [8, 9], fault diagnosis [10], monitoring and control [11, 12].

The present work uses a back propagation ANN (BPNN) for prediction of combustion parameters (ID, CD, PP and HR) by changing fuel injection pressure, injection timing, compression ratio and load. However, the combustion parameters depend on various operating and design variables such as compression ratio, fuel-air ratio, inlet pressure and temperature of air, turbulence, engine load, engine speed, injection pressure and timing. In this study, the impact of compression ratio, load, fuel injection pressure and injection timing only are considered to study simultaneous variation on combustion parameters and their prediction at different levels of operating conditions. Numerous researchers reported the effects of one or a few of the design and operating parameters such as CR, IP, IJT and load on combustion parameters but not all are considered. The present work considers all the four significant parameters. There is no work reported hither to, toward the prediction of combustion parameters with these variables. This inspires the authors to developing a BPNN for the prediction of combustion parameters.

Ignition Delay (ID). Ignition delay (ID) is stated as the time gap between commencement/start of injection (SOI) and commencement/start of combustion (SOC) in diesel engines, which may be expressed either in crank angle degrees (CAD) or milliseconds. Ignition delay (ID) expressed in milliseconds depends on speed of the engine in rpm, while that expressed in terms of CAD, is independent of speed, which attracted to adapt in the present work. Further, the usage of CAD enables the present work to use in future at any rpm whereas usage of milliseconds may not produce appropriate results.

Shorter ignition delay is preferred for the smooth running (for less fuel consumption) of engine as well as to reduce the knock. Knock is a result of abnormal combustion which enhances fuel consumption for given power. The values of IJT for short ignition delay lie in a range of SOI (start of injection) beyond which, ignition delay increases [13] however it decreases with rise in compression ratio, load and fuel injection pressure due to increase in temperature and density of the gas mixture [14]. The ignition delay is taken as 0–5 % [15, 16] of energy conversion time in the present work. SOI, determined by injection timing and SOC. CAD, where 5 % of cumulative heat release is noticed is considered as SOC. ID in CAD is given by

$$ID = [SOI - SOC]^\circ$$

Combustion Duration (CD). CD is given by period between the commencement/start of combustion (SOC) and the completion/end of combustion (EOC) in CAD. CD in crank angle degrees is given by $CD = [EOC - SOC]^\circ$ where EOC is CAD at end of combustion. EOC is determined from heat release data (similar to ID) given the CAD where 95 % of cumulative heat releases is observed. Shorter combustion duration is preferred since it results in PP nearest to top dead center (TDC). The effect of variables IJT, IP, CR and load on combustion duration is same as that on ignition delay.

Peak Pressure (PP). Peak pressure is the maximum cylinder pressure attained during the combustion process nearest to and after TDC. It directly influences the brake power and fuel consumption of the engine. A higher value of peak pressure and its occurrence nearest to TDC are preferred. The PP increases with an increase in load, CR and IP [17, 18] whereas with the advance of IJT, PP increases to certain extent and then decreases. The peak pressure in the present work is taken from pressure crank angle data.

Heat Release (HR). Heat release (HR) is the amount of thermal energy liberated during the combustion process. According to Heywood [13], combustion continues into the expansion stroke up to 31°. HR per degree crank angle is taken from the data acquisition system. Here, the HR is taken as the sum total of HR/CAD nearest to TDC (where positive value of heat released is observed) till significant positive values of HR. Further it is observed that heat release increases as CR, IP and load increase but increases with an advance in IJT up to certain extent and then decreases.

Artificial Neural Network (ANN). For solving problems which are complicated to crack by conventional modeling methods, ANN's are widely used. ANN's does not require any explicit mathematical equations for modeling of physical phenomena in a complex system. Biological neuron in the human brain can do an enormous amount of computations in a very short time utilizing billions of neurons. These neurons are interconnected to each other in the form of complex network and the mechanism is not known fully yet. Observations on the biological neuron motivated evolution of artificial neuron. ANN is similar to the biological neural network but with a less, manageable number of neurons which are employed for forecasting/prediction, function approximation, classification and pattern recognition etc. The basic elements artificial neural networks are neurons, which process the information.

A simple ANN is shown in Fig. 1. It comprises of two input neurons (x_1, x_2) and one output neuron (y) which are joined by weights (w_1, w_2). Weight is the knowledge used by the ANN for solving a problem. Based on above parameters, net input is calculated as

$$Net = x_1 w_1 + x_2 w_2 \tag{1}$$

In general, it can be written as

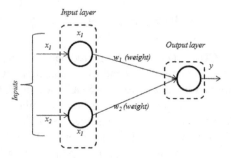

Fig. 1. A simple artificial neural net

$$Net\ input = Net = \sum_i x_i w_i \tag{2}$$

The output is calculated from net input by applying activation function. Different types of activation functions are available. Most widely used are sigmoidal functions. Binary sigmoidal function or log-sigmoidal function (ranges between 0 to 1) represented by the Eq. (3) and bipolar sigmoidal function or tan-sigmoidal function (ranges between −1 to +1) represented by the Eq. (4).

$$f(x) = \frac{1}{1 + \exp(-\sigma x)} \tag{3}$$

$$b(x) = 2f(x) - 1 = \frac{1 - \exp(-\sigma x)}{1 + \exp(-\sigma x)} \tag{4}$$

where σ is called steepness parameter. Neural networks are adjusted, or trained, so that a particular input leads to specific output as illustrated in Fig. 2.

The network weights are adjusted until the output signals match the target supplied. This adjustment procedure of weights is called learning and there are different rules for learning. For complex problems ANN's have hidden layer(s) with some neurons in addition to input and output layers. This type of networks is called as multi layer

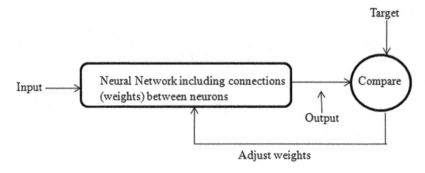

Fig. 2. Procedure in ANN

networks. Widely used multi layer networks for prediction are recurrent networks as well as feed forward networks. In the feed forward networks, information is passed in the direction of the input layer to the output layer. Neurons of a particular layer are linked to neurons of the subsequent layer. Neurons in the same layer are not connected among themselves. Hence, output depends only on inputs received from previous layers and weights. The present work employs a feed forward network. There are different types of algorithms and in the present work batch gradient descent ("traingd"), batch gradient descent momentum ("traingdm"), adaptive learning rate ("traingda"), Levenberg-Marquardt ("trainlm") are attempted to train the network. The gradient of the performance function is used in all algorithms, to determine adjustments for weights and biases to minimize performance function. Back propagation technique is used to determine this gradient. The objective of all algorithms is to minimize the performance function, which is achieved by adjusting the weights and biases. Back propagation technique is explained in the subsequent discussion. Data is normalized in the range [−1, 1] by using Eq. (5) and supplied to the network for better training.

$$y = (\frac{y_{max} - y_{min}}{x_{max} - x_{min}}) * (x - x_{min}) + y_{min} \tag{5}$$

Tangent-Sigmoid transfer function presented by Eqs. (6) and (7) are selected for the hidden layer.

$$b(x) = \frac{1 - \exp(-\sigma x)}{1 + \exp(-\sigma x)} \tag{6}$$

$$b'(x) = \frac{\sigma}{2}[(1 + b(x))(1 - b(x))] \tag{7}$$

Error function is the measure of network performance. Mean Squared Error (MSE) is given by Eq. (8).

$$MSE = \frac{1}{N}\sum_{K=1}^{N} e(k)^2 \tag{8}$$

Where $e(k) = t(k) - a(k)$.

t(k) is the target from experimental data and a(k) is the output predicted by ANN and N is the number of elements in output vector. MSE is set as 0.001. Application of algorithm for back propagation theorem is presented in the following steps. Back propagation algorithm updates weights as well as biases of the network so that the performance function fall at a faster rate i.e. the negative of the gradient. The four stages of back propagation algorithm are initialization of weights, feed forward, back propagation of errors and updating weights and biases.

The network weights as well as biases are updated through back propagation algorithm; in such a way that performance function decreases rapidly that is the negative of the gradient. Back propagation algorithm presented below is taken from the reference [19].

Initialization of weights

Step 1: From training algorithm weights are initialized.

Step 2: Do steps 3–10, while stopping condition is false.

Step 3: Do steps 4–9 for each training pair.

Feed forward

Step 4: The input signal x_i received by each input unit is transmitted to all units in the subsequent layer i.e. hidden layer.

Step 5: Each hidden unit (z_j, $j = 1...$ p) sums its weighted input signals as given in the Eq. (9).

$$z_{-inj} = v_{oj} + \sum_{i=1}^{n} x_i v_{ij} \tag{9}$$

Activation function presented in Eq. (10) is applied to $z_{in\,j}$ and these signals are send to all units in the subsequent layer i.e. Output layer

$$Z_j = f\left(z_{inj}\right) \tag{10}$$

Step 6: Eq. (11) is used to sum weighted input signals for each output unit (y_k, k = 1, ..., m) s its weighted input signals and output signals are calculated by applying activation function given by the Eq. (12)

$$y_{-ink} = w_{ok} + \sum_{j=1}^{p} z_j w_{jk} \tag{11}$$

$$Y_k = f(y_{-ink}) \tag{12}$$

Back Propagation of Errors

Step 7: A target pattern is received by each output unit, which corresponds to an input pattern, to calculate the error term using the Eq. (13).

$$\delta_k = (t_k - y_k)f(y_{-ink}) \tag{13}$$

Step 8: Delta inputs of each hidden layer are summed up from the units in the layer above using the Eq. (13) and using the Eq. (15) the error term is calculated.

$$\delta_{-inj} = \sum_{k=1}^{m} \delta_j w_{jk} \tag{14}$$

$$\delta_j = \delta_{-inj}f(z_{-inj}) \tag{15}$$

Updating Weights and Biases

Step 9: Bias and weights (j = 0,........, p) of each output (y_k, k = 1,......., m) unit are updated and Eq. (16) presents the weight correction term and (17) the bias correction term.

$$\Delta W_{jk} = \alpha \delta_k z_j \tag{16}$$

$$\Delta W_{ok} = \alpha \delta_k \tag{17}$$

Therefore

$$W_{jk}(new) = W_{jk}(old) + \Delta W_{jk}, \text{ and}$$
$$W_{ok}(new) = W_{ok}(old) + \Delta W_{ok}$$

The bias as well as weights (i = 0,….., n) of all hidden units (z_j, j = 1,…., p) are updated and Eq. (18) presents the weight correction term and (19) the bias correction term.

$$\Delta V_{ij} = \alpha \delta_j x_i \tag{18}$$

$$\Delta V_{oj} = \alpha \delta_j \tag{19}$$

Therefore

$$V_{ij}(new) = V_{ij}(old) + \Delta V_{ij},$$

$$V_{oj}(new) = V_{oj}(old) + \Delta V_{oj} \tag{20}$$

Step 10: Test the stop condition.
Minimization of errors or number of epochs etc. may be the stopping condition.

The two important training parameters which require discussion at this point of time are learning rate and momentum constant. The values of weights and biases are controlled by learning rate during training. Rapid learning may be achieved with higher learning rate but it may result in oscillation of weights where as lower rates of learning results in slow learning. To reduce oscillations and divergence, there must be little deviation in weight vector. The momentum used during training is controlled by parameter "momentum constant". This is a frequently used technique for avoiding the network trapped in a shallow minimum. To achieve faster convergence weight update formula is added with momentum. In order to use momentum, weights of previous patterns must be saved. The formula for updating weights of the back propagation network with moment is

$$w_{jk}(t+1) = w_{jk}(t) + \alpha \delta_k z_j + \mu[w_{jk}(t) - w_{jk}(t-1)] \tag{21}$$

$$v_{jk}(t+1) = v_{jk}(t) + \alpha \delta_j x_i + \mu[v_{ij}(t) - v_{ij}(t-1)] \tag{22}$$

μ is the momentum constant within the range of $0 < \mu < 1$.

In the present work values of learning rate is taken as 0.3 and momentum constant are taken as 0.9.

The knowledge of the effect of the combined variation of CR, IJT, IP on combustion parameters is essential for engine designers. However conducting the experiments consume a lot of time and money, and this can be saved by the use of ANN for prediction. Previous work reported effect of any one or two variables (out of CR, IJT and IP) on combustion parameters. The prediction of combustion parameters using ANN is also not found in previous investigations. The objective of present work is to fill this gap in research is to predict combustion parameters for various conditions of CR, IJT, IP and load.

2   Experimental Setup

Experimental investigations are carried out on a four-stroke, single-cylinder, direct injection and water cooled diesel engine with variable compression ratio. The specifications are presented in Table 1.

Table 1. Specifications of the engine

Make of the engine	Kirloskar
Number of cylinders	Single (01)
Type of cooling	Water cooling
Combustion	Direct injection
Bore	80 nm
Stroke	110 nm
Compression Ratio	Variable (15–20)
Power	5 hp
Rated speed	1500 rpm
Fuel injector opening pressure	200 bar
Fuel injection timing	24° before TDC
Type of loading	Electrical loading

The engine is coupled to AC alternator with the loading bank for experimentation purpose. AC alternator is fixed to the engine flywheel and the engine is mounted on a mild steel channel frame and further mounted on anti-vibration mounts. A panel board is used to fix the burette with a 3-way stopcock, digital RPM indicator and u-tube manometer. The Load is varied by varying resistance. The fuel is supplied from the main fuel tank to the measuring burette. An air drum is arranged on the panel frame and connected to the engine through an air hose. The air drum facilitates a magnified orifice and pressure pick up points are connected to end u-tube manometer limbs. The difference in manometer readings is taken at different loads. A piezo - electric transducer is flush mounted in the cylinder head and used to measure cylinder pressure. An optical encoder is employed to record rotation of the crank shaft. Pressure crank angle data is obtained with the help of a high speed data acquisition system. To eliminate effect of cycle to cycle variation, average of pressure crank angle data is recorded for 100 successive cycles is taken. Combustion parameters like heat release, mass fraction burnt, and combustion duration are calculated using averaged data. All digital indicators are connected to PC via RS232 to RS485 converters for data acquisition.

2.1 Experiment Procedure

Experiments are conducted at 4-different injection timings, viz. 22, 24, 26 and 28 degrees before TDC. Thickness of the metallic shims is varied which are inserted between fuel pump and engine block to change static fuel injection timing. At each injection time setting experiments are conducted at four different injector opening pressures, namely 180, 200, 220 and 240 bars. Opening pressure of the fuel injector is adjusted with the help of a injection pressure test rig. At each injector opening pressure experiments are conducted at four compression ratios, i.e. 15, 16.5, 18 and 19. At each compression ratio five loads are considered viz. 0 %, 20 %, 40 %, 60 % & 80 % loads. Therefore, 320 experiments are conducted at different set of conditions and combustion parameters are determined. The complete data is divided into two sets viz. training set and test set randomly in a proportion of 85 % & 15 % respectively. 85 % of data is used for training the network. Numerous trails have been conducted to train the network by varying training algorithm ("trainlm", "traingd", "traingda", "traingdm" etc.), the number of hidden layers (1–2), the number of nodes in the hidden layer (3–22) and activation function (tansig/logsig). After arriving at satisfactory architecture ANN is tested with 15 % of data to check its validity and capability to predict for unknown inputs.

3 Results and Discussions

As stated before objective of this work is prediction of combustion parameters, in the present section discussion presented is based on the results.

Prediction with Artificial Neural Networks. Artificial neural networks are widely used for prediction in various fields of engineering and science due their capability to predict with more accuracy. In the present work, a back propagation neural network is designed with four inputs namely, IJT, IP, CR and load and four output parameters namely, ID, CD, PP and HR. Matlab 7.7 version software is used for training and testing. 320 experiments are conducted and data sets are collected. 272 data sets (85 % of data) are used for the purpose of training the network and randomly selected 48 data sets (15 % of data) are used for testing the network. For improving efficiency of neural network data is normalized in the range −1 to +1. Numerous trials with different network parameters like transfer function, training algorithm, number of nodes in hidden layers, learning rate and momentum factor are carried out and based on co-relation coefficient value for the prediction, best neural network is selected. The best neural network (NN) elements are: tan-sigmoid transfer function, trainlm algorithm, learning rate 0.3, momentum constant 0.9 with 19 neurons in the hidden layer. Neural network (NN) with these elements is trained with Mean Squared Error (MSE) 0.003 (Fig. 3a). Co-relation coefficient for training the network is 0.99209, test and validation are 0.99213 and 0.98939 during training, as shown in Fig. 3(b).

After training neural network is tested with 48 sets of unknown data and co-relation coefficient is 0.9302 and co-relation coefficients for individual output parameters are 0.98924 for ignition delay, 0.98924 for combustion duration, 0.99445 for peak pressure and 0.9909 for heat release as shown in Figs. 4, 5, 6, 7, 8 and 9.

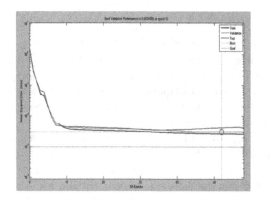 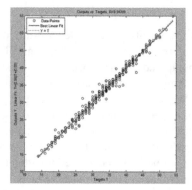

Fig. 3. (. a), (b). Performance of network during the training process indicating mse and co-relation coefficient after simulation.

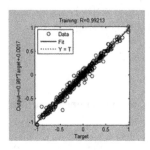 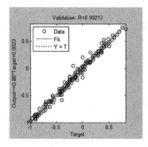 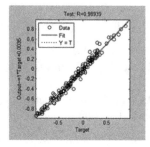

Fig. 4. Co-relation coefficients during training of network.

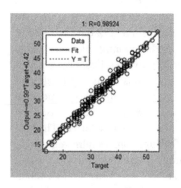 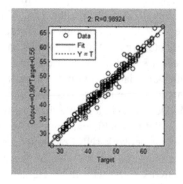

Fig. 5. Co-relation coefficient for the prediction of ID

Fig. 6. Co-relation coefficient for the prediction of CD

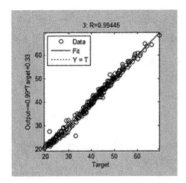

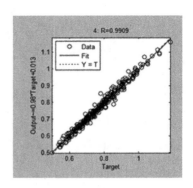

Fig. 7. Co-relation coefficient for the prediction of PP

Fig. 8. Co-relation coefficient for the prediction of HR

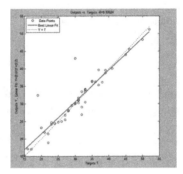

Fig. 9. Co-relation coefficient of prediction for unseen data

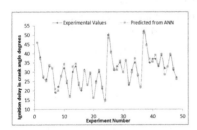

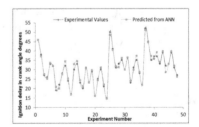

Fig. 10. Predicted vs experimental values of ID

Fig. 11. Predicted vs experimental values of CD

Figures 10, 11, 12 and 13 show predicted vs experimental values of ID, CD, PP and HR.

The average error range for prediction of each parameter is presented in Table 2. It is observed that the neural network with 4–19–4 architecture with "trainlm" learning algorithm is capable to forecast ID, CD, PP and HR with good precision and the

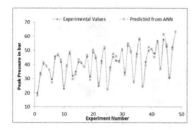

Fig. 12. Predicted vs experimental values of PP

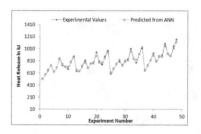

Fig. 13. Predicted vs experimental values of HR

Table 2. Average error range for prediction of parameters

Parameter	Average error range for prediction
ID	−9.87 to +10.5
Combustion duration	−9.71 to +7.47
Peak Pressure	−8.06 to +8.14
Heat Release	−6.78 to +5.7

network can be used to predict at any unknown set of conditions of IJT, IP, CR and load. The engine designers can get data from the neural network and need not conduct experiments.

4 Conclusions

A back propagation neural network (BPNN) is designed, trained and tested to predict combustion parameters of diesel engine for different IJT, IP, CR and load conditions.

There is very good agreement between experimental values and neural network (NN) predicted values. Neural networks can reduce the effort for conducting experiments and proved as an efficient tool for predicting combustion parameters.

References

1. Ma, Z., Huang, Z., Li, C., Wang, X., Miao, H.: Effects of fuel injection timing on combustion and emission characteristics of a diesel engine fueled with diesel-propane blends. Energy Fuels **21**(3), 1504–1510 (2007)
2. Sonar, D., et al.: Performance and emission characteristics of a diesel engine with varying injection pressure and fuelled with raw mahua oil (preheated and blends) and mahua oil methyl ester. Clean Technol. Environ. Pol. **17**(6), 1499–1511 (2014)
3. Hwang, J., Qi, D., Jung, Y., Bae, C.: Effect of injection parameters on the combustion and emission characteristics in a common-rail direct injection diesel engine fueled with waste cooking oil biodiesel. Renewable Energy **63**, 9–17 (2014). doi:10.1016/j.renene.2013.08. 051. Elsevier. ISSN 0960-1481

4. Sharma, A. Sivalingam, M.: Impact of fuel injection pressure on performance and emission characteristics of a diesel engine fueled with jatropha methyl ester tyre pyrolysis blend. SAE Technical Paper 2014-01-2650 (2014). doi:10.4271/2014-01-2650

5. Hwang, J., Qi, D., Jung, Y., Bae, C.: Effect of injection parameters on the combustion and emission characteristics in a common-rail direct injection diesel engine fueled with waste cooking oil biodiesel. Renewable Energy **63**, 9–17 (2014). Elsevier. ISSN 0960-1481. http://dx.doi.org/10.1016/j.renene.2013.08.051

6. Nagaraja, S., Sooryaprakash, K., Sudhakaran, R.: Investigate the effect of compression ratio over the performance and emission characteristics of variable compression ratio engine fueled with preheated palm oil - diesel blends. Procedia Earth Planet. Sci. **11**, 393–401 (2015). ISSN 1878-5220. http://dx.doi.org/10.1016/j.proeps.2015.06.038

7. Liu, M.-B., He, B.-Q., Zhao, H.: Effect of air dilution and effective compression ratio on the combustion characteristics of a HCCI (homo-geneous charge compression ignition) engine fuelled with n-butanol. Energy **85**, 296–303 (2015). ISSN 0360-5442. http://dx.doi.org/10.1016/j.energy.2015.03.082

8. Kumar, J., Bansal, A.: Application of artificial neural network to predict properties of diesel –biodiesel blends. Kathmandu Univ. J. Sci. Eng. Technol. **6**(ii), 98–103 (2010)

9. Cammarata, L., Fichera, A., Pagano, A.: Neural prediction of combustion in-stability. Appl. Energy **72**, 513–528 (2002). Elsevier

10. Atkinson, C.M., Long, T.W., Hanzevack, E.L.: Virtual sensing: a neural network-based intelligent performance and emissions prediction system for on-board diagnostics and engine control. In: Diagnostics and Controls (SP-1357) International Congress and Exposition, Detroit, Michigan, 23–26 February 1998

11. Howlett, R.J.: Monitoring and control of an internal combustion engine air-fuel ratio using neural and fuzzy techniques. In: International Symposium on the Engineering of Intelligent Systems, vol. 43 (1998)

12. Hafner, M., Schuler, M., Nelles, O., Isserman, R.: Fast neural networks for diesel engine control design. Control Eng. Pract. **8**, 1211–1221 (2000)

13. Heywood, J.B.: Internal Combustion Engine Fundamentals. McGraw Hill Book Company, New York (1998)

14. Mathur, M.L., Sharma, R.P.: Internal Combustion Engine (1999)

15. Merker, G.P., Schwarz, C., Teichmann, R.: Combustion Engines Deveopment: Mixture formation, Combustion Emissions and Simulation. Springer, Heidelberg (2011)

16. Mo, Y.: HCCI heat release rate and combustion efficiency: a coupled KIVA multi zone modeling study. Ph.d. dissertation, The University of Michigan (2008)

17. Elkassaby, M., Nemitallah, M.A.: Studying the effect of compression ratio on an engine fueled with waste oil produced biodiesel/diesel fuel. Alexandria Eng. J. **52**, 1–11 (2013)

18. Investigation on effect of variation in compression ratio on performance and combustion characteristics of C.I engine fuelled with Palm Oil Methyl Ester (POME) and its blends. Simul. Glob. J. Res. Eng. Automot. Eng. **12**(3) (2012). Version 1.0

19. Sivanandam, S.N., Sumathi, S., Deepa, S.N.: Introduction to Neural Networks using MATLAB 6.0. Tata McGraw Hill Education Private Limited (2006)

20. Elkassaby, M., Nemitallah, M.A.: Studying the effect of compression ratio on an engine fueled with waste oil produced biodiesel/diesel fuel. Alexandria Eng. J. **52**(1), 1–11 (2013). doi:10.1016/j.aej.2012.11.007

21. Ma, Z., Huang, Z., Li, C., Wang, X., Miao, H.: Effects of fuel injection timing on combustion and emission characteristics of a diesel engine fueled with diesel-propane blends. Energy Fuels **21**(3), 1504–1510 (2007)

An Improved Quantum Inspired Immune Clone Optimization Algorithm

Annavarapu Chandra Sekhara Rao, Suresh Dara[✉], and Haider Banka

Department of Computer Science and Engineering,
Indian School of Mines, Dhanbad 826004, India
{rao.acs.cse,banka.h.cse}@ismdhanbad.ac.in, darasuresh@live.in

Abstract. An improved quantum inspired immune clone optimization algorithm is proposed for optimization problem. It is proposed based on the immune clone algorithm and quantum computing theory. The algorithm adopts the quantum bit to express the chromosomes, and uses the quantum gate updating to implement evolutionary of population which can take advantage of the parallelism of quantum computing and the learning, memory capability of the immune system. Quantum observing entropy is introduced to evaluate the population evolutionary level, and relevant parameters are adjusted according to the entropy value. The proposed algorithm is tested on few benchmark optimization functions and the results are compared with other existing algorithms. The simulation results show that the proposed algorithm has better convergence, robustness and precision.

1 Introduction

Many nature inspired optimized techniques have been popular in fast few decades like Simulated Annealing, Genetic Algorithms (GA), Differential Evolution (DE), Particle Swarm Optimization (PSO, Ant Colony Optimization, Firefly Algorithms, Cuckoo Search, Bat Algorithms, Harmony Search, Artificial Immune System (AIS), etc... [1]. Artificial immune system is an artificial intelligence system through imitating the immune response, immune regulation and immune memory mechanism of biological immune system with high performance, self organization and robustness [2].

In recent years, a new optimization method based on quantum inspired [3,4] has attracted wide attention, which uses the basic principles of quantum computing (encoding and update) to obtain the solution. The theoretical study shows that the quantum computing has higher computing efficiency than the classical computer. Many researchers introduce the quantum computing to the traditional intelligent optimization algorithms and get better results [5]. The combination of quantum computing and intelligent optimization algorithms is the new trend of intelligent computing [3,4]. Using immune algorithm, different application problems have been solved in last few years like different engineering optimization problems, design and manufacturing problems [6].

© Springer International Publishing AG 2016
B.K. Panigrahi et al. (Eds.): SEMCCO 2015, LNCS 9873, pp. 84–91, 2016.
DOI: 10.1007/978-3-319-48959-9_8

The artificial immune algorithm is an application of artificial immune system in optimization domain, which mainly simulates the biological immune system [7]. This algorithm uses three component terms: Antigen, Antibody and Affinity fitness. The antigen represents the objective function of the problem, the antibody represents the solution of the problem, the affinity fitness represents the matching degree of affinity and antibody and antigen, which reflects the satisfaction degree of candidate solution for the target function and constraint conditions, the repulsive force represents the similar degree between the two antibodies [2]. The antibody is optimized according to the affinity fitness and repulsive force between antibody and antigen. The antibodies with high affinity are memorized to promote the rapid convergence [8]. Immune clone algorithm [9] was proposed by De Castro and Von Zuben in 2000 with the development of AIS, which is inspired from the biological immune principle of clone selection and successfully used to solve pattern recognition, numerical optimization and TSP problem [2,7]. Many kinds of artificial immune algorithm are proposed with the development of immune system, such as immune genetic algorithm, immune agent algorithm. Improved immune algorithm has been proposed, such as immune algorithm based on bacteria, immune acetic acid algorithm based on antibody diversity, immune genetic algorithm based on immune network theory and clone selection immune algorithm.

This paper proposes the new method known as Improved quantum inspired immune clone optimization algorithms based on the immune clone algorithm and quantum computing theory. The algorithm has three characteristic. The first one is to use the quantum encoding to construct antibody to make use of the high parallel performance of quantum computation, which can express many information states using only one quantum antibody and make the antibody group quickly convergent. The second one is the use of quantum updating approach in accomplishing immune genetic operation. The third one is to use the quantum information entropy to express the evolution degree of quantum immune clone optimization algorithm, which can get higher precision. The simulation results show that the proposed algorithm improved the searching efficiency, searching accuracy and stable convergence compared with GA, DE and PSO.

2   Related Methods

This section formally describes the basics of Immune Clone Algorithm for optimization and Quantum computing to understand the proposed algorithm.

2.1   Immune Clone Algorithm

Step: 1 Encoding and initialization of antibody. Generating randomly N antibodies correspond to the problem.

Step: 2 Affinity fitness evaluation. Choosing the best m antibodies to form the memory set A_m and forming the set A_r using the rest individuals with low fitness.

Step: 3 Checking the termination conditions whether meet, if it is yes, terminating the program, otherwise going to Step 4.

Step: 4 Immune cloning operation. Doing immune cloning operator on the every individual of memory set A_m, and using the results to form the new set $T1_i$. The size of cloning for each antibody is proportional to the affinity degree.

Step: 5 Immune evolving operation. Accomplishing updating operations by crossover and mutation and getting new population $T2_i$.

Step: 6 Cloning selecting operation. Computing the fitness of the individual of set $T1_i$ and selecting the appropriate antibody to replace the parent or retain the parent, and forming a new memory set.

Step: 7 Immune dying operation. Abandoning the low fitness of antibodies and adding new randomly generated antibodies to the population in same number in order to maintain the diversity of population.

Step: 8 Antibody update. Updating the set of antibodies $A = A_m + A_r$, and returning to the STEP 2.

2.2   Quantum Computing Theory

Quantum computing is processed as in the following steps.

Step: 1 Quantum bit: The quantum bit state is represented by either 1 or 0 and the following formula is used to define it.

$$|\Psi \geq \alpha|0 + \beta|1 \tag{1}$$

The quantum clone method encodes the solutions by using quantum bit, where these bits are two complex numbers α & β, which are based on probability with 0 state and 1 state. If the $|\alpha|^2 + |\beta|^2 = 1$, $|\alpha|^2$ is the probability then quantum bit is 0 and If $|\beta|^2$ is the probability then that quantum bit is 1.

Step: 2 Quantum observation: It is a method to transform the quantum chromosome into a realistic problem solution. The method describe as follows.

(i) Generate a random uniformly distributed number, $r = rand(0, 1)$;

(ii) If the generated number $r \leq \alpha_i^2$ the i gene of individual is $x_i = 0$, else $x_i = 1$;

(iii) Repeat the same process to generate other genes in quantum observations and finally generate the solutions.

Step: 3 Quantum update: Quantum clone method updates the antiboby by using the quantum rotating, gate operating on the quantum bit, also population are updated using quantum rotating gate. The updating formula is:

$$\cup(\Theta_i) = \begin{bmatrix} cos(\Theta_i) & -sin(\Theta_i) \\ sin(\Theta_i) & cos(\Theta_i) \end{bmatrix} \tag{2}$$

3 Proposed Approach

The proposed algorithm uses Quantum Immune Clone algorithm [10,11] and integrates with quantum computing theory. Here, the quantum bit represents antibody and uses the quantum updating that evolves toward local optimum or global optimum. This section explains basic concept of Quantum immune clone algorithm and our proposed algorithm.

3.1 Quantum Immune Clone Algorithm

Quantum immune clone algorithm [11] is a probability search optimization algorithm based on quantum theory and immune clone principle. Representation of quantum states is introduced to antibody coding quantum encoding quantum update strategy and other immune operators are adopted to make the population approach towards the partial or global optimized solution. Therefore, quantum immune clone algorithm possesses the characters of artificial immune system such as specialty, memory, and diversity, and it also has superimposed and parallelism features of quantum systems. These features make the quantum immune algorithm has a significant advantage in solving the optimization problem. In recent years, quantum immune clone algorithm is applied in many fields of optimization. It has a small population size without affecting the algorithm performance, and it also has fast convergence and strong global search ability.

Immune clone algorithm mainly includes three steps, namely the cloning operation, immune genetic manipulation and clone selection. State transfers of antibody populations can be expressed as the following random process

$$A(k)cloneA'(k)immuneA''(k)selectionA(k+1) \qquad (3)$$

Quantum immune clone algorithm is based on the basic immune clone algorithm, do quantum coding for antibodies and introduce quantum update strategy in the immune gene operation.

3.2 An Improved Quantum Immune Clone Algorithm: Proposed Algorithm

An Improved quantum immune clone algorithm adjusts quantum gates updated angular step adaptively according to the measurement of quantum immune clone algorithm evolution degree, and achieves search with small step and high resolution in the vicinity of optimum solution after algorithm has evolved to a certain extent, which get the more accurate solution.

Measure of Evolution Degree: In order to adjust the parameters adaptively according to the evolution degree of algorithms, a reasonable measure must be given. Through the analysis of the principles of Quantum immune clone algorithm, it is known that with the population approaching optimum solution, each quantum bit probability amplitude tends to 1 or 0 respectively, then the observed value will accordingly become 1 or 0. Therefore, algorithms evolution degree can be evaluated quantitatively according to the quantum bit probability amplitude. As we all know, "entropy" is a basic concept in information theory which describes the degree of uncertainty. This paper uses the concept of quantum observation entropy as measure of the evolution degree. Quantum observation entropy is defined as:

$$H_Q = -2 \sum_{i=1}^{n} q_i^2(x_i) log \, q_i(x_i) \tag{4}$$

Among them, H_Q is the observation entropy value of quantum coding system, Q_I is the probability amplitude of quantum bit encoding for gene i. For a quantum encoding system with N quantum bits, the formula 4 can be rewritten as:

$$H_Q = -2 \sum_{i=1}^{n} \left[|\alpha_i|^2 \times log(|\alpha_i|) + |\beta_i|^2 \times log(|\beta_i|) \right] \tag{5}$$

N represents the length of the individual coding, $|\alpha_i|^2$ and $\beta_i|^2$ respectively represent probability that a quantum bit in state 0 and state 1.

Quantum Update Based on the Observation of Quantum Entropy: In the basic quantum algorithms, quantum gates rotation angle is fixed. With the increase of the evolution of generations, antibodies approach in direction close to the optimal solution, then the quantum gates rotation angular step should be reduced in order to increase the accuracy of the solution. Quantum observation entropy gives a specific form for quantum gates rotation step $\Delta\Theta$ to achieve:

$$\Delta\Theta_i = 0.025\pi \left[1 - k\frac{H_{Qs} - H_Q}{H_{Qs}} \right] \tag{6}$$

H_{Qs} represents quantum observation entropy of initial antibodies; H_Q represents the current antibodies quantum observation entropy; k represents the adjustment factor.

Adjustment Strategy of Quantum Gate: The adjustment strategy of quantum gate in the paper is shown in the Table 1. Firstly randomly choosing one gene i from the current individual, and then comparing the fitness function value of current individual x and current optimal individual b to determine the rotation direction of quantum gate based on the quantum bits $[\alpha_{i,j}, \beta_{i,j}]^T$ and the observation, the step of rotation angle is computed according to the formula 6.

4   Results and Discussions

We have used five benchmark testing functions to test the performance of proposed algorithm according to the existing available literature [12,13]. The used

Table 1. Quantum gate rotation strategy.

x_i	b_i	$f(x) \geq f(b)$	Θ	$\alpha\beta > 0$	$\alpha\beta < 0$	$\alpha = 0$	$\beta = 0$
0	0	True/False	0	0	0	0	0
0	1	False	0	0	0	0	0
0	1	True	$\Delta\Theta_i$	-1	$+1$	± 1	0
0	1	False	$\Delta\Theta_i$	-1	$+1$	± 1	0
1	0	True	$\Delta\Theta_i$	$+1$	-1	0	± 1
1	1	True/False	$\Delta\Theta_i$	$+1$	-1	0	± 1

function details, and parameter values is shown in the Table 2. Here, D is the dimension of the function. We have tested on two dimension values as D=20 and D=30 and results reported in Tables 3 and 4.

Table 2. Parameters and its values details.

Parameters	Algorithm			
	Proposed	GA	PSO	DE
Population size	50	50	50	50
Maximum feneration	50	50	50	50
Elite number	2	2	2	–
Cross over probability	–	0.5	–	0.5
Mutation probability	0.01	0.01	–	–
Cross factor	–	–	–	0.5

We have taken results of an average of 10 runs for each test function on each algorithm. All results reported in Tables 3 and 4. Table 3 shows the proposed algorithm results along with other existing algorithms ICA, GA, PSO and DE for comparisons where dimension $D = 20$. Similarly, results reported in Table 4 for dimension $D = 30$.

We have reported few bench mark test function optimization values and its time for proposed algorithm and few other existing algorithms. Observing from the above tables, we can say that the proposed algorithm can get better results than the other reported algorithms. The reported searching convergent time is also less than other algorithms. When the dimension increases from 20 to 30, the proposed algorithm shows better performance of global searching capability. Finally, the test results show that the proposed algorithm has obvious advantage in performance compared with other optimization algorithm such as GA, PSO and DE (Tables 3 and 4).

Table 3. Results for 5 testing functions, D = 20.

Theory		Proposed		ICA		PSO		DE	
Function	Expect result	Optimum result	Time taken	Optimum result	Time taken	Optimum result	Time taken	Optimum result	Time taken
f_1	0	797.522	0.471	4790.108	0.775	9201.077	0.684	2218.617	0.605
f_2	−8379	−7464.340	0.427	−8123.387	0.606	−2839.385	0.675	−3906.005	0.606
f_3	0	9.712	0.432	32.101	0.637	82.811	0.675	22.946	0.612
f_4	0	9.660	0.430	17.752	0.640	16.808	0.678	12.203	0.610
f_5	0	0.001	0.433	0.001	0.621	0.416	0.680	0.001	0.617

ICA-Immune Clone Algorithm, GA- Genetic Algorithm, PSO-Particle Swarm Optimization, DE-Differential Evolution

Table 4. Testing results for 5 functions, D = 30.

Theory		Proposed		ICA		PSO		DE	
Function	Expect result	Optimum result	Time taken	Optimum result	Time taken	Optimum result	Time taken	Optimum result	Time taken
f_1	0	2641.822	0.602	12780.217	0.904	17752.867	0.788	10297.009	0.749
f_2	−12569	−10531	0.561	−11513	0.719	−3142	0.855	−4560	0.861
f_3	0	27.390	0.552	108.650	0.740	160.441	0.785	95.386	0.769
f_4	0	11.210	0.567	17.873	0.729	18.654	0.775	16.361	0.749
f_5	0	0.001	0.559	0.015	0.719	1.216	0.785	0.022	0.769

ICA-Immune Clone Algorithm, GA- Genetic Algorithm, PSO-Particle Swarm Optimization, DE-Differential Evolution

Table 5. Test functions details.

Function name	Definition bound	Solution distributing
f_1− Sphere model	$-100 \leq x_i \leq 100$	$min f_1 = f_1(0, \ldots, 0) = 0$
f_2− Generalized Schwefels problem 4	$-500 \leq x_i \leq 500$	$min f_2 = f_2(-420, 9687, \ldots, -420, 9687) = 0$
f_3− Generalized Griewank	$-600 \leq x_i \leq 600$	$min f_3 = f_3(0, \ldots, 0) = 0$
f_4− Ackleys function	$-32 \leq x_i \leq 32$	$min f_4 = f_5(0, \ldots, 0) = 0$
f_5− Sum of different power	$-1 \leq x_i \leq 1$	$min f_5 = f_5(0, \ldots, 0) = 0$

5   Conclusion and Future Work

In this paper, we have proposed an improved quantum immune clone algorithm for optimization problem based on the quantum computing theory and artificial immune model. The method uses the quantum bits to encode the antibody, and adopts the quantum gate mutation adjustment strategy to implement the quantum updating. The experimental results show that the proposed method has a good diversity of population and convergence ability, which is better than the existing optimization algorithms such as GAPSO and DE algorithm.

This proposed algorithm may extends to solve machine learning problems like feature selection, classification and clustering. We are planing to perform feature selection to get optimal feature subsets from few bench mark datasets by using proposed algorithm as our future work.

References

1. Yang, X.S.: Nature-Inspired Optimization Algorithms. Elsevier, Amsterdam (2014)
2. Yue, X., Abraham, A., Chi, Z.X., Hao, Y.Y., Mo, H.: Artificial immune system inspired behavior-based anti-spam filter. Soft. Comput. **11**(8), 729–740 (2007)
3. Han, K.H., Kim, J.H.: Quantum-inspired evolutionary algorithms with a new termination criterion, h_ε; gate, and two-phase scheme. IEEE Trans. Evol. Comput. **8**(2), 156–169 (2004)
4. Han, K.H., Kim, J.H.: Quantum-inspired evolutionary algorithm for a class of combinatorial optimization. IEEE Trans. Evol. Comput. **6**(6), 580–593 (2002)
5. Xiong, Y., Chen, H.H., Miao, F.Y., Wang, X.F.: A quantum genetic algorithm to solve combinatorial optimization problem. Acta Electronica Sin. **32**(11), 1855–1858 (2004)
6. Sun, L., Luo, Y., Ding, X., Zhang, J.: A novel artificial immune algorithm for spatial clustering with obstacle constraint and its applications. Comput. Intell. Neurosci. **2014**, 13 (2014)
7. Jiao, L.C., Du, H.F.: Development and prospect of the artificial immune system. Acta Electronica Sin. **31**(10), 1540–1548 (2003)
8. Wang, L., Pan, J., Jiao, L.: The immune algorithm. Acta Electronica Sin. **28**(7), 74–78 (2000)
9. Nunes de Casto, L., Von Zuben, F.J.: An evolutionary immune network for data clustering. In: 2000 Proceedings of Sixth Brazilian Symposium on Neural Networks, pp. 84–89. IEEE (2000)
10. Bing, H., Weiwei, Q., HuaYing, L., Qing-wen, W., Xin, Z.: Multi-route planning method of low-altitude aircrafts based on qica algorithm. In: 2015 27th Chinese Control and Decision Conference (CCDC), pp. 5498–5502. IEEE (2015)
11. Nielsen, M.A., Chuang, I.L.: Quantum Computation and Quantum Information. Cambridge University Press, Cambridge (2010)
12. Andrei, N.: An unconstrained optimization test functions collection. Adv. Model. Optim. **10**(1), 147–161 (2008)
13. Huang, H., Qin, H., Hao, Z., Lim, A.: Example-based learning particle swarm optimization for continuous optimization. Inf. Sci. **182**(1), 125–138 (2012)

Diagnosis of Parkinson Disease Patients Using Egyptian Vulture Optimization Algorithm

Aditya Dixit, Alok Sharma, Ankur Singh, and Anupam Shukla$^{(\boxtimes)}$

Soft Computing and Expert System Laboratory,
ABV-Indian Institute of Information Technology, Gwalior 474015, India
a.dixit93@gmail.com, aloksharma.iiitm@gmail.com,
ankursingh1993@gmail.com, dranumpamshukla@gmail.com

Abstract. Parkinson disease(PD) is a neurological disorder which affect the nervous system of the body causing problem related to gait and speech disorder. Speech and gait serve as major parameter in diagnosis of the disease in the early stages of its symptoms. This study uses these parameters to perform a comparative study of two nature inspired algorithm for diagnosis of the Parkinson Disease. The process involves first selecting an optimal feature set for classification and then using them to classify and predict PD patients from non PD patients. Two different datasets were used consisting of gait and speech data of PD and non PD patients. Optimal Feature selection was done using Particle swarm optimization and Egyptian Vulture Optimization Algorithm. The optimal feature set was then used to classify the dataset using KNN classifier. According to the experiment EVOA outperforms PSO in the selection of the feature subset. This study thus concludes that new meta-heuristic algorithm EVOA works better than traditional PSO in diagnosis of PD patients which in real life can help to speed up the process and lessen the suffering of the patient by early detection.

Keywords: Parkinson disease(PD) · Egyptian vulture optimization algorithm(EVOA) · Particle swarm optimization(PSO)

1 Inroduction

Parkinson Disease(PD) is a chronic disorder of central nervous system which mainly affects the motor system of the body. This is caused by death of dopamine generating cell in a region of mid brain called substantia nigra. These cells are responsible for generating a neurotransmitter called dopamine which is mainly responsible for reward based behavior. Commonly it occurs in people over age of 50 [1]. Early symptoms of PD consist of motor related disorder. Motor symptoms include tremor, rigidity, slowness of movement, postural instability and speech disorder. Together motor symptoms are collectively called "parkinsonism". First detailed description of Parkinson Disease was given by English doctor James Parkinson [2].

© Springer International Publishing AG 2016
B.K. Panigrahi et al. (Eds.): SEMCCO 2015, LNCS 9873, pp. 92–103, 2016.
DOI: 10.1007/978-3-319-48959-9_9

The aim of the present study is to find/investigate a non-invasive way of diagnosis that can be easily performed and be quite accurate. The present study is motivated by the fact that telemonitoring can provide a convenient way of diagnosis for a patient without physically traveling to the hospital. This method is a great relief for PD patients. A patient can stay at home and record his/her biometrics in a machine and send it across the Internet to the doctor.

Diagnosis of disease is primarily based on symptoms and other advanced techniques like neuroimaging. There are no lab test that will certainly identify the disease.

The two major symptoms, gait and speech disorder are generally used for clinical diagnosis. These two parameters can also be used for diagnosis using computer machine.

The rest of paper is divided as follows: In Sect. 2 the methodology of the diagnosis process is given. Sect. 3 contains the experimental outcome of the diagnosis process.

1.1 Existing Method for Diagnosis of PD

Most of the existing methods used for evaluating Parkinson's disease depends largely on human expertise. The use of Unified Parkinson Disease Rating Scale (UPDRS) [3] is heavily popular for recognition and detecting severity staging of Parkinson disease. It consists of series of tests performed on the patient, and rated by the clinician according to some predefined guidelines.

Jian et al. [4], proposed gait recognition method based on SVM (Support Vector Machines). Human motion image sequence is used for extraction of width and angle information. The features of angle and width is merged and reduced by the KPCA (Kernel Principal Component Analysis). They reduced the dimensionality of gait characteristic, which can obtain the best projection direction and enhance the capacity of data classification. Then the SVM models are trained by the decomposed feature vectors. The gaits are classified by the trained SVM models.

In 2013, JochenKlucken, et al. [5] used biosensor based Embedded Gait Analysis utilizing Intelligent Technology (eGait). In eGait accelerometers and gyroscope are attached to shoes to record movement signs and leg capacity while walking.

Recent inclination in speech pattern analysis of PD patients triggered a research for building a telediagnosis tools. Erdogdu Sakar et al. [6] collected a wide range of speech samples and sound types of varying variety such as sustained vowel, sentences compiled from a set of speaking exercises for People with Parkinson(PWP). The study aims to devise a computer software for data collection and analysis to make the process of PD diagnosis easy in the Department of Neurology in Cerrahpasa Faculty of Medicine, Istanbul University.

1.2 Need for Feature Selection

Though the use of sensors to detect Parkinson disease have revolutionized the detection techniques, but the major problem that arises is the bulk amount of data that has to be processed. The Physionet.org gait database for Parkinson patients consists of 19 attributes. Other gait databases too that serves as Parkinson detection contains mighty data with large number of attributes. There is a need to extract only the optimal feature subset which may represent the entire database and classify the PD patients with normal people efficiently. Feature construction has a long research history and a large number of feature construction approaches have been developed [7]. Based on whether a classification algorithm is included in the evaluation procedure, existing feature construction methods can be broadly divided into two categories, which are wrapper approaches and filter approaches [8]. If a learning or a classification algorithm is used as a fitness evaluation function of the feature substring then this approach is called wrapper approach. In this method feature extraction algorithm exist as a wrapper around a classification algorithm. The performance of the classification algorithm is used to evaluate the goodness of the feature subsets. Usually it provide better result than filter approach. One major drawback of this approach is that it is computationally very expensive. In filter approach search process is independent of any classification algorithm. Features are selected on the basis statistical analysis. This method requires less computation but is not as accurate as wrapper method. Bing Xue et al. [9] discussed about the implementation of particle swarm optimization technique for feature construction. This paper proposes a PSO based feature construction approach using the original low level features and constructing a high level feature for binary classification problems. They constructed a single feature out of the whole dataset and experimental results conducted by them showed that a single feature can achieve a better classification rate than using all the original features. They used the advantages of PSO as a global search technique for feature construction. Instead of only being an optimization technique, they used PSO directly for classification. An improved version of PSO is used by Yuanning Liu et al. [10] for feature selection. They designed a modified multi-swarm PSO(MSPSO) to solve problems which consists of a number of sub-swarms. They used SVM optimization in combination with PSO for feature selection. A multi swarm scheduler control and monitor each sub swarm according to some rules. The objective function was developed by taking into consideration both the classification rate and F-score. The proposed method performed better than traditional PSO and genetic algorithm. The thesis which is aimed at categorizing patients needs an algorithm which can manipulate gait data.

2   Methodology

2.1   KNN Classifier

KNN classifier is one of the most simple machine learning algorithm for classification. In classification the input consist of training data which is classified on the majority vote of its k nearest neighbors. The k nearest neighbors are selected using different predefined metrics (like euclidean distance) and the object belong to the most common class among it's k nearest neighbor. If $k = 1$, then object is assigned to the class of that single nearest neighbor. Training input consists of vectors in multidimensional feature space each with a class label. In classification phase an unlabeled vector is classified by assigning the most common label among it's k neighbors.

Feature interaction becomes a problem in classification. An irrelevant feature may become important if it's complementary to another feature. On the other hand a relevant feature may be redundant due to availability of other features.

2.2   Particle Swarm Optimization

Particle swarm intelligence algorithm was introduced as an optimization technique for use in real number space by Eberhart and Kennedy in 1995 [11].

Particles or potential solutions are represented having a position and rate of the change in d-dimensional space. In PSO, a number of solutions are encoded as a swarm of particles in the search space. The initial values of a particle are randomly chosen. Each particle maintains a record of it's best position achieved since the beginning of the iteration. Also each particle has a defined neighborhood. Particles make decision based on the performance of it's neighbor and itself. Current position of the ith particle is represented by

$$x_i = \{x_{i1}, x_{i2}, ..., x_{id}\} \tag{1}$$

Current velocity of the ith particle is represented by

$$v_i = \{v_{i1}, v_{i2}, ..., v_{id}\} \tag{2}$$

Based on the pbest and gbest PSO update the particle's velocity and position. Position update equate is as follows:

$$x_{id}^{t+1} = x_{id}^t + v_{id}^{t+1} \tag{3}$$

Velocity update equation is as follows:

$$v_{id}^{t+1} = w * v_{id}^t + c_1 * r_{1i} * \left(p_{id} - x_{id}^t\right) + c_2 * r_{2i} * \left(p_{gd} - x_{id}^t\right) \tag{4}$$

where, p_{id} denotes the particle's best (pbest) position, $d \in D$ denotes the d th dimension in the search space. w is the inertia weight. c_1 and c_2 are self and global learning factors. r_{1i} and r_{2i} are values distributed uniformly in $[0, 1]$. p_{id} and p_{gd} are element of pbest and gbest in d^{th} dimension.

For problems that require optimization in discrete search space like problems that have distinction between variables a modified version of PSO was introduced called Binary PSO.

In binary version of PSO developed by Kennedy and Eberhart [12] in 1997 x_{id}, p_{id}, v_{id} are restricted to 0 and 1 only. In binary space the velocity of a particle may be described by number of bit changed per iteration. Therefore the velocity of a particle is the Hamming distance between particle at time t and time $t+1$. In BPSO velocity is defined in terms of probability. That is if

$v_{id} = 0.40$ then there is 40 % chance that x_{id} will be 1 and 60 % chance that it will be 0. v_{id} being a probability in now in $[0, 1]$. In BPSO the only change in update equation is as follows:

$$x_{id} = \begin{cases} 1 & rand() < s(v_{id}) \\ 0 & \text{otherwise} \end{cases}$$

where $rand()$ is an uniform random number from $[0, 1]$. and

$$s(v_{id}) = \frac{1}{1 + e^{-v_{id}}} \qquad (5)$$

2.3 Egyptian Vulture Optimization Algorithm

Egyptian vulture optimization algorithm is metaheursitic algorithm that was introduced to solve combinatorial problems. The algorithm is inspired by the behavior of Egyptian vulture for acquiring their food. Egyptian vulture is different from other birds in their method of hunting. The intelligent behavior of this animal is transformed into the algorithm which can then solve hard optimization problems. These amazing, adaptive, innovative act of Egyptian vulture make them as one of the most intelligent bird species. The algorithm have been used to solve problems like 0/1 knapsack [13], traveling salesman problem [14] and it's performance is studied in a similar manner. The algorithm also have scope in path planning. The primary food of Egyptian vulture is flesh but instead of eating flesh from an animal body they eat it from eggs of another bird. However to break large and strong eggs they have to toss pebbles as hammer to break it. Another interesting feature of the bird is of rolling with twigs. They have a knack for rolling objects with twigs which distinguishes them from other birds. The two main activities described above are transformed into an algorithm.

2.4 Pebble Tossing

Egyptian Vulture uses pebbles to break hard eggs of other birds. This approach is used in algorithm to introduce new solutions in the solution set randomly. Two variables that determine the extent of operation are pebble size and level of removal. Pebble size(PS) contains number of solution to be introduced. Level of removal or force of tossing(FT) denotes how many solutions are removed from solution set. Whether PS equals FT or not depends upon the problem to which algorithm is being applied. Like for problems of shortest path PS $\neq$ FT which allow solutions to be built. On the other hand problems like TSP(Traveling salesperson) where all vertices are to be the part of the final solution PS = FT. After pebble tossing the solution breaks into four cases:

- Get In and No Removal: In this new solutions are added without removing any solution.
- Get In and Removal: In this new solutions are added by removing previous solutions.

- No Get In and No Removal: Nothing is done in this case and old solution is kept as it is.
- No Get In and Removal: No new solutions are added but some are removed from the previous one.

Also point of impact is chosen randomly.

2.5 Rolling with Twigs

It is another distinguishing feature of Egyptian Vulture. They can roll objects using twigs. While hunting they roll the egg to find a weak spot to hit. Algorithmically this is transformed in to rolling the solution set. Rolling of solution set changes the position of variables thereby creating new solutions which provide better fitness and path. There are two parameters which determine the rolling of variables.

- One is degree of rolling: It determines the length of the substring which is to be rolled.
- Other is direction of roll: It determine in which direction rolling is taking place.

2.6 Change of Angle

Apart from above two operations one more operation of change of angle is performed. It derives it's analogy from the change of angle of tossing of pebble so as to experiment the breakage of egg. Change of angle can be applied at multiple points.

Although EVOA is a single agent based algorithm but it can be used as a multi agent based system where each agent is a potential solution in the search space.

2.7 Fitness Calculation

For our purpose we are using KNN classifier as a fitness function for a selected feature set.

In this particular problem of feature selection, we use EVOA algorithm to find the optimal feature subset. In binary version of this algorithm, we use a binary string consisting of only 0's and 1's. For an n-feature dataset, we have 2^n feature subsets available of which we have to consider the optimal one. A binary string of length n is represented in such a way that for every feature used in the subset, we assign '1' to the position and else assign '0' (Figs. 1 and 2).

$$\boxed{1}\boxed{1}\ldots\boxed{}\ldots\boxed{0}\boxed{0}$$

Binary String of length n.

The pseudocode of the algorithm is as follows:

Algorithm 1. Egyptian Vulture Optimization Algorithm for Feature Selection

Input: Training Data
Output: Feature String

1: **procedure** EVOA
2:     Randomly initialize a sequence of particles.
3:     Initialize fitness of each particle.
4:     $i \leftarrow 0$
5:     **while** $i < Maximumiterations$ **do**
6:         Perform pebble tossing operation.
7:         Perform rolling twigs operation.
8:         Perform change of angle operation.
9:         **for** $eachparticle$ **do**
10:            **if** fitness >fitness of the particle **then**
11:                fitness of the particle $\leftarrow$ fitness
12:                particle's best position $\leftarrow$ present position
13:            **if** $gbest$ <fitness **then**
14:                $gbest \leftarrow$ fitness
15:        $i \leftarrow i+1$
16:    $return$ the set of selected feature string.

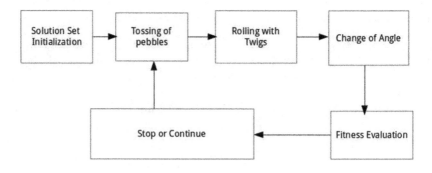

Fig. 1. Flowchart of EVOA

3   Experimental Results

The EVOA is applied over physionet gait database of Parkinson patients and classification accuracy is compared with another nature inspired algorithm PSO. It contains the measures of gait of 73 with healthy controls and 93 patients with idiopathic PD. Each foot had 7 sensors underneath it that measure force as a function of time.

The UCI speech training data consists of 20 PWP(Patients with Parkinson) and 20 healthy. The former has 6 female, 14 male and latter 10 female, 10 male patients. The people involved were suffering from Parkinson from 0 to 6 years. The test data has 28 PD patients. The entire experiment of feature selection was carried out in Enthought Canopy IDE using python 2.7. Different

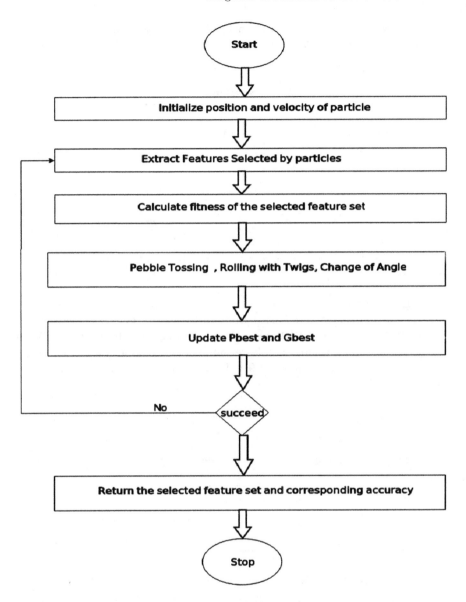

Fig. 2. Flowchart of EVOA feature selection algorithm

algorithms are then applied on these dataset and relevant features are extracted. The reduced dataset is then created using extracted feature set by wrapper method. Wrapper method uses KNN in Scikit. The performance function is f1_score as provided in scikit library [15]. The total experiment of feature selection and classification is run on Intel Core 3 CPU with 2 GB of RAM. After applying EVOA the 19 features of gait dataset is drastically reduced to 14 and 26 features of speech dataset to 5, thus achieving dimensionality reduction. The results obtained through EVOA were pretty fair than that of PSO.

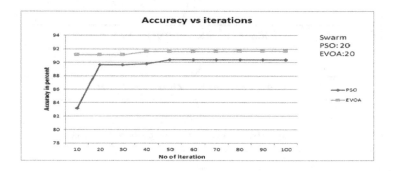

Fig. 3. Accuracy vs. Number of iteration: gait dataset

In Fig. 3 accuracy vs. number of iteration is plotted for a fixed swarm size of 20 and iterations were varied from 10 to 100 for Gait Dataset. For all iteration(10–100) accuracy of EVOA is always greater than that of PSO. EVOA converges to maximum accuracy in lesser number of iteration than PSO. In 100 iterations EVOA got an accuracy of 91.64 while PSO got an accuracy of 90.38.

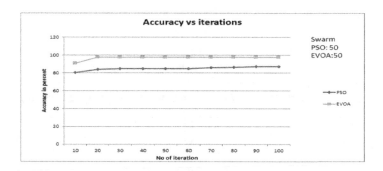

Fig. 4. Accuracy vs. Number of iteration: speech dataset

In Fig. 4, accuracy vs. number of iteration is plotted for a fixed swarm size of 50 and iterations were varied from 10 to 100 for speech Dataset. For all iteration(10–100) accuracy of EVOA is always greater than that of PSO. EVOA converges to maximum accuracy in lesser number of iteration than PSO. In 100 iterations EVOA got an accuracy of 97.87. In 100 iterations PSO got an accuracy of 87.11.

In Fig. 5, number of features vs. number of iteration is plotted for gait dataset, for a fixed swarm size of 20 and iterations were varied from 10 to 100. For all

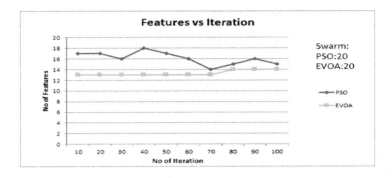

Fig. 5. Number of feature vs. Number of iteration: gait dataset

iteration(10–100) number of features selected for EVOA is always lesser than that for PSO. Out of 19 features EVOA after 100 iterations selects 14 whereas PSO selects 15 features.

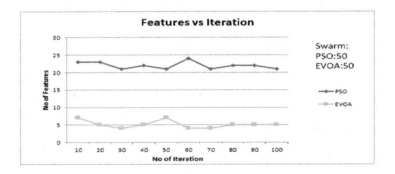

Fig. 6. Number of feature vs. Number of iteration: speech dataset

In Fig. 6, number of features vs. number of iteration is plotted for speech dataset, for a fixed swarm size of 50 and iterations were varied from 10 to 100. For all iteration(10–100) number of features selected for EVOA is always lesser than that for PSO. Out of 26 features EVOA after 100 iterations selects 5 whereas PSO selects 21 features.

Comparison Tables of EVOA and PSO

In Table 1 accuracy of two algorithms PSO and EVOA over both speech and Gait Data set is shown. Accuracy of EVOA is always greater than that of PSO.

In Table 2 number of features selected by two algorithms PSO and EVOA over both speech and Gait Data set is shown. Accuracy of EVOA is always greater than that of PSO.

Table 1. Accuracy of PSO and EVOA

Algorithm	Dataset	Accuracy
EVOA	Gait	91.64
	Speech	97.87
PSO	Gait	90.38
	Speech	87.11

Table 2. Number of features selected by PSO and EVOA

Algorithm	Dataset	Number of features
EVOA	Gait	14
	Speech	5
PSO	Gait	15
	Speech	21

References

1. Jankovic, J.: Parkinsons disease: clinical features and diagnosis. J. Neurol. Neurosurg. Psychiatry **79**(4), 368–376 (2008)
2. Langston, J.W.: Parkinsons disease: current and future challenges. Neurotoxicology **23**(4), 443–450 (2002)
3. Martínez-Martín, P., Gil-Nagel, A., Gracia, L.M., Gómez, J.B., Martínez-Sarriés, J., Bermejo, F.: Unified parkinson's disease rating scale characteristics and structure. Mov. Disord. **9**(1), 76–83 (1994)
4. Ni, J., Liang, L.: A gait recognition method based on KFDA and SVM. In: 2009 International Workshop on Intelligent Systems and Applications, ISA 2009, pp. 1–4. IEEE (2009)
5. Klucken, J., Barth, J., Kugler, P., Schlachetzki, J., Henze, T., Marxreiter, F., Kohl, Z., Steidl, R., Hornegger, J., Eskofier, B., et al.: Unbiased and mobile gait analysis detects motor impairment in Parkinsons disease. PloS ONE **8**(2), e56956 (2013)
6. Sakar, B.E., Isenkul, M.E., Sakar, C.O., Sertbas, A., Gurgen, F., Delil, S., Apaydin, H., Kursun, O.: Collection and analysis of a Parkinson speech dataset with multiple types of sound recordings. IEEE J. Biomed. Health Inform. **17**(4), 828–834 (2013)
7. Liu, H., Motoda, H.: Feature Extraction, Construction, Selection: A Data Mining Perspective. Springer, New York (1998)
8. Xue, B., Zhang, M., Browne, W.N.: Multi-objective particle swarm optimisation (pso) for feature selection. In: Proceedings of the 14th Annual Conference on Genetic and Evolutionary Computation, pp. 81–88. ACM (2012)
9. Xue, B., Zhang, M., Dai, Y., Browne, W.N.: PSO for feature construction and binary classification. In: Proceedings of the 15th Annual Conference on Genetic and Evolutionary Computation, pp. 137–144. ACM (2013)
10. Liu, Y., Wang, G., Chen, H., Dong, H., Zhu, X., Wang, S.: An improved particle swarm optimization for feature selection. J. Bionic Eng. **8**(2), 191–200 (2011)
11. Kennedy, J.: Particle swarm optimization. In: Sammut, C., Webb, G.I. (eds.) Encyclopedia of Machine Learning, pp. 760–766. Springer, New York (2010)

12. Kennedy, J., Eberhart, R.C.: A discrete binary version of the particle swarm algorithm. In: 1997 IEEE International Conference on Systems, Man, and Cybernetics. Computational Cybernetics and Simulation, vol. 5, pp. 4104–4108. IEEE (1997)

13. Sur, C., Sharma, S., Shukla, A.: Egyptian vulture optimization algorithm-a new nature inspired meta-heuristics for knapsack problem. In: Meesad, P., Unger, H., Boonkrong, S. (eds.) The 9th International Conference on Computing and Information Technology (IC2IT2013), pp. 227–237. Springer, Heidelberg (2013)

14. Sur, C., Sharma, S., Shukla, A.: Solving travelling salesman problem using egyptian vulture optimization algorithm – a new approach. In: Kłopotek, M.A., Koronacki, J., Marciniak, M., Mykowiecka, A., Wierzchoń, S.T. (eds.) IIS 2013. LNCS, vol. 7912, pp. 254–267. Springer, Heidelberg (2013). doi:10.1007/978-3-642-38634-3_28

15. Pedregosa, F., Varoquaux, G., Gramfort, A., Michel, V., Thirion, B., Grisel, O., Blondel, M., Prettenhofer, P., Weiss, R., Dubourg, V., et al.: Scikit-learn: machine learning in python. J. Mach. Learn. Res. **12**, 2825–2830 (2011)

Variance Based Particle Swarm Optimization for Function Optimization and Feature Selection

Yamuna Prasad[1]([✉]), K.K. Biswas[1], M. Hanmandlu[1],
and Chakresh Kumar Jain[2]

[1] Indian Institute of Technology, New Delhi, Delhi, India
yprasad@cse.iitd.ac.in
[2] Jaypee Institute of Information Technology, Noida, India

Abstract. Soft computing based techniques have been widely used in multi-objective optimization problems such as multi-modal function optimization, control and automation, network routing and feature selection etc. Feature Selection (FS) in high dimensional data can be modeled as multi-objective optimization problem to reduce the number of features while improving the overall accuracy. Generally, the traditional local optimization methods may not achieve this twin goal as there are many locally optimal solutions. Recently, various flavors of Particle Swarm Optimization (PSO) have been successfully applied for function optimization. The main issue in these variants of PSO is that it gets stuck in local optimum.

In this paper, we have developed a novel variant of PSO which controls the velocity of particles in a swarm. We have named the proposed method as Variance Particle Swarm Optimization (VPSO) henceforth. In VPSO, the velocity is influenced by the variance of the population. When the variance of the population is high, particles make use of exploitation and vice versa. This reduces the effect of swamping in local optimum. We have validated VPSO method for function optimization and feature selection. Our proposed VPSO method achieves significantly better results against the various PSO methods on eight publicly available benchmark functions optimization and on five publicly available benchmark datasets for feature selection.

Keywords: Function optimization · Feature selection · Support Vector Machine (SVM) · Particle Swarm Optimization (PSO)

1 Introduction

Soft computing based approaches such as Particle Swarm Optimization (PSO), Genetic Algorithm (GA) and Ant Colony Optimization (ACO) etc. play significant role in many multi-objective optimization problems. Examples of multi-objective optimization problems include multi-modal function optimization, control and automation, network routing and feature selection etc. [2,7,11,14]. In these methods a set of candidate solution is generated randomly (or based on

© Springer International Publishing AG 2016
B.K. Panigrahi et al. (Eds.): SEMCCO 2015, LNCS 9873, pp. 104–115, 2016.
DOI: 10.1007/978-3-319-48959-9_10

some local heuristics) as an initial step. In the succeeding iterations, these solutions are refined based on the fitness criteria of particles (candidates). In early iterations, particles explore the large search space and in later iterations they exploit the search space to refine their solutions.

In the literature, Various tools and methods have been developed with different variants of PSO for multi-modal function optimization namely, SPSO[1], POPOT[2], fully informed particle swarm (FIPS) [20], comprehensive learning particle swarm optimizer (CLPSO) [18] and heterogeneous comprehensive learning particle swarm optimization (HCLPSO) [19]. These methods vary in the heuristics and random number generation procedure.

The problem of feature selection (FS) is to find a minimal subset of features from the data which maximizes the classification accuracy. Searching for such optimal subset is computationally intractable (search space is exponential) [10, 16, 21]. The key concept behind FS is to remove the irrelevant and redundant features from the training data for improving the prediction accuracy.

The existing feature selection techniques can be divided into three different categories. Filter based methods depend on the statistical estimation of the importance of features (or subset of features) and are oblivious to the classifier being used [1, 8, 21]. Wrapper based methods use classification accuracy to select the relevant subset of features [15–17, 23]. Soft computing based approaches for feature selection fall under this category. In the embedded methods, feature selection metric is directly incorporated in the objective function of the classifier [3, 24–26]. In practice, wrapper based methods are more popular due to their improved accuracy despite the computational complexity.

In the literature, many variants of PSO have been developed for feature selection. Recently, authors in [23] have proposed two variants of PSO with Support Vector Machine (SVM) classifier which uses rule based fitness criterion. This rule based fitness criterion incorporates the cross-validation accuracy, testing accuracy and the number of selected features by a particle. They have shown that their method outperforms many of the state-of-art of PSO variants for feature selection.

In this paper, we propose the variance based PSO (VPSO) for multi-modal function optimization and feature selection. We conduct experiments on eight publicly available benchmark functions[3] namely Sphere, Greiwank, Rosenbrock, Rastragin, Tripod 2D, Ackley, Schwefel 2.2 and Neumaie functions. We have compared VPSO method with various PSO based function optimization methods. The proposed method achieves the lowest error in most of the cases. We have also employed VPSO for feature selection. We show that the proposed method achieves minimal subset of features while not losing on overall accuracy. We

---

[1] http://www.particleswarm.info/Programs.html.

[2] http://code.google.com/p/popot.

[3] http://www.sfu.ca/~ssurjano/optimization.html,   https://code.google.com/p/popot/.

perform extensive evaluation of the proposed approach on five publicly available benchmark UCI[4] repository datasets.

The key contributions of our work can be summarized as follows:

1. A novel way to control the velocity term in PSO using population variance.
2. Validation with the existing state-of-the-art PSO variants for function optimization and feature selection.

The rest of the paper is organized as follows:

We describe the background for PSO approach in Sect. 2. The proposed Variance based PSO is presented in Sect. 3. Experimental results are described in Sect. 4. We conclude our work in Sect. 5.

2 Particle Swarm Optimization

Particle swarm optimization (PSO) method has been successfully applied in many continuous and discrete optimization problems. PSO simulates the social and cognitive behavior of birds, bees or a school of fishes. In this method, each particle (candidate) in swarm (population) is represented by a vector in multi-dimensional search space.

The PSO is a population based search algorithm based on the simulation of the social behavior of birds, bees or a school of fishes. This algorithm originally intends to graphically simulate the graceful and unpredictable choreography of a bird folk. Each individual within the swarm is represented by a vector in multidimensional search space. Each particle has an associated velocity vector according to which it moves in the multi-dimensional search space. Further, particles also keep track of the best solutions achieved by them (local best solution) and also keep track of the best solution found so far (global best solution). The movement of particles is influenced by local best and global best solutions. The algorithm starts with initializing a random values for particles and fixed value of velocity and in the succeeding iterations solutions achieved by the particles in previous iterations are refined based on heuristics. This process is repeated till the desired results are achieved or the specified number of iterations is exhausted. The detailed description of PSO method is available in [13].

2.1 Binary PSO

The PSO was mainly developed for continuous valued search spaces. Further, it has been extended to work for discrete valued search spaces [22].

In binary PSO, each particle represents its position in binary values which are 0 or 1 instead of real values. Each particle's value can then be changed from one to zero or vice versa. In binary PSO the velocity of a particle defined as the probability that a particle might change its state to one.

---

[4] archive.ics.uci.edu/ml/datasets.html.

In a n-dimensional space, i^{th} particle is defined by vector $X_i = (x_{i1}, x_{i2}, x_{i3}, \ldots, x_{in})$ where x_{in} represents position in n^{th} dimension of ith particle position. Similarly, velocity vector is defined as $V_i = (v_{i1}, v_{i2}, v_{i3}, \ldots, v_{in})$ where v_{in} represents velocity in n^{th} dimension for i^{th} particle. The local best position of ith particle is represented by vector $Pos_i = (p_{i1}, p_{i2}, p_{i3}, \cdots, p_{in})$ and the global best position found so far is represented by vector $Pos_g = (pg_{i1}, pg_{i2}, pg_{i3}, \ldots, pg_{in})$. Particle moves are influenced by both local best and global best positions and velocity of ith particle at $(k+1)^{th}$ iteration for d^{th} dimension is updated by:

$$v_{id}^{k+1} = (\omega v_{id}^{k}) + r_1\, C_1\, (Pos_{id} - x_{id}) + r_2\, C_2\, (Pos_{gd} - x_{id}) \tag{1}$$

where $i = 1, 2, 3 \ldots m$; m being the total number of particles, $d = 1, 2, 3, \ldots n$, d being the dimension in multidimensional space, r_1 and r_2 being the two random numbers in the interval $[0,1]$ and C_1 and C_2 are constants known as social and cognitive parameters respectively. These C_1 and C_2 influence the local and global best position of the particle. ω represents inertia weight.

The position of ith particle is updated as follows:

$$x_{id}^{k+1} = x_{id} + v_{id}^{k} \tag{2}$$

2.2 BPSO for Feature Selection

When BPSO is used as in the case of feature selection [23], particle's position is denoted by vector of binary values i.e. 0,1, which indicate whether a feature should be selected or not. This means for n dimensional search space, the particle position is denoted by a vector of n binary values. Velocity is updated by Eq. (1) and particle's position is updated based on the output when the velocity is fed to a sigmoid function as in Eq. (3) [23]. However, the sigmoid function makes the final decision whether the position should be updated to 0 or 1. The sigmoid function is defined as follows:

$$S(v_{id}^{k+1}) = \frac{1}{1 + e^{-v_{id}^{k+1}}} \tag{3}$$

and the position of particle is updated as follows:

$$x_{id}^{k+1} = \begin{cases} 1 & \text{if } S(v_{id}^{k+1}) > r; \\ 0 & \text{otherwise.} \end{cases} \tag{4}$$

where, r is a random number generated in the range $[0,1]$ and S (v_{id}^{k+1}) is the sigmoid value obtained using velocity at $(k+1)^{th}$ iteration. When S (v_{id}^{k+1}) is greater than r, then the corresponding feature gets selected otherwise it is not selected.

3   Proposed Variance Based Particle Swarm Optimization

To deal with the problem of swamping in local minimum, we use dynamic strategy to update the particle's velocity. A small population variance, signifies that particles are tending to converge to a point which may be a possible local minimum. In order to get rid of getting trapped to this minimum, the velocity of the particles should be increased which makes the particles to steer out from this local trap. This enhances the exploration in a large search space. Therefore, in the proposed strategy, when population variance is high, particles exploit more (tendency to converge) and when it is low, particles explore large search space. Thus, this strategy exhibits a dynamic control over both the exploration and exploitation.

In the proposed VPSO, the velocity of ith particle is computed according to Eq. (1) and after that it is dynamically updated by Eq. (5) as follows:

$$v_{id}^{k+1} = v_{id}^{k+1} \times \exp^{-\lambda \times \text{variance}_k} \tag{5}$$

where variance_k represents the variance at k^{th} iteration. $\lambda \geq 0$ is a weight parameter which provides a relative weight to the population variance. Further, particle's state is computed by Eq. (4). The VPSO method is outlined in Algorithm 1.

3.1   VPSO Algorithm

In this subsection, we present the proposed VPSO algorithm. The algorithm (Algorithm 1) starts with initializing the population randomly and computes fitness of the particles in steps 1 to 3. The variance (σ^2) is computed in step 5. The steps from 7 to 20 solves the standard BPSO problem with a difference in step 17, where we incorporate the population variance of the previous iterations in the velocity to control both exploration and exploitation. Finally, we return the best particle in step 25 of the VPSO algorithm.

3.2   Time Complexity

Let T be the number of maximum iterations, S be the number of particles and f be the complexity of computing fitness of a particle. The time complexity of Algorithm 1 is $O(TSf)$ (similar to standard BPSO approach).

4   Experiments

We have divided our experiments into two parts. The first part demonstrates experiments on eight benchmark function optimization problems while the second part exhibits the applicability of VPSO for feature selection on five benchmark classification datasets.

Algorithm 1. VPSO Algorithm

Input: Number of particles S, Particles X in n-dimensional search space, Velocity vector V, Maximum Iteration T, dataset or function D and parameters C_1, C_2, ω.

Output: Global best particle Pos_g

1: Initialize X using uniform random number generator.
2: Initialize velocity vector V with some constant positive (0.1) and $\lambda = 1$.
3: Compute the fitness f(X_i) of the ith particle and assign it to Pos_i. (For function optimization it may be the objective value and for feature selection it may be $f(X_i) = \alpha * (100 - accuracy)/100 + (1 - \alpha) * (n - |F|)/n$ where $|F|$ represents the size of selected feature set.).
4: $Pos_g = \max_i(Pos_i)$ and $iteration = 1$.
5: Compute the variance σ^2 of the population fitness $f(X)$
6: Calculate local best and global best position of the particles.
7: **Repeat**
8:     **for** $i = 1$ to S **do**
9:         **If** $(f(X_i) < f(Pos_i))$ **then**
10:             $Pos_i = X_i$.
11:         **endif**
12:     $Pos_g = \max_i(Pos_i)$.
13:     **endfor**
14:     **for** $i = 1$ to S **do**
15:         **for** $d = 1$ to n **do**
16:             $v_{id} = \omega * v_{id} + C_1 * r_1 * (p_{id} - x_{id}) + C_2 * r_2 * (pg_{id} - x_{id})$.
17:             $v_{id} = v_{id} \times \exp^{-\lambda \times \sigma^2}$
18:             $x_{id} = \begin{cases} 1 & \text{if } S(v_{id}) > r, \text{ Compute } S() \text{ using (3)}; \\ 0 & \text{otherwise.} \end{cases}$
19:         **endfor**
20:     **endfor**
21:     Compute the fitness f(X_i).
22:     Compute the variance σ^2 of the population fitness $f(X)$.
23:     $iteration = iteration + 1$.
24: **Until** $iteration < T$
25: **Return** Global best particle Pos_g.

4.1 Function Minimization

We have validated the proposed VPSO method on eight publicly available benchmark functions. The description of these functions are presented in Table 1.

We have compared the proposed VPSO method with SPSO 2006, SPSO 2011 (http://www.particleswarm.info/Programs.html), POPOT 2006 and POPOT 2011 (http://code.google.com/p/popot) methods. The parameters like the number of dimensions and λ values with the initial range of particle values are given in Table 1. λ used in Eq. (5) depends on the benchmark function being optimized and is tuned separately for every benchmark function using the linear search in the range 0 to 1. The value for ω parameter is kept at 0.9 in all the experiments.

Table 1. Parameters of functions used

Name	# Dimension	Range	Evaluations	λ
Sphere	30	$[-100, 100]$	75000	7.8×10^{-4}
Greiwank	30	$[-600, 600]$	75000	8.9×10^{-3}
Rosenbrock	30	$[-30, 30]$	75000	5.8×10^{-4}
Rastragin	30	$[-5.12, .5.12]$	75000	4.3×10^{-4}
Tripod 2D	30	$[-100, 100]$	100000	4.3×10^{-4}
Ackley	30	$[-30, 30]$	80000	8.2×10^{-5}
Schwefel-2.2	30	$[-10, 10]$	75000	6.9×10^{-3}
Neumaier	40	$[1600, 1600]$	40000	8.7×10^{-3}

The value of parameters C_1 and C_2 is kept at 2 throughout the experiments. The maximum number of iterations is taken as 100000.

The mean error is presented in Table 2 and the corresponding standard deviation is presented in Table 3. It is observed from Table 2 that the proposed VPSO method has the lowest error in comparison to all other methods for most of the cases. It can also be noted that the standard deviation is also very low. The p-values using Wilcoxon rank sum test for VPSO method against SPSO and POPOT methods are 0.78 and 0.49 respectively. From Table 4, it can be observed that VPSO method has high success rates in most of the cases. Further, the minimum error achieved during the optimization is represented in Table 5. The dash ($-$) in Table 5 represents the non-availability of the results. The VPSO method outperforms all other methods in terms of minimum error.

Table 2. Mean error

Fun	SPSO 2006	POPOT 2006	SPSO 2011	POPOT 2011	VPSO
0	9.3×10^{-3}	9.3×10^{-2}	4.7×10^{-2}	4.7×10^{-2}	$\mathbf{9.2 \times 10^{-3}}$
1	5.1×10^{-2}	5.1×10^{-2}	4.7×10^{-2}	4.7×10^{-2}	$\mathbf{4.4 \times 10^{-2}}$
2	**98.5**	98.8	102.6	102.3	98.6
3	53.8	52.2	**50.8**	54.1	53.1
4	0.5	0.5	0.4	0.4	**0.2**
5	1.2	1.1	1.2	**0.6**	1.0
6	9.5×10^{-5}	9.6×10^{-5}	1.4	1.1	$\mathbf{9.5 \times 10^{-6}}$
7	1933.1	2803.2	**921.5**	1328.3	1931.2

Table 3. Standard deviation

Fun	SPSO 2006	POPOT 2006	SPSO 2011	POPOT 2011	VPSO
0	6.6×10^{-4}	6.1×10^{-4}	6.4×10^{-4}	7.7×10^{-4}	5.9×10^{-4}
1	1.7×10^{-2}	4.8×10^{-2}	1.9×10^{-3}	2.3×10^{-3}	4.1×10^{-2}
2	2.6	3.1	28.7	30.8	1.8
3	8.2	6.7	6.7	10.0	5.9
4	0.6	0.6	0.6	0.6	0.4
5	0.9	0.8	0.8	0.7	0.8
6	6.0×10^{-6}	4.2×10^{-6}	1.3	1.1	4.0×10^{-6}
7	1729.8	2292.7	900.9	31254.3	1629.9

Table 4. Success rate (in %)

Function	SPSO 2006 (%)	POPOT 2006 (%)	SPSO 2011 (%)	POPOT 2011 (%)	VPSO (%)
0	100.00	100.00	100.00	100.00	100.00
1	90.30	92.50	99.00	**99.50**	96.00
2	98.60	99.00	92.20	93.50	**100.00**
3	64.20	74.20	**90.40**	63.90	72.00
4	55.20	56.50	64.00	68.60	**73.00**
5	0.00	0.00	0.00	0.00	0.00
6	100.00	100.00	0.00	0.20	100.00
7	0.00	0.00	0.00	0.00	0.00

Table 5. Minimum error

Function	SPSO 2006	POPOT 2006	SPSO 2011	POPOT 2011	VPSO
0	0.006	0.009	0.009	0.009	0.009
1	0.036	0.007	0.012	0.039	0.0323
2	90.900	97.150	98.760	96.500	83.560
3	47.290	42.780	32.830	46.400	46.557
4	1.00×10^{-5}	—	—	1.92×10^{-5}	8.000×10^{-6}
5	0.00	1.155	8.37×10^{-5}	3.990×10^{-5}	0.000
6	6.00×10^{-5}	9.840×10^{-5}	9.750×10^{-5}	9.940×10^{-5}	4.700×10^{-5}
7	69.624	—	—	56.180	129.160

4.2   Application of VPSO for Feature Selection

We have tested the proposed VPSO method for feature selection on five publicly available benchmark UCI datasets [9]. The description of these datasets is given in the following subsection.

Table 6. Average accuracy

Methods	Sonar	SPECT	Ionosphere	WDBC	Perkinson
BPSO	98.5 ± 0.03	88.11 ± 0.03	98.58 ± 0.03	95.66 ± 0.06	88.33 ± 0.3
PSO-SVM [12]	96.15	-	97.33	95.61	-
BPSO-SVM [22]	-	84.64	-	**98.42**	89.23
NPSO-SVM [22]	-	83.52	-	97.89	**90.77**
CBPSOC [6]	93.27	-	93.45	97.54	-
CBPSOT [6]	95.75	-	96.02	97.54	-
EABC-SVM [5]	91.54 ± 0.78	-	95.63 ± 0.38	97.25 ± 0.71	-
VPSO (proposed)	**99.25 ± 0.03**	**88.49 ± 0.03**	**98.74 ± 0.03**	95.87 ± 0.08	88.49 ± 0.3

Dataset. In this subsection, we describe the details of the datasets used in our experimental study. Sonar and Ionosphere datasets are physical science datasets having 208 and 251 samples with 60 and 34 features respectively, SPECT is cardiac Single Proton Emission Computed Tomography image dataset having 267 samples with 22 features, WDBC is a breast cancer (diagnostic) dataset having 569 samples with 30 features and Perkinson is the relative CPU performance dataset having 197 samples with 23 features.

Methodology. We have computed 10-fold cross-validation accuracy for the purpose of comparison. In the 10-fold cross-validation, the dataset is randomly divided into ten parts. Nine parts are kept for training and the remaining part is kept for testing. This process is repeated ten times such that each of the parts should serve as testing set once. The average testing accuracy is reported. We have normalized all the data in the range [0, 1].

We have used Support Vector Machine (SVM) with RBF kernel from Libsvm library [4] to compute the accuracy and fitness. The parameter λ is tuned using the linear search starting from 0.00 to 1.00 with increments of 0.01. The best values of parameter λ are 0.01, 0.03, 0.37, 0.24 and 0.03 for Sonar, SPECT, Ionosphere, WDBC and Perkinson datasets respectively. The value for ω parameter is set to 0.9. The value of parameters C_1 and C_2 is kept at 2. The number of maximum iteration is fixed to 100. The value of parameter α is kept at 0.9. The values of gamma and cost parameters of SVM are tuned using grid search [4]. The proposed VPSO and standard BPSO methods are implemented in C language. All our experiments were run on a Intel Core^{TM} i5 (3.10 GHz) machine with 8 GB RAM.

Accuracy. Table 6 represents the average accuracy and the corresponding number of features are presented in Table 7. The proposed VPSO approach outperforms all the other methods for Sonar, SPECT and Ionosphere datasets. Further, the VPSO method performs marginally better than the BPSO method for all datasets. It can also be observed from Table 7 that the number of features selected by VPSO is significantly less than the BPSO method for Ionosphere,

Table 7. Average number of features

Methods	Sonar	SPECT	Ionosphere	WDBC	Perkinson
BPSO	32	13	21	13	8
PSO-SVM [12]	34	-	15	13	-
BPSO-SVM [22]	-	9	-	18	12
NPSO-SVM [22]	-	10	-	14	12
CBPSOC [6]	**22**	-	**12**	12	-
CBPSOT [6]	26	-	15	15	-
EABC-SVM [5]	27	-	13	13	-
VPSO (proposed)	32	**9**	18	**11**	**5**

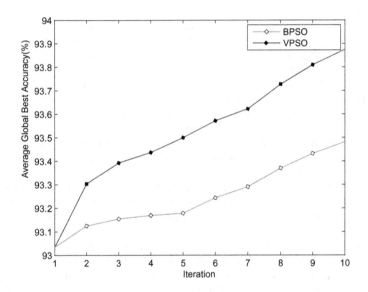

Fig. 1. Global best mean accuracy in ten iterations for ten splits of WDBC dataset

SPECT, WDBC and Perkinson datasets. For SPECT and WDBC datasets, VPSO method requires less number of features in comparison to all other methods. The p-value using Wilcoxon rank sum test is 0.39 when VPSO is compared against BPSO method.

Figure 1, plots the average of global best accuracies for ten splits in ten iterations. From Fig. 1, it can be observed that VPSO method has superior average accuracy over the BPSO method.

5   Conclusion and Future Work

We have presented a novel variant of PSO method which automatically controls both exploration and exploitation. The proposed method achieves significantly better results for multi-modal function optimization and feature selection than those of the state-of-the-art PSO optimization tools and binary PSO method.

One of the key directions for future work involves providing an extensive comparisons with other state-of-the-art function optimization methods such as CLPSO, FIPS and HCLPSO etc. on a variety of shifted and rotated benchmark problems. Other direction includes extending our approach for working with high dimensional datasets. A third direction deals with coming up with a map-reduce framework for our proposed approach.

References

1. Bekkerman, R., Yaniv, R.E., Tishby, N., Winter, Y.: Distributional word clusters vs. words for text categorization. J. Mach. Learn. Res. **3**, 1183–1208 (2003)
2. Belew, R.K., McInerney, J., Schraudolph, N.N.: Evolving networks: using the genetic algorithm with connectionist learning. In: Langton, C.G., Taylor, C., Farmer, J.D., Rasmussen, S. (eds.) Artificial Life II, pp. 511–547. Addison-Wesley, Redwood City (1992)
3. Breiman, L., Friedman, J.H., Olshen, R.A., Stone, C.J.: Classification and Regression Trees. Wadsworth, Belmont (1984)
4. Chang, C.C., Lin, C.J.: LIBSVM: A Library for Support Vector Machines (2001). http://www.csie.ntu.edu.tw/~cjlin/libsvm
5. Chen, G., Zhang, X., Wang, Z.J., Li, F.: An enhanced artificial bee colony-based support vector machine for image-based fault detection. Math. Prob. Eng. **2015**, 12 (2015)
6. Chuang, L.Y., Yang, C.H., Li, J.C.: Chaotic maps based on binary particle swarm optimization for feature selection. Appl. Soft Comput. **11**(1), 239–248 (2011)
7. Dorigo, M., Blum, C.: Ant colony optimization theory: a survey. Theoret. Comput. Sci. **344**(23), 243–278 (2005)
8. Forman, G.: An extensive empirical study of feature selection metrics for text classification. J. Mach. Learn. Res. **3**, 1289–1305 (2003)
9. Frank, A., Asuncion, A.: UCI machine learning repository (2010)
10. Guyon, I., Elisseeff, A.: An introduction to variable and feature selection. J. Mach. Learn. Res. **3**, 1157–1182 (2003)
11. Huang, C.L.: ACO-based hybrid classification system with feature subset selection and model parameters optimization. Neurocomputing **73**(1–3), 438–448 (2009)
12. Tu, C.-J., Chuang, L.Y., Chang, J.Y., Yang, C.H.: Feature selection using PSO-SVM. IAENG Int. J. Comput. Sci. **33**(1), 111–116 (2007)
13. Kennedy, J., Eberhart, R.C.: Particle swarm optimization. In: Proceedings of the IEEE International Conference on Neural Networks, pp. 1942–1948 (1995)
14. Khanesar, M., Teshnehlab, M., Shoorehdeli, M.: A novel binary particle swarm optimization. In: Mediterranean Conference on Control Automation, MED 2007, pp. 1–6, June 2007
15. Kohavi, R., Becker, B., Sommerfield, D.: Improving simple Bayes. Silicon Graphics Inc., Mountain View, CA, Technical report, Data Mining and Visualization Group (1997)
16. Kumar, P.G., Victoire, A.T.A., Renukadevi, P., Devaraj, D.: Design of fuzzy expert system for microarray data classification using a novel genetic swarm algorithm. Expert Syst. Appl. **39**(2), 1811–1821 (2012)

17. Langley, P.: Selection of relevant features in machine learning. In: Proceedings of the AAAI Fall Symposium on Relevance, pp. 140–144. AAAI Press (1994)
18. Liang, J., Qin, A., Suganthan, P., Baskar, S.: Comprehensive learning particle swarm optimizer for global optimization of multimodal functions. IEEE Trans. Evol. Comput. **10**(3), 281–295 (2006)
19. Lynn, N., Suganthan, P.N.: Heterogeneous comprehensive learning particle swarm optimization with enhanced exploration and exploitation. Swarm Evol. Comput. **24**, 11–24 (2015)
20. Mendes, R., Kennedy, J., Neves, J.: The fully informed particle swarm: simpler, maybe better. IEEE Trans. Evol. Comput. **8**(3), 204–210 (2004)
21. Peng, H., Long, F., Ding, C.: Feature selection based on mutual information: criteria of max-dependency, max-relevance, and min-redundancy. IEEE Trans. Pattern Anal. Mach. Intell. **27**, 1226–1238 (2005)
22. Prasad, Y., Biswas, K.K.: PSO - SVM based classifiers: a comparative approach. In: Ranka, S., Banerjee, A., Biswas, K.K., Dua, S., Mishra, P., Moona, R., Poon, S.-H., Wang, C.-L. (eds.) IC3 2010. CCIS, vol. 94, pp. 241–252. Springer, Heidelberg (2010). doi:10.1007/978-3-642-14834-7_23
23. Prasad, Y., Biswas, K.K., Jain, C.K.: SVM classifier based feature selection using GA, ACO and PSO for siRNA design. In: Tan, Y., Shi, Y., Tan, K.C. (eds.) ICSI 2010. LNCS, vol. 6146, pp. 307–314. Springer, Heidelberg (2010). doi:10.1007/978-3-642-13498-2_40
24. Tan, M., Wang, L., Tsang, I.W.: Learning sparse SVM for feature selection on very high dimensional datasets. In: Proceedings of the Twenty-Seventh International Conference on Machine Learning, pp. 1047–1054 (2010)
25. Varma, M., Babu, B.R.: More generality in efficient multiple kernel learning. In: Proceedings of the Twenty-Sixth International Conference on Machine Learning, pp. 1065–1072 (2009)
26. Weston, J., Mukherjee, S., Chapelle, O., Pontil, M., Vapnik, V.: Feature selection for SVMS. In: Advances in Neural Information Processing Systems (NIPS 2013), vol. 13, pp. 668–674 (2001)

Analysis of Next-Generation Sequencing Data of miRNA for the Prediction of Breast Cancer

Indrajit Saha[1,2,3](✉), Shib Sankar Bhowmick[4], Filippo Geraci[1],
Marco Pellegrini[1], Debotosh Bhattacharjee[4],
Ujjwal Maulik[4], and Dariusz Plewczynski[3]

[1] Institute of Informatics and Telematics, National Research Council, Pisa, Italy
[2] National Institute of Technical Teachers' Training and Research, Kolkata, India
[3] Centre of New Technologies, University of Warsaw, 02-097 Warsaw, Poland
indrajit@nitttrkol.ac
[4] Department of Computer Science and Engineering,
Jadavpur University, Kolkata, India

Abstract. Recently, Next-Generation Sequencing (NGS) has emerged as revolutionary technique in the fields of '-omics' research. The Cancer Research Atlas (TCGA) is a great example of it where massive amount of sequencing data is present for miRNA and mRNA. Analysing these data could bring out some potential biological insight. Moreover, developing a prognostic system based on this newly available sequencing data will give a greater help to cancer diagnosis. Hence, in this article, we have made an attempt to analyse such sequencing data of miRNA for accurate prediction of Breast Cancer. Generally miRNAs are small non-coding RNAs which are shown to participate in several carcinogenic processes either by tumor suppressors or oncogenes. This is the reason clinical treatment of the breast cancer patient has changed nowadays. Thus, it is interesting to understand the role of miRNAs for the prediction of breast cancer. In this regard, we have developed a technique using Gravitation Search Algorithm, which optimizes the underlying classification performance of Support Vector Machine. The proposed technique is able to select the potential features, in this case miRNAs, in order to achieve better prediction accuracy. In this study, we have achieved the classification accuracy upto 95.29 % by considering $\simeq$1.5 % miRNAs of whole dataset automatically. Thereafter, a list of miRNAs is created after providing a rank. It is found from the list of top 15 miRNAs that 6 miRNAs are associated with the breast cancer while in others, 5 miRNAs are associated with different cancer types and 4 are unknown miRNAs. The performance of the proposed technique is compared with seven other state-of-the-art techniques. Finally, the results have been justified by the means of statistical test along with biological significance analysis of selected miRNAs.

Keywords: Breast cancer · Gravitation search algorithm · MicroRNA · Support vector machine · The Cancer Research Atlas

---

I. Saha and S.S. Bhowmick—Joint first authors and contributed equally.

B.K. Panigrahi et al. (Eds.): SEMCCO 2015, LNCS 9873, pp. 116–127, 2016.
DOI: 10.1007/978-3-319-48959-9_11

1   Introduction

Next-Generation Sequencing (NGS) [1] is one of the emerging techniques that allows the researchers to study biological systems deeper for its high-throughput, scalability and speed. NGS provides in-depth information of complex genomic which was never possible before using traditional DNA sequencing technologies. NGS methods include whole-genome sequencing, exome sequencing, total RNA and mRNA sequencing, targeted RNA sequencing, small RNA and non-coding RNA sequencing, methylation sequencing and ChIP sequencing. It has been revolutionised back in 2005 when Genome Analyser was developed. This analyser can produce 84 kilobase (kb) to 1 gigabase (gb) of sequencing data in a single run. Later in 2014, it increases upto 1.8 Terabase (tb) after introducing HiSeqX^{TM} Ten. It can sequence over 45 genomes in a single day. However, cost is the biggest disadvantage of this emerging technique in order to available widely. In this regard, NGS tool, called Illumina MiSeq, is quite effortable to achieve the similar goal and provide a clinical assistance in diagnosis of various critical diseases like cancer. Hence, in this article, we have analyzed the latest Illumina MiSeq provided miRNA sequencing data to predict the Breast Cancer more accurately. Since the breast cancer is one of the popular cancer types in women around the globe while statistic says 31 % of all cases [2], hence, we have opted this to study in this article.

It is known that miRNAs are small non-coding RNAs of ∼22-nucleotides in length. Mostly miRNAs repress translation or promote degradation of messenger RNAs (mRNAs) by forming imperfect base pairing on the 3′ untranslated region (3′ UTR) of target mRNAs [3]. Thus, miRNAs are involved in suppressing expression of hundreds of genes and are one kind of regulators of different biological processes. More importantly, biological processes like differentiation and tissue morphogenesis are regulated by miRNAs. Additionally, miRNAs are found to have roles in diseases like cancer [4], diabetes [5], infectious disease [6] or various neurodegenerative disorders [7]. Furthermore, coexpression analysis between neighboring miRNAs [8], identification of a set of miRNAs derived from common primary transcripts [9], specificity of miRNA in particular tissue in order to know the development of cancer [10] and the prediction of miRNA targets [11] have been studied. However, cancer prediction studies using NGS data of miRNA is very limited. Hence, this fact also motivated us to analyse the newly available sequencing data of miRNA to predict the breast cancer.

This paper introduces a supervised technique that can automatically find miRNAs as features in order to improve the prediction accuracy. For this purpose, well-known global optimization technique called Gravitational Search Algorithm (GSA) [12] is used. It encodes the features, in this case miRNAs, in its agent and tries to optimize underlying classification accuracy of Support Vector Machine (SVM) [13] using such selected features. Hence, this technique can automatically identify potentially relevant miRNAs as well as predict the cancer type more accurately. The proposed technique has been validated by measuring accuracy, precision, sensitivity, specificity, F-measure, Matthews correlation coefficient (MCC) and area under the ROC curve (AUC) values in comparison with feature selection techniques like SNR [14], Welch's t-test [15], non-parametric test like Wilcoxon ranksum test [16], Joint Mutual Information (JMI) [17], minimum Redundancy Maximum Relevance (mRMR) [18], Mutual Information Feature Selection (MIFS) [19] in conjugation with SVM for all six methods as well as SVM itself alone. Finally, statistical significance of the results and the selected top miRNAs are reported along with their biological significance.

2   Gravitation Search Algorithm Integrated Support Vector Machine

Evolutionary Algorithms have the potential to adapt in dynamic environment through the previously acquired knowledge. Gravitation Search Algorithm (GSA) [12] is one of them which is quite popular nowadays for its simplicity, effectiveness as well as for its successful application in various fields of science and engineering. Hence, GSA is used here to design the proposed method that can find the relevant features as well as improve the prediction accuracy by optimizing underlying classification task of support vector machine. This section describes the proposed technique in detail.

2.1   Population Initialization

GSA starts with initial population, $X_i(t)$ where $i = 1, 2, \ldots, P$, P is the population size and t signifies the current time-stamp, and a member of the population is called agent. Each agent is having d number of positions, $\{x_i^1(t), x_i^2(t), \ldots, x_i^d(t)\}$. In this study, length of the agent is $l = \sqrt{d}$, where each position of an agent is encoded by a real number within $[0, 1]$ randomly. Thereafter, a threshold $\theta = 0.5$ is used to prepare a set of active features. Note that in worst case after applying the threshold, minimum number of active features is set to 2. Figure 1 depicts the encoding scheme of an agent.

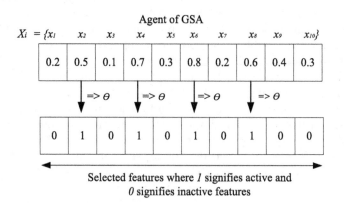

Fig. 1. Encoding scheme of an agent

2.2   Fitness Computation

Here active features use the feature indices of original data from the feature space of $\{1, 2, \ldots, n\}$ randomly, where the duplicate features are not considered. Thereafter, such features are used to compute the fitness of an agent, $ft_i(t)$ where $i = 1, 2, \ldots, P$. For this purpose, SVM is used with the 10-fold cross-validation (FCV) scheme. The average accuracy is considered in order to assign a fitness to an agent. After computing the fitness, gravitational constant $\mathcal{G}(t)$, *best* and *worst* parameters are updated using the following equations.

$$\mathcal{G}(t) = \mathcal{G}_0 e^{-\alpha \frac{t}{T}} \tag{1}$$

where $\mathcal{G}_0$ is the initial gravitational constant, α is a constant, t is the current iteration and T is the total number of iterations.

$$best(t) = max_{i \epsilon \{1, \ldots P\}} ft_i(t) \tag{2}$$

$$worst(t) = min_{i \epsilon \{1, \ldots P\}} ft_i(t) \tag{3}$$

2.3   Mass and Gravitational Force Computation

According to GSA, there are three different masses associated with each agent like **Active gravitational mass** $(\mathcal{M}_a)$, is a measure of the strength of the gravitational field due to a particular object. **Passive gravitational mass** $(\mathcal{M}_p)$, is a measure of the strength of an object's interaction with the gravitational field and **Inertial mass** $(\mathcal{M}_i)$, is a measure of an object resistance to change its state of motion when a force is applied. It is also known that agent with heavier mass is more efficient as it can move slowly in the search space, so that exploration can be done more deeply. It is assumed that gravitational and inertia masses are equal, $\mathcal{M}_{ai} = \mathcal{M}_{pi} = \mathcal{M}_{ii} = \mathcal{M}_i$ and the values are computed as follows.

$$m_i(t) = \frac{ft_i(t) - worst(t)}{best(t) - worst(t)} \tag{4}$$

$$\mathcal{M}_i(t) = \frac{m_i(t)}{\sum_N^1 m_i(t)} \tag{5}$$

With the use of above masses, gravitational force acting on i-th agent from j-th agent in d dimension is computed as follows.

$$\mathcal{F}_{ij}^d(t) = \mathcal{G}(t) \frac{\mathcal{M}_{pi}(t) \times \mathcal{M}_{aj}(t)}{\mathcal{R}_{ij}(t) + \varepsilon} (x_j^d(t) - x_i^d(t)) \tag{6}$$

where $\mathcal{M}_{aj}(t)$ is the active gravitational mass related to the j-th agent, $\mathcal{M}_{pi}(t)$ is the passive gravitational mass related to the i-th agent, $\mathcal{G}(t)$ is gravitational constant, ε is a small constant and $\mathcal{R}_{ij}(t)$ is the Euclidian distance between the two agents i and j. To make the GSA stochastic in nature, the total gravitational

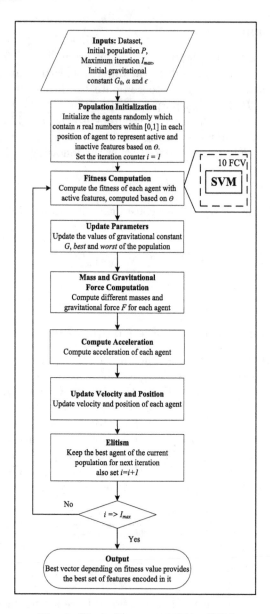

Fig. 2. Block diagram of GSA+SVM

force is computed as weighted sum of all the forces that has been acted from other agents in d dimension.

$$\mathcal{F}_i^d(t) = \sum_{j=1, j\neq i}^{N} rand_j \mathcal{F}_{ij}^d(t) \tag{7}$$

where $rand_j$ is a uniformly distributed random number, generated in the range [0, 1]. After computing the total gravitational force, it is used to compute the acceleration as follows.

$$a_i^d(t) = \frac{\mathcal{F}_i^d(t)}{\mathcal{M}_{ii}(t)} \tag{8}$$

where $\mathcal{M}_{ii}(t)$ is the inertial mass of the i-th agent.

2.4   Updating Velocity and Position

The velocity of an agent is calculated as a fraction of its current velocity added to its acceleration as follows.

$$v_i^d(t+1) = rand_i \times v_i^d(t+1) + a_i^d(t) \tag{9}$$

where v_i^d presents the velocity of i-th agent in d dimension. Then, the position of i-th agent in d dimension is calculated as follows.

$$x_i^d(t+1) = x_i^d(t) + v_i^d(t+1) \tag{10}$$

2.5   Elitism

The best agent of the current population based on the fitness is kept for the next iteration. Above processes from fitness computation is repeated until stopping criterion is met, i.e., maximum iteration is reached. The above procedure in shown in the diagram of Fig. 2.

2.6   Ranking of miRNAs Selected by GSA+SVM

The GSA+SVM has been executed 50 times in order to prepare a list of miRNAs. After getting 50 sets of miRNAs, a weight is computed based on their appearance in the list, e.g., if miRNA 'A' belongs to 33 lists out of 50, then its weight is computed as $33/50 = 0.66$. It enables us to identify miRNAs that appear more frequently in the selected feature list. From there, we have reported top fifteen miRNAs.

3   Experimental Results

3.1   Dataset

The experiments have been carried out on sequencing data of miRNA which is publicly available at TCGA[1] in the name of Breast Invasive Carcinoma (BRCA). The current dataset contains expression values of 1047 miRNAs for 1098 patient. After analysing the patient bar-code, 104 normal and 994 cancer patients have been identified. However, as this dataset looks imbalance, we have

---

[1] https://tcga-data.nci.nih.gov/tcga/.

further analysed the other patient's bar-code of different cancer types from the same TCGA website. As a result, we got additional 721 normal patients. Altogether, 825 normal patients have been collected which is comparable with 994 breast cancer patients. Therefore, the size of new data becomes 1047 × 1819. This is a two class dataset.

3.2 Parameters Settings and Performance Metrics

The GSA has been run with the parameters of initial population $P = 50$, maximum iteration $I_{max} = 50$, initial gravitational constant $\mathcal{G}_0 = 100$, $\alpha = 20$ and $\epsilon = 0.0001$. The RBF (Radial Basis Function) kernel is used for SVM. The parameters of kernel function, γ, and the trade-off between training error and margin, called C, are set to be 0.5 and 2.0, respectively. This is kept same whenever the SVM is used. The parameters of the current method as well as the other methods have been set after following the literature [20]. The performance of all the methods is evaluated using accuracy, precision, sensitivity, specificity, F-measure, Matthews correlation coefficient (MCC) and area under the ROC curve (AUC) values.

3.3 Results

The classification accuracy of all the methods is obtained through 10-fold cross-validation. This is reported in Table 1. It is clearly seen from the table that GSA+SVM outperforms the others methods by achieving 95.29 % accuracy while SNR+SVM, t-test+SVM, RankSum+SVM, JMI+SVM, mRMR+SVM, MIFS+SVM and SVM achieved 81.46 %, 81.24 %, 80.76 %, 83.68 %, 82.74 %, 80.41 %, and 70.43 %, respectively. To achieve this accuracy, GSA+SVM is considered only ≃1.5 % miRNAs of whole dataset. Similar results are also visible for other metrics. Additionally, ROC plot for all the methods are shown in Fig. 3. It also shows from Table 1 that in AUC value GSA+SVM outperformed other methods. Moreover, as the GSA+SVM is executed 50 times, a list of miRNAs is prepared after providing a rank based on their appearance in 50 lists. The reason to have 50 iterations is that to see whether any changes are occurring in the list of miRNAs or not while considering altogether. It is observed that the inclusion of new miRNAs has been stopped after 50 iterations. In a process, around 16 % miRNAs of whole dataset are found in the list of ranking. On the other hand, for the other feature selection methods, same 15 top miRNAs are considered to compute the classification accuracy. However, in case of SVM only, result of 10-fold cross-validation is shown on whole dataset. Also during the 10-fold cross-validation, the ratio of 3:2 for cancer and non-cancer patients is maintained in each fold.

The statistical significance of the results produced by the proposed method with respect to the results of other methods is shown using the non-parametric test like Friedman test [21], at 5 % significance level. Average ranks produced by Friedman test are 1, 4, 5, 6, 2, 3, 7 and 8 for GSA+SVM, SNR+SVM, t-TEST+SVM, RankSum+SVM, JMI+SVM, mRMR+SVM, MIFS+SVM and

Table 1. Prediction accuracy for top fifteen selected miRNAs

Method	Accuracy (%)	Precision (%)	Sensitivity (%)	Specificity (%)	F-Measure (%)	MCC	AUC
GSA+SVM	**95.29**	**95.75**	**95.80**	**96.97**	**96.24**	**0.93**	**0.961**
SNR+SVM	81.46	84.07	87.98	85.23	87.52	0.85	0.865
t-test+SVM	81.24	85.13	87.86	84.69	86.15	0.84	0.834
RankSum+SVM	80.76	84.15	85.81	82.74	86.86	0.82	0.812
JMI+SVM	83.68	88.88	88.59	88.01	88.73	0.88	0.897
mRMR+SVM	82.74	86.44	88.16	86.46	87.80	0.87	0.886
MIFS+SVM	80.41	83.31	85.06	82.26	85.32	0.81	0.782
SVM	70.43	77.48	76.67	77.61	72.99	0.80	0.771

SVM methods, respectively. It is clear once again that the proposed method has an advantage in ranking produced. Moreover, ranks are used to compute Chi-Square value and its corresponding p-value, i.e., 26.50 and 1.8074e−04, respectively. It indicates the acceptance of alternative hypothesis, i.e., the accuracy of GSA+SVM is statistically significant and has not occurred by chance. These results also signify the performance of GSA+SVM for the selection of miRNAs and for the prediction of Breast Cancer is better and worth to study.

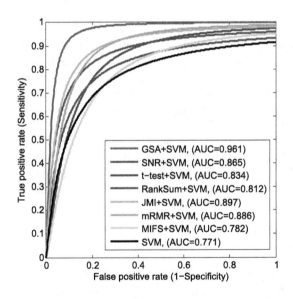

Fig. 3. ROC plots of different feature selection methods

From the ranked list of miRNAs, top 15 miRNAs have been considered for the analysis of biological significance. In this study, we have tried to find the known cancer association of these selected miRNAs. For this purpose, very recently published miRcancer[2] database [22] is used. It is very interesting to see that in

---

[2] http://mircancer.ecu.edu.

Table 2. Cancer type association of GA+SVM selected miRNAs

miRNA	Assigned Weight	Up/Down in cancerous samples	Number of targets	Associated cancer type
hsa-mir-183	0.98	up	4676	Gastric cancer, Colorectal cancer, Lung cancer, Breast cancer, Prostate cancer, HepatoCellular carcinoma, Bladder cancer
hsa-mir-182	0.95	up	4416	Gastric cancer, Colorectal cancer, Lung cancer, Breast cancer, Prostate cancer, Overian cancer, Bladder cancer, HepatoCellular carcinoma
hsa-mir-139	0.72	down	3482	Colorectal cancer, Lung cancer, Breast cancer, HepatoCellular carcinoma
hsa-mir-23b	0.68	down	5492	Gastric cancer, Prostate cancer, Overian cancer, Bladder cancer
hsa-mir-10b	0.68	down	3661	Gastric cancer, Colorectal cancer, Lung cancer, Breast cancer, Oral cancer, HepatoCellular carcinoma
hsa-mir-133b	0.68	down	2976	Gastric cancer, Colorectal cancer, Lung cancer, Prostate cancer, Bladder cancer
hsa-mir-204	0.68	down	5362	Gastric cancer, Colorectal cancer, Lung cancer, Breast cancer, Prostate cancer, HepatoCellular carcinoma
hsa-mir-21	0.67	down	2666	Oral cancer, Gastric cancer, Colorectal cancer, Lung cancer, Breast cancer, Prostate cancer, HepatoCellular carcinoma, Overian cancer, Pancreatic cancer
hsa-mir-25	0.67	up	3934	Gastric cancer, Colorectal cancer, Lung cancer, Overian cancer HepatoCellular carcinoma
hsa-mir-27b	0.67	up	5386	Oral cancer, Gastric cancer, Lung cancer, Overian cancer
hsa-mir-486	0.65	down	2760	Lung cancer, HepatoCellular carcinoma

the list of top 15 miRNAs, 6 miRNAs are associated with the breast cancer and other cancer types while 5 miRNAs are only associated with different cancer types and 4 are unknown miRNAs whose cancer association types are unknown yet. These 4 miRNAs are *hsa-mir-4303*, *hsa-mir-133a-1*, *hsa-mir-190b* and *hsa-mir-4298*, while other 11 miRNAs are reported with their cancer association types in Table 2. It is seen from the table that miRNAs, *hsa-mir-183*, *hsa-mir-182*, *hsa-mir-139*, *hsa-mir-10b*, *hsa-mir-204* and *hsa-mir-21*, are associated with 7, 8, 4, 6, 6, 9 different type of cancers including breast cancer according to miRcancer database. Therefore, these results give us an indication about the importance of the selected miRNAs association with different cancer types along with the breast cancer as well as a roadmap to study 4 unknown miRNAs in pathology.

4   Conclusion

In this paper Gravitational Search Algorithm has been embedded with SVM classifier in order to find potential miRNA that can classify the cancer class from the normal one efficiently so that the cancer prediction of new patient can be done quickly and accurately. In this work, our experiments were focused on the prediction of breast cancer since it is still one of the most common. The use of dataset is also novel. This is a next-generation sequencing data of miRNA, available at The Cancer Research Atlas. The results of the developed method, GSA+SVM, has been compared with SNR+SVM, t-test+SVM, RankSum+SVM, JMI+SVM, mRMR+SVM, MIFS+SVM and SVM in terms of accuracy, precision, sensitivity, specificity, F-measure, Matthews correlation coefficient and area under the ROC curve values. It is found that GSA+SVM consistently outperforms the other methods. The results of the developed method is also justified by a statistical significance test called, Friedman test. GSA+SVM also ranks a set of miRNAs. In the list of top 15 miRNAs, 11 miRNAs are there whose cancer association type is known. They are *hsa-mir-183*, *hsa-mir-182*, *hsa-mir-139*, *hsa-mir-23b*, *hsa-mir-10b*, *hsa-mir-133b*, *hsa-mir-204*, *hsa-mir-21*, *hsa-mir-25*, *hsa-mir-27b* and *hsa-mir-486*. It is validated through recently developed known cancer association database, called miRcancer. It is found that these miRNAs are not only involved in breast cancer but they also have a role in other cancers like gastric cancer, oral cancer, pancreatic cancer, lung cancer, colon cancer, prostate cancer, Liver cancer, etc.

As a scope of further research, 4 unknown miRNAs can be studied further. More advance and sophisticated tools can be developed using multi-objective [23] feature selection technique. Other than GSA, different metaheuristic techniques like Differential Evolution [24] can be studied. Current developed method can be used for gene selection [20], binding activity prediction of protein-peptide [25–27]and protein-protein iteration prediction [28].

Acknowledgment. This work was carried out during the tenure of an ERCIM 'Alain Bensoussan' Fellowship Programme as well as partially supported by the Polish National Science Centre (Grant number UMO-2013/09/B/NZ2/00121 and 2014/15/B/ST6/05082), COST BM1405 and BM1408 EU actions.

References

1. Grada, A., Weinbrecht, K.: Next-generation sequencing: methodology and application. J. Invest. Dermatol. **133**(8), e11 (2013)
2. Miller, T., Ghoshal, K., Ramaswamy, B., Roy, S., Datta, J., Shapiro, C., Jacob, S., Majumder, S.: MicroRNA-221/222 confers tamoxifen resistance in breast cancer by targeting p27Kip1. J. Biol. Chem. **283**(44), 29897–29903 (2008)
3. Bartel, D.: MicroRNAs: target recognition and regulatory functions. Cell **136**, 215–233 (2009)
4. Jacobsen, A., Silber, J., Harinath, G., Huse, J., Schultz, N., Sander, C.: Analysis of microRNA-target interactions across diverse cancer types. Nat. Struct. Mol. Biol. **20**(11), 1325–1332 (2013)
5. Bang-Berthelsen, C., Pedersen, L., Fløyel, T., Hagedorn, P., Gylvin, T., Pociot, F.: Independent component and pathway-based analysis of miRNA-regulated gene expression in a model of type 1 diabetes. BMC Genomics **12**(1), 97 (2011)
6. Song, H., Wang, Q., Guo, Y., Liu, S., Song, R., Gao, X., Dai, L., Li, B., Zhang, D., Cheng, J.: Microarray analysis of microRNA expression in peripheral blood mononuclear cells of critically ill patients with influenza A (H1N1). BMC Infect. Dis. **13**(1), 257 (2013)
7. Hunsberger, J., Fessler, E., Chibane, F., Leng, Y., Maric, D., Elkahloun, A., Chuang, D.: Mood stabilizer-regulated miRNAs in neuropsychiatric and neurodegenerative diseases: identifying associations and functions. Am. J. Transl. Res. **5**(4), 450–464 (2013)

8. Baskerville, S., Bartel, D.: Microarray profiling of microRNAs reveals frequent coexpression with neighboring miRNAs and host genes. RNA **11**(3), 241–247 (2005)
9. Rodriguez, A., Griffiths-Jones, S., Ashurst, J., Bradley, A.: Identification of mammalian microRNA host genes and transcription units. Genome Res. **14**(10a), 1902–1910 (2004)
10. Sun, Y., Koo, S., White, N., Peralta, E., Esau, C., Dean, N., Perera, R.: Development of a micro-array to detect human and mouse microRNAs and characterization of expression in human organs. Nucleic Acids Res. **32**, e188 (2004)
11. Grimson, A., Farh, K., Johnston, W., Garrett-Engele, P., Lim, L., Bartel, D.: MicroRNA targeting specificity in mammals: determinants beyond seed pairing. Mol. Cell **27**(1), 91–105 (2007)
12. Rashedi, E., Nezamabadi-Pour, H., Saryazdi, S.: GSA: a gravitational search algorithm. Inf. Sci. **179**(13), 2232–2248 (2009)
13. Boser, B.E., Guyon, I.M., Vapnik, N.V.: A training algorithm for optimal margin classifiers. In: Proceedings of the 5th Annual Workshop on Computational Learning Theory, pp. 144–152 (1992)
14. Golub, T.R., Slonim, D.K., Tamayo, P., Huard, C., Gassenbeek, M., Mesirov, J.P., Coller, H., Loh, M.L., Downing, J.R., Caligiuri, M.A., Bloomeld, D.D., Lander, E.S.: Molecular classification of cancer: class discovery and class prediction by gene expression monitoring. Science **286**, 531–537 (1999)
15. Bickel, P.J., Doksum, K.A.: Mathematical Statistics: Basic Ideas and Selected Topics. Holden-Day, San Francisco (1977)
16. Hollander, M., Wolfe, D.A.: Nonparametric Statistical Methods, vol. 2. Wiley, New York (1999)
17. Yang, H., Moody, J.: Feature selection based on joint mutual information. In: Proceedings of the International Symposium on Advances in Intelligent Data Analysis, pp. 22–25 (1999)
18. Peng, H., Long, F., Ding, C.: Feature selection based on mutual information: criteria of max-dependency, max-relevance, and min-redundancy. IEEE Trans. Pattern Anal. Mach. Intell. **27**(8), 1226–1238 (2005)
19. Battiti, R.: Using mutual information for selecting features in supervised neural net learning. IEEE Trans. Neural Networks **5**(4), 537–550 (1994)
20. Lancucki, A., Saha, I., Lipinski, P.: A new evolutionary gene selection technique. In: Proceedings of the International IEEE Conference on Evolutionary Computing, pp. 1612–1619 (2015)
21. Friedman, M.: A comparison of alternative tests of significance for the problem of m rankings. Ann. Math. **11**, 86–92 (1940)
22. Xie, B., Ding, Q., Han, H., Wu, D.: miRCancer: a microRNA-cancer association database constructed by text mining on literature. Bioinformatics **29**(5), 638–644 (2013)
23. Saha, I., Maulik, U., Plewczynski, D.: A new multi-objective technique for differential fuzzy clustering. Appl. Soft Comput. **11**(2), 2765–2776 (2011)
24. Saha, I., Plewczynski, D., Maulik, U., Bandyopadhyay, S.: Improved differential evolution for microarray analysis. Int. J. Data Min. Bioinform. **6**(1), 86–103 (2012)
25. Saha, I., Rak, B., Bhowmick, S.S., Maulik, U., Bhattacharjee, D., Koch, U., Lazniewski, M., Plewczynski, D.: Binding activity prediction of cyclin-dependent inhibitors. J. Chem. Inf. Model. **55**(7), 1469–1482 (2015)

26. Bhowmick, S.S., Saha, I., Mazzocco, G., Maulik, U., Rato, L., Bhattacharjee, D., Plewczynski, D.: Application of RotaSVM for HLA class II protein-peptide interaction prediction. In: Proceedings of the 5th International Conference on Bioinformatics, pp. 178–185 (2014)
27. Mazzocco, G., Bhowmick, S.S., Saha, I., Maulik, U., Bhattacharjee, D., Plewczynski, D.: MaER: a new ensemble based multiclass classifier for binding activity prediction of HLA Class II proteins. in: Proceedings of the 6th International Conference on Pattern Recognition and Machine Intelligence, pp. 462–471 (2015)
28. Saha, I., Zubek, J., Klingström, T., Forsberg, S., Wikander, J., Kierczak, M., Maulik, U., Plewczynski, D.: Ensemble learning prediction of protein-protein interactions using proteins functional annotations. Mol. BioSyst. **10**(4), 820–830 (2014)

Genetic Algorithm Based Speed Control
of Electric Vehicle with Electronic Differential

Nair R. Deepthi[(✉)] and J.L. Febin Daya

VIT/Select, Chennai, India
{deepthi.rnair2014,febindaya.jl}@vit.ac.in

Abstract. This paper discus about speed control of electric-vehicle (EV) Permanent Magnet Synchronous Motor (PMSM) drive using Electronic Differential Controller (EDC) and Genetic Algorithm (GA) tuning. EV are electrically powered by rechargeable batteries there by making it eco friendly and leading to its growing interest among customers. When a vehicle is driven along a curved road, the speed of the inner wheel should be less than the outer wheel. This type of controlling is done by EDC, which supplies necessary torque for each driving wheel and allows different wheel speeds in any curve and distribute the power to the wheel motor according to the steering angle. The control structure is based on the Field oriented control (FOC) for each front wheel-motor. In this work, the propulsion system consists of two PMSM for the two front driving wheels and, GA is implemented for optimizing PI controller parameters. Simulations is carried out in MATLAB SIMULINK.

Keywords: Electric vehicles (EV) · Permanent Magnet Synchronous Motor (PMSM) drive · Field oriented control (FOC) · Electronic differential · Genetic Algorithm (GA)

1 Introduction

Since 1960 to present, attempts have been made to produce practical electric vehicles to overcome the disadvantages of internal combustion engine (ICE) and to improve the fuel economy and reduce the tailpipe emissions. EV's were developed [1], to solve environmental and energy problems caused by the use of ICE vehicles. The EV propulsion system consists of an electric motor, which is powered by rechargeable battery, rather than a gasoline engine. The electric vehicle has the following subsystems Electric motor, Power electronic driver, Rechargeable battery [2], Fig. 1.

The main technology for EV is Electric Drive [3]. Electric drives can be classified into four major group's i.e. DC, Induction, Synchronous Reluctance, and Permanent Magnet (PM). Their fundamental topologies are different [4]. DC motors, are prominently used in EV propulsion due to their simple control principle. But the main problem associated with dc drives, is their maintenance cost for commutators and brushes, which makes them less reliable for EV. Induction Machine can widely be used for EV due to reasonable cost, higher reliability, and maintenance-free operation. The advancement of micro-computer and the Vector control principle (Field oriented control - FOC) led to attractiveness of Induction Machine for EV. Synchronous

© Springer International Publishing AG 2016
B.K. Panigrahi et al. (Eds.): SEMCCO 2015, LNCS 9873, pp. 128–142, 2016.
DOI: 10.1007/978-3-319-48959-9_12

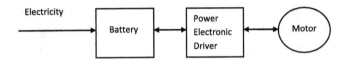

Fig. 1. Electric vehicle propulsion system

Reluctance drives have advantages like simple construction, low manufacturing cost, and excellent torque speed characteristics, but their design and control are difficult and they exhibit acoustic-noise problems. Now-a-days Permanent Magnet (PMSM and BLDC) drives due to their inherent advantages like high efficiency, larger torque to inertia ratio, power density are becoming more attractive with the invention of high-energy permanent-magnet (PM) materials and can be competitor to induction drives for EV application [19]. This paper focuses on the use of PMSM drive for Electric vehicle. The salient features of PMSM drive system are [5],

(1) High operational efficiency.
(2) Small size and lower in weight.
(3) Robustness and high dynamic performance in terms of response times and power conversion.
(4) Larger torque to inertia ratio and power density.
(5) Absence of rotor losses

The principle of vector control can be applied for controlling the speed of an Electric Vehicle [6]. The mathematical equations governing the motor dynamics is taken into consideration for this method. Calculations required are more in comparison to a standard control scheme. A DSP (digital signal processor) can solve this computational complication. This type of controlling is only possible if a precise knowledge of the instantaneous rotor flux is obtainable, which is easier in PMSM than in induction motor as the position of the rotor flux is uniquely determined by that of the rotor position in the PMSM.

In the case of speed control of any vehicle moving along a curved road, the speed of the inner wheel should be different from that of the outer wheel to ensure vehicle stability. This is done by a differential system which provides the vehicle wheel with independent driving forces. In the conventional configuration of an electric vehicle, the mechanical differential gear is replaced by an Electronic Differential (ED) system. The ED calculate the difference in the inner and outer wheel speeds, where the two wheels are controlled independently by two PMSM [7] (Fig. 2).

A PMSM drive has nonlinear characteristic due to motor dynamics, parameter variation and load characteristics. This problem could be overcome by applying an optimization technique to the PI controller in speed control loop of the Vector controlled PMSM model.

GA [8] is one such optimization technique based on "Darwin's principle of survival of the fittest". GA mimics the process of natural evolution. GA based optimization can be used in the control of systems for which an exact mathematical model cannot be obtained at all. The objective of optimization is to improve the rise time, settling time, overshoot, and steady state error in the dynamic response of the system.

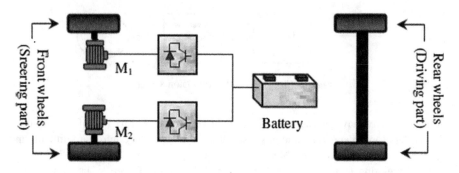

Fig. 2. Electric vehicle structure with independent front wheel

2 Mathematical Model of PMSM

For the dynamic modeling of a non-salient PMSM, some assumption needs to be considered [11, 12].

- Core losses (eddy current and hysteresis) are negligible.
- No external source connected to the rotor and hence variation of rotor flux with respect to time is negligible and taken constant.
- Stator winding will produce sinusoidal magneto motive force.
- Saturation effect is neglected.

Rotor reference frame is chosen to derive the model of PMSM as the position of rotor magnets can be used to obtain stator voltages and current. When rotor reference frame is considered the dq equivalent stator windings are transformed to reference frame moving at rotor speed [9]. The three phase stator voltage equation is given as:

$$
\begin{aligned}
u_a &= R_a\,i_a + \frac{d\lambda_a}{dt} \\
u_b &= R_b\,i_b + \frac{d\lambda_b}{dt} \\
u_c &= R_c\,i_c + \frac{d\lambda_c}{dt}
\end{aligned}
\tag{1}
$$

where R_a, R_b, R_c represents stator winding resistance which are equal for a balanced three phase system, u_a, u_b, u_c represents the three phase stator voltages, i_a, i_b, i_c represents three phase stator currents, and λ_a, λ_b, λ_c represents three phase stator flux linkages. [9]. Also

$$
\begin{aligned}
\lambda_a &= L_{aa}\,i_a + L_{ab}\,i_b + L_{ac}\,i_c + \lambda_{ma} \\
\lambda_b &= L_{ba}\,i_a + L_{bb}\,i_b + L_{bc}\,i_c + \lambda_{mb} \\
\lambda_c &= L_{ca}\,i_a + L_{cb}\,i_b + L_{cc}\,i_c + \lambda_{mc}
\end{aligned}
\tag{2}
$$

As there is no saliency, self inductance is independent of the rotor position. Hence $L_{aa} = L_{bb} = L_{cc}$.

Similarly mutual inductance can be written as: $L_{ab} = L_{bc} = L_{ca} = L_{ac} = L_{cb} = L_{ba}$.

Where, L_{aa}, L_{bb} and L_{cc} represent self-inductances of the stator a, b and c phase respectively. L_{ab}, L_{bc} and L_{ca} mutual inductances between the ab, bc and ac phases respectively [3]. λ_{ma}, λ_{mb} and λ_{mc} are the flux linkages that change depending on the rotor angle established in the stator a, b, and c phase windings respectively due to the presence of the permanent magnets on the rotor.

2.1   Three Phase to Two Phase Transformation

Park Transformation. This transformation is used in AC machines to convert three phase quantities into two phase quantity. In a balanced three-phase, star-connected machine:

$$f_a + f_b + f_c = 0 \tag{3}$$

Where, f_a, f_b and f_c represents either current, voltage or flux linkage [10].

The three phase to two phase transformation is called Park transformation. In the machine side forward Park transformation is applied whereas in the control side Inverse Park transformation is applied [6].

Forward Park Transformation: Here the three phase quantities, f_a, f_b and f_c are transformed to two phase quantity in the stationary reference frame (SRF) i.e., $f_{\alpha,\beta}$ using the transformation matrix T_{abc}

$$f_{\alpha\beta} = T_{abc} \cdot f_{abc} \tag{4}$$

$$\begin{bmatrix} f_\alpha \\ f_\beta \end{bmatrix} = \frac{2}{3} \begin{bmatrix} 1 & \cos\gamma & \cos 2\gamma \\ 0 & \sin\gamma & \sin 2\gamma \end{bmatrix} \begin{bmatrix} f_a \\ f_b \\ f_c \end{bmatrix} \tag{5}$$

Where, $\gamma = \frac{2\pi}{3}$.

The two phase quantity in SRF is then transformed to 2 phase quantity in rotating reference frame (RRF) i.e., f_d, f_q using unit vectors.

$$\begin{bmatrix} f_d \\ f_q \end{bmatrix} = \begin{bmatrix} \cos\theta r & -\sin\theta r \\ \sin\theta r & \cos\theta r \end{bmatrix} \begin{bmatrix} f_\alpha \\ f_\beta \end{bmatrix} \tag{6}$$

θr is the angle between SRF and RRF.

Inverse Park Transformation: Here the two phase quantity f_d, f_q in RRF is transformed to two phase quantity in SRF using unit vectors

$$\begin{bmatrix} f_\alpha \\ f_\beta \end{bmatrix} = \begin{bmatrix} \cos\theta r & -\sin\theta r \\ \sin\theta r & \cos\theta r \end{bmatrix} \begin{bmatrix} f_d \\ f_q \end{bmatrix} \tag{7}$$

Now the two phase quantity in SRF is transformed back to three phase quantity using the transformation matrix, T_{abc}^{-1}.

$$f_{abc} = T_{abc}^{-1} \cdot f_{\alpha\beta} \tag{8}$$

$$\begin{bmatrix} f_a \\ f_b \\ f_c \end{bmatrix} = \frac{2}{3} \begin{bmatrix} 1 & 0 \\ \cos\gamma & \sin\gamma \\ \cos 2\gamma & \sin 2\gamma \end{bmatrix} \begin{bmatrix} f_\alpha \\ f_\beta \end{bmatrix} \tag{9}$$

Applying park transformation (i.e., from Eqs. 4–9) to the current, voltages and flux linkage variables of Eq. (1) we get the mathematical model of PMSM in d-q axis

$$u_d = R_s i_d - L_q \omega_r i_q + L_d \rho i_d \tag{10}$$

$$u_q = R_s i_q + L_q \rho i_q + L_d \omega_r i_d + \omega_r \psi_f \tag{11}$$

$$\rho = \frac{d}{dt}$$

Where, 'ψ_f' is the permanent magnet flux.

Electromagnetic torque is,

$$\tau_e = \frac{3}{2} \frac{P}{2} [L_d - L_q] i_d i_q \tag{12}$$

Rotor Speed Change,

$$\frac{d\omega_r}{dt} = \frac{1}{J} [\tau_e - \tau_L] = \frac{\left\{ \frac{3}{2} \frac{P}{2} [L_d - L_q] i_d i_q - \tau_L \right\}}{J} \tag{13}$$

Where ω_r, τ_L, J, L_d, L_q, P, i_d, i_q represents rotor speed, load torque, moment of inertia, d axis inductance, q axis inductance, number of poles, direct axis current, quadrature axis current respectively.

3 Vector Control of PMSM

It is one of the speed control techniques used in AC machines. The inherent coupling effect (both torque and flux being function of voltage and frequency), existing in scalar control can be eliminated with vector control technique. By this method the torque and flux can be independently controlled by Park Transform(transforming the three phase (abc) quantity to two phase (dq) quantity). Now the d axis component can be used to control flux and q axis component can be used to control torque. Figure 3 represents the vector control principle [20, 21].

From phasor Fig. 4, stator current is the vector sum of i_α and i_β. i_α is the current component shown on the stationary reference frame, i_β is perpendicular to i_α. The

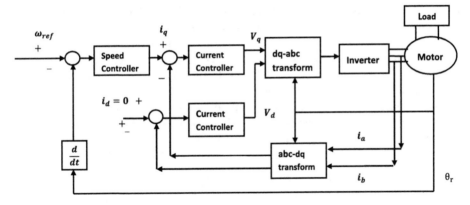

Fig. 3. Block diagram of vector controlled PMSM drive

stationary reference frame is at an angle θr from rotating reference frame. The stator current 'i$_s$ 'can be resolved onto the rotating reference frame, thereby obtaining horizontal and vertical components. The horizontal component of stator current is called field component 'i$_f$' and the vertical component is called torque component 'i$_T$'. Now 'i$_f$' can be used to control rotor flux 'λ$_r$' and 'i$_T$'can be used to control torque 'τ$_e$'

$$i_s = i_\alpha + i_\beta \qquad (14)$$

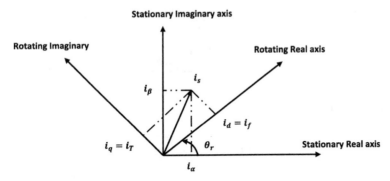

Fig. 4. Phasor diagram representing stationary reference frame to rotating reference frame transformation

4 Modeling of Electronic Differential Controller

EDC is used for independent control of the driving wheels using a speed control method such that wheels connected to EDC can be driven at different speed. The main difficulty in the design of EV is the stability of the vehicle when cornering. Here two separate PMSM drive on the front wheels with vector control technique is proposed for EV application. The EDC takes the difference between the two wheels and if any speed difference exists, it considers steering angle and vehicle speed as input parameters for calculating the required speed for the two wheels [13].

When the vehicle is driven on a straight road the two front wheel speed is same. But when travelling a curved road their exist a speed difference between the two wheels as the velocities of the two wheels are different. In such a case the inner wheel speed is lesser than the outer wheel speed, Fig. 6.

The wheel speed is a function of the speed by which the vehicle moves and the radius of the curve, R. [7]. The structure of EDC is shown in Fig. 5. Hence,

Speed of the left wheel,

$$V_L = \omega_V \left[R + \frac{d_W}{2} \right] \tag{15}$$

Speed of the right wheel,

$$V_R = \omega_V \left[R - \frac{d_W}{2} \right] \tag{16}$$

Where, d_W is the distance between wheels of the same axle.

Radius, R of the curve can be said as function of wheel base L_W and steering angle δ.

$$R = \frac{L_W}{\tan \delta} \tag{17}$$

$$\omega_{r_L} = \frac{L_W + \frac{d_W}{2} \tan \delta}{L_W} \omega_V \tag{18}$$

$$\omega_{r_R} = \frac{L_W - \frac{d_W}{2} \tan \delta}{L_W} \omega_V \tag{19}$$

Angular speed difference is,

$$\Delta\omega = \omega_{R_L} - \omega_{R_R} = \frac{\omega_V d_W \tan \delta}{L_W} \tag{20}$$

$$\begin{aligned} \text{If } \delta &> 0, \quad \text{turn right} \\ \delta &= 0, \quad \text{go straight} \\ \delta &= 0, \quad \text{turn left} \end{aligned} \tag{21}$$

As the vehicle approaches a curve the effect of steering angle, δ comes into act. The EDC will work in such a way as to reduce the speed of the inner wheel and to increase the outer wheel speed. In Fig. 7 k1 and k2 represents the gearbox ratio which is taken to be 0.5 and −0.5 respectively [14, 15].

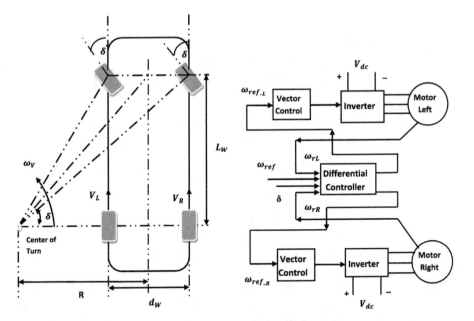

Fig. 5. Electronic differential structure for electric vehicle

Fig. 6. Block diagram of system for controlling the drive front wheel.

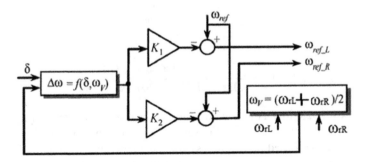

Fig. 7. Block diagram of electronic differential system

5   Optimal Tuning of PI Controller Using Genetic Algorithm

In FOC of PMSM there exist two main loops (inner and outer loop). The inner loop is the current loop and the outer loop is the speed loop. The speed control loop gives torque component reference, i_q^*, and the current control loop gives reference values of d and q axis voltages. The control action for both current and speed controller is performed by PI controllers [16, 17]. Though PI controllers are the simplest and most efficient controller, it has some disadvantages like undesirable overshoot, parameter variation etc. As the parameter variation in the outer loop is dominant compared to the

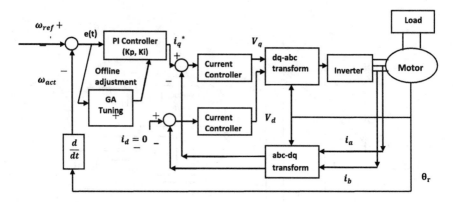

Fig. 8. Speed control of PMSM with offline GA based tuning of PI controller

inner loop, the inner loop uses PI controller while the outer loop uses PI controller whose values are optimized using GA, Fig. 8.

The approximate transfer function obtained after neglecting effect of inverter, and park transform for vector controlled PMSM is given in Eq. (22). This transfer function is subjected to genetic algorithm and after genetic operation the optimized Kp and Ki values are obtained, shown in Table 1.

Table 1. Kp and Ki values obtained using conventional PI and GAPI

Controller	Kp	Ki
PI	1	100
GAPI	9.99	99.63

$$G(s) = \frac{7.69s^2 + 206.8s - 1789}{0.03s^3 + 7.71s^2 + 207.1s - 1789} \tag{22}$$

Using GA [22, 23] first a random population is selected consisting of much number of individuals called the parent chromosome. The individuals in the population are given a fitness value. Based on this fitness value the individuals are subjected to some GA operations like reproduction, crossover and mutation. The individuals that survive after undergoing these operations are called offspring chromosomes. The chromosomes are represented using binary strings. In crossover two parents are selected and swap certain strings of the parent to create a better offspring. In mutation certain strings of the parents are altered to obtain better offspring [18].

The steps in creating genetic algorithm are given below, Fig. 9.

1. Initially generate a random population of individuals for a fixed size.
2. The fitness of each of the individual is then evaluated.
3. The fittest individual from the population is selected based on the fitness value.
4. A probabilistic method (like Roulette Wheel selection, Stochastic Universal sampling, normalized geometric selection, Tournament selection) is used for reproduction.
5. Crossover operation is implemented on the reproduced individuals.

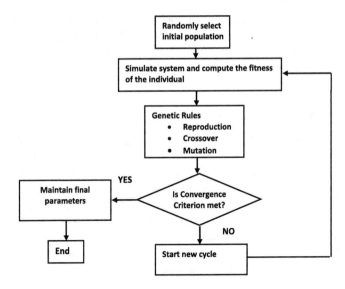

Fig. 9. Steps involved in Genetic Algorithm

6. Now Mutation operation is implemented on the crossover individual.
7. Step 2 is repeated until convergence criterion is met.

6 Objective Function

Objective functions are created based on error performance criterion. The aim of optimization is to minimize the objective function. The objective functions used were ITAE, IAE, ISE, and MSE [8]. After comparing the performance of these objective functions MSE is chosen as the performance criterion for this project, as it outperforms other objective function in terms of rise time, overshoot and settling time.

$$\text{MSE} = \frac{1}{n}\sum_{i=1}^{n}(e(t))^2 \tag{23}$$

Where $e(t) = \omega_{ref} - \omega_{act}$, is the difference in speed, n is the number of iterations. Based on this objective function the fitness of each individual is determined. Here the fitness function is selected as 1/MSE, once the maximum number of generations is reached or when the specified convergence criterion is satisfied the genetic algorithm terminates.

7 Result and Discussion

The performance of GA based PI controller for vector controlled PMSM for EV application is investigated in simulation using MATLABR2013a. The speed controller which is usually a conventional Zeigler Nichols tuned PI controller, in here is replaced by an offline Genetic algorithm tuned PI controller. The performance of both PI and GAPI are compared. The response of the drive for both conventional and GA based PI are shown. The result of conventional PI and GA based PI controller are compared for different cases in simulation.

7.1   Varying Speed and Varying Load

Here speed of 500 rpm and 700 rpm is applied at time t = 0 s and t = 0.06 s and the load torque applied is TL = 1 N.m and 3 N.m at t = 0.02 s and t = 0.05 s. In simulation, PI controller tuned drive has overshoot, undershoot and steady state error, while GA based PI controller has no overshoot no undershoot and no steady state error due to the load disturbance. Only the stator current of GAPI varies due to the load applied. The response of GAPI is better compared to conventional PI. The corresponding simulated stator current as well as load torque response is shown. Figure 10 represents PI controller tuned drive at varying speed and varying load. Figure 11 represents GAPI tuned drive at varying speed and varying load.

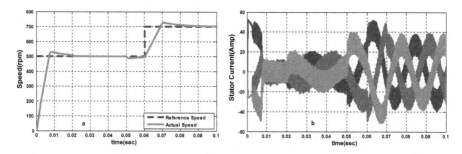

Fig. 10. Simulated dynamic response of motor operating for variable speed and varying load with PI controller, (a) Speed response. (b) Stator current

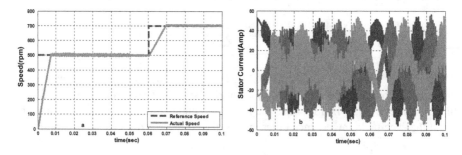

Fig. 11. Simulated dynamic response of motor operating for variable speed and varying load with GA optimized PI controller, (a) Speed response. (b) Stator current

From the above simulated responses it is observed that GAPI gives a much better performance compared to conventional PI. Hence we can use GAPI for obtaining a better performance in speed control of PMSM and then use it in an Electric vehicle application with the use of a Differential controller. The performance of Electronic Differential Controller for Electric vehicle driven by two PMSM attached to the front wheel using GA based PI controller on Vector controlled PMSM is evaluated. Different cases are considered for simulation using GAPI on vector controlled PMSM with differential controller for EV application.

7.2 Case A: Vehicle Moving on Left Curved Road

When the vehicle approaches a curved path, the steering angle, δ needs to be changed. If it is a left curve, the steering angle becomes negative and by condition stated in Eq. (21), the speed of the left motor(inner tire) is made less than the speed of the right motor(outer tire) by the Differential Controller. Reference speed of 700 rpm at t = 0 s is applied to the drive. At t = 0.02 s a left curve approaches and the steering angle is adjusted such that the vehicle wheels turn to the left curve. Figure 12b and Fig. 12a represents that the speed of the right wheel has increased and speed of the left wheel has decreased respectively. The corresponding simulated stator current, as well as Electromagnetic Torque response is shown in Figs. 13 and 14.

7.3 Case B:Vehicle Moving on a Right Curved Road

When the vehicle approaches a right curved path, the steering angle, δ changes and the speed of the right tire (inner tire) is made less than the speed of the left tire(outer tire) by the Differential Controller. Reference speed of 700 rpm is applied to the drive. At t = 0.02 s a right curve approaches and the steering angle is adjusted such that the vehicle wheels turn to the right curve. Figure 15b and Fig. 15a represents that the speed of the right wheel has decreased and speed of the left wheel has increased respectively. The corresponding simulated stator current, as well as Electromagnetic Torque response is shown in Figs. 16 and 17. Figures 15, 16 and 17 represents simulated response of GAPI on FOC PMSM with EDC for EV on a right curved road.

Simulation Result of Case A

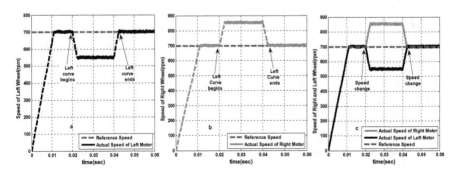

Fig. 12. Speed response for vehicle moving on left curved road with GAPI and EDC (a) Left wheel (b) Right wheel (c) Left and Right wheel together

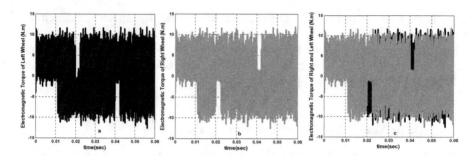

Fig. 13. Electromagnetic torque response for vehicle moving on left curved road with GAPI and EDC (a) Left wheel. (b) Right wheel. (c) Left and Right wheel together

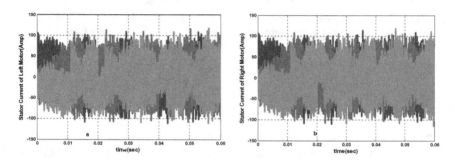

Fig. 14. Stator current response for vehicle moving on left curved road with GAPI and EDC (a) Left Motor. (b) Right Motor

Simulation Result of Case B

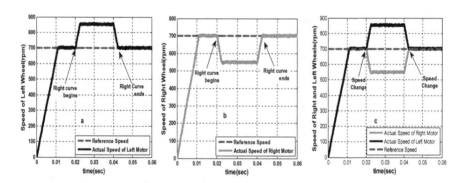

Fig. 15. Speed response for vehicle moving on right curved road with GAPI and EDC (a) Left wheel. (b) Right wheel. (c) Left and Right wheel together

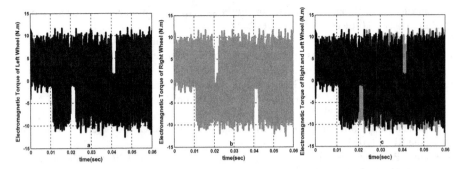

Fig. 16. Electromagnetic torque response for vehicle moving on right curved road with GAPI and EDC (a) Left wheel. (b) Right wheel. (c) Left and Right wheel together

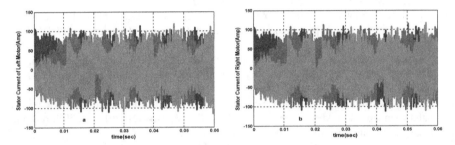

Fig. 17. Stator current response for vehicle moving on right curved road with GAPI and EDC (a) Left motor. (b) Right motor

A Appendix: Motor Parameters

Resistance $0.18\ \Omega$, d–axis inductance 0.000835H, q–axis inductance 0.000835H, Permanent magnet flux 0.07145 Wb, Pole pairs 4.

References

1. Rajashekara, K.: History of electric vehicles in general motors. IEEE Trans. Ind. Appl. **30**, 897–904 (1994)
2. Chan, C.C., Chau, K.T.: Power electronics challenges in electric vehicles. In: Proceedings of the International Conference on Industrial Electronics, Control, and Instrumentation, IECON 1993 (1993)
3. Pillay, P., Krishnan, R.: Control characteristics and speed controller design for a high performance permanent magnet synchronous motor drive. IEEE Trans. Energy Convers. **19** (1), 151–159 (2004)
4. Chau, K.T., Chan, C.C., Liu, C.: Overview of permanent-magnet brushless drives for electric and hybrid electric vehicles. IEEE Trans. Ind. Electron. **55**(6), 2246–2257 (2008)

5. Rahman, M.A., Zhou, P.: Analysis of brushless permanent magnet synchronous motors. IEEE Trans. Ind. Electron. **43**(2), 256–267 (1996)
6. Bose, B.K.: Power Electronics and AC Drives. Prentice-Hall, Englewood Cliffs (1986)
7. Ravi, A., Palani, S.: Robust electronic differential controller for an electric vehicle. Am. J. Appl. Sci. **10**(11), 1356–1362 (2013). ISSN: 1546-9239, ©2013 Science Publication
8. Elmas, C., Akcayol, M.A.: Genetic PI controller for a permanent magnet Synchronous motor. In: International XIIth Turkish Symposium on Artificial Intelligence and Neural Networks – TAINN 2003 (2003)
9. Krishnan, R.: Electric Motor Drives: Modeling, Analysis, and Control. Prentice-Hall, Upper Saddle River (2003)
10. Krause, P., Wasynczuk, O., Sudhoff, S., Pekarek, S.: Analysis of Electric Machinery and Drive Systems. Wiley, New York (2013)
11. Kulkarni, S.S., Thosar, A.G.: Mathematical modeling and simulation of permanent magnet synchronous machine. Int. J. Electron. Electr. Eng. **1**(2), 66–71 (2013)
12. Abu-Rub, H., Iqbal, A., Guzinski, J.: High Performance Control of AC Drives with MATLAB/Simulink Models. Wiley, Chichester (2012)
13. Hartani, K., Bourahla, M., Miloud, Y., Sekour, M.: Electronic differential with direct torque fuzzy control for vehicle propulsion system. Turk. J. Electr. Eng. Comput. Sci. **17**(1), 21–38 (2009)
14. Haddoun, A., Benbouzid, M.E.H., Diallo, D., Abdessemed, R., Ghouili, J., Srairi, K.: Modeling, analysis, and neural network control of an EV electrical differential. IEEE Trans. Ind. Electron. **55**(6), 2286–2294 (2008)
15. Draou, A.: A simplified sliding mode controlled electronic differential for an electric vehicle with two independent wheel drives. Energ. Power Eng. **5**, 416–421 (2013). Published Online August 2013. http://www.scirp.org/journal/epe
16. Kunto, W.W., Jeong, S.: Genetic algorithm tuned PI controller on PMSM simplified vector control. J. Cent. South Univ. **20**, 3042–3048 (2013). doi:10.1007/s117710131827x
17. Uddin, M.N., Abido, M.A., Rahman, M.A.: Real-time performance evaluation of a genetic-algorithm-based fuzzy logic controller for IPM motor drives. IEEE Trans. Ind. Appl. **41**(1), 246–252 (2005)
18. Pant, M., Thangaraj, R., Abraham, A.: Optimal tuning of PI speed controller using nature inspired heuristics. In: Eighth International Conference on Intelligent Systems Design and Applications (2008)
19. Zhu, Z.Q., Howe, D.: Electrical machines and drives for electric, hybrid, and fuel cell vehicles. IEEE Trans. Ind. Electron. **95**(4), 746–765 (2007)
20. Casadei, D., Profumo, F., Serra, G., Tani, A.: FOC and DTC: two viable schemes for induction motors torque control. IEEE Trans. Power Electron. **17**(5), 779–787 (2002)
21. Rehman, H.U., Xu, L.: Alternative energy vehicles drive system: control, flux and torque estimation, and efficiency optimization. IEEE Trans. Veh. Technol. **60**(8), 3625–3634 (2011)
22. Salmasi, F.R.: Control strategies for hybrid electric vehicles: evolution, classification, comparison, and future trends. IEEE Trans. Veh. Technol. **56**(5), 2393–2404 (2007)
23. Da Silva, W.G., Acarnley, P.P., Finch, J.W.: Application of GA to online tuning of electric drive speed controller. IEEE Trans. Ind. Electron. **47**(1), 217–219 (2000)

An Ant Colony Optimization Approach for the Dominating Tree Problem

Shyam Sundar[1], Sachchida Nand Chaurasia[2], and Alok Singh[2(✉)]

[1] Department of Computer Applications, National Institute of Technology Raipur,
Raipur 492010, Chhattisgarh, India
ssundar.mca@nitrr.ac.in
[2] School of Computer and Information Sciences, University of Hyderabad,
Hyderabad 500046, Telangana, India
{mc10pc13,alokcs}@uohyd.ernet.in

Abstract. Dominating tree problem (DTP) seeks a tree DT with minimum total edge weight on a given edge-weighted, connected, and undirected graph so that each vertex of the graph is either a member of DT or adjacent to at least one of the vertices in DT. It is a $\mathcal{NP}$-Hard problem and finds its root in providing virtual backbone for routing in wireless sensor networks. For this problem, this paper proposes an ant colony optimization (DT-ACO) approach which is different from an existing ant colony optimization (ACO) approach for the DTP. The differences lie in new strategies for two components, viz. solution construction and update of pheromone trails. These new strategies help DT-ACO in exploring high quality solutions in much lesser time in comparison to existing ACO approach as well as another swarm-based metaheuristic approach for the DTP in the literature. Computational results show that DT-ACO outperforms these two swarm-based approaches in terms of solution quality and execution time both.

Keywords: Dominating tree problem · Combinatorial optimization · Ant Colony Optimization · Heuristic · Swarm intelligence

1 Introduction

Dominating tree problem (DTP) is a recent one among many new $\mathcal{NP}$-Hard combinatorial optimization problems in the domain of wireless sensor networks (WSNs). Given a connected, edge-weighted and undirected graph $G = (V, E)$, where V and E are the set of vertices and the set of edges respectively, and a non-negative weight function $w : E \rightarrow \Re^+$ over E, the DTP seeks on this graph G a tree DT of minimum total edge weight so that each vertex of G either belongs to DT or is adjacent to at least one of vertices in DT. Vertices in DT are termed as dominating vertices, whereas vertices which are not part of DT are termed as non-dominating vertices. It should be noted that vertices and nodes are used interchangeably in this paper.

© Springer International Publishing AG 2016
B.K. Panigrahi et al. (Eds.): SEMCCO 2015, LNCS 9873, pp. 143–153, 2016.
DOI: 10.1007/978-3-319-48959-9_13

DTP has its root in providing virtual backbone for routing in WSNs [1,2]. Since a non-dominating node is atleast one hop away from one of dominating nodes of DT in the wireless network, so a set of dominating nodes of DT (solution) to this problem can be used for the purpose of storing routing information in WSNs. In this mechanism, a message can be sent from a source node to a destination node through a series of hops: the message is first passed to the dominating node in DT which is nearest to the source node, then it is routed through DT to the dominating node closest to the receiver, and, finally it is forwarded to the receiver. The advantage of this mechanism is that dominating nodes used for providing a virtual backbone are few in numbers in comparison to the total number of nodes in the network, thereby resulting less overhead on the size of routing table. Also, such scheme does not require routing table recalculations if topological changes in the network do not have impact on any of the dominating nodes.

2   Related Work

DTP is a recent variant of connected dominating set problem [3–7] and is proven to be $\mathcal{NP}$-Hard [1,2]. The papers in the early literature, e.g. [3–7] have studied the problem of constructing a routing backbone in WSNs with the intention of minimizing the energy consumption. However, instead of considering weight on each edge, these earlier papers considered the weight on each node. Zhang et al. [2] and Shin et al. [1] pointed out first time that energy consumption in routing, in fact, is directly associated with the energy consumed by edges on the route. This led to the introduction of DTP [1,2] with the objective of minimizing energy consumption of routing. They proved inapproximability result and developed a quasi-polynomial ($|V|^{O(lg|V|)}$) algorithm for the DTP. Later, a number of problem-specific heuristics [1,2,8–10] and a number of metheuristic techniques [8–10] have been proposed in the literature.

In this paper, a hybrid ant colony optimization (ACO) approach is proposed for the DTP. ACO, which is inspired by foraging behavior of real ants, is a well-known swarm intelligence technique for finding high quality solutions for combinatorial optimization problems. Hereafter, the proposed hybrid ACO approach will be referred to as DT-ACO. This DT-ACO is different from the ACO approach for the DTP [10] in the literature mainly on two components: solution construction and update of pheromone trails. New strategies, which will be discussed in subsequent sections, are devised in the components of ACO and help in exploring high quality solutions in much lesser time in the search space in comparison to existing ACO approach [10] as well as other swarm-based metaheuristic approach, i.e., artificial bee colony algorithm [10] for the DTP in the literature. DT-ACO has been tested on a set of various instances. Computational results shows the effectiveness of DT-ACO over these two swarm-based approaches in the literature.

The remainder of this paper is structured as follows: Sect. 3 describes our proposed approach, viz. DT-ACO, whereas Sect. 4 reports computational results. Finally, Sect. 5 contains some concluding remarks.

3   DT-ACO

Ant colony optimization (ACO) is a well-known swarm intelligence technique for finding high quality solutions for combinatorial optimization problems. It is motivated by the collective intelligent behaviour shown by real ants while foraging. The real ants, while walking from their nest to food sources and vice versa, deposit on the terra ferma a chemical compound known as pheromone. This forms a pheromone trail which is used for stigmergetic communication. Since other ants are able to sense such pheromone on the paths, therefore, the presence of such pheromone on the paths affects the decision making of ants about the paths chosen by them. Ants probabilistically select the paths marked by strong pheromone concentrations. Pheromone is a volatile chemical substance. Its evaporation decreases the intensity of pheromone trails and helps in path exploration. The ants tracing the shortest path are the first to reach the food and to start their return to the nest, thereby resulting large concentration of pheromone on this shortest path in comparison to longer paths. Such strong pheromone concentration stimulates more ants to follow this shortest path again, which in turn, leads to accumulation of more pheromones. After some time, almost entire colony of ants starts following the same path. Thus, pheromone trail-depositing and trail-following behavior aids the ants in discovering the shortest path between their nest and food source. This behavior emerge from cooperation among individuals of the whole colony. Such feature of real ant colonies has been exploited in developing ACO algorithms in order to find high quality solutions for difficult combinatorial optimization problems.

ACO is a stochastic search technique in which artificial ants cooperate in finding high quality solutions through the means of the pheromone trails – that are accumulated through search experience – and heuristic information of a given optimization problem. Ant System which was the first version of ACO was originally developed by Dorigo *et al.* [11–13]. Later, many diverse variants of ACO such as ant colony system (ACS) [14,15], $MAX - MIN$ Ant System (MMAS) [16,17], and multiple pheromone concept [18] have been proposed in the literature. A more comprehensive description of various variants of ACO algorithms and their applications can be studied in [19].

Similar to [10], this paper considers only pheromone on each vertex of the graph. Subsequent subsections give details of other features of DT-ACO.

3.1   Solution Construction

Each artificial ant constructs a solution through an incremental approach. In the solution construction procedure, initially S is an empty set, and all vertices $\in V$ are labeled as unmarked. Also, a vertex is selected uniformly at random from V and is added to S. This vertex is labeled as marked, and also all vertices adjacent to this selected vertex are labeled as marked. After this, at each step, the ant k constructs a solution by selecting an adjacent unselected vertex v to one, say u, of selected vertices in S. The selection of this unselected vertex v is determined

---

Algorithm 1. Pseudo-code for solution construction procedure

Initialize $S \leftarrow \phi$;

$Mark[i] \leftarrow 0 \; \forall i \in V$;   //All vertices in V are unmarked

Initialize $TMV \leftarrow 0$;

//TMV provides a count of the total number of marked vertices in V

Select a vertex $v1$ randomly;

$S \leftarrow v1$;

$Mark[v1] \leftarrow 1$; $TMV \leftarrow TMV + 1$;

   //vertex v1 is marked and TMV is incremented

for $j \leftarrow 1$ **to** $Adj[v1]$ **do**

    $\lfloor \quad Mark[j] \leftarrow 1; TMV \leftarrow TMV + 1;$

while $(TMV \neq |V|)$ **do**

    Select a vertex $v \notin S$, adjacent to a vertex $u \in S$ probabilistically according
    to equation 1;

    $S \leftarrow S \cup \{v\}$;

    for $j \leftarrow 1$ **to** $Adj[v]$ **do**

        if $(Mark[j] == 0)$ **then**

           $\lfloor \quad Mark[j] \leftarrow 1; TMV \leftarrow TMV + 1;$

---

probabilistically with the help of pheromones and heuristic information. The probability of selecting v with respect to u in S is determined as follows:

$$p_{uv}^k = \frac{[\tau_v]^\alpha [\eta_v]^\beta}{\displaystyle\sum_{u \in S} \sum_{w \in Adj[u]} [\tau_w]^\alpha [\eta_w]^\beta} \tag{1}$$

where τ_v is the pheromone concentration on the vertex v, $Adj[u]$ is the set of unselected adjacent vertices to u, and η_v is the heuristic term which is equal to $\frac{DU\,Adj[v]}{DAdj[v] \times w_{uv}}$. Here $DU\,Adj[v]$ is the degree (count) of unmarked adjacent vertices of v; $DAdj[v]$ is the degree of adjacent vertices of v and w_{uv} is the weight of an edge connecting u and v. α and β are two parameters which determine the relative influence of pheromone trail and the heuristic information respectively in the solution process. Here this probabilistic decision rule plays an important role in exploring the problem search space and also helps in finding high quality solutions in less time. When v is selected, it is added to S, and all unmarked vertices adjacent to v are labeled as marked. This iterative procedure continues until all vertices of the graph are labeled as marked.

It is to be noted that only edge weight is considered as heuristic information in the ACO [10]. The motivation behind considering a mixed strategy of selecting $\frac{DU\,Adj[v]}{DAdj[v]}$ for an unselected vertex v adjacent to $u \in S$ and edge weight in this DT-ACO is that both strategies complement each other, thereby aiding DT-ACO in finding high quality solutions in less time in comparison to the ACO [10] (see Table 1). The more the value $\frac{DU\,Adj[v]}{DAdj[v]}$, the lesser would be the number of dominating vertices in the solution, as the more number of unmarked vertices will be labeled as marked resulting more number of non-dominating vertices, and the number of iterations would be less. In addition, the lesser the edge weight w_{uv} of an edge (u, v), the more would be the possibility of selection of this edge. It could be also observed that if the number of dominating vertices becomes less, then the overhead of applying pruning procedure repeatedly (a computationally expensive procedure) on the current solution and again applying pruning procedure repeatedly on the solution (minimum spanning tree or DT) which is constructed by Prim's algorithm [11] on the subgraph of G induced by the set of dominating vertices of the current solution (see next paragraph for description) would be less, thereby reducing the overall computational time (see Table 1). The pseudo-code for solution construction procedure is given in Algorithm 1

When a solution is constructed, a pruning procedure, similar to [10], is applied on the current solution. This pruning procedure proceeds by examining all dominating vertices with degree one in the current solution one-by-one whether these candidate vertices can be pruned while respecting feasibility of DT. If a candidate vertex, say dv_1, with degree one in DT is found, then it is examined whether all non-dominating vertices adjacent to dv_1 are also adjacent to other dominating vertices in the solution. If it happens, the edge connecting this dominating vertex can also be removed from DT of the solution, which in turn, further minimizes the total edge weight of the solution. The pruned vertex dv_1 now becomes a non-dominating vertex. This pruning procedure is applied repeatedly so that no dominating vertex with degree one is left for pruning.

It is possible even after applying pruning procedure on the current solution that the total edge weight of current solution may not be minimum [10]. The reason behind this one is the selection of edge(s) with higher weight during construction of the solution. If it happens, then it is also possible that if Prim's algorithm [20] is applied to construct a minimum spanning tree on the subgraph of G induced by the set of dominating vertices of current solution, then the total edge weight of current solution may be minimized further. Since one can construct numerous dominating trees on a given set of dominating vertices, but a dominating tree constructed from Prim's algorithm will always be minimum.

Pruning procedure is again applied repeatedly on the solution (minimum spanning tree or DT) so that no dominating vertex with degree one is left for pruning, as there is possibility that one or more dominating vertices would be pruned due to construction of new DT after applying Prim's algorithm on the subgraph of G induced by the set of dominating vertices of the current solution. If pruning takes place, it would further minimize the total edge weight of the current solution.

Update of Pheromone Trails: When all ants have constructed their solutions in a particular iteration (say t), the pheromone trails are updated by first decreasing the pheromone value on each vertex (component) of the graph by a constant factor, and then augmenting the pheromone values on those vertices that are present in the iteration's best solution (S^{ib}). The pheromone trails which are updated by the iteration's best ant on the vertices of the graph are as follows:

$$\tau_v(t+1) = \rho\,\tau_v(t) + \Delta\tau_v^{ib} \tag{2}$$

where ρ is the persistence rate and $\Delta\tau_v^{ib}$ is the amount of pheromone that iteration's best ant ib deposits on vertex v due to iteration's best solution S^{ib}. The purpose of parameter ρ is to prevent unrestricted deposition of the pheromone trails, thereby, helping the DT-ACO to forget the bad choices it might have made previously. In fact, if a vertex is not selected by the ants, the pheromone value which is associated with it decreases exponentially over the number of iterations. $\Delta\tau_v^{ib}$ is defined as follows:

$$\Delta\tau_v^{ib} = \begin{cases} Q1, & \text{if } v \in S^{ib}; \\ 0, & \text{otherwise.} \end{cases} \tag{3}$$

where $Q1$ is a parameter to be determined empirically. This equation explains that vertices, which are part of S^{ib}, would receive more pheromone and are therefore more likely to be selected by ants in future iterations of the DT-ACO.

In addition, pheromone on vertices of the best-so-far solution (global best solution (S^{gb})) [18,21] is also augmented every IT^{th} iteration in the following way:

$$\Delta\tau_v^{gb} = \begin{cases} Q2, & \text{if } v \in S^{gb}; \\ 0, & \text{otherwise.} \end{cases} \tag{4}$$

where $Q2$ is a parameter to be determined empirically. This helps to focus the search around S^{gb}.

The lower pheromone trail limit τ_{min} is explicitly set so that each vertex has some chance to get selected. However, no upper pheromone trail limit is set. It is to be noted that only iteration's best ant is used to update the pheromone trails in ACO [10].

4   Computational Results

DT-ACO has been implemented in C and executed on a Linux with the configuration of 3.0 GHz Core 2 Duo system with 2 GB RAM. Like [10], DT-ACO has been also executed on each test instance 20 independent times. Also the computer system used to execute DT-ACO is same as used for executing the ABC and ACO approaches of [10].

To evaluate the performance of our approach, we have use the same instances as used in [10]. These instances have the following characteristics: each instance is a disc graph, $G = (V, E)$ where each disk denotes the transmission range of each node. The weight w_{uv} of each edge e_{uv} in E is set to $C_v \times d_{uv}^2$, where d_{uv} is the Euclidean distance between nodes u and v, and C_v is a random constant. We have taken C_v to be 1. The assumption is that $|V|$ nodes are distributed randomly in a $500\,\text{m} \times 500\,\text{m}$ area and each node has the transmission range of $100\,\text{m}$. For each value of $|V| \in \{50, 100, 200, 300, 400, 500\}$, three different test instances are generated, thereby yielding a total of 18 test instances.

4.1   Parameter Settings

Setting of parameters plays an important role in the success of any stochastic search technique. Determining an optimal combination of parameter values is in itself an $\mathcal{NP}$-hard problem. However, it is always possible to set the value of each parameter in such a manner so that good results can be obtained on most instances. For DT-ACO, various parameters and their roles are listed below:

- pop_ant: Number of ants
- α: Governs the importance given to pheromone concentration on vertices in comparison to themselves and in comparison to heuristic term
- β: Governs the importance given to heuristic values of vertices in comparison to themselves and in comparison to pheromone concentration on vertices
- ρ: Trail persistence
- $Q1$: The amount of pheromone deposited on each vertex present in iteration's best solution
- $Q2$: The amount of pheromone deposited on each vertex present in best solution found so far since the beginning of the algorithm
- τ_{min}: Minimum amount of pheromone permissible on a vertex
- IT: Number of iterations after which the pheromone is augmented on each vertex present in best solution found so far since the beginning of the algorithm

The value of the afore-mentioned parameters are chosen empirically after a large number of trials. The chosen values provide good results on all instances but they are in now way optimal parameter values for all instances. These values are $pop\_ant = 25$, $\alpha = 1, \beta = 1, \rho = 0.97$, $Q1 = 0.05$, $Q2 = 0.05$, $\tau_{min} = 0.001$, and $IT = 10$. All pheromone values are initialized to 10. Such a pheromone initialization leads to a wider exploration of the search space during initial iterations. We have allowed DT-ACO to execute for 2000 generations.

4.2   Comparison of DT-ACO with ACO and ABC

Being a swarm-based metaheuristic technique, DT-ACO has been compared with two swarm-based metaheuristic techniques in the literature, i.e., ACO [10] and artificial bee colony approach (ABC) [10] in order to show its effectiveness and robustness. Table 1 presents the best known value (BKV), average solution quality (Avg), standard deviation (SD) of solution values, average number of dominating vertices (ANDV) and average total execution time (ATET) for each test instance, which are obtained through ABC, ACO and DT-ACO. Note that the best values are reported in bold font in this table. In subsequent two paragraphs of this subsection, we compare the performance of DT-ACO with ABC and ACO approaches. Next paragraph is about comparison between DT-ACO and ABC, whereas the paragraph after that is about comparison between DT-ACO and ACO.

In Table 1, considering all 18 instances, comparing with ABC, DT-ACO is better on eleven instances, equal on six instances, and worse on one instance in terms of BKV, whereas DT-ACO is better on thirteen instances, equal on

Table 1. Results of ABC, ACO and DT-ACO approaches for the DTP

Instance	ABC					ACO					DT-ACO				
	BKV	Avg	SD	ANDV	ATET	BKV	Avg	SD	ANDV	ATET	BKV	Avg	SD	ANDV	ATET
50_1	1204.41	1204.41	0.00	19.00	25.57	1204.41	1204.41	0.00	19.00	2.41	1204.41	1204.41	0.00	19.00	2.91
50_2	1340.44	1340.44	0.00	21.00	21.46	1340.44	1340.44	0.00	21.00	4.18	1340.44	1340.44	0.00	21.00	3.00
50_3	1316.39	1316.39	0.00	19.00	22.99	1316.39	1316.39	0.00	19.00	2.50	1316.39	1316.39	0.00	19.00	3.09
100_1	1217.47	1218.15	0.69	18.45	28.64	1217.47	1217.47	0.00	19.00	12.71	1217.47	1217.47	0.00	19.00	9.77
100_2	1128.40	1128.42	0.09	17.90	27.58	1152.85	1152.85	0.00	17.00	10.86	1128.40	1143.21	11.80	16.65	7.71
100_3	1252.99	1253.14	0.23	19.70	28.39	1253.49	1253.49	0.00	19.00	8.96	1253.49	1254.75	1.80	18.65	8.82
200_1	1206.79	1209.52	2.69	18.25	84.10	1206.79	1207.61	3.58	18.05	81.13	1206.79	1211.52	2.73	17.25	31.17
200_2	1216.41	1219.74	2.15	18.90	87.78	1216.23	1217.73	2.61	17.65	78.72	1216.23	1216.65	1.83	17.15	29.28
200_3	1253.02	1258.06	3.42	22.15	90.44	1247.25	1248.94	2.99	20.90	97.93	1247.25	1252.39	5.05	20.10	35.28
300_1	1229.97	1237.47	2.89	21.75	145.17	1228.24	1243.70	9.71	22.85	352.89	1223.67	1230.13	5.13	20.50	87.32
300_2	1182.52	1200.79	7.82	19.60	162.59	1176.45	1193.95	10.51	21.10	260.30	1170.85	1171.85	1.84	18.85	75.12
300_3	1257.21	1271.20	6.74	20.50	145.75	1261.18	1276.75	9.27	24.60	251.91	1249.54	1260.85	6.03	20.00	79.97
400_1	1223.61	1241.75	7.88	21.90	263.13	1220.62	1237.45	9.50	26.05	600.74	1211.33	1219.80	7.69	20.45	152.61
400_2	1220.54	1235.29	6.97	22.45	249.39	1209.69	1246.14	21.41	24.40	591.44	1201.16	1211.15	9.63	19.50	130.40
400_3	1266.41	1276.80	4.59	22.30	216.95	1254.10	1270.34	9.42	25.85	530.58	1256.02	1268.50	7.30	21.15	123.92
500_1	1233.14	1241.60	4.56	21.40	379.72	1219.66	1240.05	9.17	26.50	1163.20	1200.06	1218.31	13.46	20.60	229.41
500_2	1245.59	1258.33	5.40	22.35	364.04	1273.86	1295.51	13.39	28.65	1031.81	1238.81	1248.83	7.09	20.70	215.61
500_3	1249.17	1278.67	11.96	21.60	338.25	1232.71	1259.08	20.03	24.35	917.73	1231.81	1257.42	10.88	20.10	197.99

three instances, and worse on two instances in terms of Avg. In terms of ATET, DT-ACO is faster than ABC on all instances.

Similarly, comparing with ACO, DT-ACO is better on ten instances, equal on seven instances, and worse on one instance in terms of BKV, whereas DT-ACO is better on twelve instances, equal on four instances, and worse on two instances in terms of Avg. In terms of ATET, DT-ACO is much faster than ACO on most of the instances (specially as the size of instances increases). It is to be noted that the total number of solutions generated in ACO [10] (20 (pop_ant) × 2500 (generations) = 50000 solutions) is same as in DT-ACO (25 (pop ant) × 2000 (generations) = 50000 solutions). Despite of having same number of solutions generated, DT-ACO is much faster than ACO [10]. The reason behind this one is that the heuristic used in solution construction (see Sect. 3.1) plays a crucial role in finding a solution (DT) with very less number of dominating vertices, thereby reducing the overhead of applying pruning procedure repeatedly (a computationally expensive procedure) on the current solution and again applying pruning procedure on the solution (minimum spanning tree or DT) which is constructed by Prim's algorithm [20] on the subgraph of G induced by the set of dominating vertices of the current solution. This overall reduces the computational time (see Table 1).

Overall, it can be observed through the results reported in Table 1 that DT-ACO shows the superiority over ABC and ACO on most of the instances in terms of solution quality and computational time. Computational results justify the usefulness of new strategies devised in two components – solution construction and update of pheromone trails – of DT-ACO, as these new strategies help intuitively in exploring high quality solutions in problem search space in much lesser time in comparison to ABC and ACO approaches in the literature [10].

In addition, the performance of DT-ACO has been also checked against ABC and ACO in terms of average number of dominating vertices (ANDV) as the number of dominating vertices impacts the performance of any routing protocols based on virtual backbone. Table 1 clearly shows that ANDV obtained by DT-ACO is quite less on most of the instances in comparison to ABC and ACO.

5   Conclusions

We have proposed an ant colony optimization approach (DT-ACO) for the DTP. DT-ACO has been compared with two state-of-the-art swarm-based metaheuristic approaches, viz. artificial bee colony (ABC) approach and ant colony optimization (ACO) approach. The proposed DT-ACO differs from the existing ACO approach [10] mainly on two components, viz. the manner in which new solutions are constructed and update of pheromone trails. Computational results justify the usefulness of new strategies devised for solution construction and pheromone trails update, as these new strategies help DT-ACO in locating high quality solutions in problem search space in a much lesser time in comparison to ABC and ACO approaches available in the literature. Overall, DT-ACO performed much better in comparison to these two existing swarm-based approaches in terms of solution quality and computational time both.

Our approach once again emphasized the importance of a properly designed heuristic term while constructing a solution via ACO. All the information available about the problem under investigation should be considered while designing the heuristic term. Approaches similar to our approach can be developed for other dominating set based problems also.

References

1. Shin, I., Shen, Y., Thai, M.T.: On approximation of dominating tree in wireless sensor networks. Optim. Lett. **4**, 393–403 (2010)
2. Zhang, N., Shin, I., Li, B., Boyaci, C., Tiwari, R., Thai, M.T.: New approximation for minimum-weight routing backbone in wireless sensor network. In: Li, Y., Huynh, D.T., Das, S.K., Du, D.-Z. (eds.) WASA 2008. LNCS, vol. 5258, pp. 96–108. Springer, Heidelberg (2008). doi:10.1007/978-3-540-88582-5_12
3. Guha, S., Khuller, S.: Approximation algorithms for connected dominating sets. Algorithmica **20**, 374–387 (1998)
4. Park, M., Wang, C., Willson, J., Thai, M.T., Wu, W., Farago, A.: A dominating and absorbent set in wireless ad-hoc networks with different transmission range. In: Proceedings of the 8th ACM International Symposium on Mobile Ad Hoc Networking and Computing (MOBIHOC) (2007)
5. Thai, M.T., Tiwari, R., Du, D.-Z.: On construction of virtual backbone in wireless ad hoc networks with unidirectional links. IEEE Trans. Mob. Comput. **7**, 1–12 (2008)
6. Thai, M.T., Wang, F., Liu, D., Zhu, S., Du, D.-Z.: Connected dominating sets in wireless networks with different transmission ranges. IEEE Trans. Mob. Comput. **6**, 721–730 (2007)
7. Wan, P.J., Alzoubi, K.M., Frieder, O.: Distributed construction on connected dominating set in wireless ad hoc networks. In: Proceedings of the Conference of the IEEE Communications Society (INFOCOM) (2002)
8. Chaurasia, S.N., Singh, A.: A hybrid heuristic for dominating tree problem. Soft Comput. **20**, 377–397 (2016)
9. Sundar, S.: A steady-state genetic algorithm for the dominating tree problem. In: Dick, G., et al. (eds.) SEAL 2014. LNCS, vol. 8886, pp. 48–57. Springer, Heidelberg (2014). doi:10.1007/978-3-319-13563-2_5
10. Sundar, S., Singh, A.: New heuristic approaches for the dominating tree problem. Appl. Soft Comput. **13**, 4695–4703 (2013)
11. Dorigo, M., Maniezzo, V., Colorni, A.: Positive feedback as a search strategy, Technical Report 91-016. Dipartimento di Elettronica, Politecnico di Milano, Milan, Italy (1991)
12. Dorigo, M.: Optimization, learning and natural algorithms. Ph.D. thesis. Dipartimento di Elettronica, Politecnico di Milano, Italy (1992). [in Italian]
13. Colorni, A., Dorigo, M., Maniezzo, V.: Ant system: optimization by a colony of cooperating agents. IEEE Trans. Syst. Man Cybern. Part B **26**(1), 29–41 (1996)
14. Gambardella, L.M., Dorigo, M.: Ant colonies for the traveling salesman problem. BioSyst. **43**, 7381 (1997)
15. Gambardella, L.M., Dorigo, M.: A cooperative learning approach to the traveling salesman problem. IEEE Trans. Evol. Comput. **1**, 5366 (1997)
16. Stützle, T., Hoos, H.H.: Improving the ant system: a detailed report on the $\mathcal{MAX} - \mathcal{MIN}$ ant system, Technical report AIDA-96-12, FG Intellektik, FB Informatic, TU Darmstadt, Germany (1996)

17. Stützle, T., Hoos, H.H.: $\mathcal{MAX} - \mathcal{MIN}$ ant system. Future Gener. Comput. Syst. **16**, 889–914 (2000)
18. Sundar, S., Singh, A.: New heuristics for two bounded-degree spanning tree problems. Inf. Sci. **195**, 226–240 (2012)
19. Dorigo, M., Stützle, T.: Ant Colony Optimization. MIT Press, Cambridge (2004)
20. Prim, R.C.: Shortest connection networks and some generalizations. Bell Syst. Tech. J. **36**, 1389–1401 (1957)
21. Stützle, T., Hoos, H.H.: New heuristic approaches for the dominating tree problem. Future Gener. Comput. Syst. **16**, 889–914 (2000)

Multi-objective Power Dispatch Using Stochastic Fractal Search Algorithm and TOPSIS

Hari Mohan Dubey[1(✉)], Manjaree Pandit[1], B.K. Panigrahi[2],
and Tushar Tyagi[1]

[1] Department of Electrical Engineering,
Madhav Institute of Technology and Science, Gwalior, India
harimohandubeymits@gmail.com, tshrtyg@gmail.com,
manjaree_p@hotmail.com
[2] Department of Electrical Engineering,
Indian Institute of Technology Delhi, New Delhi, India
bkpanigrahi@ee.iitd.ac.in

Abstract. This paper presents solution of multi objective economic and emission dispatch (MOEED) problem using stochastic fractal search algorithm (SFSA). Fractals are self repeating natural patterns like DNA, leaves of a tree etc. SFSA is a novel optimization algorithm which utilizes the concept of fractals for exploring and searching the problem domain for finding the optimal solution. Fractals are created around a random initial solution by employing a suitable stochastic technique. The generated particles then explore the search space in an efficient manner using diffusion property of random fractal. For overall fitness evaluation of the multiple Pareto optimal solutions TOPSIS (technique for order preference similar to an ideal solution) is employed. To validate the performance of the proposed method on practical constrained optimization problems analysis has been carried out on standard 10 and 13 generating unit systems. Results of stochastic fractal search algorithm with weighted sum method (SFSA_WS) are compared with SFSA with TOPSIS (SFSA_TOP) method. The results obtained by both cases are also compared with those available in recent literature, which confirms the potential of SFSA_TOP for solution of MOEED problems.

Keywords: Meta-heuristic · Economic emission dispatch · Fractals

1 Introduction

In recent years the awareness about environmental protection and generation of clean energy is quite high among policy makers in the Power Sector. The thermal power plants release several contaminants in the atmosphere and pollute the air. After passing of the U.S. clean air act amendments of 1990, utilities have changed their generation strategies, to carry out optimal dispatch not just at minimum cost but also at reduced levels of emission. In the past the only objective of the electricity generating stations

© Springer International Publishing AG 2016
B.K. Panigrahi et al. (Eds.): SEMCCO 2015, LNCS 9873, pp. 154–166, 2016.
DOI: 10.1007/978-3-319-48959-9_14

was to reduce the production cost of electricity, but now they are forced to minimize production cost as well as level of emission.

The economic dispatch problem is one of the most important optimization problems in era of the modern power system. Solution of this problem is a purposeful task, and attracts several researchers to work in this area. Considering emission, the classical economic dispatch problem has now been converted to multi objective economic emission dispatch. The solution of MOEED lies in three ways, the first approach is to consider the emission as a constraint with some tolerable limit but this approach suffers the difficulty of getting good trade off relations between emission and cost.

The second approach is to consider the emission as another objective in addition to the cost and apply single objective optimization methods to minimize the aggregated function obtained by a weighted linear combination of both objectives. This is called weighted sum approach in which different weights are assigned to the cost and emission and a Pareto-optimal front is obtained, by running the algorithm with different weights. The third approach is multi-objective approach where both objectives are treated separately as competing objectives which are simultaneously minimized by using a multi-objective algorithm.

Conventional optimization approaches like goal programming [1] and weighted min-max method [2] are used to solve multi objective optimization problems.

Several methods are available which are applied to solve the MOEED problem with the help of evolutionary algorithms, like differential evolution (DE) [3], Bacterial Foraging Algorithm (BFA) [4] and Gravitational Search Algorithm (GSA) [5]. Finding the best compromise solution out of the large number of Pareto optimal solutions of a complex multi-objective problem is a tedious task. A time-varying Gaussian membership function based fuzzy selection method has been used in [6] to select the best solution using a 3-step, 5, class fuzzy mechanism.

In this paper stochastic fractal search algorithm (SFSA) developed by Hamid Salimi in 2015 [7] is applied to solve the MOEED problem. The SFSA is a novel evolutionary algorithm inspired by the natural phenomenon of growth that utilizes mathematical concept called fractal which is based on diffusion which improves the exploration capacity of the algorithm. For overall fitness evaluation of the multiple Pareto optimal solutions TOPSIS is employed here.

2   Mathematical Formulation

The goal of multi objective economic and emission dispatch (MOEED) problem is to find an optimal dispatch solution for the available generating units in a power system, such that cost and emission both are minimized such that all the equality and inequality constraints are satisfied.

Cost and emission are independent functions and hence it is a bi-objective problem. By using the weighted sum approach of multi-objective optimization this can be converted into a single objective problem. The objective functions and associated operating constraints are as below.

2.1 Cost Function for Economic Dispatch Problem

The fuel cost function with for the m number of generators can be expressed as:

$$\text{Min F}_t = \sum_{i=1}^{m} \left[\left(a_i \times P_i^2 + b_i \times P_i + c_i \right) + \left| d_i \sin \left[\left(P_i^{min} - P_i \right) \right] \right| \right] \quad (\$ /h) \qquad (1)$$

Where, a_i, b_i, c_i are the cost coefficients of the ith generator, P_i is the real power dispatched by the ith generator, d_i and e_i are used to depict the effect of valve-point loading (VPL). P_i^{min} is the minimum possible dispatch from the ith unit.

2.2 Function for Emission Dispatch

The mathematical function for total emission released from the burning of fossil fuels can be expressed as:

$$\text{Min E}_t = \sum_{i=1}^{m} \left[\left(\alpha_i \times P_i^2 + \beta_i \times P_i + \gamma_i \right) + \zeta_i \times \exp(\lambda_i \times P_i) \right] \quad \text{ton/h} \qquad (2)$$

α_i, β_i, λ_i, ζ_i and λ_i represents the emission coefficients of ith generator.

2.3 Power Balance Constraints

The total power generated by all associated generators must meet the load demand and the losses occurred in the transmission lines. Thus the power balance equation expressed as:

$$\sum_{i=1}^{m} P_i = P_D + P_L \qquad (3)$$

Where P_D is the total demand and P_L is the loss in transmission network. The losses occurred during the transmission can be calculated by B-coefficient matrix as:

$$P_L = \sum_{i=1}^{m} \sum_{j=1}^{m} P_i B_{ij} P_j + \sum_{i=1}^{m} B_{oi} P_i + B_{oo} \qquad (4)$$

2.4 Generation Limits Constraints

The generated power of each generator must remain within their maximum (P^{max}) and minimum (P^{min}) operating limits and expressed as:

$$P_i^{min} \leq P_i \leq P_i^{max} \qquad (5)$$

2.5   Formulation of Economic Emission Dispatch Problem

The bi-objective function is converted into a single objective problem by incorporating a weight factor w.

$$F_{TOTAL} = w \times F_t + (1 - w) \times E_t \qquad (6)$$

Where F_{TOTAL} is the total cost in \$/h. w is adjusted between 0 and 1 depending on the importance assigned to an objective. F_t is the total fuel cost and E_t is the total emission.

3   Stochastic Fractal Search Algorithm

A fractal is a natural or graphical pattern which repeats itself at every scale, such as patterns on sea shells, electrical discharge patterns made in the sky by lightening, repeated patterns on broccoli, designs on peacock wings etc. Mathematical sets which have a self-similar structure are also referred to as fractals. Stochastic fractal search algorithm (SFSA), is an optimization algorithm which conducts the search for the best solution by creating randomly distributed fractals all over the search domain. A search agent is placed at the center and then diffusion is used for creating similar patterns again and again like a leaves of tree and then creating whole branch of similar patterns. Such pattern can be found in nature like growth of algae and the structure of DNA. The growth of fractals can be modeled using mathematical technique called diffusion limited aggregation (DLA) [16]. The random fractals can be generated by using any of the stochastic processes such as Brownian motion, Levy flight, Gaussian walks, percolation clusters, self-avoiding walks, and the Brownian tree [7]. The SFSA algorithm has two key steps, diffusion process and updating process, which are explained below.

3.1   Diffusion Process

Here each particle diffuses around its position and creates other points in the search space. This process ensures the exploitation property of an algorithm and increases the probability of finding local minima.

New particles are generated from the diffusion process using statistical methods like either Levy flight or Gaussian walks. However Levy flight method converges faster than Gaussian walk but Gaussian walk is favorable for finding global minima. For diffusion limited aggregation Gaussian walk is used here and expressed as:

$$GW_1 = gaussian(\mu_{BP}, \sigma) + \varepsilon \times BP - \varepsilon' \times q_i \qquad (7)$$

$$GW_2 = gaussian(\mu_q, \sigma) \qquad (8)$$

Where ε and ε' are uniformly distributed numbers between 0 and 1, q_i and BP are i^{th} point and best point in the group respectively. $\mu_{BP} = |BP|$ and $\mu_q = |q_i|$,

σ is the standard deviation represented as:

$$\sigma = \frac{\log(g)}{g} \times (q_i - BP) \tag{9}$$

The factor $\frac{\log(g)}{g}$ reduces the size of the Gaussian jumps as iteration (g) progresses during simulation.

3.2 Updating Process

Considering a constrained optimization problem of D dimensions (number of variables), the points are initialized in space within their upper limit (UL) and lower limit (LL) as:

$$q_i = LL + \varepsilon \times (UL - LL) \tag{10}$$

Where q_j is a vector of dimension D.

After initialization of all points in the search space, their fitness are evaluated and the best point (BP) is identified, then this point is diffused around the current position and new points are generated by (7). Then ranking is done for all points based on their fitness. Each point i in search space has assigned a probability which follows uniform distribution as:

$$q_{ai} = \frac{rank(q_i)}{N} \tag{11}$$

Where, $rank(q_i)$ is the rank of point q_i among the other points in the group and N is the number of points in the group.

For each point q_i in group based on either condition $P_{ai} < \varepsilon$ is satisfied or not, the jth component of q_i is updated according to the equation below otherwise it remains unchanged.

$$q_i' = q_r(j) - \epsilon \times (q_t(j) - q_i(j)) \tag{12}$$

q_i' is the new modified position of q_i, q_r and q_t are random selected points in the group, $\varepsilon \in (0, 1)$.

In second updating process, the position of the point is changed with respect to the position of other points in the group. It helps to improve the quality of exploration.

All points obtained from the first updating are ranked again according to the Eq. (11). If $q_{ai} < \varepsilon$ for the ith position is held for a new point q_i', the current position of q_i' is modified according to the Eqs. (13) and (14) as depicted below otherwise remains unchanged.

$$q_i'' = q_i' + \varepsilon' \times (q_t' - BP) \; if \; \varepsilon' \leq 0.5 \tag{13}$$

$$q_i'' = q_i' + \varepsilon' \times (q_t' - q_r') \; if \; \varepsilon' > 0.5 \tag{14}$$

Where q_t' and q_r' are random selected points obtained from the first updating process, ε' is random number generated by the Gaussian distribution. If the fitness if new solution is found to be better then only q_i'' is replaced by q_i'.

4 TOPSIS

TOPSIS is a technique for order preference by similarity to an ideal solution (TOPSIS) [8]. It is used as the decision making scheme for conflicting objectives. It facilitates the user or decision maker to find the best compromise solution between the different objectives which is similar to the ideal solution. TOPSIS try to find the shortest geometric distance from the ideal solution. Its procedure can be sum up in the following steps.

Step-1 The normalized decision Matrix is formed as below:

$$r_{ij} = \frac{x_{ij}}{\sqrt{sum(x_{ij}^2)}} for \; i = 1, 2, - - - m; \; j = 1, 2, - - - n \tag{15}$$

Where, r_{ij} and x_{ij} are normalized and original decision matrix. m is number of different solutions and n is the of objective values.

Step-2 Compute the weight normalized matrix with weights as per the decision maker to different attributes. Weight normalized values are calculated as:

$$\vartheta_{ij} = W_j \times r_{ij} \tag{16}$$

W_j is weight assigned to jth attribute and ϑ_{ij} is the weighted normalized decision matrix.

Step-3 Here positive ideal solution and negative ideal solution are identified as per (17) and (18) respectively.

$$A^+ = [v_1^+, v_2^+, - - - v_n^+]; \; v_j^+ = \{\max(v_{ij}) \; if \; j \in J; \; \min(v_{ij}) \; if \; j \in J'\} \tag{17}$$

$$A^- = [v_1^-, v_2^-, - - - v_n^-]; \; v_j^- = \{\min(v_{ij}) \; if \; j \in J; \; \max(v_{ij}) \; if \; j \in J'\} \tag{18}$$

Step-4 The separation measures from positive and negative ideal values are computed as per (19) and (20) respectively.

$$S_i^+ = \sqrt{\sum_{j=1}^{n} \left(v_{ij} - v_j^+ \right)^2} \tag{19}$$

$$S_i^- = \sqrt{\sum_{j=1}^{n} \left(v_{ij} - v_j^- \right)^2} \tag{20}$$

Step-5 with respect to their respective closeness the TOPSIS rank is evaluated as:

$$S_i = \frac{S_i^-}{S_i^+ + S_i^-} \tag{21}$$

Higher values of TOPSIS rank signifies that the corresponding solution is close to the ideal solution.

5   Implementation of SFSA in Economic Emission Dispatch Problem

Step-1 All points (solution) are generated within the lower/upper limits with the help of the equation given below.

$$\text{Points} = P_i^{min} + \text{rand}(NP, D) \times \left(P_i^{max} - P_i^{min} \right) \tag{22}$$

NP is number of search agents and D is the number of units for that particular system.

Step-2 fitness of all the points are evaluated by (6) which must satisfy the operating constraints (3) and (5) and then ranking of points in has been done on the basis of the Eq. (11) to obtain the best point (BP).

For TOPSIS ranking if single objective function alone required to be minimized among multi objective function then, the weight factor for particular to be assign as one, where as for other objective remains zero. On the other hand if all objective function say n, needed to be minimized simultaneously, the weight assign to each objective is 1/n to evaluate best compromise solution (BCS).

Step-3 The best point obtained above is diffused around its surrounding position to create another point in the search space as per (7) and (8).

Step-4 Diffused points are evaluated on the basis of their fitness as per (6) which must satisfy the associated operating constraints and the re-ranking has been done. To improve the fitness of the points obtained above another process called updating process is performed. In updating process the points obtained are by (12).

They are ranked again as per step-2, till the termination criterion has not been met, If the termination criterion is not met then from step-1 to step-4 are repeated again.

6 Simulation Results

For test cases of MOEED problem the SFSA_WS and SFSA_TOP are implemented in MATLAB 7.8 and the system configuration is Intel core i5 processor with 2 GHz speed and 4 GB RAM. SFSA has mainly two main parameters, Search Agents (NP) and the maximum diffusion number (MDN). For ten unit their effect are investigated. Simulation analysis has been carried out with variation in NP and MDN keeping iteration 500 over twenty repeated trials. The outcomes of analysis are presented Table 1. It was observed that with NP = 50 and MDN = 2 the Standard deviation of cost is found to be low and are considered to be as optimum parameter for analysis.

Table 1. Effect of variation in parameters

NP	MDN	Min Cost ($/h)	Ave Cost ($/h)	Max Cost ($/h)	S.D	CPU (sec)
25	2	111497.675	111497.838	111498.160	0.1403	4.73
	4	111497.716	111497.835	111498.026	0.1029	6.33
	6	111497.639	111497.869	111498.083	0.1459	7.83
50	2	**111497.630**	**111497.677**	**111497.711**	**0.0256**	8.37
	4	111497.655	111497.683	111497.737	0.0271	11.34
	6	111497.642	111497.684	111497.780	0.0392	14.31
100	2	111497.751	111497.821	111497.965	0.0642	15.38
	4	111497.697	111497.746	111497.850	0.0799	21.01
	6	111497.668	111497.778	111497.897	0.0678	26.62

S.D.: Standard deviation

6.1 *Test Case 1:* 10 Unit System

This test case has ten thermal generating units with non-smooth cost function and emission. VPL effects are included in the cost function. Transmission line losses are also considered here. The entire data for this system is adopted from [5] with power demand of 2000 MW. The simulation result obtained by SFSA in terms of minimum cost is 111497.630825 $/h where as minimum emission is 4572.16811 ton/h. Table 2 depicts the optimum power generation for each individual case i.e. best Cost Solution (ELD), Best Emission Solution (EED) and best compromise solution (BCS).

For multi objective case best compromise solution are found to be 113020.5375 ($/h) and 4159.5302 (ton/h) by SFS_TOP whereas 112820.0351 ($/h) and 4185.5751 (ton/h) by SFS_WS. The comparison of results are made in terms of best cost best emission and BCS with most resent reported method as Real Coded Chemical Reaction algorithm (RCCRO) [9], Backtracking search optimization (BSA) [10] and other in Table 3. Figure 1 depicts the convergence characteristic for 10unit system and its pareto front is depicted in Fig. 2.

Table 2. Optimum power dispatch by Ten unit system for the power demand of $P_D = 2000$ MW

Unit no	ELD	EED	BCS (WS)	BCS (TOPSIS)
1	55.0000	55.0000	54.99994	54.9999
2	80.0000	79.9991	79.99990	79.9999
3	106.9398	81.1365	86.34781	85.8704
4	100.5749	81.4024	84.61540	84.2748
5	81.5010	160.0000	130.09042	134.3331
6	83.0231	239.9999	147.74948	152.9883
7	300.0000	294.4696	299.99906	299.9906
8	340.0000	297.2785	319.57290	317.6779
9	470.0000	396.7198	439.15688	435.8209
10	470.0000	395.5883	442.07658	438.3974
Total O/P (MW)	2087.03	2081.59	2084.60	2084.40
Loss (MW)	87.03	81.59	84.60	84.40
Cost ($/h)	111497.630825	116412.75739	112820.0351	113020.5375
Emission (ton/h)	4572.16811	3932.199367	4185.5751	4159.5302

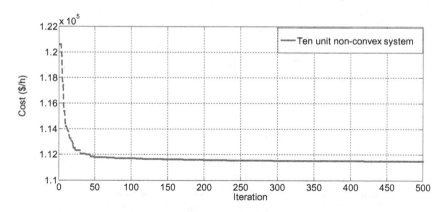

Fig. 1. Cost convergence for the 10 unit system

Table 3. Comparison of results for ten unit system

Method	ELD		EED		BCS	
	Cost ($/h)	Emis. (ton/h)	Cost ($/h)	Emis. (ton/h)	Cost ($/h)	Emis. (ton/h)
DE [3]	111500.00	4581.00	116400.00	3923.00	134800.00	4124.9000
PDE [3]	NA[#]	NA	NA	NA	135100.00	4111.4000
NSGA-II [5]	NA	NA	NA	NA	113540.00	4130.2000
SPEA-2 [5]	NA	NA	NA	NA	113520.00	4109.1000
RCCRO [9]	111497.6319	4571.9552	116412.4441	3932.2433	113355.745	4121.0684
BSA [10]	111497.6308	4572.193	116412.444	3932.2430	113126.751	4146.7285

(*continued*)

Table 3. (*continued*)

Method	ELD		EED		BCS	
	Cost ($/h)	Emis. (ton/h)	Cost ($/h)	Emis. (ton/h)	Cost ($/h)	Emis. (ton/h)
SFSA	**111497.6308**	4572.1681	116412.7573	**3932.1993**	NA	NA
SFSA_WS	NA	NA	NA	NA	**112820.0351**	**4185.5751**
SFSA_TOP	NA	NA	NA	NA	**113020.5375**	**4159.5302**

NA: Not available, BCS: Best Compromise Solution

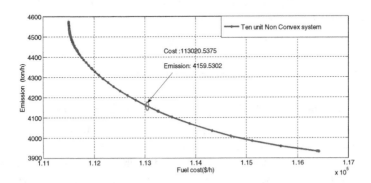

Fig. 2. Pareto optimal front for the 10 unit system

6.2   *Test Case 2:* **13unit System**

This test case has thirteen thermal generating units with non-smooth cost function and emission. Valve point loading effects are included in the cost function. Transmission line losses are not considered here. The entire data for this system is adopted from [11] with power demand of 1800 MW. The simulation result obtained by SFSA in terms of minimum cost is 17960.3661 $/h where as minimum emission is 57.11173 ton/h. Table 4 depicts the optimum power generation for scheduling three individual cases as best cost solution, best emission solution and best compromise solution (BCS).

Table 4. Optimum power dispatch by thirteen unit system for the power demand of $P_D = 1800$ MW

Unit (MW)	ELD	EED	BCS (WS)	BCS (TOPSIS)
P1	628.3185	80.14933	269.3337	179.9021
P2	149.5997	165.49676	224.4067	299.1531
P3	222.7491	165.49676	230.7312	299.0787
P4	109.8666	154.05212	159.7396	109.9257
P5	60.0000	154.05211	110.1409	158.7779
P6	109.8666	154.05211	109.8854	109.9768

(continued)

Table 4. (*continued*)

Unit (MW)	ELD	EED	BCS (WS)	BCS (TOPSIS)
P7	109.8666	154.05211	109.9356	108.1612
P8	109.8666	154.05212	159.8139	159.8583
P9	109.8666	154.05211	160.1238	109.8431
P10	40.0000	119.40235	40.4862	77.6774
P11	40.0000	119.40235	77.6891	40.0805
P12	55.0000	112.86988	92.5265	55.1700
P13	55.0000	112.86989	55.1870	92.3633
Total O/P (MW)	1800.00	1800.00	1800.00	1800.00
cost ($/h)	17960.3661	19140.89426	18087.7755	18071.7050
Emission (ton/h)	460.99962	57.11173	96.8685	89.6176

Table 5. Comparison of results for thirteen unit system

Method	ELD		EED		BCS	
	Cost ($/h)	Emis. (ton/h)	Cost ($/h)	Emis. (ton/h)	Cost ($/h)	Emis. (ton/h)
CDEMD [12]	17961.9440	NA	NA	NA	NA	NA
ACHS [13]	17963.8292	NA	NA	NA	NA	NA
θ-PSO [14]	17,963.8297	NA	NA	NA	NA	NA
TLBO [15]	18141.6	NA	NA	NA	NA	NA
BBOT [11]	17960.346	461.479	19098.756	58.241	18081.483	95.3095
SFSA	17960.3661	460.99962	19140.89426	57.11173	NA	NA
SFSA_WS	NA	NA	NA	NA	18087.7755	96.8685
SFSA_TOP	NA	NA	NA	NA	18071.7050	89.6176

NA: Not available

The comparison of results are made with improved differential evolution approach based on cultural algorithm and diversity measure (CDEMD) [12], hybrid harmony search with arithmetic crossover operation (ACHS) [13], θ-PSO [14] and most recently reported method teaching learning based optimization (TLBO) [15].

For multi objective case best compromise solution are found to be 18071.7050 ($/h) and 89.6176 (ton/h) by SFS_TOP whereas 18087.7755 ($/h) and 96.8685 (ton/h) by SFS_WS which is compared with Biogeography based optimization technique (BBOT) [11] in Table 5. The cost convergence characteristic for 13unit system and its pareto optimum front are depicted in Figs. 3 and 4 respectively.

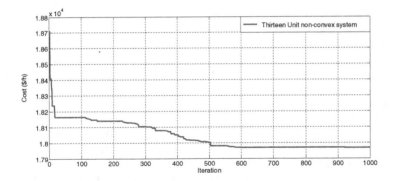

Fig. 3. Cost convergence of 13 unit system

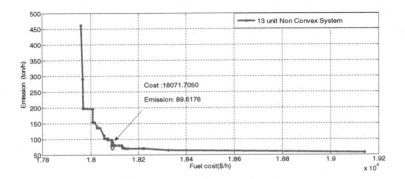

Fig. 4. Pareto optimal front of 13 unit system

7 Conclusion

In this paper a novel Stochastic Fractal search algorithm using TOPSIS is applied to solve MOEED problems. Here TOPSIS is utilized as overall ranking tool to identify the best compromise solution which equally satisfies the two conflicting objectives, cost and emission. The approach has been tested on two standard test cases and results are compared with other reported methods available in recent literature. It is observed that the solution obtained by SFSA and SFSA_TOP are better than other contemporary meta-heuristics for the tested problems. The SFSA is found to be promising. To get best compromise solution the weighted sum approach is also quite popular. More over the SFSA_TOP can be effectively used for more complex and constrained MOEED problems.

References

1. Nanda, J., Kothari, D.P., Linga Murthy, K.S.: Economic emission load dispatch through goal programming techniques. IEEE Trans. Energy Convers. **3**(1), 26–32 (1988)
2. Palanichamy, C., Babu, N.S.: Analytical solution for combined economic and emissions dispatch. Electric Power Syst. Res. **78**, 1129–1137 (2008)
3. Basu, M.: Economic environmental dispatch using multi-objective differential evolution. Appl. Soft Comput. **11**, 2845–2853 (2011)
4. Pandit, N., Tripathi, A., Tapaswi, S., Pandit, M.: An improved bacterial foraging algorithm for combined static/dynamic environmental economic dispatch. Appl. Soft Comput. **12**, 3500–3513 (2012)
5. Güvenç, U., Sönmez, Y., Duman, S., Yörükeren, N.: Combined economic and emission dispatch solution using gravitational search algorithm. Scientia Iranica D **19**(6), 1754–1762 (2012)
6. Pandit, M., Chaudhary, V., Dubey, H.M., Panigrahi, B.K.: Multi-period wind integrated optimal dispatch using series PSO-DE with time-varying Gaussian membership function based fuzzy selection. Electr. Power Energy Syst. **73**, 259–272 (2015)
7. Salimi, H.: Stochastic fractal search: a powerful metaheuristic algorithm. Knowl. Based Syst. **75**, 1–18 (2015)
8. Hwang, C.L., Yoon, K.: Multiple Attribute Decision Making: Method and Applications. Springer-Verlag, New York (1981)
9. Bhattacharjee, K., Bhattacharya, A., Dey, S.H.: Solution of economic emission load dispatch problems of power systems by real coded chemical reaction algorithm. Electr. Energy Syst. **59**, 176–187 (2014)
10. Bhattacharjee, K., Bhattacharya, A., Dey, S.H.: Backtracking search optimization based economic environmental power dispatch problems. Electr. Power Energy Syst. **73**, 830–842 (2015)
11. Rajasomashekar, S., Arvindhbabu, P.: Biogeography based optimization technique for best compromise solution of economic emission dispatch. Swarm Evol. Comput. **7**, 47–57 (2012)
12. Coelho, L.S., Thom Souza, R.C., Mariani, V.C.: Improved differential evolution approach based on cultural algorithm and diversity measure applied to solve economic load dispatch problems. Math. Comput. Simul. **79**, 3136–3147 (2009)
13. Niu, Q., Zhang, H., Wang, X., Li, K., Irwin, G.W.: A hybrid harmony search with arithmetic crossover operation for economic dispatch. Electr. Power Energy Syst. **62**, 237–257 (2014)
14. Hosseinnezhad, V., Babaei, E.: Economic load dispatch using θ-PSO. Electr. Power Energy Syst. **49**, 160–169 (2013)
15. Banerjee, S., Maity, D., Chanda, C.K.: Teaching learning based optimization for economic load dispatch problem considering valve point loading effect. Electr. Power Energy Syst. **73**, 456–464 (2015)
16. Witten, T.T., Sander, L.: Diffusion limited aggregation. Phys. Rev. B **27**, 56–86 (1983)

Particle Swarm Optimization
for the Deployment of Directional Sensors

Pankaj Singh, S. Mini$^{(\boxtimes)}$, and Ketan Sabale

National Institute of Technology Goa, Farmagudi, Goa, India
pankajnitg@gmail.com, mini2min2002@yahoo.co.in, ketansabale1@gmail.com

Abstract. Directional sensors are a special class of sensors that have special characteristics, such as the angle of sensing. Hence the techniques or methods that are used to solve problems in traditional disk-based sensing models may not be applicable to directional sensor networks. Random deployment of directional sensor nodes usually fails where the number of sensors are limited or have less sensing capability. This paper addresses coverage enhancement of applications that use directional sensor nodes. We assume that the number of directional sensor nodes are less than the number of objects to be covered in the region. The main aim is to identify the optimal/near optimal deployment locations of the directional sensor nodes such that the coverage is maximized. We use Particle Swarm Optimization (PSO) algorithm to compute the deployment locations of the nodes. The experimental results reveal that PSO is a promising method to solve this problem.

Keywords: Wireless sensor networks · Directional sensor networks · Sensor deployment · Particle swarm optimization

1 Introduction

Wireless Sensor Networks (WSNs) have attracted tremendous research interests recently because of its vast applications. In a WSN, sensors are deployed in certain geographic region to cover certain specific point-locations (objects or targets) or the entire area. Sensors, generally battery powered, have limitations on energy. Sensors can have circular sensing model (disk based) or non-circular sensing model. In real applications, due to equipment constraints or environmental impairments or as required by the application, certain sensors may only sense directionally and facilitate a sector-like sensing range, which are termed directional sensors. Some examples are video sensors, ultrasonic sensors, infrared sensors, multimedia and smart phone camera. The sensing ability of directional sensors is limited by a sector region of some radius r and the targets are detected only if they are located within the sensing sector. A target is said to be covered by a directional sensor if the object lies within the sensing sector (of predefined radius) of the sensor.

Sensor nodes are usually randomly deployed [1] for regions that are inaccessible. A large number of sensor nodes will be required for this purpose. However,

© Springer International Publishing AG 2016
B.K. Panigrahi et al. (Eds.): SEMCCO 2015, LNCS 9873, pp. 167–175, 2016.
DOI: 10.1007/978-3-319-48959-9_15

this is may not be effective if the sensors are limited. If the region is accessible and the sensor nodes are limited (due to cost factor or other constraints), it is better to adopt a deterministic deployment scheme wherein the optimal deployment locations are pre-computed. With directional sensors, it is even more advantageous since there are several factors that affect the total number of objects that can be covered. The sensing range of the sensor and the sector which the sensor can sense are the major factors.

Figure 1 shows a sample random deployment of four directional sensors in a region where objects are to be covered. It can be seen that only one object is covered. If a deterministic deployment scheme is adopted, more objects can be covered.

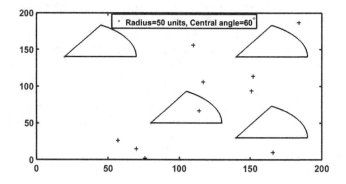

Fig. 1. A sample random deployment

This paper addresses the placement of directional sensor nodes in a given region. A directional sensor node will henceforth be referred as a sensor node. We assume that the region is accessible and the sensor nodes can be deployed at the pre-computed deployment locations. It is also assumed that the number of sensor nodes to be deployed is less than the number of objects to be covered. The optimal/near optimal locations of deployment are computed using Particle Swarm Optimization [2,3].

The rest of the paper is organized as follows: Sect. 2 presents an overview of the related research. The problem is formulated in Sect. 3. Section 4 describes the proposed approach. The results are reported and discussed in Sect. 5. Section 6 concludes the paper.

2   Related Work

There have been several research efforts on tackling problems pertaining to directional sensor networks. Maximum Coverage with Minimum Sensors (MCMS) problem of directional sensor networks is addressed in [1]. The aim is to maximize the coverage of targets whereas the number of sensors to be activated is minimized. Centralized and distributed algorithms to solve this problem are proposed. A Sensing Neighborhood Cooperative Sleeping (SNCS) protocol which performs adaptive scheduling is also proposed. Scheduling sensor nodes is the common way of prolonging network lifetime in directional sensor networks as in traditional WSNs. [4] is a survey on directional sensor networks and addresses various design issues and challenges for directional sensors network. Coverage enhancement algorithms organize the working directions of sensor nodes and determine a set of active nodes once after the initial deployment. However, active nodes need to be replaced by inactive nodes repeatedly and vice versa.

Other scheduling algorithms are proposed in [5,6]. These methods help to save energy and prolong the network lifetime, which are essential for sensor networks. If coverage of all the targets are required, the number of sensors should be reasonably high for scheduling to be feasible. Several other scheduling algorithms have also been proposed to increase the network lifetime of directional sensor networks.

A directional sensor model is proposed in [7] where each sensor is fixed to one direction and analyzes the probability of full area coverage. In [8], another directional sensor model is proposed, where a sensor is allowed to work in several directions. In order to maximize the area of coverage of randomly deployed sensors, which is an NP-complete problem, a method DGreedy is proposed in [9]. Coverage problem of directional sensor networks is addressed in [10]. The optimal area coverage problem is proved to be NP-complete in [11]. A method based on greedy approximation algorithm for Optimal Coverage in Directional Sensors Network (OCDSN) problem is also proposed.

The deployment positions play a crucial role in attaining maximum coverage of the objects. This paper concerns deterministic deployment of directional sensor nodes when the number of sensor nodes are limited. It aims at maximizing the coverage of targets (or objects). The deployment locations are computed using Particle Swarm Optimization. Other algorithms like Differential Evolution (DE) [12] and improved PSO [13] can also be used to solve this problem.

3   Problem Definition

Given a region R and n sensors $S = \{S_1, S_2, \ldots, S_n\}$ to monitor m targets $T = \{T_1, T_2, \ldots, T_m\}$, the objective is to identify the optimal deployment locations of S such that the maximum number of targets are covered. If the sensor S_i, $1 \leq i \leq n$, is at position (x_1, y_1) and the object T_j is at position (x_2, y_2), then S_i can sense T_j iff both the following conditions are satisfied.

– The distance d_{ij} between S_i and T_j is less than or equal to the sector radius r.

$$\sqrt{(x_1 - x_2)^2 + (y_1 - y_2)^2} \leq r \tag{1}$$

– The angle (in counter clockwise direction) between the sensor, the object and the horizontal line through the origin of the sensor, is greater than or equal to the start angle and less than the sum of central angle and start angle.

This can be formulated as a single objective optimization problem where the objective function F is given by,

$$F = \forall S_i(max(coverage(T)))$$ (2)

4   Proposed Approach

Algorithm 1.

1: Initialize particles
2: **repeat**
3: **for** all particles **do**
4:       Calculate the fitness value
5:       **if** the fitness value is better than the best fitness value (*pbest*) in history **then**
6:             Set current value as the new *pbest*
7:       **end if**
8: **end for**
9: Choose the particle with the best fitness value of all the particles as the *gbest*
10: **for** each particle **do**
11:       Calculate particle velocity according to velocity update equation (Equation(3))
12:       Update particle position according to position update equation (Equation(4))
13: **end for**
14: **until**(maximum iterations or minimum error criteria is not attained)

The coverage area of directional sensors make the directional sensors different from conventional sensor networks. The deployment positions of directional sensors critically affect coverage of the objects (or targets). We use Particle Swarm Optimization (PSO) to compute the optimal/near-optimal deployment locations.

PSO is one among the many stochastic optimization techniques. It is inspired by bird flocking and fish schooling. The swarm of s potential solutions are known as particles. A group of particles move in a search space where there many possible solutions. Each particle will have a position vector and a velocity vector associated to it. In addition to it, each particle can also memorize its own best position identified so far and also the best position that has been found by the communication with its neighbors [2]. The fitness function is evaluated in PSO as in all the other evolutionary algorithms [3]. The best value associated with each particle is known as *pbest* and the best value over all the particles is known as *gbest*.

The search for the global solution is carried out in an nd-dimensional hyperspace, where n is the number of optimal parameters that are to be determined. A particle i occupies position x_{id} and velocity v_{id} in the dth dimension of the hyperspace, $1 \leq i \leq s$ and $1 \leq d \leq nd$. Each particle is evaluated through an objective function $f(x_1; x_2; \ldots; x_{nd})$, where $f : \mathbb{R}^{nd} \to \mathbb{R}$.

Since this work is concerned with a maximization problem, the algorithm tries to maximize the fitness function. In each iteration tr, velocity v and position x are updated using Eqs. (3) and (4). The process of updation is repeated iteratively till some predefined number of iterations or till an acceptable *gbest* is obtained.

$$v_{id}(tr + 1) = w.v_{id}(tr) + \varphi_1.r_1(tr).pbest_{id} - x_{id}$$
$$+\varphi_2.r_2(tr).(gbest_d - x_{id}) \tag{3}$$
$$x_{id}(tr + 1) = x_{id}(tr) + v_{id}(tr + 1) \tag{4}$$

Here, φ_1 and φ_2 are constants, and $r_1(tr)$ and $r_2(tr)$ are random numbers uniformly distributed in $[0, 1]$.

The basic steps of PSO [3] are shown in Algorithm 1.

5 Results and Discussion

We consider a 100×100 grid for experimentation. The number of sensors are varied between 5 to 20 and the number of objects are varied between 10 to 55. The sensing range of the nodes is 30 or 50 units, the start angle is either $0°$ or $30°$, and the central angle is $30°$ or $60°$. Each parameter is changed by keeping all the other parameters fixed. The population size is 10, number of iterations is 1000 and the number of runs is 3. For each deployment configuration, three instances are considered. Simulations are carried out using MatLab.

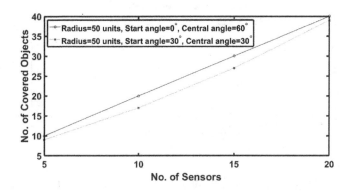

Fig. 2. No. of sensors vs. No. of objects covered for fixed radii (No. of objects $= 2 \times$ No. of sensors)

Figure 2 shows the plot of number of sensors vs. the number of objects covered for some particular setting of parameters. The total number of objects deployed in the region is twice the number of sensors. The radius is fixed as 50 units. When the start angle is $0°$ and central angle is $60°$, there is an increase in the number of objects that are covered, as to compared to a start angle of $30°$ and central angle of $30°$. This is because the sensing sector will be larger in the first set up than in the second one.

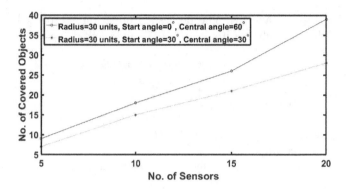

Fig. 3. No. of sensors vs. No. of objects covered for fixed radii (No. of objects = 2 × No. of sensors)

Similar to the assumption in Fig. 2, Fig. 3 considers the number of objects deployed in the region as twice the number of sensors. The configuration with start angle 0° and central angle 60° can cover more objects than the one with start angle 30° and central angle 30°.

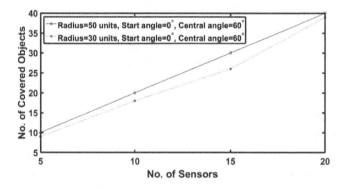

Fig. 4. No. of sensors vs. No. of objects covered for different radii (No. of objects = 2 × No. of sensors)

Figure 4 shows the results while varying radii. When the radius is 50 units, more objects could be covered, compared to when the radius is 30 units. The start angle and the central angle are fixed as 0° and 60° respectively, for both the cases.

The same is observed when the start angle is at 30° and the central angle is fixed at 30°. When the radius is increased, it is evident that more number of objects can be covered (Fig. 5).

Table 1 shows the results when the number of sensors is 5. Initial experiments are carried out with 10 objects. The radius is taken as 50 units. The start angle

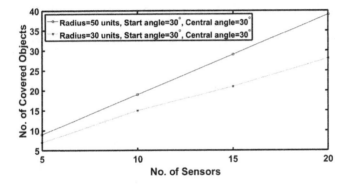

Fig. 5. No. of sensors vs. No. of objects covered for different radii (No. of objects $= 2 \times$ No. of sensors)

Table 1. Experimental results (No. of sensors $= 5$)

Sensors	Objects	r	Start Angle (°)	Central Angle (°)	Instance	No. of covered objects		
						Best	Mean	Standard Deviation
5	10	50	0	60	1	10	10	0
					2	10	10	0
					3	10	10	0
			30	30	1	9	8.3333	0.5774
					2	9	9	0
					3	9	9	0
		30	0	60	1	8	8	0
					2	9	9	0
					3	9	9	0
			30	30	1	6	6	0
					2	6	6	0
					3	7	6.6667	0.5774
	15	50	0	60	1	14	14	0
					2	14	14	0
					3	14	14	0
			30	30	1	12	12	0
					2	12	12	0
					3	12	12	0
		30	0	60	1	11	11	0
					2	11	11	0
					3	11	11	0
			30	30	1	9	9	0
					2	9	9	0
					3	9	9	0

Table 2. Experimental results (No. of sensors $= 20$)

Sensors	Objects	r	Start angle (°)	Central angle (°)	Instance	No. of covered objects		
						Best	Mean	Standard Deviation
20	50	50	0	60	1	50	49.33	0.57
					2	50	50	0
					3	50	50	0
			30	30	1	44	44	0
					2	44	44	0
					3	44	44	0
		30	0	60	1	43	43	0
					2	43	43	0
					3	43	43	0
			30	30	1	33	33	0
					2	33	33	0
					3	33	33	0
	55	50	0	60	1	55	55	0
					2	55	55	0
					3	55	55	0
			30	30	1	52	52	0
					2	52	52	0
					3	52	52	0
		30	0	60	1	48	47.33	1.15
					2	48	48	0
					3	48	48	0
			30	30	1	33	33	0
					2	40	40	0
					3	40	40	0

and central angle are changed to observe the change in the number of targets that can be covered. When the start angle is 0° and central angle is 60°, all the ten objects can be covered. But when the start angle is shifted to 30° and the central angle is reduced to 30°, not all the ten objects could be covered for all the three instances under consideration. When the radius is reduced to 30 units, even when the start angle is 0° and central angle is 60°, there are objects that could not be covered. The coverage reduces further when the start angle is increased and the central angle is decreased. When the number of objects deployed in the region is increased to 15, complete coverage is no possible with radius of 50 units and start angle 0° and central angle 60°.

The results when 20 sensors are deployed in the region, is tabulated in Table 2. The number of objects to be monitored in the region is initially fixed as 50 and then changed to 55. When the number of objects are increased, the possibility of better coverage fades. As the radius is reduced, the number of objects that can be covered also reduces.

6   Conclusion and Future Work

The disk-sensing models will sense the entire disk, whereas the directional sensors sense only a sector. Hence the placement of these nodes are crucial for obtaining maximum coverage. The problem of deploying directional sensors is addressed in this paper. The focus is to achieve maximum coverage of the objects placed. Based on particle swarm optimization, we computed the optimum deployment locations. Experimental results revealed that some parameters: radius, start angle and the central angle, had a strong influence on the overall coverage. These are sensitive parameters that play an important role in the deployment locations. In the present work, we have not changed the orientation of the sensor nodes. We propose to do this in the future. In addition we plan to use this method on a larger network and compare with other algorithms.

References

1. Ai, J., Alhussein, A.A.: Coverage by directional sensors in randomly deployed wireless sensor networks. J. Comb. Optim. **11**(1), 21–41 (2006)
2. Kennedy, J., Eberhart, R.: Particle swarm optimization. In: IEEE International Conference on Neural Networks, pp. 1942–1948 (1995)
3. Eberhart, R., Kennedy, J.: A new optimizer using particle swarm theory. In: Sixth International Symposium on Micro Machine and Human Science, pp. 39–43 (1995)
4. Guvensan, M.A., Gokhan Yavuz, A.: On coverage issues in directional sensor networks: a survey. Ad Hoc Netw. **9**(7), 1238–1255 (2011)
5. Yanli, C., Lou, W., Li, M., Li, X.-Y.: Target-oriented scheduling in directional sensor networks. In: INFOCOM (2007)
6. Cai, Y., Lou, W., Li, M., Xiang-Yang, L.: Energy efficient target-oriented scheduling in directional sensor networks. IEEE Trans. Comput. **58**(9), 1259–1274 (2009)
7. Ma, H., Liu, Y.: On coverage problems of directional sensor networks. In: Jia, X., Wu, J., He, Y. (eds.) MSN 2005. LNCS, vol. 3794, pp. 721–731. Springer, Heidelberg (2005). doi:10.1007/11599463_70
8. Zhao, J., Zeng, J.-C.: An electrostatic field-based coverage-enhancing algorithm for wireless multimedia sensor networks. In: 5th International Conference on Wireless Communications, Networking and Mobile Computing (2009)
9. Cheng, W., Li, S., Liao, X., Changxiang, S., Chen, H.: Maximal coverage scheduling in randomly deployed directional sensor networks. In: International Conference on Parallel Processing Workshops, pp. 10–14 (2007)
10. Yanli, C., Lou, W., Li, M.: Cover set problem in directional sensor networks. In: Future Generation Communication and Networking (2007)
11. Li, J., Wang, R.-C., Huang, H.-P., Sun, L.-J.: Voronoi based area coverage optimization for directional sensor networks. In: Second International Symposium on Electronic Commerce and Security, pp. 488–493 (2009)
12. Das, S., Suganthan, P.N.: Differential evolution: a survey of the state-of-the-art. IEEE Trans. Evol. Comput. **15**(1), 4–31 (2011)
13. Lynn, N., Suganthan, P.N.: Heterogeneous comprehensive learning particle swarm optimization with enhanced exploration and exploitation. Swarm Evol. Comput. **24**, 11–24 (2015)

Region Based Multiple Features for an Effective Content Based Access Medical Image Retrieval an Integrated with Relevance Feedback Approach

B. Jyothi[1(✉)], Y. MadhaveeLatha[2], P.G. Krishna Mohan[3],
and V.S.K. Reddy[4]

[1] Department of ECE, MRCET, JNTUH, Hyderabad, India
bjyothi815@gmail.com
[2] Department of ECE, MRECW, JNTUH, Hyderabad, India
madhaveelatha2009@gmail.com
[3] Department of ECE, IARE, Hyderabad, India
pgkmohan@yahoo.com
[4] Department of ECE, MRCET, Hyderabad, India
mrcet2004@gmail.com

Abstract. An efficient Content-based medical image retrieval (CBMIR) system is imperative to browse the entire database to locate required medical image. This paper proposes an effecChapHead:/Authortive scheme includes the detection of the boundary of the image followed by exploring the content of the interior boundary region with the help of multiple features. The proposed technique integrates the Texture, Shape features and the relevance feedback mechanism. Differentiate of Gabor Filter used for Texture feature extraction and Moments extract the Region based shape features. The Euclidean distance is used for similarity measure and then these distances are sorted out and ranked. The Recall rate of the medical retrieval system has been enhanced by adapting Relevance Feedback mechanism. The efficiency of the proposed method has been evaluated by using a huge data base by employing multiple features and integrating with Relevance feedback approach. Correspondingly, the Recall Rate has been enormously enhanced and Error Rate has been reduced as compared to the existing classical retrieval methods.

Keywords: Content based image retrieval · Boundary detection · Feature extraction · Relevance feedback

1 Introduction

Advancement of technology in the medical field has increased the generation and storage of medical images in database. Medical images are significant diagnosing evidence to provide important information about any disease, helps in medical education and Training and assisting Computer Aided Diagnosis Applications (CAD) [1]. To convince the exceeding needs, it is absolutely necessary to construct an effective retrieval system to retrieve similar medical images from a huge data base. Basically,

© Springer International Publishing AG 2016
B.K. Panigrahi et al. (Eds.): SEMCCO 2015, LNCS 9873, pp. 176–187, 2016.
DOI: 10.1007/978-3-319-48959-9_16

there are two methods for searching required images. They are concept based searching method and Content based searching method. The former is confronted with many challenges [2] because medical images are complex in nature. It is cumbersome to save database images which involve large manual annotations, consumption of too much time and huge expenses. The more the number of database images the more complex the problems will be. Since there are innumerable images in a given database, even a medical expert has to struggle to retrieve required images which facilitate the diagnosing process in time. To overcome these limitations, a lot of research has been taken up in the content-based image retrieval (CBIR) approaches during the last decade [3, 4]. Content based methodology addresses the issues involved in the concept based methodology. The images required by the medical expert retrieved by providing the query image whose content is similar to that of retrieved images based on their visible features such as Color, Texture and Shape used for disease analysis. Generally medical images are largely in gray scale, for diagnosing gray scale images texture & shape feature are extracted. H. Greenspan and A.T. Pinhas have discussed various CBMIR approaches in [5] and noticed that these approaches are effective for radiographic image retrieval task. The medical images can be examined more effectively by involving multiple features in spite of using solo feature. They unite the advantages of singular features ensuing in improving the retrieval system [6].

A shape feature provides useful information for identifying entities. The medical images consists of many objects, each object have specific information in it. The human can identify the objects entirely from their shapes [7]. Typically, the shapes carry semantic information [8]. The frequently used Shape demonstration techniques include Fourier descriptors [9]. The latter extracts the entire region information. The various region based methods discussed are in [10, 11]. Among the region based descriptors; moments play a significant role and are very popular. They exploit both boundary and interior content of the image.

Texture is an innate surface property of an image which gives the spatial connection to the surrounding image background. In addition it also characterizes the structural understanding of a region. Han et al. [12] proposed invariant to rotation and scale Gabor representations, Gabor features, have been particularly doing well in many computer vision and image processing applications [13]. It is extremely difficult to describe the whole content of a medical image exactly with the help of low level feature. To fill the semantic break between the low level visible features and high level observation Relevance feedback (RFB) was introduced [14].

Feature description plays a significant role in increasing the output of the retrieval scheme. In the proposed method, we have extracted the boundary of an image followed by extracting multiple feature. A boundary is a stripe that symbols the edges of an entity and partitions it from the surroundings. Medical images have deprived boundaries. Hence there are little practical problems while obtaining the medical images through scanning such noise and with reduced amount of illumination.

The image retrieval systems have a limited recall rate. A survey of RFB techniques recommends that various query modification approaches for the efficient design of the high performance retrieval system with the relevance feedback [15]. Relevance feedback is a query refinement technique that captures the user needs through the given feedback learning method. Initially the users retrieve a few relevant images in reaction to the given query image, then the users can modify the original input query automatically by using feedback process which can be done by expanding query with the information feed by feedback approach. Two basic components of relevance feedback have been evolved in research. First one based on the reweighting of query image feature vector. A second component of query image modification is based on altering the actual terms in the query image [16]. RB has initially been developed for increasing the efficiency of information system. Various relevance techniques have been discussed in [17]. User interaction with the retrieval system significantly (greatly) improves the retrieval results. RB is an effective mean to bridge the gap between.

This paper concentrates on the expansion of a novel and efficient approach for extracting characteristics about region. We expand the skeleton for image segmentation using edge following. The content of the region is to be extracted by using shape and texture features. Texture features are extracted using second order statistical feature at various orientations. Region based shape features such as Chebyshev moments are used for extracting interior detected boundary region. For a given query, the medical image retrieval system returns preliminary results based on ED as a similarity metric. If the user is not satisfied with the retrieved output, he can interact with the system by modifying the query image. In this procedure, the user make interaction with the system and selects the most relevant image for searching again based on the relevance feedback learning algorithm. The system accordingly analyzes the user feedback and returns superior results. This frame work increases the effectiveness of the retrieval system by using RFB [18]. Finally, required medical images are displayed by matching the identical features.

The remaining paper is organized as follows. Section 2 deals the CBMIR system. Section 3 deals with Features Extraction Sect. 4 presents Relevance feedback mechanism Sect. 5 focus the Results. Section 6 discuss the Conclusion of the paper.

2   CBMIR System

The structure of a classic theoretical CBMIR system is shown in Fig. 1 and discussed as follows. It consists of three steps: off-line feature extraction step, online image retrieval and feedback steps.

In offline step, the input image and database images are pre-processed for reducing noise with the help of median filter. Next the region of the object is detected by ignoring the background of the image. Later, the visible characteristics of the image is extracted by using second-order statistical components. These components are stored in the database as a feature vector along with the images. The database consists of various classes of medical images of certain human organs such as liver, lungs brain etc. We follow the suit for query image in online phase.

In online step, the retrieval system is given a query image for probing identical images. The system recovers the similar images by enumerating the analogy measure between the input image feature vector and corresponding data base images. In conclusion, the system profits the results which are majorly relevant to the input image.

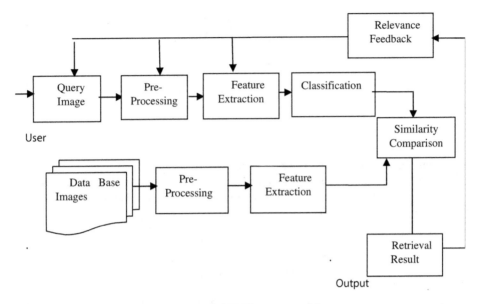

Fig. 1. Proposed CBMIR system architecture

In feedback phase the user checks whether the retrieved images are relevant or not otherwise he repeats the searching process in more effective way by using feedback learning algorithm.

3 Feature Extraction Approach

A feature describes the relevant visible information using visual features. In the proposed approach the region based features are used for describing the content of the image. For the medical images, the shape and the texture are the dominant features which can efficiently represent an image. The input image is F(i, j) where i, j are coordinates of the pixels in the image. The object region in an image recognized by means of edge following method. The region within in the detected boundary is described with the help of steerable decomposition and moments.

3.1 Boundary Detection

The Intensity Gradient and Texture map are the criteria on which the border line of the given medical image and the data base medical images are detected as follows.

$$M(i, j) = \frac{1}{M_r} \sum_{(i,j) \in N} \sqrt{M_x^2(i, j) + M_y^2(i, j)} \tag{1}$$

$$D(i, j) = \frac{1}{M_r} \sum_{(i,j) \in N} \tan^{-1} \left(\frac{M_y(i, j)}{M_x(i, j)} \right) \tag{2}$$

$$M_x(i, j) = -G_y x f(x, j) \approx \frac{\partial f(x, y)}{\partial y} \tag{3}$$

$$M_y(i, j) = -G_x x f(y, i) \approx \frac{\partial f(x, y)}{\partial x} \tag{4}$$

Where G_x and G_y difference masks of a Gaussian

The data base images as well as query image have been convolved with texture mask TM(i, j) to brighten the texture pattern which is defined as law's texture [18] on the resulting image RS(x, y).

$$TM(i, j) = M.M^T \tag{5}$$

$$M = (1, 4, 6, 4, 1)^T \tag{6}$$

$$RS(i, j) = F(i, j) * TM(i, j) \tag{7}$$

The edges can be tracked around the image as follows.

$$L_{ij}(i, j) = M_{ij}(i, j) + D_{ij}(i, j) + RS_{ij}(i, j) \tag{8}$$

3.2 Texture Pattern Extraction

Medical images are more often represented in gray level, mainly medical image surfaces demonstrates texture. This paper focuses a scale and rotation invariant texture depiction implemented with the help of steerable perishing defined in [19]. It is a extraordinary class of filter is synthesized at dissimilar orientations as a linear grouping of basis filters. The filter syntheses the image at different angles to determines the individual output of the orientations. Steerable oriented filter is a quadrature pair to permit adaptive control over phase and orientation. The filter at an orientation θ can be synthesized by linear combination of $G_1^{0^0}$ & $G_1^{90^0}$ and interpolation functions given as follows.

$$G_1^\theta = \cos(\theta) G_1^{0^0} + \sin(\theta) G_1^{90^0} \tag{9}$$

$G_1^{0^0}$ & $G_1^{90^0}$ are set of basis filters.

Cos (θ) & Sin (θ) are the Corresponding interpolation functions

$$G(x, y) = e^{-(x^2 + y^2)} \tag{10}$$

Where $G_1^{0^0} = -2xe^{-(x^2 + y^2)}$ and $G_1^{90^0} = -2ye^{-(x^2 + y^2)}$

The steering constraint is

$$F_\theta(m,n) = \sum_{k=1}^{N} b_k(\theta) A_k(m,n) \qquad (11)$$

where $b_k(\theta)$ is the interpolation function and $A_k(m, n)$ are the basis filters response at θ. Texture sequence can be extracted by applying second order from 10 oriented sub-bands as shown in Fig. 2.

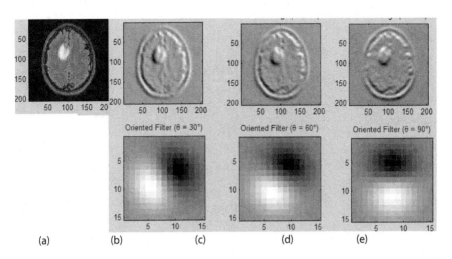

Fig. 2. The Oriented filtered images (a) The input image (b) Image with orotation of 30° (c) Image with a rotation of 60° (d) Image with a rotation of 90°

$$B(i,j) = \sum_i \sum_j I(i_1, j_1) S_i(i - I_1, j - J_1) \qquad (12)$$

Where $B_i(i, j)$ is symbolizing horizontal and S_i represents the filters at various orientations $i = 1, 2, 3, 4, 5, 6\ldots$

The second order statistical component analysis defined in [20] as follows.

Energy (E)

$$E = \sum_{i=0}^{N-1} \sum_{j=0}^{M-1} \{F(i,j)\}^2 \qquad (13)$$

Contrast(C)

$$C = \sum_{i=0}^{N-1} \sum_{j=0}^{M-1} |i - j| F(i,j) \qquad (14)$$

Inverse Difference Moment (IDM)

$$IDM = \sum_{i=0}^{N-1}\sum_{j=0}^{M-1} \frac{1}{1+(i-j)^2} F(i,j) \tag{15}$$

Entropy (E)

$$E = \sum_{i=0}^{N-1}\sum_{j=0}^{M-1} F(i,j) X \log(F(i,j)) \tag{16}$$

Correlation (Cr)

$$Cr = \sum_{i=0}^{N-1}\sum_{j=0}^{M-1} \frac{\{iXj\}X(F(i,j)-\{\mu_i X\mu_j\})}{\sigma_i X\sigma_j} \tag{17}$$

Variance (V)

$$V = \sum_{i=0}^{N-1}\sum_{j=0}^{M-1} (i-\mu)^2 F(i,j) \tag{18}$$

$$Fv = [E, C, IDM, E, Cr, V] \tag{19}$$

3.3   Shape Feature Extraction

The useful information is supplied by object shape features for image retrieval. The Object is recognized with the help of their shapes. In the proposed procedure we extricate the shape features using discrete orthogonal moments.

Chebyshev Moments: Mukundan has proposed discrete orthogonal moments to be used to do away with the bottle-necks connected to continuous orthogonal moments. According to him, Chebyshev moments are of high quality when compared with geometric, Legendre, and Zernike moments with respect to image reconstruction capability. For a digital image F(i, j) with (n + m) order and N × N size, Chebyshev moments are defined according to the subsequent relations

$$C_0(x) = 1 \tag{20}$$

$$C_1(x) = (2x - M + 1)/M \tag{21}$$

$$C_p(x) = \frac{(2p-1)C_1(x)C_{p-1}(x) - (p-1)\{1 - \frac{(p-1)^2}{M^2}\}C_{p-2}(x)}{p}; P > 1 \tag{22}$$

and the squared-norm $\rho(p, M)$ is given by

$$P(p, M) = \frac{M\left[1 - \frac{1}{M^2}\right]\left[1 - \frac{2^2}{M^2}\right]\cdots\cdots\cdots\left[1 - \frac{p^2}{M^2}\right]}{2p + 1} \; ; p = 0, 1, 2\ldots\ldots M - 1 \quad (23)$$

The Chebyshev moment of order p and repetition q is defined as:

$$S_{pq} = \frac{1}{2\pi\rho(P, n)} \sum_{r=0}^{n-1} \sum_{\theta=0}^{2\pi} C_p(r)e^{-j2\theta}f(r, \theta), \text{ where m denotes } (M/2) + 1 \quad (24)$$

4   Relevance Feedback Learning Approach

The relevance feedback (RFB) is an automatic query refinement procedure that improves the retrieval performance of CBMIR system. The RB is a very powerful technique which automatically adjusts the query image feature vector using the information fed back by the user with the formally retrieved images. In this approach we have adopted Rocchio [22] similarity based relevance feedback approach. The following Rocchio algorithm is employed to enhance the refinement of the query image for qualitative search by combining the reweighting term query image then the modified query defined as follows

$$Q_1 = Q_0 + \frac{1}{n_1}\sum_{i=1}^{n_1} R_i - \frac{1}{n_2}\sum_{i=1}^{n_2} N_i \quad (25)$$

Where

Q_0 = initial query image feature vector
R_i = first search relevant image feature vector
N_i = first search non-relevant image feature
n1 = the no of related images
n_2 = the no of non-related images

Q_1 is the vector sum of the initial query image plus the feature vectors of the related and non- related images.

5   Experimental Results

The input dataset consists of the various images of different modality acquired from cancer research center, Frederick national laboratory, which releases and provides necessary medical images for research, gathering of medical data and personal projects and verify the various methods and results by project explorer. Our database consist of 1000 medical images of a variety of classes of various organs of the human body such as abdomen, lungs and brain etc. We have experimented the usefulness of the presented method by computing the Euclidian distance [23] between the feature vector of input image and the consequent feature of the data base images. The similarity measure between query image and target image is defined as

$$ED(Fv_1, Fv_2) = \sqrt{\sum_{\forall i} (Fv_1(i) - Fv_2(i))^2} \tag{26}$$

With the help of Recall Rate and Error Rate the effectiveness of the retrieval system have been evaluated as shown in the Figs. 3 and (4) and it also compare d with the methods defined in [24, 25] with the proposed method. From the investigational results it is understandable that the proposed approach gives outstanding results for the CBMIR systems as it compares with the existing methods shown in Fig. 5.

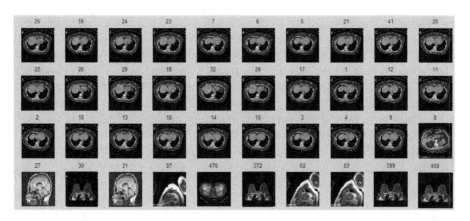

Fig. 3. Retrieved images using multiple features

$$Recall\,Rate = \frac{Number\,of\,\,Relavant\,Images\,Retrieved}{Total\,Number\,of\,\,Relavant\,Images\,in\,Database} \tag{27}$$

$$Error\,Rate = \frac{Number\,of\,Non\,Relavant\,Images\,Retrieved}{Total\,Number\,of\,Images\,Retrieved} \tag{28}$$

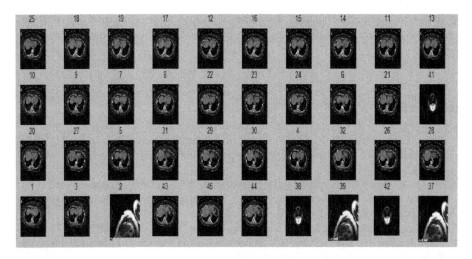

Fig. 4. Retrieved images using proposed method (Multiple features + relevance feedback method

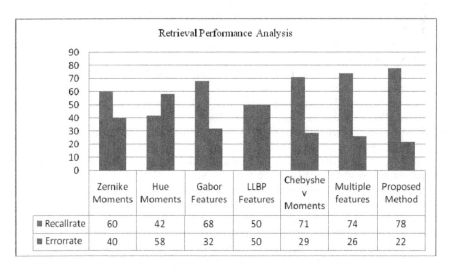

Fig. 5. The CBMIR retrieval results using different schemes

6 Discussion and Conclusion

Content extraction is a considerable task in proficient medical image retrieval. We have presented a new procedure for extracting region characteristics from an image with the help of moments and Texture Features by using steerable filter along with the integration of relevance feedback approach. It can effortlessly be executed and is computationally more efficient than the conventional methods. The results have show that the proposed approach enhances the retrieval output when compared the previous techniques. In future, this Scheme improved by considering more features for multiple diseases.

References

1. Khoo, L.A., Taylor, P., Given-Wilson, R.M.: Computer-aided detection in the United Kingdom national breast screening programme: prospective study. Radiology **237**, 444–449 (2005)
2. Muller, H., Michous, N., Bandon, D., Geissbuhler, A.: A review of content based image retrieval systems in medical applications — clinical benefits and future directions. Int. J. Med. Inform. **73**(1), 1–23 (2004)
3. Flickner, M., et al.: Query by image and video content. IEEE Comput. **28**(9), 23–32 (1995)
4. Furht, B., Smoliar, S.W., Zhang, H.J.: Image and Video Processing in Multimedia Systems. Kluwer Academic Publishers, Norwell (1995)
5. Greenspan, H., Pinhas, A.T.: Medical image categorization and retrieval for PAC Suing the GMM-KL framework. IEEE Trans. Inf. Techol. Biomed. **11**(2), 190–202 (2007)
6. Hiremath, P.S., Pujari, J.: Content based image retrieval using color, texture and shape features. In: Proceedings of the 15th International Conference on Advanced Computing and Communications, Guwahati, Inde, pp. 780–784, December 2007
7. Somkantha, K., Theera-Umpon, N.: Boundary detection in medical images using edge following algorithm based on intensity gradient and texture gradient features. IEEE Trans. Biomed. Eng. **58**(3), 567–573 (2011)
8. Manjunath, B.S., Salembier, P., Sikora, T.: Introduction to MPEG-7: Multimedia Content Description Interface. Wiley, Chichester (2002)
9. Vogel, J., Schiele, B.: Performance evaluation and optimization for content- based image retrieval. Pattern Recognit. **39**(5), 897–909 (2006)
10. Hu, M.-K.: Visual pattern recognition by moment invariants. IRE Trans. Inf. Theor. IT **8**, 179–187 (1962)
11. Mukundan, R., Ramakrishnan, K.R.: Moment Functions in Image Analysis: Theory and Applications. World Scientific Publication Co., Singapore (1998)
12. Han, J., Ma, K.K.: Rotation-invariant and scale-invariant Gabor features for texture image retrieval. Image Vis. Comput. **25**(9), 1474–1481 (2007)
13. Messer, K., et al.: Face authentication test on the BANCA database. In: International Conference on Pattern Recognition (ICPR) (2004)
14. Patil, P.B., Kokare, M.B.: Relevance feedback in content based image retrieval a review. J. Appl. Comput. Sci. Math. **10**(5), 41–47 (2011)
15. Hoi, C.H., Lyu, M.R.: A novel log based relevance feedback technique in content based image retrieval. In: proceedings of the ACM Multimedia (ACM-MM 2004), New york, USA, pp. 24–31 (2004)
16. Cheng, E., Jin, F., Zhang, L.: Unified relevance feedback framework for web image retrieval. IEEE Trans. Image Process. **18**(6), 1350–1357 (2009)
17. Zhou, X.S., Hung, T.S.: Relevance feedback in image retrieval: a comprehensive review. In: A Review for ACM Multimedia System Journal Shoter Version, IEEE CVPR 2001, workshop on Content Based Access Image and Video Libravies(LBAIVL)

18. Rui, Y., Huang, T.S., Ortega, M., Mehrotra, S.: Relevance feedback: a power tool for interactive content-based image retrieval. IEEE Trans. Circuits Syst. Video Technol. 8(5), 644–655 (1998)
19. wang, X.-Y, Yu, Y.-J., Yang, H.-Y.: An effective image retrieval scheme using color, texture and shape features. Comput. Stand. Interfaces CSI, p. 10. 02706
20. Jyothi, B., MadhaveeLatha, Y., Mohan, P.G.K.: Multidimetional feature space for an effective content based medical image retrieval. In: IACC-2015, pp. 67–71 (2015)
21. Mukundan, R., Ong, S.H., Lee, P.A.: Image analysis by tchebichef moments. IEEE Trans. Image Process. 10(9), 1357–1364 (2001)
22. Kumar, P.: Image retrieval relevance feedback algorithms: trends and techniques. Int. J. Sci. Eng. Technol. 2(1), 13–21 (2013). (ISSN: 22771581)
23. El-Naga, I., Yang, Y., Galatsanos, N.P., Nishikawa, R.M., Wernick, M.N.: A similarity learning approach to content-based image retrieval: application to digital mammography. IEEE Trans. Med. Imaging 23(10), 1233–1244 (2004)
24. Petpon, A., Srisuk, S.: Face recognition with local line binary pattern. In: 2009 Fifth International Conference on Image and Graphics, 978-0-7695-3883-9/09. IEEE Computer society (2009)
25. Kamarainen, J.-K., Kyrki, V., Kalviainen, H.: Invariance properties of Gabor filter based features-overview and applications. IEEE Trans. Image Process. 15(5), 1088–1099 (2006)

Robot Workcell Layout Optimization Using Firefly Algorithm

Akif Muhtasim Alim[1], S.G. Ponnambalam[1(✉)], and G. Kanagaraj[2(✉)]

[1] Advanced Engineering Platform and School of Engineering,
Monash University Malaysia, 46150 Bandar Sunway, Malaysia
sgponnambalam@monash.edu
[2] Department of Mechanical Engineering,
Thiagarajar College of Engineering, Madurai, India
gkmech@tce.edu

Abstract. This paper propose firefly algorithm for optimizing the distance travel of a robot arm for a given sequence of operations by determining the relative positions and orientations of the stations in the workcell. B-Star-Tree and Sequence Pair representation schemes are used to generate the initial layouts. For a given sequence of operations, the firefly algorithm was able to achieve a layout that yields a near minimum distance of travel. Minimising the total distance travel of the robot arm indirectly minimises the cycle time of the robot workcell. Simulation results show the sequence pair representation method performs better efficiency among the two methods applied in terms of reducing the distance.

1 Introduction

The robot workcell can be defined as a manufacturing cell consisting of one or many robots which act as the center-piece and the fundamental member of the cell. The robot interacts with stations, which may include vibratory bowls, index tables and conveyer belts, and transports and affects the assembly of the different parts from one station to another. This requires the robot to move to specific access points of each individual machine. Thus, positions of these access points contribute to the productivity of the workcell. The advantages of such a workcell include a high output and the flexibility to adapt to changes due to manufacturing and market demands. As such the design and planning of the layout with the objective of minimizing robot, travel distance is essential to establish the efficiency of the robotic workcell [1].

Robots are widely known for being very flexible and easily reprogrammable. In a manufacturing system, a robot generally handles assembly tasks which include a sequence of operations between a set of stations. To increase the productivity of such tasks, the cycle time needs to be reduced. The cycle time of a task in a robot workcell depends on the speed and acceleration of the robot and the path taken by the robot arm to complete the task [2]. The increasing need for automated manufacturing cells for higher productivity and quality of products requires very fast and efficient planning methods to design an appropriate workcell layout for a particular manufacturing task [3]. With the introduction of robots in modern day manufacturing workcells,

© Springer International Publishing AG 2016
B.K. Panigrahi et al. (Eds.): SEMCCO 2015, LNCS 9873, pp. 188–200, 2016.
DOI: 10.1007/978-3-319-48959-9_17

optimization of robotic workcell layout is essential in ensuring the minimization of the product cycle time. To reduce the cycle time, one factor that can be optimized is the distance travelled by the robot to complete a particular sequence of operations. The distance depends on the placement of the stations around the robot so as to make the robot's movement minimum in order to reach the target machines. The sequence of operations and the access points in each of the station also affect the distance travelled by the robot and the cycle time it takes. The robot and the stations are placed in such a way that the complete shop floor layout is optimized with respect to the robot arm movements in a collision free manner. To achieve an integrated design process for workcells, an automatic layout planning tool is required.

Tay and Ngoi (1996) proposed a spatial representation system [2] to generate a layout. The spatial representation method which represents shapes and dimensions of stations, the robot work envelope and the floor space, can represent L-shaped and T-shaped stations (shapes with 90° or 180° straight edges) and use many small squares to represent circles or polygons. The B*-Tree (B-star-tree) model has been proposed in [3]. The method is based on ordered binary trees to model compacted floor plans. It follows the position of each of the station in the tree to place them on the workspace. Hiroshi and Fujiyoshi introduced a block placement method called sequence pair in 1996 [4]. Xiaoping et al. proposed a fast evaluation of sequence pair in block placement by longest common subsequence computation in 2001 [5]. A sequence pair is a pair of sequences of n elements representing a list of n blocks and its structure is represented using a meta-grid. Siang et al. (2005) proposed to use GA to optimize a robot workcell layout [1] by calculating the distance covered by a robot arm. Adel El-Baz (2004) attempted to use the genetic algorithm for facility layout problems of different manufacturing environments [6]. Simulated annealing method adopted [7, 8] to optimize an assembly workcell layout where the cycle time for completing a given sequence of operations has been minimized. Yasuhiro et al. (2003), proposed particle swarm optimization to optimize the layout of manufacturing cells and the allocation of transport robots [9]. Yap et al. (2014) developed a virtual reality based programming for an industrial robotic work cell layout to improve the human-machine interface [10]. An augmented reality-based robotic work cell layout developed in [11] which eliminate the need for extensive programming knowledge. Differential evolution (DE) algorithm for facility layout problem and compare their results with well known genetic algorithm [12]. Jian and Ping developed a simplified mathematical model for robot cell layout problem with an objective of minimal cycle time and solved by the approach of GA [13].

2 Methodology

2.1 B-Star Tree Representation

The B*-Tree model requires an initial tree and the layout is plotted based on the tree. The tree is formed using an initial sequence which consists of the number of stations. Based on the random sequence the tree is randomly generated and the layout is then generated. So let's say for example the problem consists of 6 stations and the sequence for the 6 stations is as shown in Fig. 1. Based on the sequence the random tree is generated. Here, the station 1 is set as the root node and using the subsequent stations a sequence of predecessors is formed. The root node does not require any predecessors (set to 0) and no position. The condition for the predecessors is that each station can have 2 or less number of branches. Each of the branches which are left or right are assigned positions and a position '0' means the station is on the left of the predecessor and a position '1' means the right of the predecessor. The predecessors and the positions are shown in Table 1.

Table 1. Data required forming tree

Station sequence	Predecessors	Positions
1	0	–
2	1	0
5	2	0
3	1	1
4	3	0
6	3	1

Fig. 1. Sequence of stations

To create the layout the information about each of the station's dimensions is also required and the following describes how the tree helps create the layout in a step by step method (Fig. 2). The layout is viewed from the top as an X-Y coordinate system. Station number 1 is the one placed first since that is the root node as shown in Fig. 3(a) and its bottom left coordinate is selected as (0, 0) which is the starting point of the layout. Then using the B*-tree the rest of the stations are placed based on its predecessor and its position. The predecessor column says stations 2 and 3 have station 1 as predecessor. Position of station 2 is '0' which means it will be placed on the right of station 1 and position of station 3 is '1' so it is placed above station 1. The placements are shown in Fig. 3(b) and (d) respectively. When a station has a position '0', its starting x-coordinate is where its predecessor's width ends. Let x_b and x_e be the starting and end x-coordinate and the letters i and j represent the current station and the predecessor respectively. The formulas for calculating the x-coordinates will be given as follows:

$$x_{1i} = x_{2j} \tag{1}$$

$$x_{2i} = x_{1j} + w_i \tag{2}$$

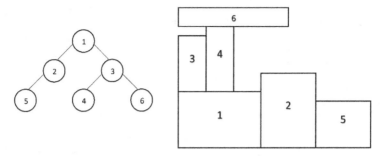

Fig. 2. B-Star-Tree and subsequent layout

Here w_i is the width of the current station. So station 2 has starting x-coordinate of 9 which is the end of station 1 and its end coordinate is $9 + 6 = 15$. The number 6 is from the dimensions where the width of station 2 is 6. Using the two x-coordinates an x-span is created. So for station 2 the x-span is [9, 15]. The starting y coordinate is taken as the maximum y value within the x-span of the current station in the previous contour, C.

$$y_{1i} = \max(y_{all\_c}) \tag{3}$$

$$y_{2i} = y_{1j} + h_i \tag{4}$$

Here h_i is the height of the current station being placed. To find the starting height of station 2, the maximum value of 'y 'is taken between the x-span [9, 15] from the existing contour. The contour is the perimeter of all the coordinates denoted by C. The maximum height as found from C in Fig. 3(a) is 0 within the x-span. The height of the station is then added to find the end y-coordinate of the current station being placed.

Using the dimensions of the stations provided the placement of the next stations is decided and the overall perimeter of the stations are noted down. While selecting which station to be placed next, the pattern that is followed is all stations on the left of the root node are placed first and then the stations on the right. If sub-stations have branches then those are executed first. For example the tree shows station 6 is a direct branch of station 3 but station 5 will be placed first since it is the branch on the left. Figure 3 shows the each of the stations being placed one by one and the respective perimeter is shown by the "bold black line". The coordinates of these lines are shown below each of the figures.

2.2   Sequence Pair Representation

A sequence pair is a pair of sequences of n elements representing a list of n blocks. The sequence pair structure is actually a meta-grid. Given a sequence pair (X, Y), a 45 degree oblique grid as shown in Fig. 4(a) can be constructed. For example, consider the sequence pair (X, Y) = (<4 3 1 6 2 5>, <6 3 5 4 1 2>). The two sequences are placed along the two axis of a grid and each of the station's intersection is found (Fig. 4(a)). It

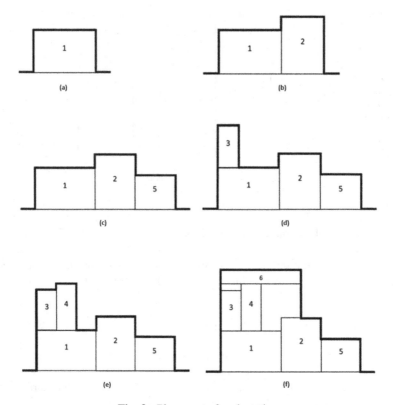

Fig. 3. Placement of each station

is repeated for all the other stations. The grid is rotated 45° counter-clockwise to give the oblique grid. This is used to create the vertical and horizontal graphs shown in Figs. 5(a) and 6(b). For every block, the plane is divided by the two crossing slope lines into four cones as shown in Fig. 4(b). Block 2 is in the right cone of block 1 then

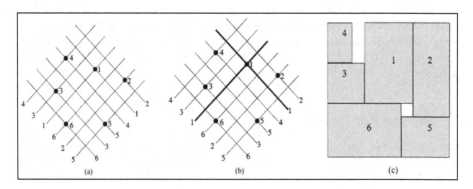

Fig. 4. (a) Oblique grid (b) four cones of block 1 (c) corresponding packing. Dimensions for the six blocks are 1 (4 × 6), 2 (3 × 7), 3 (3 × 3), 4 (2 × 3), 5 (4 × 3) and 6 (6 × 4)

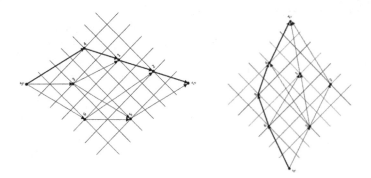

Fig. 5. (a) Horizontal (b) vertical constraint graphs

it is to the right of block 1 (Fig. 5). In general the sequence pair imposes the relationship between each of blocks as follows–

$$\left(\ldots\ldots.b_i\ldots.b_j\ldots\ldots\right), \left(\ldots\ldots.b_i\ldots.b_j\ldots\ldots\right) \rightarrow b_i \text{ is to the left of } b_j$$
$$\left(\ldots\ldots.b_j\ldots.b_i\ldots\ldots\right), \left(\ldots\ldots.b_i\ldots.b_j\ldots\ldots\right) \rightarrow b_i \text{ is below } b_j$$

If pair 1 is reversed, meaning the first pair (4 3 1 6 2 5) becomes (5 2 6 1 3 4) then using the first rule can be written as

$$\left(\ldots\ldots.b_i\ldots.b_j\ldots\ldots\right), \left(\ldots\ldots.b_i\ldots.b_j\ldots\ldots\right) \rightarrow b_i \text{ is below } b_j$$

The starting and ending point is added to the horizontal and vertical graphs. The horizontal graph is constructed as follows

(1) $V = \{s_h\}U\{t_h\}U\{v_i | i = 1, \ldots, n\}$ where v_i corresponds to a block, s_h is the source node representing left boundary and t_h is the sink node representing right boundary
(2) $E = (s_h, v_i)$ and (v_i, t_h) for each module i, and (i, j) if and only if i is on the left of j
(3) Vertex weight equals the width of block i for vertex v_i but zero for s_h and t_h.

The vertical and horizontal graphs are used to calculate the coordinates of each of the blocks. The longest common subsequence for weighted sequence pair is found next. It is taken to avoid overlap of the blocks. A weighted sequence is a sequence whose elements are in a given set S, while every element $s_i \in S$ has a weight. Given two sequences X and Y, a sequence Z is a common subsequence of X and Y if Z is a subsequence for both X and Y. For example, (1 2) is the common subsequence of (1 5 2) and (2 4 1 2 5). Note that element repetition and sequences with unequal lengths are allowed. The length of a common subsequence $Z = (z_1, z_2 \ldots z_n)$ is $\sum_{i=1}^{n} w(z_i)$. The longest common sequence can also determine the position of an individual block. The x-coordinate of module i is given by the longest path length from source s_h to node i in the horizontal constraint graph and the y-coordinate of module i can be computed from the vertical constraint graph. So for the example above, the using the horizontal constraint graph from Fig. 5(a), the x-coordinates will be–

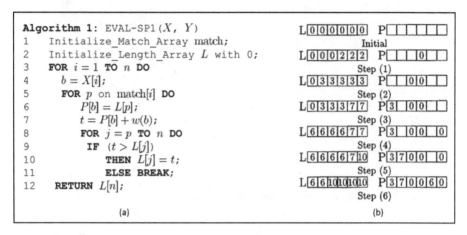

```
Algorithm 1: EVAL-SP1 (X, Y)
1     Initialize_Match_Array match;
2     Initialize_Length_Array L with 0;
3     FOR i = 1 TO n DO
4         b = X[i];
5         FOR p on match[i] DO
6             P[b] = L[p];
7             t = P[b] + w(b);
8             FOR j = p TO n DO
9                 IF (t > L[j])
10                    THEN L[j] = t;
11                    ELSE BREAK;
12    RETURN L[n];
```

(a)

(b)

Fig. 6. (a) Algorithm for coordinate calculation (b) corresponding coordinates

Module 4: $x_4 = 0$
Module 3: $x_3 = 0$
Module 6: $x_6 = 0$
Module 1: $x_1 = $ max $(x_4 + w_4, x_3 + w_3) = $ max $(0 + 2, 0 + 3) = 3$
Module 2: $x_2 = x_1 + w_1 = 3 + 4 = 7$
Module 5: $x_5 = $ max $(x_6 + w_6, x_3 + w_3) = $ max $(0 + 6, 0 + 3) = 6$

Using the vertical constraint graph from Fig. 6(b), the y-coordinates will be–

Module 6: $y_6 = 0$;
Module 5: $y_5 = 0$;
Module 3: $y_3 = y_6 + h_6 = 0 + 4 = 4$
Module 1: $y_1 = $ max $(y_5 + h_5, y_6 + h_6) = $ max $(0 + 3, 0 + 4) = 4$
Module 2: $y_2 = y_5 + h_5 = 0 + 3 = 3$
Module 4: $y_4 = $ max $(y_5 + h_5, y_3 + h_3) = $ max $(0 + 3, 4 + 3) = 7$

The fastest way to calculate the coordinates is by using a very well-known algorithm. The algorithm (Fig. 6(a)) is used to program the calculation of the coordinates of each of the blocks.

Assuming that the blocks are named 1, 2 ... n and the input sequence pair is (X, Y), then both X and Y are permutations of (1, 2 ... n). The weight w_b is equal to the width of the block 'b' being placed. Block position array P[b], b = 1, 2 ... n, is used to record the x coordinate of block 'b'. For each index i in X, we need a list of corresponding j indexes such that $X[i] = Y[j]$. The array match $[i]$, $i = 1, 2, ..., $n, is constructed for this purpose, i.e. match $[i] = j$ if $X[i] = Y[j]$. The length array L $[1 ... n]$ is used to record the length of candidates of the longest common sequence. The algorithm is shown in Fig. 6(a) and as an example Fig. 6(b) shows the steps took to compute the longest common sequence of sequence pair (<4 3 1 6 2 5>, <6 3 5 4 1 2>) in determining the x coordinate of each block. When the algorithm ends, the array P $[1 ...$ 6] records the blocks' x coordinates.

2.3   Objective Function

The objective function is to minimize the distance travelled by the robot for a particular sequence of operation. The mid points of each of the stations have already been assumed as the access points of the stations. So the robot arm will go from one station's mid-point to another's and the Euclidean distance is calculated between the two stations and all the distances are added up to give the total distance. The formula can be written as:

$$distance = \sum_{i=1}^{n} D_{ij} \tag{5}$$

Where D_{ij}, is the distance between the access points of current station i and the next station j in the sequence and n is the length of the operation sequence.

3   The Firefly Algorithm

Firefly algorithm is a nature based metaheuristic algorithm which follows the mating behavior of fireflies. Naturally a female firefly with lower brightness tends to move towards a male firefly of higher brightness in order to mate. For this problem, the brightness or intensities are the distances from each layout. Whenever a firefly with a lower distance is found, it tries to move towards that firefly.

Firefly algorithm follows the following idealized rules–

- All fireflies are unisex, so one firefly will be attracted to other fireflies regardless of their sex.
- Attractiveness is proportional to a firefly's brightness. Thus for any two flashing fireflies, the less bright one will move towards the brighter one. The attractiveness is proportional to the brightness, both of which decrease as their distance increases. If there is no brighter one than a particular firefly, it will move randomly.
- The brightness of a firefly is affected or determined by the landscape of the objective function.

For an initial population of n, there are n number of intensity values I. The algorithm works such that it takes the first intensity value, meaning the first distance, and compares with all the other distances and whenever a distance lower than itself is found, it tries to move towards that using the algorithm. The movement is actually of the sequences which create the layout shown in Fig. 7. The sequence is optimized so as to become the exact sequence which gives the lowest distance.

The movement of a firefly i attracted to another more attractive (brighter/lower distance) firefly j is determined by–

$$x_i^{t+1} = x_i^t + \beta_0 e^{-\gamma r_{ij}^2}\left(x_j^t - x_i^t\right) + \alpha \epsilon_i^t \tag{6}$$

Where

x_i^{t+1} is the new sequence

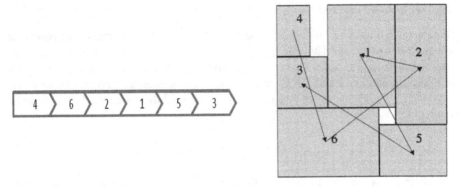

Fig. 7. Robot movements according to operation sequence

x_i^t is the current sequence being optimized
x_j^t is the sequence firefly trying to move towards
$\epsilon_i^t = (\text{rand} - 0.5)$

$$r_{ij} = \sqrt{\sum_{k=1}^{d} (x_{i,k} - x_{j,k})^2} \tag{7}$$

There are three initial parameters which need to be set – alpha, beta and gamma. Gamma, γ is the fixed light absorption coefficient which is user defined and remains fixed during the entire simulation. Alpha, α, the randomness parameter and beta, β, the attractiveness parameter varies as the algorithm runs according to the Eqs. (8) and (9).

$$\alpha = \alpha_0 \theta^t \tag{8}$$

$$\beta = \frac{\beta_0}{1 + \gamma r^2} \tag{9}$$

Where

$r = r_{ij}$
θ is the randomness reduction constant $-\theta \in [0, 1]$
t is the pseudo time $-t \in [0, t_{max}]$

The following explains how the equations of the algorithm are applied–

The B-star-tree only requires only one sequence to start creating the layout. The tree itself is randomly made as described before. And for sequence pair, each layout requires two sequences. So for example consider a scenario of an initial population of 5 which in turn gives 5 distances as shown below–

814.3   195.7   798.3   1417.9   216.5

An initial population of 5 means the outer loop of i and the inner loop of j in the algorithm will run 5 times. Consider B-star-tree method first which requires only one sequence. So let's say when i is 1, it is considering the distance 814.3 which is achieved from an initial sequence of let's say (2 5 3 1 4 6). The inner loop j will run from 1 to 5. When j is 1 and 4 and the distance is the same or greater, the algorithm will not run. But when j is 2, 3 or 5, the program will find that the distances are lower and the algorithm will run.

So let's consider $j = 2$. Initially, alpha and beta are set to 1 and gamma is set to 0.001 for example. Using these values, the firefly 1 will try to move to firefly 2. So for example the sequence which gives a distance of 195.7 is (6 2 1 3 5 4). The distance r_{ij} will be calculated first as follows–

$$r_{ij} = \sqrt{\sum (x_{i,k} - x_{j,k})^2}$$

$$r_{ij} = \sqrt{\begin{aligned}[(2-6)^2 + (5-2)^2 + (3-1)^2 + \\ (1-3)^2 + (4-5)^2 + (6-4)^2]\end{aligned}}$$

The value of r_{ij} is input to the movement equation. The movement formula will look like this–

$$x_i^{t+1} = x_i^t + \beta_0 e^{-\gamma r_{ij}^2}\left(x_j^t - x_i^t\right) + \alpha \epsilon_i^t$$

$$x_i^{t+1} = (2\ 5\ 3\ 1\ 4\ 6) + 1\left(e^{-0.001\left(r_{ij}^2\right)}\right)\left(\begin{aligned}(6\ 2\ 1\ 3\ 5\ 4) \\ -(2\ 5\ 3\ 1\ 4\ 6)\end{aligned}\right) + 1(\epsilon_i^t)$$

Where ϵ is found using (rand – 0.5). The resulting 6 numbers will be in decimals so the numbers are rounded off and numbers more than the number of stations or repeated are replaced with the missing stations and a new sequence is achieved.

When sequence pair method is considered all the steps remain the same except that there are two sequences for each distance and two sequences for the distance it is comparing to. The subtractions occur between the first sequences of each i and j.

4   Results and Discussion

Figure 8(a) shows the initial layout randomly created which gave the largest distance and its corresponding B-Star-Tree. Figure 8(b) shows the optimized layout where the distance for the same firefly is plotted after every generation. The only parameter that can be varied is gamma which is 0.001 for this solution. For an initial layout of 50, there is 50 fireflies and distance of one firefly is observed. To get the best results, the firefly (sequence) which gives the worst distance is observed to see how much it is optimized. Both the optimization graphs show some sort of randomness even when the

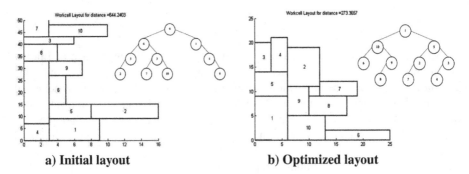

a) Initial layout   b) Optimized layout

Fig. 8. B-Star-Tree method

best fit line is stable and has saturated. This is due to some of the parameters inside the algorithm which are still random. The equation using which α and ε vary in random which causes the randomness in the distances towards the end. The other parameter which is controlled by the user is gamma, γ. From running simulations, it has been observed that increasing gamma value causes more randomness within the results and distance may not be the optimum all the time.

The number of generations used for each of the methods is 60, but the graphs have shown that the objective function optimizes within 10 generations. It can be concluded based on observations that the efficiency of the Firefly Algorithm is very high. The reason for this is maybe because of the double loop of i and j in the pseudo code where 2500 calculations are taking place for an initial population of 50 for 1 generation. So the efficiency becomes high.

From Fig. 8, it can be seen that the initial distance of 644.2401 has been gradually reduced and the minimum distance within the 60 generations is 273.3657 for the B-Star-Tree method. Figure 9(a) similar patterns are observed for the sequence pair method where the initial distance of 1261.0933 has been reduced to 195.6559.

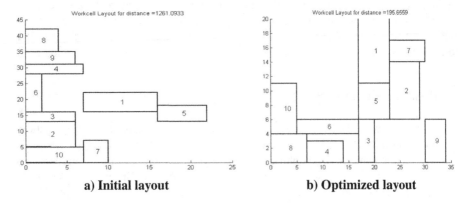

a) Initial layout   b) Optimized layout

Fig. 9. Sequence Pair method

The percentage of reduction can be calculated as

$$Percentage\,reduction = \frac{Initial\,distance - Final\,distance}{Initial\,distance} \times 100 \qquad (10)$$

The percentage reduction obtained from B-Star-Tree layout is 57.57 % and Sequence Pair method is 84.48 %. Hence, the Sequence Pair method has a higher reduction of distance and it has a better efficiency with the firefly algorithm. Even though the layout looks more compact in case of the optimized B-Star-Tree layout (Fig. 8), it does not necessarily mean it will give a lower distance. The distance only depends on the placements of the stations and the sequence of operations. The optimized Sequence Pair layout (Fig. 9) shows that the stations are not exactly compact, but the distance is still much lower than the B-Star-Tree. So it can be said the Sequence Pair method is more efficient and more effective.

5 Conclusion

In this paper, a fire fly algorithm is proposed to optimize the robot workcell layout. Two layout representation schemes, the B-Star-Tree method and the Sequence Pair method, are used to generate the initial layouts. The firefly algorithm is successfully implemented to optimize each of the layouts in collision free movements. From the obtained results in can be concluded that the Sequence Pair method has the better efficiency and effectiveness among the two methods applied in terms of reducing the distance. A fruitful scope for further research on other factors affecting the cycle time including the acceleration, speed and movement of the robot can also be optimized to give a better solution.

Acknowledgment. This research is supported by University Grant Commission, New Delhi under research Grant No. F-30-1/2014/RA-2014-16-OB-TAM-5658 (SA-II).

References

1. Sim, S.-K., Tay, M.-L., Khairyanto, A.: Optimisation of a robotic workcell layout using genetic algorithms. In: ASME 2005 International Design Engineering Technical Conferences and Computers and Information in Engineering Conference, pp. 921–930 (2005)
2. Tay, M.M., Ngoi, B.: Optimising robot workcell layout. Int. J. Adv. Manufact. Technol. **12**, 377–385 (1996)
3. Chung, Y., Chang, Y., Wu, G., Wu, S.: B*-tree: a new representation for non-slicing floor plans. In: Proceedings of Design Automation Conference, pp. 458–463 (2000)
4. Murata, H., Fujiyoshi, K., Nakatake, S., Kajitani, Y.: VLSI module placement based on rectangle-packing by the sequence-pair. IEEE Trans. Comput. Aided Des. Integr. Circuits Syst. **15**, 1518–1524 (1996)
5. Tang, X., Tian, R., Wong, D.: Fast evaluation of sequence pair in block placement by longest common subsequence computation. IEEE Trans. Comput. Aided Des. Integr. Circuits Syst. **20**, 1406–1413 (2001)

6. El-Baz, M.A.: A genetic algorithm for facility layout problems of different manufacturing environments. Comput. Industr. Eng. **47**, 233–246 (2004)
7. Jajodia, S., Minis, I., Harhalakis, G., Proth, J.-M.: CLASS: computerized layout solutions using simulated annealing. Int. J. Prod. Res. **30**, 95–108 (1992)
8. Barral, D., Perrin, J.-P., Dombre, E., Liegeois, A.: Simulated annealing combined with a constructive algorithm for optimising assembly workcell layout. Int. J. Adv. Manuf. Technol. **17**, 593–602 (2001)
9. Yamada, Y., Ookoudo, K., Komura, Y.: Layout optimization of manufacturing cells and allocation optimization of transport robots in reconfigurable manufacturing systems using particle swarm optimization. In: Proceedings of 2003 IEEE/RSJ International Conference on Intelligent Robots and Systems (IROS 2003), pp. 2049–2054 (2003)
10. Yap, H.J., Taha, Z., Dawal, S.Z.M., Chang, S.-W.: Virtual reality based support system for layout planning and programming of an industrial robotic work cell, (2014). doi:10.1371/journal.pone.0109692
11. Pai, Y.S., Yap, H.J., Singh, R.: Augmented reality–based programming, planning and simulation of a robotic work cell. Proc. Inst. Mech. Eng. Part B: J. Eng. Manuf. **229**, 1029–1045 (2015)
12. Tao, J., Wang, P., Qiao, H., Tang, Z.: Facility layouts based on differential evolution algorithm. In: Proceedings of IEEE International Conference on Robotics and Biomimetics (ROBIO), pp. 1778–1783 (2013)
13. Jian, Z., Ai-Ping, L.: Genetic algorithm for robot work cell layout problem. In: Proceedings of IEEE World Congress on Software Engineering, pp. 460–464 (2009)

Particle Swarm Optimization
Based on the Winner's Strategy

Shailendra S. Aote[1], M.M. Raghuwanshi[2(✉)], and L.G. Malik[3]

[1] Department of CSE, RCOEM, Nagpur, India
shailendra_aote@rediffmail.com
[2] YCCE, Nagpur, India
m_raghuwanshi@rediffmail.com
[3] CSE, GHRCE, Nagpur, India
lgmalik@rediffmail.com

Abstract. This paper presents particle swarm optimization based on winner's strategy (PSO-WS). Instead of considering gbest and pbest particle for position update, each particle considers its distance from immediate winner to update its position. If this strategy performs well for the particle, then that particle updates its position based on this strategy, otherwise its position is replaced by its immediate winner particle's position. Dimension dependant swarm size is used for better exploration. Proposed method is compared with CSO and CCPSO2, which are available to solve large scale optimization problems. Statistical results show that proposed method performs well for separable as well as non separable problems.

Keywords: Particle swarm optimization · Winners strategy · Large scale optimization

1 Introduction

As many researchers are attracted towards the field of optimization, many optimization methods starting from single objective optimization to multi-objective optimization, unimodal optimization to multimodal optimization, are proposed in past years. Optimization means problem solving in which one seeks to minimize or maximize the objective function in presence of the constraints. Difficulty in solving the problem increases with the increase in dimension size.

Particle swarm optimization (PSO) is global optimization method proposed initially by James Kennedy and Russell Eberhart [1] in 1995. The particle swarm concept originated as a simulation of simplified social system. When a flock of birds travel in the air to find the food, they maintain their velocity and position, so that they never collide each other. There is no central coordinator for the movement of flock. Movement takes place based on cooperation among each bird. Due to its simple equation and involvement of less parameter, it becomes one of the promising algorithms for solving optimization problems.

Each particle is treated as a point in a D dimensional space. The ith particle is represented as,

© Springer International Publishing AG 2016
B.K. Panigrahi et al. (Eds.): SEMCCO 2015, LNCS 9873, pp. 201–213, 2016.
DOI: 10.1007/978-3-319-48959-9_18

$$Xi = (Xi1, Xi2, \ldots\ldots\ldots, XiD)$$

The best previous position (the position giving the best fitness value) of any particle is recorded and represented as,

$$Pi = (Pi1, Pi2, \ldots\ldots, PiD)$$

The index of the best particle among all the particles in the population is represented by the symbol g. The rate of the position change (velocity) for particle i is represented as,

$$Vi = (Vi1, Vi2, \ldots\ldots\ldots, ViD)$$

The velocity and position of the particles are updated according to the following equation,

$$ViD = w * ViD + c1 * rand() * (PiD - XiD) + c2 * rand() * (PgD - XiD) \quad (1)$$

$$XiD = XiD + ViD \quad (2)$$

rand() is a random function gives value in the range [0,1]. The first part of the Eq. (1) talks about previous velocity; whereas the second part is the "cognition" part that represents the private thinking of the particle. The third part is the "social" part that represents the collaboration among the particles. Therefore, Eq. (1) is calculate the particle's new velocity according to its previous velocity and the distances of its current position from its own best experience (position) and the group's best experience. Particle moves toward a new position according to Eq. (2). The performance of each particle is measured according to a predefined fitness function, which is related to the problem to be solved.

These basic PSO equations are updated by researchers. The inertia weight w is brought into the Eq. (1) as shown in Eq. (3) by Yuhui Shi in 1998 [8]. This w helps in balancing the global search and local search. It can be a positive constant or even a positive linear or nonlinear function of time.

$$ViD = w * ViD + c1 * rand() * (PiD - XiD) + c2 * rand() * (PgD - XiD) \quad (3)$$

Initially value 0.7 was proposed for w that is further considered as dynamic for better exploration in the beginning and for fine exploitation at the end. Lots of PSO variants are proposed from its formation to till date. Efforts are put towards increase in efficiency and convergence speed. Both the things are rarely achieved in a single algorithm. Low dimensional problems are easier to solve, where as complexity increase as the increase in dimensions and modality. A niching method is introduced in EAs to locate multiple optimal solutions [2]. Distance based LIPS model [3], a memetic PSO

[4], Adaptive PSO [5], Fractional PSO [6], AGPSO [7], CSO [33] and many other techniques are proposed to handle higher dimensional and multimodal problems. In spite of these techniques, trapping in local minima and the rate of convergence are two unavoidable problems in PSO and all other EAs. Though the PSO is nature inspired algorithm, a lot of issues can still be modeled to improve the performance. Different techniques to deal with the stagnation are studied in [29–31]. They control the parameters involved in velocity update equation. To remove the problem of stagnation and to get the better performance, lot of techniques like GCPSO [9] which uses a different velocity update equation for the best particle since its personal best and global best both lie at the same point. OPSO [10] employs opposition based learning for each particle and applies dynamic Cauchy mutation on the best particle. QPSO [11] proposed a new discrete particle swarm optimization algorithm based on quantum representation of individuals, which in turn causes faster convergence. In the new method called H-PSO [12], the particles are arranged in a dynamic hierarchy that is used to define a neighborhood structure. Depending on the quality of their so-far best found solution, the particles move up or down the hierarchy. This gives good particles that move up in the hierarchy a larger influence on the swarm. George I. Evers proposed a RegPSO [13], where the problem of stagnation is removed by automatically triggering the swarm regrouping. Efforts are taken to solve multimodal problems. To solve higher dimensional problems, variants cooperative co evolution strategies like CPSO-SK and CPSO-HK [14], CCPSO [15], CCPSO2 [16] are proposed.

Following the idea in [33], where losers are updated base on winners. A pair wise is competition takes place between the particles. Different pairs among the particle are randomly formed. The problem in this strategy is that the loser in one pair may be winner for another pair. So, in this paper, instead of forming the pair randomly, we introduced the concept of immediate winner for each particle. Each particle will update the position based on immediate winners.

Rest of the paper is organized as follows. Section 2 represents the PSO with winners' strategy. Experimental results and analysis is given into Sect. 3, followed by Conclusion in Sect. 4.

2   PSO with Winners Strategy

Though, the CSO performs well on high dimensional problems, some kinds of randomness are involved to find a new generational swarm. When two particles are selected, then the loser particle is updated and winner particle is transferred to a new generation. But the loser particle may be the winner with respect to some other particles and winner may be the loser for some other competition. In order to solve optimization problems, a new PSO with winner strategy is defined here. General PSO considers gbest and pbest to update the position in each iteration. Instead of considering pbest and gbest, we consider an immediate winner particle for each. In each iteration, it first evaluates the swarm to calculate the fitness. Sort the swarm in increasing order of the fitness. The best particle follows the general velocity and position update equation, where the third part of velocity equation is absent because, the best particle itself is a gbest. Other particles, consider their immediate winner particle for position updates. Immediate winner is termed as given: if i is a current position, then i−1 is considered as winner position. This strategy is more promising as no randomness is involved to define winner as given in [33].

The velocity update equation for particle i is,

$$vel(i) = w * vel(i) + \Phi * rand * (vel(i-1) - vel(i))$$

Where Φ is clerk's coefficient that controls the swarm and w is the inertia value, which is ranging from 0.9 to 0.4. If the new position of the particle is better, that particle enters into next generation otherwise its position is replaced by its winner particle's position. Figure 1 shows the working of the proposed algorithm. There are total seven particles, which are arranged in increasing order of their fitness value (like 1, 2, 3,…). Instead of selecting two random particles and performing competition among them, first two particles are selected and competition is performed between these two. The particle '2' will update its strategy based on the particle '1'. Learning is taken place based on the winner particle. This strategy is repeated for all the particles.

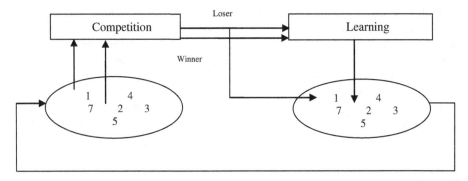

Fig. 1. Position update based on winner's strategy

The proposed algorithm is as follows

```
START
    Swarm size = Number of Dimensions
    Initialize position and velocity the swarm.
    fit = Evaluate the swarm.
    While termination criteria is not satisfied do
        Sort the swarm
        The best particle follows same velocity and position update equation as
                                        per eq. (3) and (2).
        for  j = 2 to size of swarm
            vel(j) = w*vel(j) +  Φ* rand* (vel(j-1) – vel(j))
            pos( j) = pos (j) + vel (j)
        end for
        fit1= Evaluate the swarm
        for  j = 2 to size of swarm
            if (fit1(j) < fit (j)
                        Update the position of particle
            else
                        pos(j) =pos (j-1);
            end if
        end for
    end While
End Start
```

Total m−1 comparisons are needed to find the next position of the swarm. Computational complexity of PSO-WS is $O(mn)$, where m is swarm size and n is the search dimensions.

2.1   Discussion on Selection of Value of Φ

Constriction factor (Φ) is one of the major components in the velocity update equation of loser particle. Φ is used to control the distance of previous and current velocities. To decide the value of Φ, following formulations is used.

$$d = \text{mean (distance between velocities of current particle to all other particles)}$$

$$d' = \text{distance of ith and } (i-1)\text{th particle}$$

$$\Phi = \begin{cases} \text{rand}\,(1,2) & \text{if } d' < d \\ 0 & \text{if } d' = d \\ \text{rand}\,(0,1) & \text{if } d' > d \end{cases}$$

ith particle will find the distance to (i−1)th particle and recorded as 'd''. The mean of distances is considered as d. If the d' is less than the mean distance 'd', any random value between 1 and 2 is assigned to Φ. If d' is greater than d, then the Φ is assigned with any random value between 0 and 1. Otherwise, it sets as 0, so that it will use its current velocity component for further modification.

2.2 Discussion on New Velocity Update Formula

The new velocity update formula is mainly designed for loser particle. It will not consider personal or global best for further calculations. It simply calculates the distance and direction of the winner particle, so that it will update its value based on the winner's particle velocity and position.

3 Experimental Results and Analysis

Proper parameter setting plays very important role in solving the optimization problem. One of the most important parameter is the swarm size. With the small swarm size, convergence is very fast but may cause premature convergence without exploring the search space. It doesn't mean that swarm size is large, which may cause slower convergence speed. To decide the optimum value of swarm size, the experiment is performed on all the functions defined in CEC-08. For 100 dimensions swarm size ranges from 20 to 100, for 500 dimensions the range of swarm is taken as 25–300, whereas the range of swarm size is considered as 25–500 for 1000 dimensions. The final values which are used for experimentations are 100, 300, 500 for 100, 500 and 1000

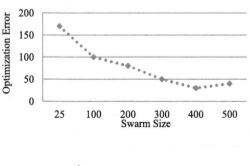

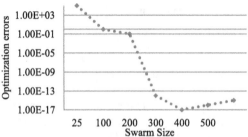

Fig. 2. Optimization error obtain by PSO-WS on (a) f2 and (b) f6 of 1000 dimensions with different swarm sizes varying from 25 to 500

dimensions respectively. Figure 2 shows the performance of f2 and f6 to decide the swarm size for 1000 dimensions.

50 independent runs are taken for each function and its mean, median, standard deviation and best value is noted for comparison. For each independent run, the

Table 1. Comparison of PSO-WS with CSO and CCPSO2 on 100 dimensions

100D	PSO−WS	CSO	CCPSO2
$CEC08_1$	7.28E − 33 (1.87E-33)	9.11E − 29(1.10E − 28) (<0.0001)	7.73E − 14 (3.23E − 14) **(0.0176)**
$CEC08_2$	6.12E + 00 (8.01E + 00)	3.35E + 01(5.38E + 00) (<0.0001)	6.08E + 00 (7.83E + 00) (0.9972)
$CEC08_3$	1.25E + 00 (3.11E + 00)	3.90E + 02(5.53E + 02) (<0.0001)	4.23E + 02 (8.65E + 02) (0.626)
$CEC08_4$	2.09E − 05 (1.17E-05)	5.60E + 01(7.48E + 00) (<0.0001)	3.98E − 02 (1.99E − 01) (0.841)
$CEC08_5$	7.20E − 05 (9.19E-05)	0.00E + 00(0.00E + 00) (0.4343)	3.45E − 03 (4.88E − 03) (0.489)
$CEC08_6$	4.61E − 16 (9.34E-16)	1.20E − 014(1.52E − 015) (<0.0001)	1.44E − 13 (3.06E − 14) (<0.0001)
$CEC08_7$	−1.93E + 01 (1.14E + 00)	−7.25E + 05(1.88E + 04) (<0.0001)	−1.50E + 03 (1.04E + 01) (<0.0001)
w/l/NC for mean		6/0/1	3/0/4
w/l/NC for std. deviation		5/1/1	3/0/4

Table 2. Comparison of PSO−WS With CSO and CCPSO2 on 500 dimensions

500D	PSO-WS	CSO	CCPSO2
$CEC08_1$	9.28E − 28 (1.29E − 29)	6.57E − 23(3.90E − 24) (<0.0001)	7.73E − 14 (3.23E − 14) **(0.009)**
$CEC08_2$	9.15E + 00 (3.21E + 00)	2.60E + 01(2.40E + 00) (<0.0001)	5.79E + 01 (4.21E + 01) (0.207)
$CEC08_3$	3.51E + 01 (1.17E + 01)	5.74E + 02(1.67E + 02) **(0.0005)**	7.24E + 02 (1.54E + 02) (<0.0001)
$CEC08_4$	4.29E − 04 (8.21E − 02)	3.19E + 02(2.16E + 01) (<0.0001)	3.98E − 02 (1.99E − 01) (0.8461)
$CEC08_5$	1.93E − 20 (5.01E − 10)	2.22E − 16(0.00E + 00) (1.000)	1.18E − 03 (4.61E − 03) (0.7792)
$CEC08_6$	5.81E-15 (8.21E − 15)	4.13E − 13(1.10E − 014) (<0.0001)	5.34E − 13 (8.61E − 14) (<0.0001)
$CEC08_7$	−7.69E + 03 (1.61E + 01)	−1.97E + 06(1.88E + 04) (<0.0001)	−7.23E + 03 (4.16E + 01) (<0.0001)
w/l/NC for mean		6/0/1	4/0/3
w/l/NC for Std. Deviation		5/1/1	4/0/3

Table 3. Comparison of PSO-WS with CSO and CCPSO2 on 1000 dimensions

1000D	PSO-WS	CSO	CCPSO2
$CEC08_1$	7.08E − 26 (3.96E − 27)	1.09E − 21(4.20E − 23) (**<0.0001**) (**<0.0001**)	5.18E − 13 (9.61E − 14) (**<0.0001**)
$CEC08_2$	4.13E + 01 (4.21E + 00)	4.15E + 01(9.74E − 01) (0.9631)	7.82E + 01(4.25E + 01) (0.3878)
$CEC08_3$	6.97E + 02 (6.31E + 01)	1.01E + 03(3.02E + 01) (**<0.0001**)	1.33E + 03(2.63E + 02) (**0.0195**)
$CEC08_4$	9.73E − 03 (6.84E − 02)	6.98E + 02(3.10E + 01) (**<0.0001**)	1.99E − 01 (4.06E − 01) (0.6458)
$CEC08_5$	3.85E − 19 (6.33E − 18)	2.26E − 16(2.28E − 17) (**<0.0001**)	1.18E − 03 (3.27E − 03) (0.7183)
$CEC08_6$	7.34E − 14 (4.23E − 15)	1.21E − 12(2.64E − 014) (**<0.0001**)	1.02E − 12 (1.68E − 13) (**<0.0001**)
$CEC08_7$	−9.18E + 03 (8.12E + 01)	−3.83E + 06(4.82E + 04) (**<0.0001**)	−1.43E + 04 (8.27E + 01) (**<0.0001**)
w/l/NC for mean		6/0/1	4/0/3
w/l/NC for Std. Deviation		5/1/1	4/0/3

maximum number of FEs, as recommended in, is set to $5000 * n$, where n is the search dimension of the test functions. In the comparisons between different statistical results, two-tailed t-tests are conducted at a significance level of $\alpha = 0.05$. The performance is compared with CSO and CCPSO-2, which are known as the state of the art algorithm for large scale optimization problems. Performance is evaluated on 100, 500 and 1000 dimensions on CEC-08 test suit [32] and shown the in Tables 1, 2 and 3 respectively.

Results of CSO & CCPSO2 are taken from [33]. Values outside the brackets show the mean performance, whereas values inside the first brackets show standard deviation. Values for CSO and CCPSO2 in second bracket shows p-value. Unpaired t-test was conducted between PSO-WS and CSO also between PSO-WS and CCPSO2. If two results are statistically significant shown in bold, then the comparision takes place. Results of test is shown in w/l/NC form, where w, l, NC stands for winning count, loser count and no conclusion count. No conclusion is made for Statistically different results.

Results show that PSO-WS outperforms on mean and standard deviation for most of the function, where statistical results are significant.

Figure 3(a–f) shows optimization results of PSO-WS, CCSPS2, CSO on 100, 500 and 1000 dimensions.

In order to get an overall picture of the scalability of PSO-WA, CSO and CCPSO2, the mean optimization errors for all test functions except $f7$ of dimensions 100, 500, and 1000 are plotted in Fig. 3. It can be seen that PSO-WS has shown the best scalability on *all the functions*.

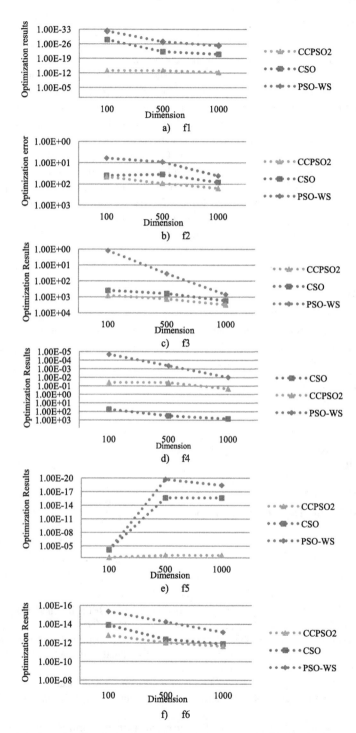

Fig. 3. Statistical results of optimization error obtain by PSO-WS, CSO and CCPSO2 on 100-D, 500-D and 1000-D *f1 to f6*

4 Conclusion and Future Work

In this paper, a new strategy based on immediate winner particle is proposed. After sorting the fitness of particles, each particle updates its position, based on the particle, which has better fitness value. If new position is better as compared to previous position, then it is accepted, otherwise its position is replaced with winner particle's position. To have a better exploration, dimension dependant swarm size is used. The proposed algorithm is compared with two state of the art algorithm for large scale optimization known as CSO and CCPSO2 on CEC-08 test suit. Statistical results show that proposed method performs extremely well on most of the functions.

Future work is to provide theoretical proof of convergence for the proposed method. The algorithm can be solved for CEC-2010 test suit. To test the scalability, proposed algorithm can be implemented up to 5000 dimensions. This method can be used to solve multiobjective optimization problems.

Appendix

Seven benchmark functions are used in CEC-2008 test suit. These functions are summarized as follows.

Unimodal Functions (2):

F1: Shifted Sphere Function
F2: Shifted Schwefel's

Multimodal Functions (5):

F3: Shifted Rosenbrock's Function
F4: Shifted Rastrigin's Function
F5: Shifted Griewank's Function
F6: Shifted Ackley's Function
F7: FastFractal "DoubleDip" Function

References

1. Kennedy, J., Eberhart, R.C.: Particle swarm optimization. In: IEEE International Conference on Neural Network, Perth, Australia 1995, pp. 1942–1948 (1995)
2. Li, X., Deb, K.: Comparing lbest PSO niching algorithms using different position update rules. In: WCCI 2010 IEEE World Congress on Computational Intelligence 18–23 July, 2010 - CCIB, Barcelona, Spain, pp. 1564–1571 (2010)
3. Qu, B.Y., Suganthan, P.N., Das, Swagatam: A distance-based locally informed particle swarm model for multi-modal optimization. IEEE Trans. Evol. Comput. **17**(3), 387–402 (2013)
4. Wang, H., Moon, I., Yang, S., Wang, D.: A memetic particle swarm optimization algorithm for multimodal optimization problems. Inf. Sci. **197**, 38–52 (2012)

5. Zhan, Z.H., Zhang, J., Li, Y.: Adaptive particle swarm optimization. IEEE Trans. Syst. Man Cybern. Part B Cybern. **39**(6), 1362–1381 (2009)
6. Kiranyaz, S., Ince, T., Yildirim, A., Gabbouj, M.: Fractional particle swarm optimization in multidimensional search space. IEEE Trans. Syst. Man Cybern. Part B Cybern. **40**(2), 298–319 (2010)
7. Mirjalili, S., Lewis, A., Sadiq, A.S.: Autonomous particles groups for particle swarm optimization. Arab. J Sci. Eng. **39**, 4683–4697 (2014)
8. Shi, Y., Eberhart, R.: A modified particle swarm optimizer. In: Proceedings of the IEEE Congress on Evolutionary Computation (CEC 1998), Piscataway, pp. 69–73 (1998)
9. van den Bergh, F.: An analysis of particle swarm optimizers, Ph.D. dissertation, Department of Computer Science, University of Pretoria, Pretoria, South Africa (2002)
10. Wang, H., et al.: Opposition-based particle swarm algorithm with cauchy mutation. In: Proceedings of the IEEE Congress on Evolutionary Computation, pp. 4750–4756 (2007)
11. Yang, S., Wang, M.: A quantum particle swarm optimization. In: Proceedings of the IEEE Congress on Evolutionary Computation (CEC 2004), pp. 320–324 (2004)
12. Janson, S., Middendorf, M.: A hierarchical particle swarm optimizer and its adaptive variant. IEEE Trans. Syst. Man Cybern. Part B Cybern. **35**(6), 1272–1282 (2005)
13. Evers, G.I., Ghalia, M.B.: Regrouping particle swarm optimization: a new global optimization algorithm with improved performance consistency across benchmarks. In: IEEE International Conference on Systems, Man and Cybernetics, pp. 3901–3908 (2009)
14. van den Bergh, F., Engelbrecht, A.: A cooperative approach to particle swarm optimization. IEEE Trans. Evol. Comput. **8**(3), 225–239 (2004)
15. Yang, Z., Tang, K., Yao, X.: Large scale evolutionary optimization using cooperative coevolution. Inf. Sci. **178**(15), 2986–2999 (2008)
16. Cui, Z.; Zeng, J.; Yin, Y.: An improved PSO with time-varying accelerator coefficients. In: Eighth International Conference on Intelligent Systems Design and Applications, Kaohsiung, pp. 638–643 (2008)
17. Ziyu, T., Dingxue, Z.: A modified particle swarm optimization with an adaptive acceleration coefficients. In: Asia-Pacific Conference on Information Processing, Shenzhen, pp. 330–332 (2009)
18. Bao, G.Q., Mao, K.F.: Particle swarm optimization algorithm with asymmetric time varying acceleration coefficients. In: IEEE International Conference on Robotics and Biomimetics, Guilin, pp. 2134–2139 (2009)
19. Dai, Y., Liu, L., Li, Y.: An intelligent parameter selection method for particle swarm optimization algorithm. In: Fourth International Joint Conference on Computational Sciences and Optimization, pp. 960–964 (2011)
20. Clerc, M., Kennedy, J.: The particle swarm: explosion, stability, and convergence in a multidimensional complex space. IEEE Trans. Evol. Comput. **6**(1), 58–73 (2002)
21. Ray, T., Yao, X.: A cooperative coevolutionary algorithm with correlation based adaptive variable partitioning. In: Proceedings of IEEE CEC, May 2009, pp. 983–999 (2009)
22. Zhao, S.Z., Liang, J.J., Suganthan, P.N., Tasgetiren, M.F.: Dynamic multi-swarm particle swarm optimizer with local search for large scale global optimization. In: Proceedings of IEEE CEC, June 2008, pp. 3845–3852 (2008)
23. Shen, X., Chi, Z., Yang, J., Chen, C.: Particle swarm optimization with dynamic adaptive inertia weight. In: International Conference on Challenges in Environmental Science and Engineering, pp 287–289 (2010)
24. Helwig, S., Branke, J., Mostaghim, S.: Experimental analysis of bound handling techniques in particle swarm optimization. In: IEEE (2011)

25. Omidvar, M.N., Li, X., Yao, X.: Cooperative co-evolution with delta grouping for large scale non-separable function optimization. In: WCCI 2010 IEEE World Congress on Computational Intelligence, 18–23 July, 2010 - CCIB, Barcelona, Spain, pp. 1762–1769 (2010)

26. Epitropakis, M.G., Plagianakos, V.P., Vrahatis, M.N.: Evolving cognitive and social experience in particle swarm optimization through differential evolution: a hybrid approach. Inf. Sci. **216**, 50–92 (2012)

27. Ratnaweera, A., Halgamuge, S.K., Watson, H.C.: Self-organizing hierarchical particle swarm optimizer with time-varying acceleration coefficients. IEEE Trans. Evol. Comput. **8** (3), 240–255 (2004)

28. Shi, Y., Eberhart, R.C.: Empirical study of particle swarm optimization. In: Proceedings of IEEE International Congress on Evolutionary Computation, vol. 3, pp. 101–106 (1999)

29. Bonyadi, M.R., Michalewicz, Z., Li, X.: An analysis of the velocity updating rule of the particle swarm optimization algorithm. J. Heuristics **20**(4), 417–452 (2014)

30. Li, X., Yao, X.: Cooperatively coevolving particle swarms for large scale optimization. IEEE Trans. Evol. Comput. **16**(2), 210–224 (2012)

31. Bonyadi, M.R., Michalewicz, Z.: A locally convergent rotationally invariant particle swarm optimization algorithm. Swarm Intell. **8**(3), 159–198 (2014)

32. Tang, K., Yáo, X., Suganthan, P.N., MacNish, C., Chen, Y.P., Chen, C.M., Yang, Z.: Benchmark functions for the CEC 2008 special session and competition on large scale global optimization, Nature Inspired Computation and Applications Laboratory, University of Science and Technology, Hefei, China, Technical report (2007). http://nical.ustc.edu.cn/cec08ss.php

33. Cheng, Ran, Jin, Yaochu: A competitive swarm optimizer for large scale optimization. IEEE Trans. Cybern. **45**(2), 191–204 (2015)

34. Zhao, S.Z., Suganthan, P.N., Das, S.: Self-adaptive differential evolution with multi-trajectory search for large scale optimization. Soft. Comput. **15**(11), 2175–2185 (2011). doi:10.1007/s00500-010-0645-4

35. Zhao, S.Z., Liang, J.J., Suganthan, P.N., Tasgetiren, M.F.: Dynamic multi-swarm particle swarm optimizer with local search for large scale global optimization. In: IEEE Congress on Evolutionary Computation, pp. 3845–3852, Hong Kong, June 2008

36. Hao, Z., Guo, G., Huang, H.: A particle swarm optimization algorithm with differential evolution. In: 2007 International Conference on Machine Learning and Cybernetics, vol. 2, pp. 1031–1035 (2007)

37. Omran, M.G., Engelbrecht, A.P., Salman, A.: Differential evolution based particle swarm optimization. In: 2007 IEEE Swarm Intelligence Symposium, SIS 2007, pp. 112–119 (2007)

38. Kennedy, J.: Small worlds and mega-minds: effects of neighborhood topology on particle swarm performance. In: IEEE, pp. 1931–1938 (2009)

39. Kennedy, J., Mendes, R.: Population structure and particle swarm performance. In: Proceedings of the Congress on Evolutionary Computation, pp. 1671–1676 (2002)

40. Mendes, R.: Population topologies and their influence in particle swarm performance, Ph.D. dissertation, Escola de Engenharia, Universidade do Minho, Portugal (2004)

41. Emara, H.M.: Adaptive clubs-based particle swarm optimization. In: American Control Conference 2009, ACC 2009, pp. 5628–5634 (2009)

42. Elsayed, S.M., Sarker, R.A. and Essam, D.L.: Memetic multi-topology particle swarm optimizer for constrained optimization. In: Proceedings of the IEEE Congress on Evolutionary Computation, pp. 1–8 (2012)

43. Gong, Y.J., Zhang, J.: Small-world particle swarm optimization with topology adaptation. In: Proceedings of the Fifteenth Annual Conference on Genetic and Evolutionary Computation Conference, pp. 25–32 (2013)

44. Liang, S., Song, S., Kong, L. Cheng, J.: An improved particle swarm optimization algorithm and its convergence analysis. In: Second International Conference on Computer Modeling and Simulation, pp. 138–141 (2010)
45. Bird, S., Li, X.: Improving local convergence in particle swarms by fitness approximation using regression. In: Tenne, Y., Goh, C.K. (eds.) Computational Intelligence in Expensive Optimization Problems, pp. 265–293. Springer, Heidelberg (2010)
46. Chen, W.N., Zhang, J., Lin, Y., Chen, N., Zhan, Z.H., Chung, H.S.H., Li, Y., Shi, Y.H.: Particle swarm optimization with an aging leader and challengers. IEEE Trans. Evol. Comput. **17**(2), 241–258 (2013)
47. Qu, B.Y., Suganthan, P.N., Das, S.: A distance-based locally informed particle swarm model for multi-modal optimization. IEEE Trans. Evol. Comput. **17**(3), 387–402 (2013)

Black Hole Artificial Bee Colony Algorithm

Nirmala Sharma[1]([✉]), Harish Sharma[1], Ajay Sharma[2],
and Jagdish Chand Bansal[3]

[1] Rajasthan Technical University, Kota, India
nirmala_rtu@yahoo.com, harish.sharma0107@gmail.com
[2] Government Engineering College, Jhalawar, Rajasthan, India
[3] South Asian University, New Delhi, India

Abstract. Artificial bee colony (ABC) is an efficient methodology to solve optimization problems. Here, in this article a modified variant of ABC, namely Black Hole ABC algorithm (BHABC) is proposed which is based on the natural space black hole (BH) phenomenon. In BHABC, the implementation of BH gives a high exploration ability while maintaining the original exploitation ability of the ABC algorithm. The suggested algorithm is judged against 12 benchmark test functions and accessed with original ABC and its two modifications, that are Best So Far ABC (BSFABC) and Modified ABC (MABC). The results reveals that BHABC is a competitive variant of ABC.

Keywords: Meta-heuristic optimization techniques · Swarm intelligence · Black hole operator

1 Introduction

The nature inspired algorithms (NIA) are metaheuristics with the ability of self persistence and collective intelligence for solving complex optimization problems, that were tedious to solve by deterministic methods. ABC algorithm is inspired by communication skills and intellectual behavior of honey bees (HBs) [5,12]. There is always a presence of odds with all the evens, ABC has an intrinsic drawback of stagnation. In ABC algorithm, HBs stops wandering towards true solution and do not results in premature convergence too [11]. To eradicating the pitfall of ABC, research is in continuous progress [3,4,6,10,14–16]

In order to obtain a high convergent algorithm and augment the exploration abilities of ABC algorithms, a natural space BH phenomenon is applied with ABC. A BH represents an area of space having a lot of mass concentrated in such a way that there is no path for an object in its vicinity to flee and clear its gravitational horizon. In this paper, BH phenomenon is incorporated into ABC. Here, the best solution is selected as BH while remaining solutions are considered as stars. Any star which comes within a predefined range of BH is swallowed by BH and diminishes permanently [9]. This new modification of algorithm is named as Black Hole Artificial Bee Colony (BHABC) algorithm.

ⓒ Springer International Publishing AG 2016
B.K. Panigrahi et al. (Eds.): SEMCCO 2015, LNCS 9873, pp. 214–221, 2016.
DOI: 10.1007/978-3-319-48959-9_19

The remaining paper is structured in following style: Sect. 2 elucidates the BH phenomenon. BHABC is explained in Sect. 3. In Sect. 4, performance of BHABC is evaluated with several benchmark functions. Finally, Sect. 5 concludes the work in a summarized way.

2   Black Hole Phenomenon

The black hole (BH) phenomenon was invented by John Michell and Pierre Laplace [13]. After the collapse of a massive star in the space, there is always a possibility for the black hole to come in the picture [8]. The lot of mass is scattered in the black hole in such a way that the gravitational power of a black hole becomes so high that any object which crosses its boundary will be swallowed by it and that object permanently dies out. Even the light cannot flee this gravitational pull.

The boundary of the BH is called the event horizon E_H which has exceptional gravitational power [17]. The E_H radius is termed as the Schwarzschild radius [8,9] and it can be calculated using Eq. 1.

$$R_s = \frac{2GM}{C} \qquad (1)$$

here G represents the gravity constant, M implies the mass of the BH and C represents the velocity of the light. R_s is known as Schwarzschild radius.

3   Black Hole ABC Algorithm

In working of ABC algorithm stagnation is that situation where the candidate solutions stop exploring the new regions and work in a very narrow region. Due to the stagnation, algorithm lost its energy of finding better solution. Stagnation may cause algorithm to converge prematurely or stuck to the local optima. The stagnation phenomena occurs when all or most of the candidate solutions come very closed to each other. In other words, when the sum of distances between any two candidate solutions become very small.

In case of stagnation, to make ABC algorithm more explorative, concept of black hole is introduced to basic version of ABC. For simulating the black hole phenomenon, all candidate solutions are considered as stars, while the solution having best fitness among all candidate solutions is chosen as a black hole. All food sources (solutions) are initialized in a random manner in the given search space as shown in Eq. 2:

$$x_{ij} = x_{lb} + rand[0, 1](x_{ub} - x_{lb}) \qquad (2)$$

here x_i symbolizes the ith food source in the populous, x_{lb} and x_{ub} are lower and upper bounds of x_i in j^{th} dimension and $rand[0, 1]$ is an evenly scattered arbitrary numeral in the bounds [0, 1].

Subsequent to initialization of solutions, the fitness value (FV) of all the candidate solutions are evaluated and the best fit food source in the current populous, is nominated as a BH and rest of the solutions form the ordinary stars. After initializing the BH and stars, the stars are attracted by the BH i.e. the solutions update their positions using the distance and direction of the BH (best solution found so far). The position update equation of the solutions is expressed by Eq. 3:

$$x_i(t+1) = x_i(t) + rand(x_{BH} - x_i(t)) \qquad (3)$$

where $x_i(t)$ and $x_i(t+1)$ represents the position of the ith solution during iteration t and $t+1$ correspondingly. x_{BH} is the position of the BH (best solution) in the search region and $rand$ is evenly scattered arbitrary numeral specified in the bounds $[0, 1]$.

The BH search strategy is described as follows: While proceeding towards the BH, a star (solution) may attain a position which may be better than the position of the BH. In such a case, the positions of the BH and the star are interchanged i.e. the star is nominated as a new BH of the search region. In addition, when a star moves towards a BH, there is always chance to cross the E_H of the BH. Therefore, the star which crosses the E_H of the BH will be absorbed in the BH. When a star is sucked by the BH, it is died out and another star is born i.e. a new solution is produced in the search area.

The distance R_E (in this paper Euclidean distance but may be any) between the star and BH is calculated and compared with the radius of the E_H. The radius of the E_H of BH is computed through applying Eq. 4:

$$R = \frac{f_{BH}}{\sum_{i=1}^{N} f_i} \qquad (4)$$

Here f_{BH} represents the FV of the BH (current best solution) and f_i is the FV of the ith star.

Like, ABC, the BHABC algorithm is also apportioned into three segments, namely employed bee segment, onlooker bee segment, and scout bee segment. The BH phenomenon is applied in the employed bee segment of the algorithm, while other segments are kept similar as in the original version of ABC. Based on the above explanation the BHABC algorithm is described in Algorithm 1.

4   Outcomes and Discussions

To verify the efficieny of intended BHABC, it is evaluated on 12 different global optimization problems (f_1 to f_{12}) as shown in Table 1.

To prove the performance of the suggested algorithm BHABC, the algorithms, BHABC, ABC, Best so far ABC (BSFABC) [2] and Modified ABC (MABC) [1] are compared through experiments over test functions. The adopted experimental setting is adopted:

Initialize the parameters: MCN (Maximum number of cycles), D (Dimension of the problem), SN (Swarm Size);
Initialize the swarm having food sources, x_i where (i=1,2,......,SN) by using Eq. (2);
cycle = 1;
while *cycle <> MCN* **do**

> • Employed Bee Segment:
>> • For every solution, evaluate the objective function;
>> • Choose the best fit solution as BH;
>> • Change the position of each star solution using equation (3);
>> `/* `$fitness_{star}$` implies the fitness of the star solution and `$fitness_{BH}$` implies the fitness of the BH solution                  */`
>> • **if** $fitness_{star} > fitness_{BH}$ **then**
>> | Interchange the position of star and BH;
>>   **end**
>>   `/* `R_{BH}` represents the radius of the event horizon `E_H` of BH while `R_E` represents the Euclidean distance amid the star solution and the BH solution                  */`
>> • **if** $R_{BH} > R_E$ **then**
>> | Generate a new food source x_i randomly in the search area ;
>>   **end**
> • Onlooker Bee Segment;
> • Scout Bee Segment;
> • Memorize the best solution evaluated so far;
> • cycle=cycle+1;

end
Output the best solution;

Algorithm 1. Black Hole Artificial Bee Colony (*ABC*)

– Number of simulations =100,
– Number of solutions or food sources ($SN = NP/2$),
– $\phi_{ij} = rand[-1,1]$

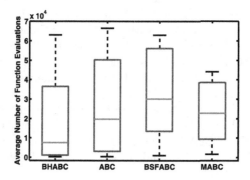

Fig. 1. AFE representation through boxplots

Table 1. Test problems, D: Dimension, AE: Acceptable Error

Objective function	Search range	Optimum value	D	AE
$f_1(x) = \sum_{i=1}^{D} x_i^2$	$[-5.12\ 5.12]$	$f(0) = 0$	30	$1.0E - 05$
$f_2(x) = \sum_{i=1}^{D} \sum_{j=1}^{i} x_j^2$	$[-65.536\ 65.536]$	$f(0) = 0$	30	$1.0E - 05$
$f_3(x) = \frac{\pi}{D}(10\sin^2(\pi y_1) + \sum_{i=1}^{D-1}(y_i - 1)^2 \times (1 + 10\sin^2(\pi y_{i+1})) + (y_D - 1)^2)$, where $y_i = 1 + \frac{1}{4}(x_i + 1)$	$[-10, 10]$	$f(-1) = 0$	30	$1.0E - 05$
$f_4(x) = [1.5 - x_1(1 - x_2)]^2 + [2.25 - x_1(1 - x_2^2)]^2 + [2.625 - x_1(1 - x_2^3)]^2$	$[-4.5, 4.5]$	$f(3, 0.5) = 0$	2	$1.0E - 05$
$f_5(x) = 100(x_2 - x_1^2)^2 + (1 - x_1)^2 + 90(x_4 - x_3^2)^2 + (1 - x_3)^2 + 10.1[(x_2 - 1)^2 + (x_4 - 1)^2] + 19.8(x_2 - 1)(x_4 - 1)$	$[-10, 10]$	$f(1) = 0$	4	$1.0E - 05$
$f_6(x) = a(x_2 - bx_1^2 + cx_1 - d)^2 + e(1 - f)\cos x_1 + e$	$-5 \leq x_1 \leq 10, 0 \leq x_2 \leq 15$	$f(-\pi, 12.275) = 0.3979$	2	$1.0E - 05$
$f_7(x) = \sum_{i=1}^{11}\left[a_i - \frac{x_1(b_i^2 + b_i x_2)}{b_i^2 + b_i x_3 + x_4}\right]^2$	$[-5, 5]$	$f(0.192833, 0.190836, 0.123117, 0.135766) = 0.000307486$	4	$1.0E - 05$
$f_8(x) = 10^5 x_1^2 + x_2^2 - (x_1^2 + x_2^2)^2 + 10^{-5}(x_1^2 + x_2^2)^4$	$[-20, 20]$	$f(0, 15) = f(0, -15) = -24777$	2	$5.0E - 01$
$f_9 = (1 - 8x_1 + 7x_1^2 - 7/3x_1^3 + 1/4x_1^4)x_2^2\exp(-x_2)$, subject to $0 \leq x_1 \leq 5, 0 \leq x_2 \leq 6$	$[0,5], [0,6]$	-2.3458	2	$1.0E - 06$
$f_{10}(x) = \sin(x_1 + x_2) + (x_1 - x_2)^2 - \frac{3}{2}x_1 + \frac{5}{2}x_2 + 1$	$x_1 \in [-1.5, 4], x_2 \in [-3, 3]$	$f(-0.547, -1.547) = -1.9133$	30	$1.0E - 04$
$f_{11}(x) = \sum_{i=1}^{5}\left(\frac{x_1 x_3 t_i}{1 + x_1 t_i + x_2 v_i} - y_i\right)^2$	$[-10, 10]$	$f(3.13, 15.16, 0.78) = 0.4 \times 10^{-4}$	3	$1.0E - 03$
$f_{12}(x) = -\sum_{i=1}^{5} i\cos((i + 1)x_1 + 1)\sum_{i=1}^{5} i\cos((i + 1)x_2 + 1)$	$[-10, 10]$	$f(7.0835, 4.8580) = -186.7309$	2	$1.0E - 05$

- limit is multiplication of Dimension of the problem and total number of solutions [1],
- The experiments for BSFABC and MABC are carried out by using parameter setting suggested by the respective inventors.

The research outcomes over considered algorithms are presented in Table 2. Table 2 shows an assessment over standard deviation (SD), mean error (ME), average number of function evaluations (AFE), and success rate (SR). Results in Table 2 reflects that BHABC outperforms most of the times in terms of reliability, efficiency, and accuracy as assessed with the ABC, BSFABC, and MABC.

Apart from these outcomes, boxplot analysis of AFE is carried out. The boxplots for BHABC and other considered algorithm are presented in Fig. 1. The analysis reveals that the interquartile range and the median of BHABC are quite low.

By considering the ME, SR, and AFE to measure the performance, the performance indices (PIs) is carried out as explained in [4,7]. The PIs are shown for the BHABC, ABC, BSFABC, and MABC through line graphs in Figs. 2(a), (b), and (c). The Figs. 2(a), (b), and (c) show results of giving weight to SR, ME, and AFE respectively.

Table 2. Assessment of the outcomes of test problems, TP: Test Problem

TP	Algorithm	SD	ME	AFE	SR
f_1	BHABC	1.03E−03	1.54E−04	44066	97
	ABC	2.10E−03	4.26E−04	66525.21	96
	BSFABC	2.97E−06	5.67E−06	62936.12	100
	MABC	5.42E−07	9.24E−06	44038.5	100
f_2	BHABC	2.56E−06	6.97E−06	28894.12	100
	ABC	2.14E−06	7.84E−06	31029.82	100
	BSFABC	2.29E−06	7.29E−06	49425	100
	MABC	6.76E−07	9.17E−06	32993	100
f_3	BHABC	1.75E−06	7.88E−06	12163.02	100
	ABC	2.85E−06	6.93E−06	10355.32	100
	BSFABC	2.52E−06	6.72E−06	26570.5	100
	MABC	7.12E−07	9.10E−06	22702.5	100
f_4	BHABC	2.95E−06	5.49E−06	7259.59	100
	ABC	2.73E−06	7.24E−06	34002.38	100
	BSFABC	1.69E−05	1.28E−05	49064.36	92
	MABC	2.94E−06	5.47E−06	9369.35	100
f_5	BHABC	1.89E−03	8.26E−03	63024.92	99
	ABC	1.07E−01	1.56E−01	200085.97	0
	BSFABC	3.19E−02	2.62E−02	153739	44
	MABC	1.25E−02	1.52E−02	146091.22	52
f_6	BHABC	6.65E−06	5.86E−06	1299.75	100
	ABC	6.87E−06	6.35E−06	3005.62	100
	BSFABC	7.19E−06	6.09E−06	29551.41	86
	MABC	6.73E−06	5.97E−06	22809.08	90
f_7	BHABC	1.65E−05	8.71E−05	62584.17	100
	ABC	7.16E−05	1.69E−04	182713.19	21
	BSFABC	7.91E−05	1.53E−04	120752.09	45
	MABC	8.10E−05	1.99E−04	185320.93	14
f_8	BHABC	5.77E−03	4.91E−01	946.24	100
	ABC	5.52E−03	4.89E−01	3145.86	100
	BSFABC	5.28E−03	4.91E−01	2800.72	100
	MABC	5.46E−03	4.91E−01	2347.19	100
f_9	BHABC	6.34E−06	6.10E−06	337.42	100
	ABC	6.19E−06	5.94E−06	428.01	100
	BSFABC	6.97E−06	6.22E−06	30539.05	85
	MABC	6.10E−06	5.33E−06	12957.85	94
f_{10}	BHABC	6.65E−06	8.83E−05	800.09	100
	ABC	6.95E−06	8.80E−05	1772.87	100
	BSFABC	6.44E−06	8.71E−05	1013.58	100
	MABC	6.79E−06	8.77E−05	1641.17	100
f_{11}	BHABC	3.07E−06	1.95E−03	4761.02	100
	ABC	2.97E−06	1.94E−03	29064.93	100
	BSFABC	2.64E−06	1.95E−03	17641.71	100
	MABC	2.96E−06	1.95E−03	9296.69	100
f_{12}	BHABC	5.78E−06	5.10E−06	7917.47	100
	ABC	5.58E−06	4.93E−06	9968.97	100
	BSFABC	5.76E−06	5.11E−06	9396.07	100
	MABC	5.37E−06	4.65E−06	26573.93	100

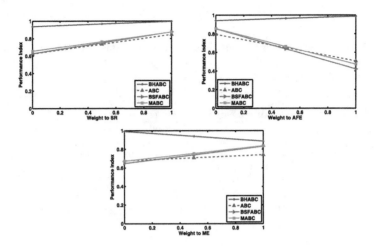

Fig. 2. Results of PIs; (a) SR, (b) AFE and (c) ME.

It is justified from Fig. 2 that PI of BHABC are better than the considered algorithms in all cases i.e. BHABC shows better performance over other considered algorithms.

5   Conclusion

This paper focusses on a new variant of ABC algorithm, namely Black Hole ABC (BHABC) algorithm. The proposed algorithm is developed by taking inspiration from the black hole (BH) phenomenon in space. The best solution among all the solutions is considered as BH. The absorption property of BH is used to enhance the exploration ability of the ABC algorithm. If any solution gets better position than the BH then the position of BH is updated accordingly. In BHABC, no new parameter is introduced hence, no need for adjusting the values of the various parameters. To evaluate the suggested algorithm, it is evaluated on the 12 benchmark functions. After analysing the outcomes, it can be stated that the BHABC will be a better choice to solve the continuous optimization problems.

References

1. Akay, B., Karaboga, D.: A modified artificial bee colony algorithm for real-parameter optimization. Inf. Sci. **192**, 120–142 (2012)
2. Banharnsakun, A., Achalakul, T., Sirinaovakul, B.: The best-so-far selection in Artificial Bee Colony algorithm. Appl. Soft Comput. **11**(2), 2888–2901 (2011)
3. Bansal, J.C., Sharma, H., Arya, K.V., Deep, K., Pant, M.: Self-adaptive artificial bee colony. Optimization **63**(10), 1513–1532 (2014)
4. Bansal, J.C., Sharma, H., Arya, K.V., Nagar, A.: Memetic search in artificial bee colony algorithm. Soft. Comput. **17**(10), 1911–1928 (2013)

5. Bansal, J.C., Sharma, H., Jadon, S.S.: Artificial bee colony algorithm: a survey. Int. J. Adv. Intell. Paradigms **5**(1), 123–159 (2013)
6. Bansal, J.C., Sharma, H., Nagar, A., Arya, K.V.: Balanced artificial bee colony algorithm. Int. J. Artif. Intell. Soft Comput. **3**(3), 222–243 (2013)
7. Bansal, J.C., Sharma, H.: Cognitive learning in differential evolution and its application to model order reduction problem for single-input single-output systems. Memetic Comput. **4**(3), 209–229 (2012)
8. Doraghinejad, M., Nezamabadi-pour, H., Sadeghian, A.H., Maghfoori, M.: A hybrid algorithm based on gravitational search algorithm for unimodal optimization. In: 2012 2nd International eConference on Computer and Knowledge Engineering (ICCKE), pp. 129–132. IEEE (2012)
9. Hatamlou, A.: Black hole: a new heuristic optimization approach for data clustering. Inf. Sci. **222**, 175–184 (2013)
10. Jadon, S.S., Bansal, J.C., Tiwari, R., Sharma, H.: Expedited artificial bee colony algorithm. In: Pant, M., Deep, K., Nagar, A., Bansal, J.C. (eds.) Proceedings of the Third International Conference on Soft Computing for Problem Solving, vol. 259, pp. 787–800. Springer, Heidelberg (2014)
11. Karaboga, D., Akay, B.: A comparative study of Artificial Bee Colony algorithm. Appl. Math. Comput. **214**(1), 108–132 (2009)
12. Karaboga, D., Basturk, B.: On the performance of artificial bee colony (ABC) algorithm. Appl. Soft Comput. **8**(1), 687–697 (2008)
13. Montgomery, C., Orchiston, W., Whittingham, I.: Michell, Laplace and the origin of the black hole concept. J. Astron. Hist. Heritage **12**, 90–96 (2009)
14. Sharma, H., Bansal, J.C., Arya, K.V.: Opposition based lévy flight artificial bee colony. Memetic Comput. **5**(3), 213–227 (2013)
15. Sharma, H., Bansal, J.C., Arya, K.V.: Power law-based local search in artificial bee colony. Int. J. Artif. Intell. Soft Comput. **4**(2), 164–194 (2014)
16. Sharma, H., Bansal, J.C., Arya, K.V., Deep, K.: Dynamic swarm Artificial Bee Colony algorithm. Int. J. Appl. Evol. Comput. (IJAEC) **3**(4), 19–33 (2012)
17. Zhang, J., Liu, K., Tan, Y., He, X.: Random black hole particle swarm optimization and its application. In: 2008 International Conference on Neural Networks and Signal Processing, pp. 359–365. IEEE (2008)

A Gravitational Search Algorithm for Energy Efficient Multi-sink Placement in Wireless Sensor Networks

P.C. Srinivasa Rao$^{(\boxtimes)}$, Haider Banka, and Prasanta K. Jana

Department of Computer Science and Engineering,
Indian Institute of Technology (ISM), Dhanbad 826004, India
pasupuleti.vasu@yahoo.in, hbanka2002@yahoo.com,
prasantajana@yahoo.com

Abstract. Optimal placement of multi-sink has been accepted an energy efficient approaches of extending the life of wireless sensor networks (WSNs). In this paper, a Gravitational Search Algorithm (GSA) based approach called GSA-MSP (Gravitational Search Algorithm based Multi-Sink Placement) for multi-sink placement for sensor network has been proposed. The algorithm has been designed with proper encoding scheme and a new fitness function. We consider the energy, Euclidian distance from the gateways to the sinks, and data rate of gateways are as parameters for the efficient design of GSA-MSP. The GSA-MSP has been tested vigorously over a varying number of sensors, gateways and sinks on various scenarios of WSNs. To show the efficacy of the GSA-MSP has been compared with some existing algorithms.

Keywords: Placement of multi-sink · Gravitational search algorithm · NP-Hard · Network lifetime

1 Introduction

Wireless sensor network (WSN) is a network of sensors, which are connected wirelessly, cooperate themselves to receive and aggregate the data from a target area and transmit to the BS [1]. Wireless sensor networks have plenty of applications such as wide spectrum of applications such as environmental monitoring, military, health and disaster management systems [2]. Due to energy constraint of sensors, energy saving of the sensors is the main crucial task for the scalable network. Clustering approach in WSNs has been well recognized technique that has been investigated rigorously [3–5]. In a cluster based WSNs, sensors are grouped into several clusters and has a representative node called cluster head (CH). The cluster heads gathering the data from sensors within their clusters, the collected data send to BS called as sink node [6]. To mitigate the WSN defects investigators have used some nodes with extra energy called as gateway nodes [7]. These gateways receive, fusing and forwarding the fused data to the BS, which serves as CHs. However, gateways also contain irreplaceable batteries and hence, at most care have been taken for saving energy of sensors. The gateway nodes are heterogeneous such that energy and data rates are different.

© Springer International Publishing AG 2016
B.K. Panigrahi et al. (Eds.): SEMCCO 2015, LNCS 9873, pp. 222–234, 2016.
DOI: 10.1007/978-3-319-48959-9_20

The placement of sink node has great effect on the energy dissipation of the WSNs [8, 9]. It may impact on other metrics such as delay, packet receipt by the BS. One of a solution is to place multi-sink, therefore gateway nodes can disseminate the aggregated data to their closest sink node with less network delay and cost of communication. However, determination of multiple sink positions is still competitive task, which may affect the routes in time sensitive cases.

Multiple sink problem has been proven to be a computational hard in nature (NP-Hard) [10]. Therefore, brute force approaches may not work efficiently for the scalable networks. GSA is one of the recent meta-heuristics which have been proven to be very effective to solve NP-hard problems in various domains because it convergence quickly, high quality of solution and ease of implementation [11]. In this work, we deal to find the optimal location of sink nodes for a given location of a gateway in clustered network. We propose a GSA for the same with proper encoding scheme and a new fitness function. The algorithm is simulated extensively over various simulation metrics and compared with some relates approaches.

The rest of the paper is organized as follows. Review of literature is provided in Sect. 2. The Sect. 3 presents the energy model, preliminaries of GSA, terminologies and network model. The methodology and GSA-MSP are presented in Sect. 4. The Sect. 5 describes the results and Sect. 6 concludes the work.

2 Reviews of Literature

Various approaches have been discussed in the literature to solve the multi-sink location problem. Two heuristic approaches have proposed by Pan et al. [12] to approximate the position of sinks. In the first approach application nodes (ANs) are homogeneous and second is for heterogeneous ANs. Homogeneous application nodes have same WSN parameters like initial energy, data transmission rates and data rate, where as heterogeneous application nodes have different network parameters. However, the computational complexity varies exponentially with the scalability of the network. Hence, the problem becomes computationally hard. In [13], the authors have proposed three algorithms for the optimal placement of sinks. The first one is best sink location (BSL), second one is maximizing the network lifetime while minimizes the number of sinks (MSMNL) and a third one for a predefined number of operation period minimizing the number of sinks (MSPOP). In [14], several sink placement strategies were presented, discussed and evaluated to achieve the goal of minimizing the maximum worst-case delay and maximizing the lifetime of a WSN. These sink placement strategies are: random sink placement (RSP), geographic sink placement (GSP), intelligent sink placement (ISP).

Some meta-heuristic based multi-sink placement algorithms have been also proposed. Among them few are well recognized like genetic algorithm based sink placement (GASP) [15]. However, it converges slowly in the initial iterations due to local trapping. In [16], a PSO is used to place multiple sink nodes. It finds the optimal position of multi-sinks with respect to different application nodes for increasing the life span of application nodes. However, only initial energy was used in the fitness function. But the energy of gateways changes for each round. Therefore, there is a need to improve the fitness function for the placement of optimal sinks. In [17], to solve the multi-sink placement problem for maximizes the lifetime of the network while minimizes the worst case delay discrete PSO (DPSO) had proposed. However, it slowly converges to a solution in the initial iterations. For the large scale network it converges slowly even in higher iterations. The optimal placement of a sink node has proposed by Md Nafees et al. [18] using PSO based technique. However, it suffers from the hotspot problem. Even it does not work for the time sensitive applications.

3 Preliminaries

3.1 Gravitational Search Algorithm

The initial swarm of agents say N_A. Each agent provides a potential solution. An agent A_i, $1 \leq i \leq N_A$ has position x_i^d and velocity v_i^d, $1 \leq d \leq D$ in the dth dimension of the search space. The dimension of each agent is same. A fitness function is used to evaluate the quality of an agent. Each agent is assigned with a random position and velocity in the initial generation. Let the position of an ith agent be represented as $X_i = \left(x_i^1, x_i^2, \ldots\ldots, x_i^D \right)$. The force acting on i^{th} agent due to j^{th} agent at time t in d^{th} dimension can be represented as follows.

$$F_{ij}^d(t) = G(t) \frac{M_{pi}(t) \times M_{aj}(t)}{R_{ij}(t)} \left(x_j^d(t) - x_i^d(t) \right) \tag{1}$$

where M_{pi} is the passive gravitational mass of ith agent, M_{aj} is the active gravitational mass of jth agent and $G(t)$ is a function such that $G(t) = G_0 \, (t_0/t_{max})^\alpha$ where G_0 is a initial gravitational constant value and α is a constant value between 0 and 1. The value of $G(t)$ decreases along with iterations, t_0 is the current iteration number and t_{max} is the maximum number of iterations. $R_{ij}(t)$ is the Euclidian distance between two agents i and j. Equation (2) gives the total force exerted by all agents on i^{th} agent in d^{th} dimension at time t.

$$F_i^d(t) = \sum_{j=1, j \neq i}^{N_A} rand_j \times F_{ij}^d(t) \tag{2}$$

where $rand_j$ is a random number in the interval [0, 1].

Gravitational and inertial masses are evaluated by the fitness evaluation. An agent with heavier mass is more efficient than other agents.

$$m_i(t) = \frac{fit_i(t) - worst(t)}{best(t) - worst(t)} + \varepsilon \tag{3}$$

where ε is a small positive value, $fit_i(t)$ is the fitness of ith agent at time t, $worst(t)$, $best$ (t) are defined as follows. For the proposed algorithm the problem is minimization case, the formulas are as follows.

$$best(t) = \max_{j \in \{1,..N_A\}} fit_j(t) \tag{4}$$

$$worst(t) = \min_{j \in \{1,..N_A\}} fit_j(t) \tag{5}$$

$$M_i(t) = \frac{m_i(t)}{\sum\limits_{j=1}^{N_A} m_i(t)} \tag{6}$$

Given that $M_{ai} = M_{pi} = M_{ii} = M_i$.

According to the Newton's second law of motion

$$a_i^d(t) = \frac{F_i^d(t)}{M_{ii}(t)} \tag{7}$$

where M_{ii} is the inertial mass of ith agent and $a_i^d(t)$ is the acceleration of ith agent in d^{th} dimension at time t.

The velocity and position of an agent can be updated as follows.

$$v_i^d(t+1) = rand_i \times v_i^d(t) + a_i^d(t) \tag{8}$$

$$x_i^d(t+1) = x_i^d(t) + v_i^d(t+1) \tag{9}$$

To balance the exploration and exploitation of the search space a function on *Kbest* is defined, its value decreases with the iteration to decrease the force acting on agents linearly to jump from the neighbor search.

3.2 Energy Model

We follow the same radio model as used in [3]. The energy dissipation of the node depends on the length of the data and distance to be sent. The energy dissipation of each sensor of the WSN for transmitting the *l*-bit data packet is given as follows.

$$E_{TX}(l,d) = \begin{cases} l \times E_{elec} + l \times \varepsilon_{fs} \times d^2, & if \ d < d_0 \\ l \times E_{elec} + l \times \varepsilon_{mp} \times d^4, & if \ d \geq d_0 \end{cases} \tag{10}$$

To run the one bit of data transmitter or receiver circuit dissipates E_{elec} of energy, amplification energy for multipath model ε_{mp} and for free space model ε_{fs} depends on the transmitter amplifier model and d_0 is the threshold transmission distance. The energy dissipated by the receiver for *l*-bit of data is as follows:

$$E_{RX}(l) = l \times E_{elec} \tag{11}$$

3.3   Network Scenario and Notations

3.3.1   Network Scenario

The sensor nodes along with some gateways are deployed randomly throughout the sensing field. Using RSSI model nodes can compute the distance to other nodes. We assume that all sensors are homogeneous.; all gateways are heterogeneous and stationary after deployment. There is a direct communication between gateways and sinks. The communication links are symmetric and wireless. A node can communicate the other node when it is within the communication range. We have used the lifetime of the network as the time to first gateway death (FGD).

3.3.2   Notations

For the ease of GSA-MSP, we first list some notations as follows.

S:	The group of sensors, i.e., $S = \{s_1, s_2, s_3, ..., s_n\}$
G:	The group of gateways, i.e., $G = \{g_1, g_2, g_3, ..., g_m\}$ where, m < n
d_{max}:	The max. transmission range of a sensor node
R_{max}:	The max. transmission range of a gateway
d_0:	Sensor threshold distance
R_0:	Gateway threshold distance
$E\ s_i$:	The initial energy of sensor s_i, $1 \leq i \leq$ n
Eg_i:	The reidual energy of gateway g_j, $1 \leq j \leq$ m
$dis\ (s_i, g_j)$:	The distance between a gateway node g_j. and sensor node s_i
$Comm(s_i)$:	The group of gateways in the range of s_i,
	i.e., $Comm(s_i) = \{g_j | \forall g_j \in G \wedge dis\ (s_i,\ g_j) \leq d_{max}\}$
$dis(g_j, SN_k)$:	The distance between a sink node SN_k and gateway node g_i
Dr_j:	The data rate of jth gateway.

4   Proposed Approach

The network setup operates in two phases. The first phase is setup phase consists of bootstrapping, clustering and multi-sink placement. Initially, all sensor nodes and gateways undergoes bootstrapping process where BS assigns unique IDs to all nodes. After that, all sensor nodes and gateways broadcast their IDs within their communication ranges such as d_{max} and R_{max} using CSMA/CA MAC layer protocol. All gateways receive the IDs of nodes within their communication range. Finally, each gateway sends the local information to BS for network setup. In the clustering phase all sensor nodes assigned to the nearest gateways, during this process all sensor nodes informed to the IDs of the gateways belong to. After that GSA-MSP is run to find the optimal locations of the multi-sink against to the heterogeneous gateways. The second phase is a steady state phase, in this phase gateways collects the data from the sensors, aggregate and send to optimal sink which are obtained from proposed algorithm. The SA-MSP is given in Fig. 1.

Algorithm : GSA based energy efficient Multi-sink placement

Input: (1) Group of heterogeneous gateways: $G = \{g_1, g_2, g_3, \ldots, g_m\}$.
       (2) Predefined swarm of agents of size: N_A.
       (3) Total no. of dimensions of an agent: $n=l$.
Result: Optimized locations of Sinks $SN = \{SN_1, SN_2, SN_3, \ldots, SN_l\}$.

Step 1: Generate inital agents A_i, $\forall i, j$, $1 \le i \le N_A$, $1 \le j \le n=l$, total sinks
              $x_i^d(0) = (p_i^d(0), q_i^d(0))$ /* Deployed locationof sink nodes*/
Step 2: *for* $t = 1$ to *Terminate*
          for $i = 1$ to N_A *do*
              Calculate *Fitness(A_i)* /* Using equation 14*/
Step 3:   Update *best* and *worst* fitness of all agents/*Using Eqs. (4), (5)*/
Step 4:   Calculate $M_i(t)$ and $a_i^d(t)$ of each agent of the system.
              Improvise velocity and position of A_i /*Using Eqs. (8), (9)*/
          endfor
      endfor
Step 5: Stop

Fig. 1. GSA based energy efficient multi-sink placement algorithm

4.1   Representation of an Agent

In GSA, an agent represents a potential solution. For multi-sink placement of the GSA-MSP, it indicates the optimal location of the sink nods against to the gateways. Let $A_i = (x_i^1, x_i^2, \ldots, x_i^n)$ be the ith agent of total agents. where each component $x_i^d = (p_i^d(t), q_i^d(t))$, $1 \le i \le N_A$, $1 \le d \le n$, denotes the location of sinks. Then the ith agent can is as follows:

$$A_i = \left[(p_i^1(t), q_i^1(t)), (p_i^2(t), q_i^2(t)), \ldots, (p_i^d(t), q_i^d(t)), \ldots, (p_i^n(t), q_i^n(t)) \right] \quad (12)$$

where N_A indicates the population of agents and n denotes the total sinks.

The dimensions, D is similar to all agents and same as number of sinks, i.e., l. Figure 2, provides the graphical representation of an agent, where SN denotes the index of the sink node and o denotes the index of location of sink node which are deployed randomly. For example, we consider 5 sinks. Assume the sensing area is 200×200 m^2. We generate the agents by assigning location to the sinks with a random number between 0 and 200, e.g., SN_1 is assigned to $(10.5, 38.1)$, SN_2 is assigned to $(131.5, 7.1)$ and so on.

4.2   Derivation of Fitness Function

The Minimal Euclidian distance: It can be defined as the distance from a gateway node to the particular sink in an agent i.e., gateways consume some part of energy

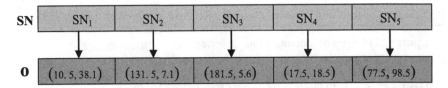

Fig. 2. An example of an agent representation

during communication with the sink nodes. To maximize the lifetime of gateways, it is necessary to reduce the distance between gateway nodes to the sink nodes.

$$\text{Minimize} f_1 = \min_{k=1}^{l} dis(g_j, SN_k) \tag{13}$$

Initially we deployed the sensors along with the gateways, after formation of clusters, we introduce the sinks against to the clustered gateway nodes. In the process of clustering, gateway nodes consume some energy while receiving and aggregated the data. Therefore, we need to consider residual energy rather than the initial energy of gateways. We derived the fitness function by considering the residual energy of gateways, data rate and Eq. (13). For maximizing the lifetime of the network we need to minimize f_1. So f_1 appears in the denominator of the below fitness Eq. (14). In the numerator of fitness function we consider the residual energy of gateways and data rate of gateways is a constant value is considered in the denominator of the fitness function.

$$\textit{Maximize Fitness} = \frac{\sum\limits_{j=1}^{m} E_{g_j}}{\sum\limits_{j=1}^{m} Dr_j(\chi_1 + \chi_2 \times f_1)} \tag{14}$$

Lifetime of Network $\propto$ *Fitness*

where χ_1, χ_2 are distance independent and dependent constants. The fitness function values are normalized within the range of 0 and 1 for optimizing the problem efficiently.

4.3   Updating of Velocity and Position

The updating of velocities and positions of agents can be done using Eqs. (8) and (9). It can be shown as follows.

Illustration. Consider the an agent as described in Fig. 2. For example, there are 10 agents ranging from A_1 to A_{10} with dimension $D = 5$ and the velocities of these agents are zero.

Let us assume that the total force acting on agent A_I due to all other agents in the first dimension of A_I be 30.5, i.e., $F_1^1(1)$ Also the inertial mass M_1 be 0.21.

Therefore, acceleration of A_1 with respect to first dimension can be written as

$$a_1^1(1) = F_1^1(1)/M_1 = 30.5/0.21 = 145.24$$

Consider A_1 as the input agent. Now compute the velocity of A_1 in the 1st dimension using Eq. (8). Also consider that $rand_I$ be 0.7. Then

$$V_{1,1}(t+1) = 0.7 \times 0 + 145.24$$

Using Eq. (9) the position is updated as follows.

$$x_{11}(t+1) = 10.5 + 145.24 = 155.74$$

The updation of velocity along X-axis of $X_{1, 1}(t)$ is shown in above calculations, and in the similar way updation of velocity along Y-axis is computed as follows.

$$V_{1,1}(t+1) = 0.7 \times 0 + 145.24; y_{11}(t+1) = 38.1 + 145.24 = 183.34.$$

Hence, the 1st dimension of A_I, i.e., $X_{1, 1}(t) = (10.5, 38.1)$ which is the position of first dimension of A_I (see Fig. 2) is updated to a another location $X_{1, 1}(t + 1) = (155.74, 183.34)$. The other dimensions of A_1 are also updated similarly. In the same way all other agents also updated.

5   Simulation Results

The GSA-MSP was analyzed using C language and the results were plotted using MATLAB (version 7.11) running on Windows 7 with chipset 2600, 3.40 GHZ CPU 2 GB RAM using Intel core i7 processor. We assume the network parameters for the proposed and comparative algorithms as shown in Table 1 for maintaining same simulation platform.

Also the GSA parameters were considered as $N_A = 30$, $Kbest = 80$, $G_0 = 800$, $\varepsilon = 0.05$, $\chi_1 = 0$, $\chi_2 = 1$, $\alpha = 0.2$ for approximating the better positions of sinks and $X_i^d(t + 1)$ is bounded by the absorption rule such that: if $X_i^d(t + 1) < 0$ then $X_i^d(t + 1) = 0$ and if $X_i^d(t + 1) > 200$ then $X_i^d(t + 1) = 200$. The performance of GSA-MSP was tested with an existing GA-based multi-sink placement algorithm [14] and some existing PSO based multi-sink placement algorithms [15, 16].

To analyze the performance of GSA-MSP algorithm, we use **A.** Total Energy Consumption, **B.** Network Lifetime, **C.** Packets receipt by BS, **D.** Number of alive gateway nodes and **E.** Convergence rate.

A. Performance Analysis in Terms of Energy Consumption.

Figures 3 and 4, demonstrates the energy dissipation of WSNs with the number of rounds with 300 sensors and 15 gateways. It is clear that if the number of sinks

Table 1. WSN parameters

Parameter	Value
Size of the sensing field	200x200 m^2
Number of sink nodes	5
Total sensor nodes	500
Energy of sensor	2 Joules
Energy of gateway	1–25 Joules
Data rate gateways 100	1–10 Kbps
E_{elec}	50 nJ/bit
ε_{fs}	10 pJ/bit/m^2
ε_{mp}	0.0013 pJ/bit/m^4
$dmax$	90 m
d_0	60 m
$Rmax$	120 m
r_0	90 m
Packet length	4000 bits
Message size	500 bits

increases energy consumption decreases. The proposed algorithm consumes less energy in both cases compared to some benchmark meta-heuristic based multi-sink placement algorithms such as DPSO, PSO and GASP. In DPSO the main focus is to reduce the maximum worst case delay. In PSO, the authors considered the initial energy of gateways only, which may hamper the lifetime of the WSN. In GASP, the quality of fitness values are not good because, it causes premature convergence in the initial iteration. Our main emphasis is on deriving the fitness function is to reduce energy consumption, in this way it consume less energy compared to existing algorithms. However, we have not considered delay metric, but our algorithm reduces the maximum worst delay also.

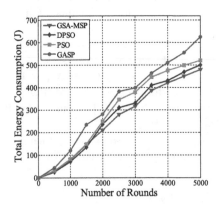

Fig. 3. Total sinks = 3

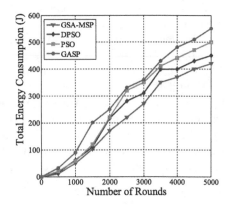

Fig. 4. Total sinks = 5

B. Performance Analysis in Terms of Network Lifetime.

From Figs. 5 and 6, it's clear that as the sink nodes increase the network lifetime. Also, we can see that as the nodes increase the life of a network decreases. Because gateways are overloaded to do extra work for sensing, aggregating and relaying the member sensor node data and send directly to the sink nodes. We have considered residual th energy of gateways while deriving the fitness function, however the existing algorithm does not consider this vital parameter which may reduce the lifetime of a network.

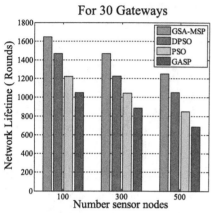

Fig. 5. Total sinks = 3

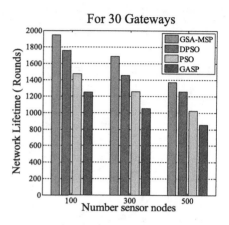

Fig. 6. Total sinks = 5

C. Performance Analysis in Terms of Packets Receipt by Sink Nodes.

Figures 7 and 8, demonstrates the performance of GSA-MSP with its comparatives in terms of packets received by the BS. It can be observed that GSA-MSP received

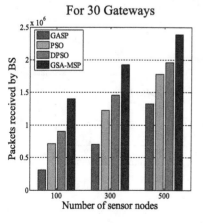

Fig. 7. Total sinks = 3

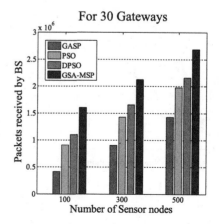

Fig. 8. Total sinks = 5

more packets compared to existing algorithms. The justification behind this is as the gateways have more network lifetime and less energy consumption. Therefore, more number of packet receipt by the sink nodes. Also, it can be observed that receipt of data packets is more when the number of sensor nodes increases.

D. Performance Analysis in Terms of Alive Gateway Nodes.

Figures 9 and 10, illustrates the total alive nodes with the rounds. We consider the 300 sensor nodes and 15 gateways. As the number of sink nodes increases the total alive nodes also increases. The GSA-MSP gives better performance over its comparatives, this is because, gateway nodes consume less energy. As the number of rounds increases less number of gateways fall down with its comparatives, this is due to as we have taken care of energy of gateways.

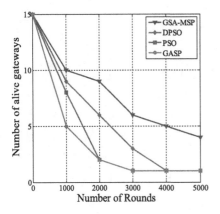

Fig. 9. Total sinks = 3

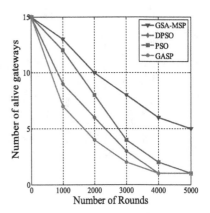

Fig. 10. Total sinks = 5

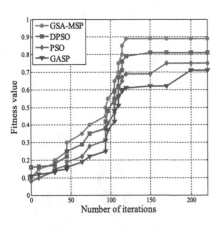

Fig. 11. Total sinks = 3

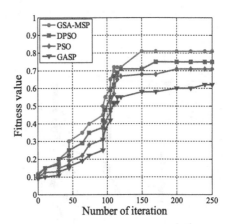

Fig. 12. Total sinks = 5

E. Performance Analysis in Terms of Convergence Rate.

In Figs. 11 and 12, we have analyzed the convergence of the GSA-MSP at two instances such that one with 3 sink nodes and other 5 sink nodes. Here also we consider the 300 sensor nodes and 15 gateways. It can be observed that GSA-MSP converges quickly with good quality of solution in both instances compared to DPSO, PSO and GASP algorithms. This is because the operators used for intensifying and diversifying the search space are simplified by using the GSA. However, as the number of sinks increases converges also quickly. The reason behind this is gateways can use less communication distance when sending the data packets.

6 Conclusion

In this paper, a GSA-MSP algorithm has been presented by considering proper encoding of an agent and a new fitness function. For the energy efficiency of the network, Euclidian distance, residual energy and data rate of gateways have been considered. The GSA-MSP has been tested vigorously over different network scenarios. For the superiority of GSA-MSP with existing algorithms such as GA and PSO based multi-sink placement approaches, we have used network lifetime, packets received by BS energy consumption, and convergence. It can be observed that the GSA-MSP out performs the existing algorithms in all such network parameters and also converges quickly.

In future work, we will consider the issue of finding the exact number of sinks for given network and also multi-hop routing with multiple sink nodes using appropriate meta-heuristics.

References

1. Akyildiz, I.F., Weilian, S., Sankarasubramaniam, Y., Cayirci, E.: A survey on sensor networks. IEEE Commun. Mag. **40**(8), 102–114 (2002)
2. Yick, J., Mukherjee, B., Ghosal, D.: Wireless sensor network survey. Comput. Netw. **52**(12), 2292–2330 (2008)
3. Rao, P.C.S., Jana, P.K., Banka, H.: A particle swarm optimization based energy efficient cluster head selection algorithm for wireless sensor networks. Wirel. Netw. doi:10.1007/s11276-016-1270-7
4. Rao, P.C.S., Banka, H.: Energy efficient clustering algorithms for wireless sensor networks: novel chemical reaction optimization approach. Wirel. Netw. doi:10.1007/s11276-015-1156-0
5. Rao, P.C.S., Banka, H.: Novel chemical reaction optimization based unequal clustering and routing algorithms for wireless sensor networks. Wirel. Netw. doi:10.1007/s11276-015-1148-0
6. Abbasi, A.A., Younis, M.: A survey on clustering algorithms for wireless sensor networks. Comput. Commun. **30**(14), 2826–2841 (2007)
7. Rao, P.C.S., Banka, H., Jana, P.K.: PSO based multiple sink placement for protracting the lifetime of wireless sensor networks. In: Satapathy, S.C., Raju, K.S., Mandal, J.K., Bhateja, V. (eds.) IC3T 2015. AISC, vol. 379, pp. 605–616. Springer, Heidelberg (2016). doi:10.1007/978-81-322-2517-1_58

8. Akkaya, K., Mohamed, Y., Waleed, Y.: Positioning of base stations in wireless sensor networks. IEEE Commun. Mag. **45**, 96–102 (2007)
9. Efrat, A., Har-Peled, S., Mitchell, J.S.: Approximation algorithms for two optimal location problems in sensor networks. In: IEEE 2nd International Conference on Broadband Networks, pp. 714–723 (2005)
10. Bogdanov, A., Maneva, E., Riesenfeld, S.: Poweraware base station positioning for sensor networks. Proc. IEEE INFOCOM **1**, 575–585 (2004)
11. Esmat, R., Hossein, N., Saeid, S.: GSA: a gravitational search algorithm. Info. Sci. **179**, 223–2248 (2009)
12. Pan, J., Cai, L., Hou, Y.T., Shi, Y., Shen, S.X.: Optimal base-station locations in two-tiered wireless sensor networks. IEEE Trans. Mob. Comput. **4**(5), 458–473 (2007)
13. Oyman, E.I., Ersoy, C.: Multiple sink network design problem in large scale wireless sensor networks. IEEE Int. Conf. Commun. **6**, 3663–3667 (2004)
14. Poe, W., Schmitt, J.B.: Minimizing the maximum delay in wireless sensor networks by intelligent sink placement. Technical report no. 362/07, University of Kaiserslautern, Germany, pp. 1–20 (2007)
15. Poe, W., Schmitt, J.B.: Placing multiple sinks in time-sensitive wireless sensor networks using a genetic algorithm. In: IEEE International Conference on Measuring, Modelling and Evaluation of Computer and Communication Systems (MMB), 2008 14th GI/ITG Conference, pp. 1–15 (2008)
16. Hong, T.P., Shiu, G.N.: Allocating multiple base stations under general power consumption by the agent swarm optimization. In: IEEE Swarm Intelligence Symposium, pp. 23–28 (2007)
17. Safa, H., El-Hajj, W., Zoubian, H.: Agent swarm optimization based approach to solve the multiple sink placement problem in WSNs. In: IEEE International Conference on Communications, pp. 5445–5450 (2012)
18. Rahman, M.N., Matin, M.A.: Efficient algorithm for prolonging network lifetime of wireless sensor networks. Tsinghua Sci. Technol. **16**(6), 561–568 (2011)

Optimum Clustering of Active Distribution Networks Using Back Tracking Search Algorithm

Reham A. Osama[1], Almoataz Y. Abdelaziz[1(✉)], Rania A. Swief[1],
Mohamed Ezzat[1], R.K. Saket[2,3], and K.S. Anand Kumar[2,3]

[1] Electric Power and Machines Department, Faculty of Engineering,
Ain Shams University, Cairo, Egypt
almoatazabdelaziz@hotmail.com
[2] Department of Electrical Engineering, Indian Institute of Technology,
Banaras Hindu University, Varanasi, Uttar Pradesh, India
rksaket.eee@iitbhu.ac.in
[3] Electrical Division, CSIR-National Aerospace Laboratories, Kodihalli,
Bangalore, Karnataka, India

Abstract. A microgrid has become the main building block of future distribution networks, demanding a systematic procedure for its optimal construction. Large distribution systems can be divided into clusters of distributed energy resources serving a group of distributed loads, known as microgrids to facilitate powerful control and operation. This paper compares the clustering of smart distribution systems into a set of microgrids based on two different objective functions. The probabilistic nature of intermittent distributed generators and loads is considered by performing a probabilistic Backward-Forward sweep power flow. The probabilistic approach aims to determine the optimal virtual cut set lines that split the system into self sufficient microgrids. The Back Tracking Search optimization algorithm is used to cluster a 69-bus distribution system with optimally allocated distributed generation units. The design concept, problem formulation, solution algorithms, probabilistic model and other graph related theories are presented in this paper.

Keywords: Clustering · Distributed energy resources · Microgrids · Self adequacy

1 Introduction

A microgrid is a localized, scalable, and sustainable power grid consisting of an aggregation of loads and corresponding generation sources capable of operating independent of the larger grid. According to IEEE standard 1547.4-2011, large distribution systems can be clustered into a number of microgrids to facilitate powerful control and operation in future distribution systems [1].

In this article, the planning stage towards a self-healing distribution system is considered by dividing the system into a set of virtual microgrids which will benefit the utility, customers and owners of distributed generators (DGs). One important

© Springer International Publishing AG 2016
B.K. Panigrahi et al. (Eds.): SEMCCO 2015, LNCS 9873, pp. 235–246, 2016.
DOI: 10.1007/978-3-319-48959-9_21

benefit/objective is the minimization of the power imbalance in microgrids that leads to self sufficient and supply secure clusters. During grid connected mode, this achieves minimum interaction between the microgrids. During disturbances, this can stop the propagation of disturbances by splitting the system into self-sufficient islands through a self-healing system reconfiguration control action. As a result, islanding will be possible with minimum load shedding.

In order to have a more feasible and robust design in the presence of the intermittent nature of DG units and loads, the impact of the uncertain variables such as solar irradiance, wind speed and load profile is addressed by a probabilistic analysis. Probabilistic Backward-Forward sweep load flow is applied to calculate the probabilistic indices that are defined for one of the objective functions.

This paper applies a very recent swarm optimization technique namely backtracking search algorithm (BSA) to the optimal clustering problem that was developed in 2013 [2]. The BSA has a unique mechanism for generating a trial individual enables it to solve numerical optimization problems successfully and quickly. The algorithm uses three basic genetic operators: selection, mutation and crossover to generate trial individuals. The BSA has a random mutation scheme and non-uniform crossover strategy in contrast with many genetic algorithms.

The paper is organized as follows. Section 2 explains the microgrid design concept; Sect. 3 presents the models used for DGs and loads; the problem formulation is given in Sect. 4; Sect. 5 explains the BSA algorithm used to solve the optimal clustering problem; Sect. 6 discusses the clustering of a 69-bus distribution system; finally the paper is concluded in Sect. 7.

2 Microgrids Design Concept and Benefits

Microgrids are known as small distribution systems connecting a group of electricity consumers to a number of distributed generation and storage units which can operate in grid connected or isolated grid modes. This paper aims to optimally design virtual microgrids in a distribution system including several dispatchable and intermittent distributed generation units. Clustering large distribution systems into smaller microgrids has many benefits to the utility, customers and DG owners [3]. Among these benefits: easier control, enhanced reliability, load routing and transfer among microgrids. An optimal design means that the real and reactive power imbalance within the microgrids is minimized. The less the transferred energy between the microgrids, or the less the generation-load imbalance within them, the more self-sufficient the microgrids will be. Thus, at normal system operation, the energy flow between these clusters is minimized as well which will make each microgrid operates with minimum interaction with others of the system. During disturbances, more loads can be supplied in case of autonomous-mode operation of microgrids in the distribution system and the energy losses on power lines connecting the microgrids will be minimized. Islanding will be possible with minimum load shedding actions. These self sufficient islands can stop the propagation of disturbances. The design of these microgrids is beneficial to optimize the overall system operational aspects.

3   Modeling of System Components

Due to the intermittent characteristics of DGs and hourly variation nature of loads, the optimal clustering of distribution systems should be based on the probabilistic approach. In this paper, DG units are modeled as a combination of photo voltaic (PV) modules, wind turbines and biomass generators. The first step is the processing of historical data. A selected period of one year is divided into four seasons, and a typical day is generated for each season in order to represent the random behavior of different renewable resources during each period. The solar irradiance for each day is modeled using Beta PDF [4] after which the probabilistic function of the output power of PV modules can be easily generated. The wind speed for each day is modeled using Rayleigh PDF which is a special case of the Weibull distribution [5]. The output power of a wind turbine can be then easily calculated. The biomass is considered to be a firm generation with constant output powers and the load. The load is modeled using the IEEE-RTS load model [6] where the hourly peak load is presented as percentage of the daily peak load. The load is represented by Gaussian PDF. Historical data is utilized in this research to generate for each season a typical day's frequency distribution of the irradiance and wind speed measurements. Each PDF is then divided into number of states. The number of states affects the accuracy and complexity of the formulation. The value of each variable in each state is the average value of the state interval. The probability of each state is obtained by evaluating the area under the curve within the state interval. The probabilistic value of a variable is accumulated considering the probability of each state. In order to get the probabilistic power flows, the deterministic load flow is run for each state and accumulated considering the probability of each state.

4   Problem Formulation

The aim of the microgrid design is to maximize the self sufficiency of the microgrids by minimizing the real and reactive power imbalance between generations and loads within each microgrid. This can be achieved using two different objectives.

4.1   First Objective

For each generation load state, the objective function to be minimized is calculated by subtracting the load level and losses from the generation at that state. The real and reactive power losses in the microgrid are assumed to be 5 % of the real and reactive load at each state [10].

The first objective function can be formulated as follows:

$$F1 = a * F_P + b * F_Q \tag{1}$$

$$F_P = \sum_{i=1}^{NMG} \sum_{j=1}^{Nstates} \sum_{k=1}^{NBus_i} \left| P_{G_{i,j,k}} - P_{L_{i,j,k}}(1 - 0.05) \right| * \sigma_i \tag{2}$$

$$F_Q = \sum_{i=1}^{NMG} \sum_{j=1}^{Nstates} \sum_{k=1}^{NBus_i} \left|Q_{G_{i,j,k}} - Q_{L_{i,j,k}}(1 - 0.05)\right| * \sigma_i \tag{3}$$

Where, the factors a and b are selected according to the system requirement for load-generation balance in the microgrids such that a + b = 1, NMG is the number of microgrids, N_{states} is the number of generation load states, N_{Busi} is the number of buses in microgrid i, σi is the probability of the state i, $P_{G\ i,j,k}$, $Q_{G\ i,j,k}$, $P_{L\ i,j,k}$ and $Q_{L\ i,j,k}$ are the active generated power and the load in state j, microgrid i and at bus k.

4.2   Second Objective

In order to minimize the power imbalance in the microgrids, two probabilistic indices are defined in the second objective function as follows:

$$F2 = \frac{a*P_{index} + b * Q_{index}}{NMG - 1} \tag{4}$$

$$P_{index} = \sum_{j=1}^{Ncutsets} \sum_{i=1}^{Nstates} \left|P_{ji}\right| * \sigma_i \tag{5}$$

$$Q_{index} = \sum_{j=1}^{Ncutsets} \sum_{i=1}^{Nstates} \left|Q_{ji}\right| * \sigma_i \tag{6}$$

Where, P_{index} and Q_{index} are probabilistic indices representing the total real and reactive power flows of the virtual cut set lines connecting the microgrids together respectively; P_{ji} and Q_{ji} are the active and reactive power flows of the cut set line j at state i; and $N_{cutsets}$ the total number of cut set lines. The denominator is to normalize the objective function. The active and reactive power flows of the cut set lines are evaluated by performing the probabilistic load flow. In this paper, the Backward-Forward Sweep load flow method [11] is used for the deterministic load flow during each state.

For the optimal microgrid construction problem, there are several constraints that has to be satisfied while selecting the virtual cut set lines that connect the microgrids together. Among these constraints are those related to the system topology that checks that all the system buses are considered in different microgrids and that all buses in each microgrid has a radial configuration. This paper applies the shortest path algorithm that has been proposed in [7]. If for a specific bus there is at least one path to another bus of the system and this applies for all system buses, this ensures that there are no unconnected buses and that all buses in microgrids are connected as a tree. One constraint is to check that any proposed cut set vector is feasible from the point that all clusters have generation units to supply the loads if islanding is required otherwise the solution is discarded. A constraint that restricts a minimum number of buses in a microgrid is required to ensure an acceptable logical design.

5   The Solution Algorithm

The BSA is a population-based iterative evolutionary algorithm designed to find a global minimum. The BSA has a single control parameter and the problem-solving performance is not sensitive to the starting value of this parameter. The BSA has five steps: initialization, selection-I, mutation, crossover and selection-II. A flowchart for the BSA algorithm is shown in Fig. 1.

5.1   Initialization

BSA initializes the population P such that:

$$P_{i,j} \leftarrow U(low_j, up_j) \tag{7}$$

For i = 1, 2, 3, ..., N and j = 1, 2, 3, ..., D, where N and D are the population size and the problem dimension, respectively, U is the uniform distribution.

5.2   Selection-I

This stage determines the historical population called oldP to be used for calculating the search direction. After oldP is determined, the order of individuals is then randomly shuffled by a permuting function.

$$oldP_{i,j} \leftarrow U(low_j, up_j) \tag{8}$$

$$oldP \leftarrow permuting(oldP) \tag{9}$$

5.3   Mutation

At this stage, the initial form of the trial population "Mutant" is generated. The historical population is used in the calculation of the search-direction matrix (oldP-P); BSOA generates a trial population, taking partial advantage of its experiences from previous generations. The parameter F controls the amplitude of the search direction matrix.

$$Mutant = P + F.(oldP - P) \tag{10}$$

5.4   Crossover

At this stage, the final form of the trial population T is generated. BSA's crossover calculates a binary integer-valued matrix (map) of size (N.D) that indicates the individuals of T to be manipulated by using the relevant individuals of P. The mix rate

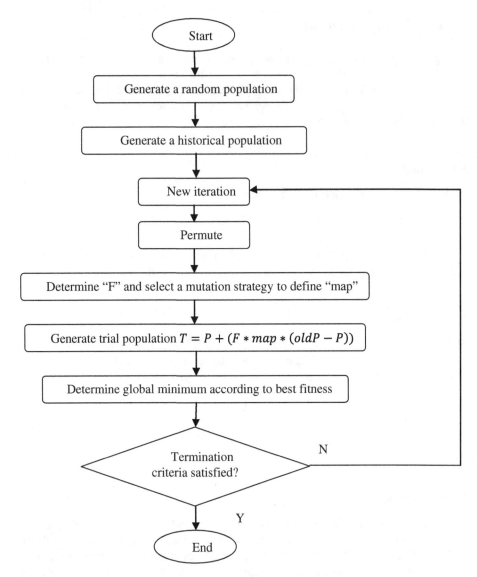

Fig. 1. The flowchart for the BSA optimization algorithm

parameter (mixrate) controls the number of elements of individuals that will mutate in a trial. Two predefined strategies are randomly used to define BSA's map. The first strategy uses mixrate. The second strategy allows only one randomly chosen individual to be mutated in each trial. BSA applies a boundary control mechanism for individuals that overflow the allowed search space limits as a result of mutation and crossover.

5.5   Selection-II

In this stage, the T that has better fitness values than the corresponding P is used to update the P, based on a greedy selection. If the best individual of P which is Pbest has a better fitness value than the global minimum value obtained so far by BSA, the global minimum is updated to be Pbest, and the global minimum value is updated to be the fitness value of Pbest.

6   Simulation Results

In this section, the BSA algorithm is used for the optimal microgrid design. The test system is a 69-bus distribution system [8] which is shown in Fig. 2.

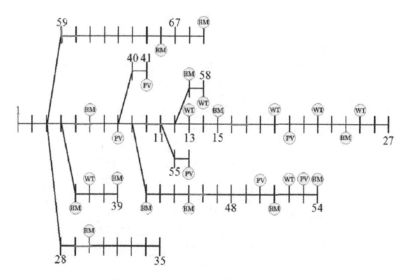

Fig. 2. The 69-bus system under study

The system is a 12.66 kV system with one supply point and 7 laterals. One study for the optimal DG allocation resulted in a penetration combination of wind, PV and biomass generators [9]. The details of the type, size and location of DG units are given in Table 1.

Table 1. DGs mix installed in the system.

DG type	Locations in the system (Buses)	Rated capacities (kW)
Wind turbine	13, 19, 22, 25, 37, 52, 58	50, 25, 25, 25, 50, 50, 25
PV module	8, 20, 41, 50, 53, 56	25, 25, 25, 25, 25, 25
Biomass DG	6, 15, 24, 30, 36, 39, 42, 45, 51, 54, 57, 66, 69	25, 50, 25, 25, 75,75, 25, 25, 50, 75, 75, 50, 25

One year of hourly historical data is used to generate the PDFs for irradiance, wind speed to obtain the distributions' parameters. The PDF for each season is then divided into number of states. In this paper, the number of states = 5.

Table 2 shows the modified load data for the system under study.

Table 2. Modified load data for the 69-bus IEEE-RTS.

Hour	Winter	Spring	Summer	Fall
12 am–1 am	0.4757	0.3969	0.64	0.3717
1–2 am	0.4473	0.3906	0.6	0.3658
2–3 am	0.426	0.378	0.58	0.354
3–4 am	0.4189	0.3654	0.56	0.3422
4–5 am	0.4189	0.3717	0.56	0.3481
5–6 am	0.426	0.4095	0.58	0.3835
6–7 am	0.5254	0.4536	0.64	0.4248
7–8 am	0.6106	0.5355	0.76	0.5015
8–9 am	0.6745	0.5985	0.87	0.5605
9–10 am	0.6816	0.6237	0.95	0.5841
10–11 am	0.6816	0.63	0.99	0.59
11 am–12 pm	0.6745	0.6237	1	0.5841
12–1 pm	0.6745	0.5859	0.99	0.5487
1–2 pm	0.6745	0.5796	1	0.5428
2–3 pm	0.6603	0.567	1	0.531
3–4 pm	0.6674	0.5544	0.97	0.5192
4–5 pm	0.7029	0.567	0.96	0.531
5–6 pm	0.71	0.5796	0.96	0.5428
6–7 pm	0.71	0.6048	0.93	0.5664
7–8 pm	0.6816	0.6174	0.92	0.5782
8–9 pm	0.6461	0.6048	0.92	0.5664
9–10 pm	0.5893	0.567	0.93	0.531
10–11 pm	0.5183	0.504	0.87	0.472
11 pm–12 am	0.4473	0.441	0.72	0.413

The parameters of the objective functions are set as a = 0.5, b = 0.5 since the reactive power has an important role in supporting the voltage profile. Mathematically, the optimum result will occur when the system is split into two virtual microgrids and the connecting power line has the minimum transferring energy. In order to have more feasible solutions (more than two micro-grids), another constraint is added at this stage only which restricts clustering the test system into a fixed number of microgrids.

The BSA is used as the solution algorithm for optimum microgrid design. The control variables are the virtual cut set lines that connect the microgrids together.

The probabilistic forward-backward sweep load flow is required to run when using the second objective function only. However, the first objective function does not need running the load flow during simulation. Table 3 shows the results of the system

Table 3. Optimal clustering results of the test system using the first objective.

NMG	Cut set vector	F1
2	28	48.625
3	28-62	79.328
4	28-62-19	221.983
5	28-62-19-12	316.942
6	28-62-20-13-10	680.190
7	28-62-20-13-10-44	2438.705

Table 4. Optimal clustering results of the test system using the second objective.

NMG	Cut set vector	F2
2	28	24.504
3	28-62	29.286
4	28-62-19	42.382
5	28-62-19-12	63.291
6	28-62-19-12-9	113.360
7	28-62-19-12-9-47	236.766

partitioning using the first objective function and Table 4 shows the clustering results using the second objective function.

It is clear that the results will be different based on the chosen number of minimum microgrids. The cut set k is the line whose end node is the node (k + 1) such that the cut set 10 is the line whose end node is 11.

It is noticeable that the clustering results for the 2 objectives have slight differences for the same number of microgrids. For example, clustering the system into 5 microgrids leads to the same cut set vector using both objectives which is [28-62-19-12]. While clustering the system into 7 microgrids leads to a cut set vector of [28-62-20-13-10-44] using the first objective and a cut set vector of [28-62-19-12-9-47] using the second objective. By comparing, it is clear that the cut set vectors when the number of microgrids is 7 is very close to each other. This result is logic because both objective functions aim at minimizing the imbalance within the microgrids. This also proves the effectiveness of the BSA. The calculated values of the objective functions are different for the same number of microgrids because the first is calculated based on the power mismatch while the second is based on the power flows.

Figures 3 and 4 show the optimal clustering with minimum number of microgrids equals to 7 using the first and second objective respectively.

The obtained results are compared to that in [9]. The authors in [9] applied the Tabu Search (TS) optimization algorithm to cluster the same test system with the same combination and distribution of DGs into 7 microgrids to maximize the system reliability and supply adequacy. Table 5 shows the difference between the optimum 6 cut set lines obtained by this paper and that obtained in [9] according to different objectives.

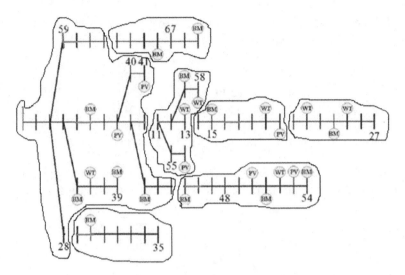

Fig. 3. Clustering the test system into 7 microgrids using the first objective

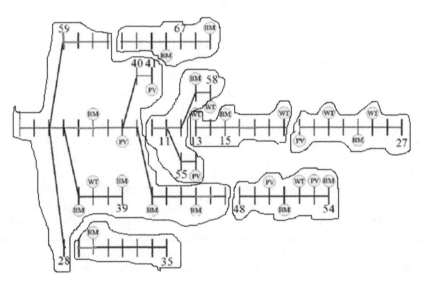

Fig. 4. Clustering the test system into 7 microgrids using the second objective

It is obvious that the optimal cut set vector as well as the objective function value are different based on the objective function used and the solution algorithm applied. Future work will include solving the optimal clustering of distribution networks using multi-objective functions that combine the most important operational aspects of distribution networks.

Table 5. Comparison for the optimum microgrid design results based on different objectives.

Objective	Cut set vector	Algorithm used	The objective function value
Maximize reliability [9]	5-10-16-29-45-59	TS	1785.2
Minimize the imbalance using the first objective function	28-62-20-13-10-44	BSA	2438.705
Minimizing the imbalance using the second objective function	28-62-19-12-9-47	BSA	236.766

7   Conclusions

This paper presented a planning strategy for optimal clustering of distribution networks into a number of self sufficient microgrids considering the probabilistic nature of DGs and loads. The back tracking search optimization is used as a solution algorithm. As shown, the BSA has a simple structure that is effective, fast and capable of solving the problem. The optimal solution is the one with the minimum power and energy imbalance in each microgrid. Two objective functions have been considered for the design problem to minimize the imbalance. The first is based on calculating the power mismatch. The second is based on calculating the flow indices. Since both objective targets maximizing the self sufficiency of microgrids, the clustering results were very close for the same number of microgrids which is logical and proves the validity and effectiveness of the BSA. It worth mentioning that the first objective does not require running the probabilistic load flow during the simulation but the second objective function requires running the probabilistic load flow which is a simulation burden.

References

1. IEEE guide for design, operation and integration of distributed resource island systems with electric power systems. IEEE Std. 1–54 (2011)
2. Civicioglu, P.: Backtracking search optimization algorithm for numerical optimization problems. Appl. Math. Comput. **219**(15), 8121–8144 (2013)
3. Arefifar, S.A., Mohamed, Y.A.I., El-Fouly, T.H.M.: Supply-adequacy-based optimal construction of microgrids in smart distribution systems. IEEE Trans. Smart Grid **3**(3), 1491–1502 (2012)
4. Salameh, Z.M., Borowy, B.S., Amin, R.A.R.A.: Photovoltaic module-site matching based on the capacity factors. IEEE Trans. Energy Convers. **1**(2), 326–332 (1995)
5. El-Saadany, E.F., Atwa, Y.M.: Probabilistic approach for optimal allocation of wind-based distributed generation in distribution systems. IET Renew. Power Gener. **5**(1), 79–88 (2011)
6. Pinheiro, J.M.S., Dornellas, C.R.R., Melo, A.C.G.: Probing the new IEEE reliability test system (RTS-96): HL-II assesment. IEEE Trans. Power Syst. **13**(1), 171–176 (1998)
7. Boris, V.C., Andrew, V.G., Tomasz, R.: Shortest paths algorithms: theory and experimental evaluation. Math. Program. **73**(2), 129–174 (1996)
8. Lasseter, R.H., Nikkhajoei, H.: Distributed generation interface to CERTS microgrid. IEEE Trans. Power Deliv. **24**(3), 1598–1608 (2009)

9. Arefifar, S.A., Mohamed, Y.A.-R.I.: DG mix, reactive sources and energy storage units for optimizing microgrid reliability and supply security. IEEE Trans. Smart Grid **5**(4), 1835–1844 (2014)
10. Savier, J.S., Das, D.: Impact of network reconfiguration on loss allocation of radial distribution systems. IEEE Trans. Power Deliv. **22**(4), 2473–2480 (2007)
11. Shirmohammadi, D., Hong, H.W., Semlyen, A., Luo, G.X.: A compensation-based powerflow method for weakly meshed distribution and transmission networks. IEEE Trans. Power Syst. **3**(2), 753–762 (1988)

Energy Efficient Clustering for Wireless Sensor Networks: A Gravitational Search Algorithm

P.C. Srinivasa Rao$^{(\boxtimes)}$, Haider Banka, and Prasanta K. Jana

Department of Computer Science and Engineering,
Indian Institute of Technology (ISM), Dhanbad 826004, India
pasupuleti.vasu@yahoo.in, hbanka2002@yahoo.com,
prasantajana@yahoo.com

Abstract. Clustering is an efficient technique for saving energy of wireless sensor networks (WSNs). In this paper, a Gravitational Search Algorithm (GSA) based approach has been presented called GSA-EEC (GSA based Energy Efficient Clustering). The algorithm is designed with an efficient encoding scheme of an and a new fitness function. For the efficient design of WSNs. we consider the Euclidian distance from the sensors to gateways and gateways to sink and residual energy of gateways. The GSA-EEC is simulated extensively with varying number of sensor and gateways and various scenarios of WSNs. To show the efficacy of the GSA-EEC, we compared with some of the benchmark clustering algorithms.

Keywords: Wireless sensor networks · Clustering · NP-hard · Gravitational search algorithm · Network life time

1 Introduction

Clustering sensor nodes is an efficient technique for conserving energy of sensor nodes [1]. In a clustered network, there are several groups of sensors called as clusters and each cluster have a representative node called cluster head (CH). The cluster heads gathering the data sensors within their clusters, fuse them and send the fused data to the base station (BS) [2]. To conquer the deficiencies of the network investigators have used special nodes called as gateways which are having similar function as that of sensors, however these nodes of more energy than sensors [3]. These gateways serve the role of cluster heads. However, they are also operated by small batteries and need to conserve the energy of these nodes. Figure 1, gives the simple model of clustered WSN.

Let us assume that there are m gateways and n sensor nodes in the network suppose with k nodes in the communication range of gateways. Therefore, k^n is the computational complexity of assignment of n sensors to m gateway nodes. Hence, classical methods are not efficient with the scalable network. GSA [4], is one of the recent nature inspired technique which can efficiently handles computational hard problems. Here, we present an efficient clustering algorithm based on GSA technique. The GSA-EEC vigorously tested with some of existing algorithms using various performance metrics.

Many papers have been reported in the literature [5–7] based clustering schemes. LEACH [8] is a representative one among them. In LEACH, CHs have been selected

© Springer International Publishing AG 2016
B.K. Panigrahi et al. (Eds.): SEMCCO 2015, LNCS 9873, pp. 247–259, 2016.
DOI: 10.1007/978-3-319-48959-9_22

Sensor node

Gateway

Base Station

Fig. 1. A clustered based WSN

with some probability. The limitation of this approach is a node with low energy may elect CH. It hampers the lifetime of the network. Therefore, huge numbers of schemes have been designed to improve LEACH. PEGASIS [9] is an efficient approach over LEACH, however, it is not scalable for large WSNs. The disadvantage of this approach is the delay. Numbers of hierarchical clustering algorithms [10–12] have also proposed to improve the network lifetime of WSN. Gupta et al. [13] have proposed a load balanced clustering approach called as LBC. LBC forms the clusters in an efficient manner, however, it ignores distance from sensor to gateways and gateways to BS, and energy of the gateway. These parameters play crucial role in reducing the energy consumption. Low et al. [14] have proposed a clustering scheme called GLBCA by using BFS, however for large scale network the execution time is high. Hussain et al. [15] have presented a GA based hierarchical clustering algorithm to choose a set of cluster heads from the normal sensor nodes. N.M. Abdul Latiff et al. [16], have designed PSO based clustering approach called PSO-C by using residual energy and intra-cluster distance as objectives, whereas in PSO-C, ignore the distance and energy metrics of gateways in the formation of clusters.

The rest of the paper is organized as follows. In Sect. 2, we have provided terminologies, preliminaries of GSA, network and energy models. The proposed algorithm GSA-EEC and methodology have been provided in Sect. 3. Section 4 contains simulation results and Sect. 5 concludes the paper.

2 Preliminaries

2.1 Overview of Gravitational Search Algorithm

The initial swarm of agents say N_A. Each agent provides a potential solution. An agent A_i, $1 \leq i \leq N_A$ has position x_i^d and velocity v_i^d, $1 \leq d \leq D$ in the dth dimension of the search space. The dimension of each agent is same. A fitness function is used to evaluate each agent for verifying the quality of the solution. In the initialization process of GSA, each agent is assigned with a random position and velocity to move in the search space. Let the position of an ith agent be represented as $X_i = (x_i^1, x_i^2, \ldots, x_i^D)$. The force acting on i^{th} agent due to j^{th} agent at time t in d^{th} dimension can be represented as follows.

$$F_{ij}^d(t) = G(t) \frac{M_{pi}(t) \times M_{aj}(t)}{R_{ij}(t)} (x_j^d(t) - x_i^d(t)) \tag{1}$$

where M_{pi} is the passive gravitational mass of ith agent, M_{aj} is the active gravitational mass of jth agent and $G(t)$ is a function such that $G(t) = G_0 (t_0/t_{max})^\phi$ where G_0 is a initial gravitational constant value and α is a constant value. The value of $G(t)$ decreases along with iterations, t_0 is the current iteration number and t_{max} is the maximum number of iterations. $R_{ij}(t)$ is the Euclidian distance between two agents i and j. Equation (2) gives the total force exerted by all agents on i^{th} agent in d^{th} dimension at time t.

$$F_i^d(t) = \sum_{j=1, j \neq i}^{N_A} rand_j \times F_{ij}^d(t) \tag{2}$$

where $rand_j$ is a random number in the interval [0, 1].

Gravitational and inertial masses are evaluated by the fitness evaluation. An agent with heavier mass is more efficient than other agents.

$$m_i(t) = \frac{fit_i(t) - worst(t)}{best(t) - worst(t)} + \varepsilon \tag{3}$$

where ε is a small positive value, $fit_i(t)$ is the fitness of ith agent at time t, $worst(t)$, $best(t)$ are defined as follows. For the proposed algorithm the problem is minimization case, the formulas are as follows.

$$best(t) = \min_{j \in \{1,..N_A\}} fit_j(t) \tag{4}$$

$$worst(t) = \max_{j \in \{1,..N_A\}} fit_j(t) \tag{5}$$

$$M_i(t) = \frac{m_i(t)}{\sum_{j=1}^{N_A} m_i(t)} \tag{6}$$

Given that $M_{ai} = M_{pi} = M_{ii} = M_i$.

According to Newton's second law of motion

$$a_i^d(t) = \frac{F_i^d(t)}{M_{ii}(t)} \tag{7}$$

where M_{ii} is the inertial mass of ith agent and $a_i^d(t)$ is the acceleration of ith agent in d^{th} dimension at time t.

The velocity and position of an agent are updated as follows.

$$v_i^d(t+1) = rand_i \times v_i^d(t) + a_i^d(t) \tag{8}$$

$$x_i^d(t+1) = x_i^d(t) + v_i^d(t+1) \tag{9}$$

To balance the exploration and exploitation of the search space a function on *Kbest* is defined, its value decreases with the iteration in order to decrease the force acting on agents to escape from neighbor regions.

2.2   Energy Model

We use the same radio model given in [8]. The energy consumption of a node depends on the length of the data and distance to be sent. The energy dissipation of each sensor of the WSN for transmitting the *l*-bit data packet is given as follows.

$$E_{TX}(l,d) = \begin{cases} l \times E_{elec} + l \times \varepsilon_{fs} \times d^2, & \text{if } d < d_0 \\ l \times E_{elec} + l \times \varepsilon_{mp} \times d^4, & \text{if } d \geq d_0 \end{cases} \tag{10}$$

To run the a bit of data, the transmitter or receiver circuit consumes E_{elec} of energy, amplification energy for multipath model ε_{mp} and for free space model ε_{fs} depends on the transmitter amplifier model and d_0 is the threshold transmission distance. The energy dissipated by the receiver for *l*-bit of data is as follows:

$$E_{RX}(l) = l \times E_{elec}$$

2.3   WSN Model and Notations

2.3.1   WSN Model

The sensor nodes along with some gateways are deployed randomly throughout the sensing field. All the nodes are stationary after deployment. Using RSSI model nodes can compute the distance to other nodes. There is a direct communication between gateways and sinks. We assume that all sensors and gateways are homogeneous. The communication links are symmetric and wireless. A node can communicate the other node when it is within the communication range. We have used the lifetime of the network as the time to first gateway death (FGD).

2.3.2   Notations

We have used some notations for ease of understanding of the GSA-EEC as follows:

S:	The group of sensors, i.e., $S = \{s_1, s_2, s_3,...., s_n\}$
G:	The group of gateways, i.e., $G = \{g_1, g_2, g_3,..., g_m\}$ where, m < n
d_0:	Sensor threshold distance
R_0:	Gateway threshold distance

d_{max}:   The max. transmission range of a sensor node
R_{max}:   The max. transmission range of a gateway
Eg_j: The reidual energy of gateway g_j, $1 \leq j \leq m$
Es_i: The initial energy of sensor s_i, $1 \leq i \leq n$
$Comm(s_i)$:   The group of gateways in the range of s_i, i.e., $Comm(s_i) = \{g_j | \forall g_j \in G \wedge$
                    dis $(s_i, g_j) \leq d_{max}\}$
$dis\ (s_i, g_j)$:   The distance between a gateway node g_j. and sensor node s_i
$dis\ (g_j, SN_k)$: The distance between a sink node SN_k and gateway node g_i
Dr_j: The data rate of jth gateway
l_{ij}:   Total no. of gateways in the range of sensor node s_i

Consider the FGD (First gateway death) is the lifetime of the network in our algorithm [17].

3 Proposed Approach

The network setup operates in two phases. The first phase is the setup phase consists of bootstrapping and clustering. Initially, all sensor nodes and gateways undergo boot-strapping process where BS assigns unique IDs to all nodes. After that, all sensor nodes and gateways broadcast their IDs within their communication ranges such as d_{max} and R_{max} using CSMA/CA MAC layer protocol. All gateways receive the IDs of nodes within their communication range. Finally, each gateway sends the local information to BS for network setup. In clustering phase BS run the proposed clustering algorithm, during this process all sensor nodes informed to the IDs of the gateways belongs to. The second phase is a steady state phase, in this phase gateways collects the data from their clusters, fuse and directly transmit to the base station. The GSA-EEC is given in Fig. 2.

3.1 Initialization and Representation of Agent

An agent denotes the potential solution. In the cluster formation of the GSA-EEC an agent indicates the assignments of sensor nodes to the proper gateways. Let $A_i = [x_{i,}^1(t),$ $x_{i,}^2(t), x_{i,}^3(t), x_{i,}^4(t), \ldots, x_{i,}^D(t)]$ be the ith agent of the swarm of agents. Each component $x_{i,}^d(t)$ maps the sensor to the gateway nodes and $1 \leq i \leq N_A$, $1 \leq d \leq D$. Then an agent can be represented as follows.

$$A_i = [x_{i,}^1(t), x_{i,}^2(t), x_{i,}^3(t), \ldots \ldots, x_{i,}^D(t)] \tag{12}$$

We initialize the each component by a randomly generated uniform distributed numbers Rand [1, 2], $1 \leq$ Rand [1, 2] ≤ 2. The component of dth dimension of an agent, i.e., $x_{i,}^d$ maps to the sensor node s_d to a g_k as follows.

Algorithm : GSA based energy efficient Clustering algorithm

Input: (1) The group of sensors : $S = \{s_1, s_2, s_3,....., s_n\}$.

(2) Set of gateway nodes: $G = \{g_1, g_2, g_3,....., g_m\}$.

(3) Predefined swarm of agents of size: N_A.

(4) Number of dimensions of an agent = Number of sensor nodes = n

Output: Optimal assignment of all sensors to gateways i.e., Optimal formation of clusters

Step 1: Initialize agents A_i, $\forall i, 1 \leq i \leq N_A$,

$A_i = [x_{i,}^1(t), x_{i,}^2(t), x_{i,}^3(t), x_{i,}^4(t),........, x_{i,}^D(t)]$ /*D = No. of sensors*/

Where $1 \leq x_{i,}^d(t) \leq 2$.

$g_k = Index\ (Comm(s_d) \times x_{i,}^d, n)$ /*Mapping function*/

$$n = \begin{cases} floor\ (Comm(s_d) \times x^d) & if\ n \leq |Comm(s_d)| \\ floor\ (Comm(s_d) \times x_i^d) - |Comm(s_d)| & otherwise \end{cases}$$

Step 2: *for* $t = 1$ to *Terminate*

for $i = 1$ to N_A *do*

2.1 Compute *Fitness*(A_i) /* From Eq. 16*/

Step 3:   Update *best* and *worst* fitness of all agents/* From Eqs. (4), (5) */

Step 4:   Calculate $M_i(t)$ and $a_i^d(t)$ of each agent of the system.

4.1 Improve velocity and position of A_i /* From Eqs. (8), (9)*/

endfor

endfor

Step 5: Stop

Fig. 2. GSA based energy efficient clustering algorithm

$$g_k = Index\left(Comm(s_d) \times x_{i,}^d, n\right).$$

$$n = \begin{cases} floor\ (Comm\ (s_d) \times x_i^d) & if\ n \leq |Comm\ (s_d)| \\ floor\ (Comm\ (s_d) \times x_i^d)) - |Comm\ (s_d)| & otherwise \end{cases} \tag{13}$$

Figure 3, represents the sample agent where g indicates the index of gateway nodes and s represents the index of sensors. The encoding process is illustrated in Sect. 3.3.

3.2 Derivation of Fitness Function

The objectives of fitness function given as follows.

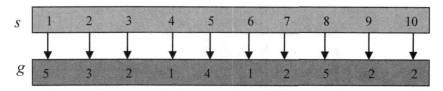

Fig. 3. Representation of a sample agent

(a) Energy of gateways: The sensors assign to gateway nodes with more residual energy gateways. The sensors can elect the gateways with more remaining energy than other nodes. The aim of this objective is to balance the energy of network and prevents the premature die of gateways.

$$\text{Objective 1 :}$$

$$\text{Maximize} f_1 = \sum_{i=1}^{n} \max_{j=1}^{l_{ij}} E_{g_j} \tag{14}$$

(b) Gateway and BS distance: The distance from sensor to gateway node and gateway to BS is considered as the second objective. A sensor can choose the gateway with minimum distance and also from the BS distance from that gateway. It can be represented as follows. It reduces the energy consumption of sensor nodes while sending the sensed data packets to BS.

$$\text{Objective 2 :}$$

$$\text{Minimize} f_2 = \sum_{i=1}^{n} \min_{j=1}^{l_{ij}} (dis(s_i, g_j) + dis(g_j, BS)) \tag{15}$$

$$\text{Minimize} \quad Fitness = \alpha \times 1/f_1 + \beta \times f_2 \tag{16}$$

where $\alpha + \beta = 1$

3.3 Illustration

Let us consider 10 sensors in the network. The mapping sensors to gateways can be explained in Tables 1 and 2. This is clear from the Fig. 3 that s_1 is assigned to g_5 and s_2 selected as g_3 and so on.

4 Simulation Results

The GSA-EEC was analyzed using C language and the results are plotted using MATLAB running on Windows 7 on an Intel core i7 processor with chipset 2600, 3.4 GHZ CPU 2 GB RAM. We have considered the parameters as used in [8], for the simulation as given in Table 3.

Table 1. Sensor nodes with list of possible gateway nodes

Sensor nodes	Comm(s_d)	$|Comm(s_d)|$
s_1	$\{g_1, g_2, g_3, g_4, g_5\}$	5
s_2	$\{g_1, g_3, g_4, g_5\}$	4
s_3	$\{g_4, g_5\}$	2
s_4	$\{g_2\}$	1
s_5	$\{g_1, g_2, g_4, g_5\}$	4
s_6	$\{g_1, g_5\}$	2
s_7	$\{g_1, g_2, g_3\}$	3
s_8	$\{g_1, g_2, g_3, g_4, g_5\}$	5
s_9	$\{g_1, g_4\}$	2
s_{10}	$\{g_2, g_4, g_5\}$	3

Table 2. Assignment of sensor nodes to the gateways

Sensor nodes	x_i^d	n	Assigned gateways
s_1	1.12	5	5
s_2	1.82	3	3
s_3	1.11	2	2
s_4	2.00	1	1
s_5	1.21	4	4
s_6	1.29	1	1
s_7	1.87	2	2
s_8	1.19	5	5
s_9	1.49	2	2
s_{10}	1.91	2	2

Table 3. WSN Parameters

Parameter	Value
Area of sensor field	200×200 m^2
Location of BS	((100,100) & (200, 200)
Total number sensors	500
Energy of sensor	1 J
Energy of gateway	5 J
E_{elec}	50 nJ/bit
ε_{fs}	10 pJ/bit/m^2
ε_{mp}	0.0013 pJ/bit/m^4
d_{max}	100 m
d_0	86 m
R_{max}	150 m
r_0	129 m
Data Packet length	4000 bits
Message size	500 bits

We have extensively tested the GSA-EEC with varying number of sensors and various scenarios. However, we have presented two of them are for WSN#1, the placement of BS at (100, 100) and for WSN#2, the placement of BS at (200, 200).

Also the GSA parameters were considered as $N_A = 50$, $Kbest = 270$, $G_0 = 1500$, $\alpha = 0.6$, $\phi = 0.2$, $\varepsilon = 0.05$ and $x_i^d(t + 1)$ is bounded by the absorption rule as: if $x_i^d(t + 1) < 0$ then $x_i^d(t + 1) = 0$ and if $x_i^d(t + 1) > 200$ then $x_i^d(t + 1) = 200$. The performance of the proposed algorithm is tested with some existing algorithms such as LBC [13], GLBCA [14], GA [15] and PSO-C [16].

The following metrics are used to test the performance of the algorithms.

A. Total Energy Consumption.
B. Lifetime of network.
C. Packet receipt by base station
D. Number of alive gateways
E. Convergence rate

A. Performance analysis in terms of Total Energy Consumption

Figure 4, demonstrates the total energy consumption of the network at 300 sensors and 24 gateways with the number of rounds. It is clear that the GSA-EEC outperforms the existed approaches. Because GSA-EEC saving energy by reducing the distance between sensors to gateways and also gateways to sensors. Whereas as in PSO-C, ignore the distance and energy metrics of gateways in the formation of clusters. In the same way GA, GLBCA and LBC form the clusters in an efficient manner, however they ignore the distance from sensor to gateway and gateway to the base station and energy of gateway in the assignment of member sensors to the gateways. These parameters plays crucial role in reducing the energy consumption.

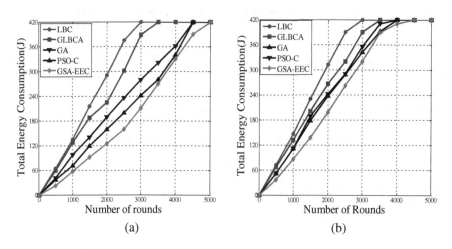

Fig. 4. Total energy consumption for (a) WSN#1 (b) WSN#2

B. Performance analysis in terms of the Lifetime of Network

Figure 5, explains the network lifetime along with various numbers of sensor nodes. It is clear that GSA-EEC performs better than the existing algorithm. The justification behind this is we were taking care of energy of gateways by deriving the novel fitness function. The possibility of FGD is more when the number of sensors increases because gateways consumes more energy for sensing, aggregating and relaying the data to BS directly.

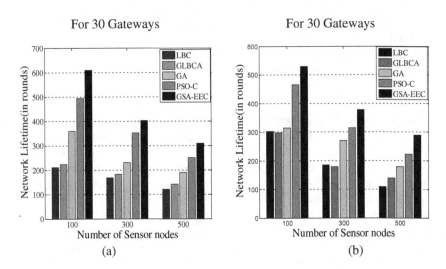

Fig. 5. Network Lifetime for (a) WSN#1 (b) WSN#2

C. Performance analysis in terms of packets receipt by Base station

Figure 6, demonstrates the performance of the proposed algorithm in terms of packets received by the BS. It can be observed that GSA-EEC received more packets compared to existing algorithms. Also, it can be observed that receipt of data packets is more when the number of sensor nodes increases. This is due to the fact that GSA-EEC more the lifetime of the network and consumes less energy.

D. Performance analysis in terms of a live gateways

Figure 7, describes the alive nodes versus rounds. We consider the 300 sensor nodes and 24 gateways. The change of BS position from center to corner of target field the number of alive gateways decreases. The proposed algorithm GSA-EEC outperforms the existed clustering algorithms LBC, GLBCA, GA and PSO-C in both cases.

E. Performance analysis in terms of convergence

The GSA-EEC is tested in terms of convergence over a varying number of sensor nodes from 100-500. For example, we consider the convergence of the proposed algorithm with 300 sensors and 24 gateways as shown in Fig. 8. It can be observed that GSA-EEC shows better quality of solution and faster convergence compared to PSO-C and GA. The reason for the quick convergence is due to the fact that the use of appropriate operators for intensifying and diversifying the search space compared to existing GA and PSO meta-heuristics.

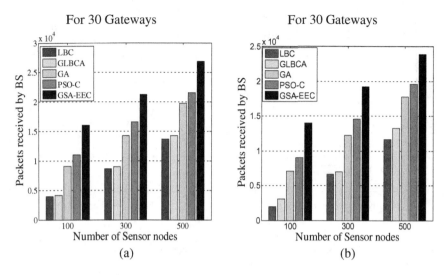

Fig. 6. Packets received by BS (a) WSN#1 (b) WSN#2

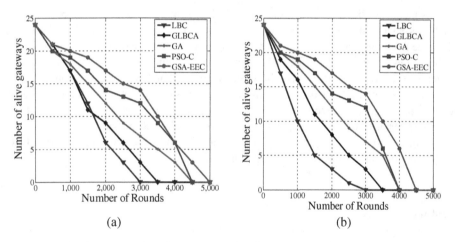

Fig. 7. Number of alive gateways for (a) WSN#1 (b) WSN#2

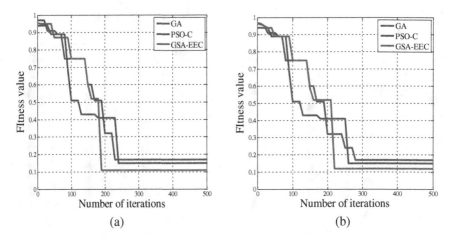

Fig. 8. Convergence rate for (a) WSN#1 (b) WSN#2

5   Conclusion and Future Work

In this paper, we have presented GSA based clustering algorithms and we have shown that it is energy efficient. We have considered various parameters such as Euclidian distance from the sensors to gateways and gateways to sink, energy of gateways for the efficient design of the GSA-EEC. The proposed algorithm is simulated vigorously over different scenarios of WSNs. To show the superiority of GSA-EEC with its comparatives, we have used various performance metrics such as network lifetime, energy consumption, packets received by the base station and convergence. The GSA-EEC shows superiority over its comparatives in terms of all such metrics.

In future work, we target to design an efficient routing scheme for the GSA-EEC using suitable nature inspired Optimization technique.

References

1. Yick, J., Mukherjee, B., Ghosal, D.: Wirel. Sens. Netw. Surv. Comput. Netw. **52**(12), 2292–2330 (2008)
2. Ashouri, M., Yousefi, H., Basiri, J., Hemmatyar, A.M.A., Movaghar, A.: PDC: prediction-based data-aware clustering in wireless sensor networks. J. Parallel Distrib. Comput. **81**, 24–35 (2015)
3. Srinivasa Rao, P.C., Banka, H., Jana, P.K.: PSO-based multiple-sink placement algorithm for protracting the lifetime of wireless sensor networks. In: Satapathy, S.C., Raju, K.,Srujan, Mandal, J.K., Bhateja, V. (eds.). AISC, vol. 379, pp. 605–616Springer, Heidelberg (2016). doi:10.1007/978-81-322-2517-1_58
4. Esmat, R., Hossein, N., Saeid, S.: GSA: a gravitational search algorithm. Inf. Sci. **179**, 223–2248 (2009)

5. Sabet, M., Naji, H.R.: A decentralized energy efficient hierarchical cluster-based routing algorithm for wireless sensor networks. AEU Int. J. Electron. Commun. **69**(5), 790–799 (2015)
6. Sert, S.A., Bagci, H., Yazici, A.: MOFCA: multi-objective fuzzy clustering algorithm for wireless sensor networks. Appl. Soft Comput. **30**, 151–165 (2015)
7. Abbasi, D.S., Abouei, J.: Toward cluster-based weighted compressive data aggregation in wireless sensor networks. Ad Hoc Netw. (2015). doi:10.1016/j.adhoc.2015.08.014
8. Heinzelman, W.B., Chandrakasan, A.P., Balakrishnan, H.: Energy efficient communication protocol for wireless microsensor networks. In: Proceedings of the 33rd Hawaii International Conference on System Sciences, p. 10 (2000)
9. Lindsey, S., Raghavendra, C.S.: PEGASIS: power efficient gathering in sensor information systems. In: Proceedings of the IEEE Aerospace Conference, Vol. 3, pp. 1125–1130 (2002)
10. Srinivasa Rao, P.C., Jana, P.K., Banka, H.: A particle swarm optimization based energy efficient cluster head selection algorithm for wireless sensor networks. Wirel. Netw. doi:10.1007/s11276-016-1270-7
11. Srinivasa Rao, P.C., Banka, H.: Energy efficient clustering algorithms for wireless sensor networks: novel chemical reaction optimization approach. Wirel. Netw. doi:10.1007/s11276-015-1156-0
12. Srinivasa Rao, P.C., Banka, H.: Novel chemical reaction optimization based unequal clustering and routing algorithms for wireless sensor networks. Wirel. Netw. doi:10.1007/s11276-015-1148-0
13. Gupta, G., Younis, M.: Load-balanced clustering of wireless sensor networks. In: IEEE International Conference on Communications, ICC 2003, vol. 3, pp. 1848–1852. IEEE (2003)
14. Low, C.P., Fang, C., Ng, J.M., Ang, Y.H.: Efficient load-balanced clustering algorithms for wireless sensor networks. Comput. Commun. **31**(4), 750–759 (2008)
15. Hussain, S., Matin, A.W., Islam, O.: Genetic algorithm for hierarchical wireless sensor networks. J. Netw. **2**(5), 87–97 (2007)
16. Latiff, N.M.A., Tsemenidis, C.C., Sheriff, B.S.: Energy-aware clustering for wireless sensor networks using particle swarm optimization. In: Proceedings of the 18th Annual IEEE International Symposium on Personal, Indoor and Mobile Radio Communications, pp. 1–5 (2007)
17. Dietrich, I., Dressler, F.: On the lifetime of wireless sensor networks. ACM Trans. Sens. Netw. **5**(1), 1–38 (2007)

Hybridizing Cuckoo Search with Bio-inspired Algorithms for Constrained Optimization Problems

G. Kanagaraj[1(✉)], S.G. Ponnambalam[2], and A.H. Gandomi[3]

[1] Department of Mechanical Engineering, Thiagarajar College of Engineering,
Madurai, India
gkmech@tce.edu
[2] Advanced Engineering Platform, School of Engineering, Monash University
Malaysia, 46150 Bandar Sunway, Malaysia
sgponnambalam@monash.edu
[3] BEACON Center for the Study of Evolution in Action,
Michigan State University, East Lansing, MI 48824, USA
gandomi@msu.edu

Abstract. Constrained optimization problems are complex and highly nonlinear, optimal solutions of practical interest may not even exist. This paper investigates the hybridization of a standard Cuckoo search (CS) algorithm with genetic algorithm (GA) and particle swarm optimization (PSO) algorithm. A new hybrid algorithms by adding positive properties of GA and PSO to the CS algorithms (denoted as CS-GA and CS-PSO, respectively) are proposed to solve for constrained optimization problems. According to the life style of cuckoo birds, each cuckoo will lay more than one egg at a time and always searching a better place to lay the eggs not to be discovered by the host birds, in order to increase the chance of eggs survival rate. By including evolution principles of GA or swarm intelligence of PSO in CS, it is possible to increase the optimization search space. The performance of hybrid algorithms developed in this paper is first tested with a well-known Himmelblau's function and then further validated by solving four classical constrained optimization problems. Optimization results fully demonstrate the efficiency of the proposed approaches.

1 Introduction

Optimization algorithms have been extensively used in constrained design optimization problems. Meta-heuristic methods such as evolutionary computation and swarm intelligence algorithms are attractive because they are rather simple to implement and have better global search abilities than gradient-based optimizers [1]. The general formulation of a constrained optimization problem is:

$$\text{Optimise: } f(\mathbf{X})$$
$$\text{Subject to:}$$
$$g_i(\mathbf{X}) \geq 0, i = 1, 2, \ldots N, \tag{1}$$
$$h_j(\mathbf{X}) = 0, j = N + 1, \ldots M,$$
$$l_i \leq x_i \leq u_i$$

© Springer International Publishing AG 2016
B.K. Panigrahi et al. (Eds.): SEMCCO 2015, LNCS 9873, pp. 260–273, 2016.
DOI: 10.1007/978-3-319-48959-9_23

Where $X = [x_1, x_2, \ldots\ldots x_N]^T$ is the design vector including N optimization variables (continuous, integer or discrete) each of which may range between the lower and upper bounds l_i and u_i; $f(\mathbf{X})$ is the objective function; $g_j(\mathbf{X})$ and $h_j(\mathbf{X})$, respectively, are the inequality and equality constraints (the latter can be replaced by the inequality constraint $|h_j(X) - \varepsilon| \leq 0$ where ε is a tolerance limit set by the user).

Most design optimization problems include many design variables and complicated constraints. Non-linearity often results in multimodal response. For this reason, modern meta-heuristic algorithms were developed to carry out global search trying to increase computational efficiency, solve larger problems, and implement robust optimization codes [2]. The search efficiency of meta-heuristic algorithms can be attributed to the fact that they mimic the best features available in nature from the most various sources ranging from biology [3] to physics [4]. However, there not exist meta-heuristic algorithms intrinsically able to find the global optimum for any kind of real world large-scale problems. Nature-inspired algorithms, based on the selection of the fittest, adaptation to changes, and genetic mechanisms in biological systems which have evolved by natural selection over millions of years are continuously proposed by researchers that continue to find asymptotically better meta-heuristic algorithms for specific design problems.

Evolutionary computation and swarm intelligence algorithms are the main categories of bio-inspired meta-heuristic optimization algorithms. Various algorithms were successfully utilized in solving optimization problems: for example, genetic algorithms (GA) [5, 6], Particle swarm optimization (PSO) [7, 8], Ant Colony Optimization (ACO) [9], Interior search algorithm (ISA) [10], Differential Evolution (DE) [11, 12], Firefly Algorithm (FA) [13, 14], Bat Algorithm (BA) [15, 16] etc. Another biology-inspired meta-heuristic algorithm successfully applied in many engineering problems [17, 18] is Cuckoo Search (CS). CS, developed in 2009 by Yang and Deb [19], reproduces the behavior of some cuckoo species in combination with the Levy flight behavior of some birds and fruit flies. Cuckoo search has recently attracted increasing attention because of its simple formulation, easy implementation and small number of internal parameters involved in the algorithm formulation. Hybridization of CS with other meta-heuristic algorithms was proven to be a viable approach [20, 21]. In this paper, cuckoo search is hybridized with standard GA or PSO (the resulting algorithms are denoted as CS-GA and CS-PSO, respectively). The performance of the new hybrid algorithms developed in this research is first evaluated by Himmelblau's test function and then further validated by solving four design bench mark problems. Numerical results confirm the validity of the proposed approaches. The remainder of the paper is organized as follows: Sect. 2 describes the brief idea of cuckoo search and in details of the proposed hybrid CS-GA and CS-PSO algorithms. Test problems and optimization results are presented in Sect. 3. Section 4 summarizes the main findings of the present study and outlines directions for further research.

2   Cuckoo Search Algorithm

Cuckoo search (CS) algorithm is based on the obligate brood-parasitic behavior of some cuckoo species in combination with the Lévy flight behavior of some birds and fruit flies. In standard CS, the following three idealized rules are used:

1. Each cuckoo lays one egg at a time, and dumps it in a randomly chosen nest.
2. The nests with high quality of eggs (solutions) will survive to the next generation.
3. The number of available host nests is fixed, and a host can discover an alien egg with a probability $p_a \in [0, 1]$. In this case, the host bird can either throw the egg away or abandon the nest so as to build a completely new nest in a new location.

The above three rules can be transformed into the following search methodology:

1. An egg represents a solution and is stored in a nest.
2. The cuckoo bird searches the most suitable nest to lay eggs (solution) in order to maximize eggs survival rate. The high quality eggs (best solutions near to optimal value) which are more similar to the host bird's eggs have the opportunity to develop (next generation) and become a mature cuckoo.
3. The host bird discover the alien egg (worse solutions away from optimal value) with a probability $p_a \in [0, 1]$ and these eggs are thrown away or the nest is abandoned, and completely new nest is built in a new location. Otherwise, the egg grows up and is alive for the next generation. New eggs (solutions) lay by a cuckoo chooses the nest by Lévy flights around the current best solutions.

2.1   Lévy Flight

In nature, animals search for food in a random or quasi-random way. In general, the foraging path of an animal is effectively a random walk because the next move is based on the current location/state and the transition probability to the next location. Which direction it chooses depends implicitly on a probability which can be modeled mathematically. For example, various studies have shown that the flight behavior of many animals and insects has demonstrated the typical characteristics of Lévy flights [22]. A study by Reynolds and Frye [23] shows that fruit flies or Drosophila melanogaster explore their landscape using a series of straight flight paths punctuated by a sudden 90° turn, leading to a Lévy-flight-style intermittent scale-free search pattern. Even light can be related to Lévy-flights [24]. Subsequently, such behavior has been applied to optimization and optimal search, and preliminary results show its promising capability [25]. Lévy Flight is performed to generate new solution stochastically.

$$x_i(t + 1) = x_i(t) + \alpha \oplus \text{Lévy}(\beta) \tag{2}$$

where $\alpha > 0$ is the step size which should be related to the scale of the problem of interest. In order to accommodate the difference between solution qualities, it can be set [26].

$$\alpha = \alpha_0 \left[x_j(t) - x_i(t) \right] \tag{3}$$

where α_0 is a constant while the term in the bracket corresponds to the difference of two selected solutions. This mimics the fact that similar eggs are less likely to be discovered and newly generated solutions are proportional to their differences. The product $\oplus$. means entry-wise multiplications. Lévy flight is essentially a Markov chain in which the random steps are drawn from a Lévy distribution [15]. The generation of the Lévy distribution can be achieved by Mantegna's algorithm. Mantegna's algorithm produces random noise according to a symmetric Lévy stable distribution [27]. A symmetric Lévy stable distribution is ideal for Lévy flights as the direction of the flight should be random [15].

In Mantegna's algorithm, the step length can be calculated as

$$\text{Lévy}(\beta) \sim \frac{u}{|v|^{\frac{1}{\beta}}}, \tag{4}$$

Where u and v are drawn from normal distributions. That is.

$$u \sim N\left(0, \sigma_u^2\right), \quad v \sim N\left(0, \sigma_v^2\right), \tag{5}$$

$$\sigma_u = \left\{ \frac{\Gamma(1+\beta)\sin\left(\frac{\pi\beta}{2}\right)}{\Gamma\left[\frac{(1+\beta)}{2}\right]\beta 2^{\frac{\beta-1}{2}}} \right\}^{\frac{1}{\beta}}, \quad \sigma_v = 1 \tag{6}$$

where the distribution parameter $\beta \in [0.3, 1.99]$.

For the best cuckoo laying eggs, the step size, α used is

$$\alpha = \alpha_c \left[bestnest(t) - x_i(t) \right] \tag{7}$$

where α_c is a constant.

According to the life style of cuckoo birds, each cuckoo will lay more than one egg at a time and always searching a place to lay the eggs not to be discovered by the host birds, in order to increase the chance of eggs survival. The evolution principles of GA in CS used to lay more eggs from a cuckoo and swarm intelligence of PSO in CS used to update their position according to PSO equation. The proposed hybrid CS-GA and CS-PSO are described in the following section.

2.2 Hybrid CS-GA Algorithm

Genetic Algorithms (GA) employ random choice to carry out a highly exploitative search, striking a balance between exploration of the feasible domain and exploitation of "good" solutions [28]. The rationale of developing the CS-GA algorithm is to combine the advantages of Cuckoo Search and GA in order to mimic the real life style of cuckoo birds. Each cuckoo lays more than one egg at a time and dumps them in a randomly chosen nest always searching the best place to lay eggs not to be discovered by the host birds. This increases the probability of eggs survival. The GA crossover operator is used to reproduce more eggs for each cuckoo. We select two parents and generate two offspring for them. Cuckoo birds mimic the color and pattern of the host bird in order to protect eggs from being recognized by the host birds. Therefore, cuckoo birds will have a mutation in their genes to supply this need. Thus, the GA mutation operator is added for all cuckoo birds. GA selection strategy is used to select the survived cuckoos among all the produced cuckoos and eggs. After the new generations of eggs that have grown to cuckoo bird, these mature birds in their real life immigrate to a better environment for their lifetime via Lévy flight and so forth. In addition, the destination place has limited capacity for them to build their nests. The flow chart proposed hybrid CS-GA is presented in Fig. 1.

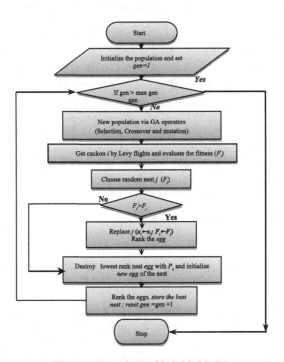

Fig. 1. Flow chart of hybrid CS-GA

2.3   Hybrid CS-PSO Algorithm

Particle swarm optimization (PSO), developed by Kennedy and Eberhart in 1995 [29], is a population based algorithm inspired by the social interaction and communication in a flock of birds. In PSO, a member of the swarm (population) is called a particle, and the objective of each particle is to discover the optimal point in a continuous search space as it moves from one point to another during the search process. Each particle moves around in the search space with a velocity. During the movement, each particle adjusts its position according to its own experience (p_{best}) and the most successful particle experience (g_{best}).

The velocity and position are updated using the following equations.

$$V_{t+1} = wV_t + C_1 U_1 (p_{best} - x_t) + C_2 U_2 (g_{best} - x_t) \qquad (8)$$

$$x_{t+1} = x_t + V_{t+1} \qquad (9)$$

Where w is called the inertia coefficient used to balance exploration versus exploitation of the solution space. Values of w close to 1 usually encourage exploration of new areas in the solution space, while for small values of w such as $w < 0.4$, the search shifts to the exploitation mode. Parameters C_1 and C_2 are called cognition and social coefficients, respectively, and they are very important for facilitating convergence in PSO. Based on an empirical study [29] as well as theoretical results [30], it is recommended to set C_1 and C_2 such that $C_1 + C_2 < 4$. U_1 and U_2 are uniform random numbers uniformly distributed between 0 and 1.x_t is current position of the particle. The process is repeated until a satisfactory solution is found. The flowchart of proposed hybrid CS-PSO is presented in Fig. 2.

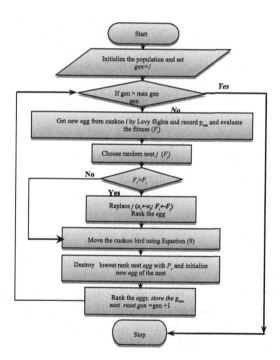

Fig. 2. Flow chart of hybrid CS-PSO

Swarm intelligence of PSO was introduced in CS to modify the third search rule. If alien eggs are discovered by the host bird they will be thrown away or the host bird will abandon its nest and build a new nest elsewhere. The cuckoo bird always looks for a better place where to lay eggs in order to better hide them. The present CS-PSO algorithm introduces the communication between cuckoo birds. The main goal of this communication is to inform each other from their position and help each other to migrate to a better place to build the nest. Each bird will record the personal experience as p_{best} during its own life. The p_{best} among all the birds is called g_{best}. Cuckoo birds migrate to the new position according to Eq. (9).

3 Test Problems and Results

The proposed hybrid CS-GA and CS-PSO algorithm were initially tested a well-known Himmelblau's test function, and then applied to five optimization problems. Optimization runs were carried out on a 2.4 GHz Intel® -64 Core(TM) 2 CPU 6600 computer with 2 GB of RAM memory. Optimization algorithms were implemented in MATLAB. For each test case, 30 independent runs were performed.

3.1 Himmelblau's Problem

This problem has originally been proposed by Himmelblau's [31] and it has been widely used as a benchmark nonlinear constrained optimization problem. In this problem, there are five design variables $[x_1, x_2, x_3, x_4, x_5]$, six nonlinear inequality constraints, and ten boundary conditions. The problem can be stated as follows:

$$Min: f(X) = 5.3578547x_3^2 + 0.8356891x_1x_5 + 37.293239x_1 - 40792.141$$
$$Subject\,to: 0 \le g_1 \le 92, 90 \le g_2 \le 110, 20 \le g_1 \le 25$$
$$g_1 = 85.334407 + 0.0056858x_2x_5 + 0.0026x_1x_4 - 0.0022053x_3x_5$$
$$g_2 = 80.51249 + 0.0071317x_2x_5 + 0.0029955x_1x_2 + 0.0021813x_3^2 \tag{10}$$
$$g_3 = 9.300961 + 0.0047026x_3x_5 + 0.0012547x_1x_3 + 0.0019085x_3x_4$$
$$78 \le x_1 \le 102, 33 \le x_2 \le 45, 27 \le x_3, x_4, x_5 \le 45$$

The problem was solved by Himmelblau [31] using generalized gradient method and several other methods such as Genetic Algorithm (GA) [32], particle swarm optimization (PSO) [33], Bat algorithm (BA) [34], evolutionary algorithms (EA) [35] and Cuckoo search (CS) [17]. Table 1 summarizes the optimal results obtained by CS-GA and CS-PSO algorithm. Table 2 compares the results obtained by CS-GA and CS-PSO, as well as other methods reported in the literature. It is obvious that the result obtained using CS-GA is better than the best feasible solution and CS-PSO obtained the same results previously reported.

3.2 Cantilever Beam Design Problem

This problem is a good benchmark to verify the capability of any algorithm for solving continuous, discrete, and/or mixed variable structural design problems. It was originally presented by Thanedar and Vanderplaats [36] with ten variables, and it has been

Table 1. Optimal result for Himmelblau's problem

Proposed algorithms	Design variables [x₁–x₅]	Objective function f(X)	No. of evaluations	Avg. time (s)
CS-GA	78.0, 33.0, 29.9999, 45.0, 36.7640714	−30664.8112	15000	3.1624
CS-PSO	78.0, 33.0, 29.9953, 45.0, 36.7758081	−30665.5374	10000	2.9832

Table 2. Statistical comparison results for Himmelblau's problem

Methods	Best	$0 \leq g_1 \leq 92$	$90 \leq g_2 \leq 110$	$20 \leq g_3 \leq 25$
GGM	−30373.9490	N/A	N/A	N/A
GA	−30005.7000	91.65619	99.53690	20.02553
PSO	−30665.539	92.00000	98.8405	20.00000
BA	−30665.4922	91.99990	98.84039	20.00001
EA	−30665.539	92.00000	98.8405	20.00000
CS	−30665.2327	91.99996	98.84067	20.00036
CS-GA	−30664.8112	91.9981971	98.8383447	20.0000
CS-PSO	−30665.5374	92.00000	98.84050	20.0000

solved with continuous, discrete and mixed variables in different cases in the literature [37]. The problem can be expressed as follows:

$$Min\, f(\mathbf{X}) = 0.0624(x_1 + x_2 + x_3 + x_4 + x_5)$$

$$\text{Subject to: } g(\mathbf{X}) = \frac{61}{x_1^3} + \frac{37}{x_2^3} + \frac{19}{x_3^3} + \frac{7}{x_4^3} + \frac{1}{x_5^3} - 1 \leq 0 \tag{11}$$

The best solutions obtained using CS-GA, CS-PSO, CS [17] and generalized convex approximation methods (GCA) [38] are listed in Table 3. As it is seen, the solution found out by CS-GA and CS-PSO is slightly better than basic CS and GCA methods.

Table 3. Best solutions of the cantilever beam design problem

Method	Design variables					f(X)
	x_1	x_2	x_3	x_4	x_5	
GCA	6.0100	5.3000	4.4900	3.4900	2.1500	1.3400
CS	6.0089	5.3049	4.5023	3.5077	2.1504	1.33999
CS-GA	6.016016	5.309174	4.494330	3.501475	2.152665	**1.339956**
CS-PSO	6.016016	5.309174	4.494330	3.501475	2.152665	**1.339956**

3.3   Tubular Column Design Problem

A uniform column of tubular section to carry a compressive load $P = 2500$ kgf at minimum cost [39]. The column is made of a material that has a yield stress σ_y of 500 kgf cm^{-2}, a modulus of elasticity E of 0.85×10^6 kgf cm^{-2}, and a density ρ of 0.0025 kgf cm^{-3}. The length L of the column is 250 cm. The stress included in the column should be less than the buckling stress (constraint g_1) and the yield stress (constraint g_2). The mean diameter of the column is restricted between 2 and 14 cm (constraint g_3 and g_4), and columns with thickness outside the range 0.2–0.8 cm are not commercially available (constraint g_5 and g_6). The cost of the column includes material and construction costs and can be taken as $9.82dt + 2d$, where d is the mean diameter of the column in centimeters and t is tube thickness. The optimization model of this problem can be expressed as follows:

$$Minimize\ f(d,t) = 9.82dt + 2d$$

$$\text{Subject to } g_1 = \frac{P}{\pi dt\sigma_y} - 1 \leq 0; \quad g_2 = \frac{8PL^2}{\pi^3 Edt(d^2 + t^2)} - 1 \leq 0 \quad g_3 = \frac{2.0}{d} - 1 \leq 0;$$

$$g_4 = \frac{d}{14} - 1 \leq 0; \qquad g_5 = \frac{0.2}{t} - 1 \leq 0; \qquad g_6 = \frac{t}{0.8} - 1 \leq 0$$

$$(12)$$

Table 4 illustrates the statistical results for the tubular column problem. It is seen that the optimal solution found by CS-GA and CS-PSO slightly better than solution provided by CS [17].

Table 4. Statistical results for the tubular column problem

Design variables	Proposed CS-GA	Proposed CS-PSO	Gandomi et al. [17]
d(cm)	5.451157	5.451132	5.45139
t(cm)	0.2919655	0.2919744	0.29196
g1	-0.21×10^{-6}	-0.2×10^{-4}	-0.0241
g2	-0.49×10^{-6}	-0.1×10^{-4}	-0.1095
g3	-0.633105	-0.633103	-0.6331
g4	-0.610631	-0.610633	-0.6106
g5	-0.314987	-0.315008	-0.3150
g6	-0.635043	-0.635032	-0.6351
$f(X)$	26.53133	26.53169	26.53217

3.4   Three Bar Truss Design Problem

This three bar truss design problem was first presented by Nowcki [40]. The volume of a statically loaded 3-bar truss is to be minimized subject to stress (σ) constraints on each of the truss members. The objective is to evaluate the optimal cross sectional areas (A_1, A_2). The mathematical formulation is given as below:

Min: $f(A1, A2) = (2\sqrt{2}A1 + A2)I$

Subject to $g_1 = \dfrac{\sqrt{2}A_1 + A_2}{\sqrt{2}A_1^2 + 2A_1A_2}P - \sigma \leq 0;\ g_2 = \dfrac{A_2}{\sqrt{2}A_1^2 + 2A_1A_2}P - \sigma \leq 0;\ g_3 = \dfrac{1}{A_1 + \sqrt{2}A_2}P - \sigma \leq 0$ $\qquad$ (13)

Where $0 < A1 < 1$ and $0 < A2 < 1$; $P = 2$ kN/cm^2, $\sigma = 2$ kN/cm^2 and $1 = 100$ cm.

The available algorithms solving this problem include swarm strategy (SS) [41], social behavior inspired optimization technique (SBO) [42] DE with dynamic stochastic selection (DEDS) [43], hybrid evolutionary algorithm with adaptive constraint handling (HEAA) [44], DE with level comparison (DELC) [45],CS [17] and GA with flexible allowance technique (GAFAT) [18].

The results of these algorithms are listed in Table 5. It can be seen that the best function value 263.8958 obtained by CS-GA and CS-PSO is the best function value and the same as the results obtained by GAFAT.

Table 5. Statistical results of three bar truss design problem

Algorithms	A_1	A_2	$f(X)$
CS [17]	0.78867	0.40902	263.9716
GAFAT [18]	0.7886751338	0.4082482928	263.8958434
SS [41]	0.795	0.395	264.3
SBO [42]	0.7886210370	0.4084013340	263.8958466
DEDS [43]	0.7886751359	0.4082482868	263.8958434
HEAA [44]	0.3567292035	0.0516895376	263.8958434
DELC [45]	0.7886751287	0.4082483070	263.8958434
CS-GA	0.7886751	0.4082483	263.8958
CS-PSO	0.788675134	0.40824828	263.8958433

3.5   Corrugated Bulkhead Design Problem

This problem is as an example of minimum-weight design of the corrugated bulkheads for a tanker. The variables of the problem are width (b), depth (h), length (l), and plate thickness (t). The minimum-weight requires the solution of the following optimization problem:

$$\text{Min: } f(b,h,l,t) = \frac{5.665t(b + 1)}{b + \sqrt{(1^2 - h^2)}} \qquad (14)$$

Subject to

$g_1 = th\left(0.4b + \tfrac{1}{6}\right) - 8.94(b + \sqrt{(1^2 - h^2)}) \geq 0;$

$g_2 = th^2\left(0.2b + \tfrac{1}{12}\right) - 2.2\left[8.94\left(b + \sqrt{(1^2 - h^2)}\right)\right]^{\frac{4}{3}} \geq 0$

$g_3 = t - 0.0156b - 0.15 \geq 0;$

$g_4 = t - 0.01561 - 0.15 \geq 0;$ $\qquad\qquad$ $g_5 = t - 1.05 \geq 0;\ g_6 = 1 - h \geq 0$

Where $0 \leq b, h, l \leq 100$ and $0 \leq t \leq 5$.

The minimum-weight and the statistical values of the corrugated bulkhead are given in Table 6. For this problem, Ravindran et al. [46] reported the minimum value of 6.84241 using a random search method. As it is seen, the best objective value reported by Gandomi et al. [17] is the best one but they did not consider the fifth constrained due to it is duplication of lower bound for t. A comparison of the results shows that CS-GA performs better in terms of solution quality than CS-PSO.

Table 6. Statistical results of corrugated bulkhead design problem

Design variables	Current research		Gandomi et al. [17]	Ravindran et al. [46]
	CS-GA	CS-PSO	CS	N/A
b (cm)	57.69231	57.69221	37.1179498	–
h (cm)	34.11410	34.11411	33.0350210	–
l (cm)	57.69231	57.68935	37.1939476	–
t (cm)	1.050000	1.05	0.7306255	–
g_1	239.3241	239.3391	23.35377	–
g_2	0.66909E−03	0.65168	33.21697	–
g_3	0.36000E−07	0.15E−05	0.1585483E−02	–
g_4	0.36000E−07	0.46E−04	0.3999174E−03	–
g_5	0.000000	0.00000	–	–
g_6	23.57821	23.57524	4.158927	–
$f(\mathbf{X})$	6.841343	6.841409	5.894331	6.84241

4   Conclusion

Hybridized version of cuckoo search with well-known GA and PSO algorithms proposed and tested in this paper. In standard CS, each cuckoo lays one egg at a time, but in this CS-GA algorithm, in order to lay more eggs genetic strategy used. To reduce the chance of eggs to be discovered by host bird mutation operator was used. Since there is limitation in number of nests the selection operator was used to select all cuckoos. This will increase the search space and reduce the fitness average in the population during the algorithm's performance. GA ensures to pass the best solutions onto the next iteration/generation, and there is no risk that the best solutions are being cast out of the population. The exploitation moves are within the neighborhood of the best solutions locally. CS-GA uses a balanced local search and global search.

The swarm intelligence behavior of PSO is built with standard CS in order to guide the cuckoo for selecting the best place to lay the egg. This will increase the best eggs for survival. From the simulation results our comparisons with a large number of comparator algorithms indicated that the proposed hybrid CS-GA and CS-PSO can provide outstanding results for solving optimization problems. Although the number of variables and types of problems solved in this work are limited and hence cannot substantiate the range of scope of application of the algorithm, the authors believe that the algorithm's working principles and features are appealing and its searching efficiency can be further improved constrained handling techniques adopted in [47, 48] with future development work and experimentation. Additionally, future research will investigate the performance of the hybrid CS with other optimization algorithms in solving unconstrained and constrained multi-objective optimization problems as well as real world applications.

Acknowledgment. This research is supported by University Grant Commission, New Delhi under research Grant No. F-30-1/2014/RA-2014-16-OB-TAM-5658 (SA-II).

References

1. Gandomi, A.H., et al. (eds.): Metaheuristic Applications in Structures and Infrastructures, Chap. 1. Elsevier, Waltham (2013)
2. El-Ghazali, T.: Metaheuristics: From Design to Implementation. Wiley, Chichester (2009)
3. Gandomi, A.H., Alavi, A.H.: Krill herd: a new bio-inspired optimization algorithm. Commun. Nonlinear Sci. Numer. Simul. **17**(12), 4831–4845 (2012)
4. Kaveh, A., Talatahari, S.: A novel heuristic optimization method: charged system search. Acta Mech. **213**, 267–289 (2010)
5. Goldberg, D.E.: Genetic Algorithms in Search, Optimization, and Machine Learning. Addison Wesley, Reading (1989)
6. Pezeshk, S., Camp, C.V.: State of the art on the use of genetic algorithms in design of steel structures, Chap. 3. In: Burns, S. (ed.) Recent Advances in Optimal Structural Design, 55–79 (2002)
7. Kennedy, J., Eberhart, R.C.: A discrete binary version of the particle swarm algorithm. In: Proceedings of the Conference on Systems, Man, and Cybernetics SMC97, pp. 4104–4108 (1997)
8. Gopalakrishnan, K.: Particle swarm optimization in civil infrastructure systems: state-of-the-art review and case study, Chapt. 3. In: Gandomi, A.H., et al. (eds.) Metaheuristic Applications in Structures and Infrastructures. Elsevier, Waltham, MI (2013)
9. Dorigo, M., Di Caro, G.: Ant colony optimization: a new meta-heuristic. In: Proceedings of the Congress on Evolutionary Computation (1999)
10. Gandomi, A.H.: Interior search algorithm (ISA): a novel approach for global optimization. ISA Trans. **53**, 1168–1183 (2014)
11. Storn, R., Price, K.: Differential evolution-a simple and efficient heuristic for global optimization over continuous spaces. J. Global Optim. **11**, 341–359 (1997)
12. Kitayama, S., Arakawa, M., Yamazaki, K.: Differential evolution as the global optimization technique and its application to structural optimization. Appl. Soft Comput. **11**, 3792–3803 (2011)
13. Yang, X.S.: Nature-Inspired Metaheuristic Algorithms. Luniver Press, Frome (2008)
14. Talatahari, S., Gandomi, A.H., Yun, G.J.: Optimum design of tower structures by firefly algorithm. Struct. Des. Tall Spec. Build. **23**, 350–361 (2014). doi:10.1002/tal.1043
15. Yang, X.-S.: A new metaheuristic bat-inspired algorithm. In: González, J.R., Pelta, D.A., Cruz, C., Terrazas, G., Krasnogor, N. (eds.) NICSO 2010. SCI, vol. 284, pp. 65–74. Springer, Heidelberg (2010)
16. Gandomi, A.H., Yang, X.S., Talatahari, S., Alavi, A.H.: Bat algorithm for constrained optimization tasks. Neural Comput Appl. **22**, 1239–1255 (2013). doi:10.1007/s00521-012-1028-9

17. Gandomi, A.H., Yang, X.S., Alavi, A.H.: Cuckoo search algorithm: a metaheuristic approach to solve structural optimization problems. Eng. Comput. **29**, 17–35 (2013). doi:10.1007/s00366-011-0241-y
18. Gandomi, A.H., Talatahari, S., Yang, X.S., Deb, S.: Design optimization of truss structures using cuckoo search algorithm. Struct. Des. Tall Spec. Build. **22**, 1330–1349 (2013). doi:10.1002/tal.1033
19. Yang, X.S., Deb, S.: Cuckoo search via Levy flights. In: World Congress on Nature and Biologically Inspired Computing (NaBIC 2009), pp. 210–214. IEEE Publications (2007)
20. Kanagaraj, G., Ponnambalam, S.G., Jawahar, N.: A hybrid cuckoo search and genetic algorithm for reliability–redundancy allocation problems. Comput. Ind. Eng. **66**(4), 1115–1124 (2013)
21. Kanagaraj, G., Ponnambalam, S.G., Jawahar, N., Nilakantan, J.M.: An effective hybrid cuckoo search and genetic algorithm for constrained engineering design optimization. Eng. Optim. **46**(10), 1331–1351 (2014)
22. Pavlyukevich, I.: Lévy flights, non-local search and simulated annealing. J. Comput. Phys. **226**, 1830–1844 (2007)
23. Reynolds, A.M., Frye, M.A.: Free-flight odor tracking in Drosophila is consistent with an optimal intermittent scale-free search. PLoS ONE **2**, 354 (2007)
24. Barthelemy, P., Bertolotti, J., Wiersma, D.S.: A Lévy flight for light. Nature **453**, 495–498 (2008)
25. Shlesinger, M.F.: Mathematical physics: search research. Nature **443**, 281–282 (2006)
26. Yang, X.S., Deb, S.: Multi-objective cuckoo search for design optimization. Comput. Oper. Res. **40**, 1616–1624 (2011)
27. Leccardi, M.: Comparison of three algorithms for Levy noise generation, p. 5. ENOC, Eindhoven (2005)
28. Goldberg, D.E.: Genetic Algorithms in Search, Optimization, and Machine Learning. Addison-Wesley, Reading (1989)
29. Eberhart, R., Kennedy, J..: A new optimizer using particle swarm theory. In: IEEE Sixth International Symposium on Micro Machine Human Science (1995)
30. Ozcan, E., Mohan, C.: Particle swarm optimization: surfing the waves. In: Proceedings of the IEEE congress on evolutionary computation (CEC), pp. 1939–1944. IEEE, Piscataway (1999)
31. Himmelblau, D.M., Clark, B.J., Eichberg, M.: Applied Nonlinear Programming. McGraw-Hill, New York (1972)
32. Homaifar, A., Qi, C.X., Lai, S.H.: Constrained optimization via genetic algorithms. Simulation **62**, 242–253 (1994)
33. He, S., Prempain, E., Wu, Q.H.: An improved particle swarm optimizer for mechanical design optimization problems. Eng. Optim. **36**, 585–605 (2004)
34. Yang, X.S., Gandomi, A.H.: Bat algorithm: a novel approach for global engineering optimization. Eng. Comput. **29**(5), 464–483 (2012).
35. Carlos, A., Coello, C.: Constraint-handling using an evolutionary multiobjective optimization technique. Civil Eng. Syst. **17**, 319–346 (2000)
36. Thanedar, P.B., Vanderplaats, G.N.: Survey of discrete variable optimization for structural design. J. Struct. Eng. **121**, 301–306 (1995)
37. Lamberti, L., Pappalettere, C.: Move limits definition in structural optimization with sequential linear programming. Part II: numerical examples. Comput. Struct. **81**, 215–238 (2003)
38. Chickermane, H., Gea, H.C.: Structural optimization using a new local approximation method. Int. J. Numer. Meth. Eng. **39**, 829–846 (1996)
39. Rao, S.S.: Engineering Optimization: Theory and Practice. Wiley, Hoboken (2009)

40. Nowacki, H.: Optimization in pre-contract ship design. In: Lind, F.K., Williams, T.J. (eds.) Computer Applications in the Automation of Shipyard Operation and Ship Design, vol. 2, pp. 327–338. Elsevier, New York (1974)
41. Ray, T., Saini, P.: Engineering design optimization using a swarm with an intelligent information sharing among individuals. Eng. Optim. **33**, 735–748 (2001)
42. Ray, T., Liew, K.M.: Society and civilization: an optimization algorithm based on the simulation of social behavior. IEEE Trans. Evol. Comput. **7**, 386–396 (2003)
43. Zhang, M., Luo, W., Wang, X.: Differential evolution with dynamic stochastic selection for constrained optimization. Inf. Sci. **178**, 3043–3074 (2008)
44. Wang, Y., Cai, Z., Zhou, Y., Fan, Z.: Constrained optimization based on hybrid evolutionary algorithm and adaptive constraint-handling technique. Struct. Multidiscip. Optim. **37**, 395–413 (2009)
45. Wang, L., Li, L.: An effective differential evolution with level comparison for constrained engineering design. Struct. Multidiscip. Optim. **41**, 947–963 (2010)
46. Rekalitis, G.V., Ravindran, A., Ragshell, K.M.: Engineering Optimization: Methods and Applications. Wiley, New York (1983)
47. Mallipeddi, R., Suganthan, P.N.: Ensemble of constraint handling techniques. IEEE Trans. Evol. Comput. **14**(4), 561–579 (2010)
48. Saha, C., Das, S., Pal, K., Mukherjee, S.: Fuzzy rule-based penalty function approach for constrained optimization. IEEE Trans. Cybern. doi:10.1109/TCYB.2014.2359985

A Hybrid Genetic Algorithm Using Dynamic Distance in Mutation Operator for Solving MSA Problem

Rohit Kumar Yadav[(✉)] and Haider Banka

Department of Computer Science and Engineering,
Indian School of Mines, Dhanbad 826004, India
rohit.ism.123@gmail.com, hbanka2002@yahoo.com

Abstract. In this paper, a hybrid Genetic Algorithm for solving multiple sequence alignment problems is proposed. Two new mechanisms have been introduced, i.e., one to generate the initial population and the second one is used during mutation operation. Here, the initial populations have been generated by Needleman Wunsch pair-wise alignment method. In the second step, the UPGMA method is used to generate the Guide tree with the help of two different matrix such as dynamic distance and edit distance matrix. The performance of the proposed method has been tested on publicly available benchmark datasets (i.e. Bali base) with some of the existing methods such as PRRP, CLUSTALX, SB–PIMA, MULTALIGN, SAGA, RBT-GA. We find that proposed method is better in most of cases and where it is not better at least close to best solution.

Keywords: Multiple sequence alignment · Genetic algorithm · Pair-wise alignment · Edit distance · Dynamic distance

1 Introduction

Bioinformatics gives a platform to develop algorithms and software to understand biological data. Bioinformatics is an interdisciplinary subject which combines computer science, mathematics and all engineering to study and process of biological data. Hence, in other words, we can say that Bioinformatics describe as an application of computational methods to solve biological problems [1]. Multiple Sequence Alignment (MSA) is the most remarkable and challenging problem in Bioinformatics. It is an extension of pair-wise sequence alignment to absorb more than two sequences at a time. Since in MSA align more than two sequences at a time. It should be worth noted that the solution of sequence problem is infeasible in polynomial time when the number and length of the sequence dramatically increases. Therefore, the problem of MSA leads to NP-Hard [2]. Theoretically, the potential of dynamic programming is appropriate to solve any number and length of the sequences. Practically, it is computationally expensive in both time and memory when the number of sequences is more than two. Hence, numerous existing methods are being developed to solve the MSA problem in appropriate time [3, 4]. In the progressive alignment method, first two sequences are chosen and then these two sequences are aligned using the dynamic

© Springer International Publishing AG 2016
B.K. Panigrahi et al. (Eds.): SEMCCO 2015, LNCS 9873, pp. 274–286, 2016.
DOI: 10.1007/978-3-319-48959-9_24

programming method. After that we replace the resulting pairwise alignment in giving multiple sequence alignment. It is guaranteed that progressive alignment gives solution in the reasonable amount of time. But the drawback is resulting alignment is not necessarily optimal in each case because the result depends on the initial alignment.

Probabilistic method such as Hidden Markov Model (HMM) is another possibility for solving MSA problem. In recent years, HMM achieved significant popularity in many fields [5]. It has been also applied in MSA [6, 7]. HMMER [8] is also a method to solve MSA problem using HMM. HMM is creating an operation of gap insertion and deletion to align the sequences. But the problem behind this method is there is no predestination algorithm to find optimally trained HMM.

Stochastic optimization method such as simulated annealing (SA) [9, 10] and Evolutionary methods [11–13, 17, 18] are alternative options of HMM to solve MSA problem. These approaches execute a series of steps to updating the alignment using some operator in each generation and also improve the objective function which quantify the quality of MSA for finding the optimal alignment.

In this paper, a GA based approach is proposed to incorporate pair-wise alignment method in initial generation, while the UPGMA based method is used in mutation operator in the intermediate generations. Two proximity measures such as dynamic distance and edit distance find the Phylogenetic tree.

2 Preliminaries

2.1 Minimum Edit Distance

Suppose we have two strings

INTENTION

EXECUTION

Then minimum edit distance is the minimum number of operations (delete, insert and substitution) to convert one sequence to another.

INTE $*$ NTION

$*$ EXE CUTION

DSS IS

Hence the minimum Edit distance between these sequences is 5.

2.2 PAM Matrix

A PAM matrix is a 20 * 20 matrix which gives the score between one of the twenty standard amino acids. In Bioinformatics, PAM matrices are regularly used as substitution matrices to score sequence alignments for proteins. In PAM matrix, each row and columns gives a score which is dependent on similarity of protein elements.

This score is calculated through biological phenomenon. This is dependent the series of one or more point mutation not only due a possibility.

3   Proposed Algorithm

In this proposed method first we generate initial population using Needleman and Wunsch algorithm in place of simple random initialization. After that we create child population using crossover and modified mutation operator and also define criteria for stopping.

3.1   Initial Generation

In this step, we have generated initial population by using the Needleman and Wunsch algorithm. Figure 1 is the process to generate an initial population. We have also taken one example to generate an initial population.

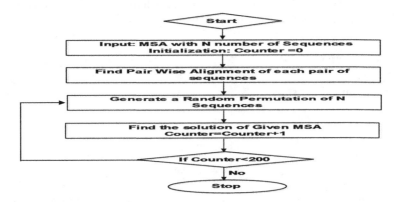

Fig. 1. Flow chart to generate an initial population using pair-wise alignment method

Suppose that the given MSA with 4 numbers of sequences:

PQRS

QRST

RSTU

STUV

Now, we are generating initial population using Needleman and Wunsch algorithm. According to this method we have to used three steps for finding the alignment. First one is Matrix Initialization, Matrix fill score and Trace back. We have defined all steps one by one.

Since First pair (1,2) is

PQRS

QRST

3.1.1 Matrix Initialization (N + 1, M + 1)

Where N is the length of the first sequence and M is the length of second sequence. Fill zeroes in the first row and first column. It is given in Fig. 2(a).

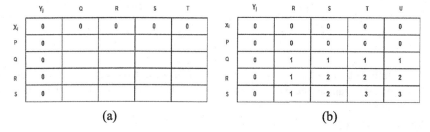

	Y_j	Q	R	S	T		Y_j	R	S	T	U
X_i	0	0	0	0	0	X_i	0	0	0	0	0
P	0					P	0	0	0	0	0
Q	0					Q	0	1	1	1	1
R	0					R	0	1	2	2	2
S	0					S	0	1	2	3	3

(a)   (b)

Fig. 2. Matrix initialization and score

3.1.2 Matrix Fill Scores

$$C[i,j] = \begin{cases} 0, & \text{if } i = 0 \text{ or } j = 0 \\ C[i-1, j-1]+1, & \text{if } i, j > 0 \text{ and } x_i = y_j \\ \text{Max}(C[i, j-1], C[i-1, j]), & \text{if } i, j > 0 \text{ and } x_i \neq y_j \end{cases}$$

Using this algorithm we find the matrix score, which is given in Fig. 2(b).

3.1.3 Trace Back

Symbolic representation of the trace back process is given below.

S.No	Equation	Symbolic Representation
1	$Xi=Yj$	↖
2	$C[i1,j] \geq C[i,j-1]$	↑
3	$C[i-1,j] < C[i,j-1]$	←

Now our matrix is given in Fig. 3(a).

After this process, we trace the path according to our arrow sign, it is shown in Fig. 3(b).

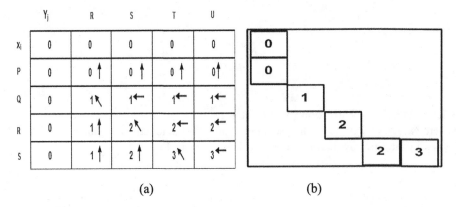

(a)   (b)

Fig. 3. Trace back and path

According to this path we find the alignment of these two sequences. For vertical entry we put the gap in second sequence and for horizontal put the gap in the first sequence and for diagonal no gap.

So our Alignment becomes

$$ABCD\_$$
$$\_BCDE$$

Since in this problem 4 sequence so we have $4 * (4 - 2)/2 = 6$ pairs.

Now we can generate a random permutation. Since in this example 4 sequences. So we can generate a random permutation from 1 to 4. Suppose we generate Random permutation (3, 4, 1, and 2).

Then first pair (3, 4) and second pair (1, 2) is

$$RSTU\_$$
$$\_STUV$$
$$PQRS\_$$
$$\_QRST$$

Now convert this MSA as is given our problem

$$PQRS\_$$
$$\_QRST$$
$$RSTU\_$$
$$\_STUV$$

This is solution of giving MSA.

According to flow chart we can generate K number of solutions. Hence our initial population has been created.

3.2   Fitness Function

In this section we find the fitness function of corresponding MSA using sum of pair method. Here, we calculate column score by summing the product of each pair of symbols. For calculating fitness score of complete MSA summed over all column score by using 1.

$$T = \sum_{k=1}^{K} S_k \text{ Where } T_k = \sum_{i=1}^{N-1} \sum_{j=i+1}^{N} Cost(A_i, A_j) \tag{1}$$

Here, T is the cost of multiple alignments. K is the length (columns) of the alignment, S_k is the cost of the kth column of K length and N is the number of sequences.

Cost (A_i, A_j) is the alignment score between two aligned sequences A_i and A_j when $A_i \neq$ "_" and $A_j \neq$ "_". Then Cost (A_i, A_j) is determined from the percentage of acceptable mutations matrix (PAM) [15]. Also, when $A_i =$ "_" and $A_j =$ "_" then Cost $(A_i, A_j) = 0$. Finally, the cost function Cost (A_i, A_j) includes the sum of the substitution costs of the insertion/deletions when $A_i =$ "_" and $A_j \neq$ "_" or $A_i \neq$ "_" and $A_j =$ "_" = 1.

3.3   Child Generation

(1) Crossover
(2) Mutation

3.3.1   Crossover

Two dimensional matrix of binary string is used to show each alignment. Where every row represented by a sequence and each column is represented by protein sequence. After that we put the value 1 in place of gap – and put value 0 in place of protein sequence. An example of the encoding is represented by Fig. 4. Now according to Fig. 4 first one is the initial MSA. Now according to pair wise alignment we put the gap in initial MSA problem which is described in initial generation sequences. Now we find the initial alignment of given multiple sequences. According to encoding scheme in place of protein sequence we put element 0 and in place of gap we put element 1. After that in representation of chromosome we have taken value of every column. According to Fig. 4 the value of the first column is 000. Now we have taken decimal equivalent of this binary representation. So our first column value is 0. Similarly we have taken binary representation of 4th column and we find that decimal equivalent of this column is 4. Hence we can find the decimal equivalent of binary representation of each and every column. So now our chromosome is 0 1 0 4 2 0 0.

In the selection process two solutions are selected by tournament selection procedure. This process is given in [16]. Its procedure is that first Encode the MSA problem, according to Binary encoding scheme which is given in Fig. 4. After this process, we choose a column position randomly. Suppose a third position chosen

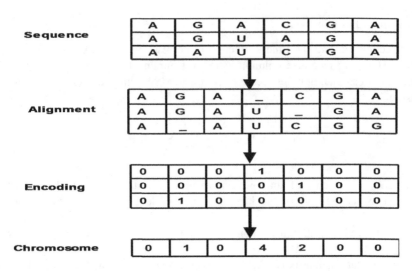

Fig. 4. Chromosome representation of individual solution of MSA

randomly and interchange the element in both chromosome solutions. Now again decode the chromosome solution and put the gap, according to binary decoding. Then put the original sequence. However, we have considered only best solution in next generation.

3.3.2 Mutation

On solution is selected by the probability rate of mutation in our mutation process. After the selection of solution we have generated two different type of distance matrix. These matrix are known as Dynamic distance matrix and Edit distance matrix.

(A) Dynamic distance:- This distance is calculated by the use of two sequences. This distance is equivalent to ratio of number of mismatch element and total number of alignment.

Dynamic distance = Number of mismatch elements/Total number of alignment length

Now we have taken one example to show that how we have calculated distance matrix.

PQRS_

_QRST

RSTU_

_STUV

Now we have to find pair wise alignment of each and every sequences. Hence we find the alignment of first pair (1, 2) according to pair wise alignment method. Then first pair (1, 2) is

PQRS_

_QRST

In our first pair mismatching element is 2 and total number of alignment length is 5. So according to formula of dynamic distance method distance between first pair of sequences is 2/5.

Similarly according to pair wise alignment method we can find alignment of pair (1, 3) is

PQRS__

__RSTU

Since number of mismatching element in pair (1, 3) alignment is 4 and total number of alignment length is 6. Hence distance between second pair of sequence is 4/6. Similarly we can find distance between each and every pair of given solution. Figure 5 is showing distance between each and every pair of given solution.

	1	2	3
2	2/5		
3	4/6	2/5	
4	6/7	4/6	2/5

Fig. 5. Dynamic distance matrix

(B) Edit distance:- The minimum number of editing operation (insertion, deletion, substitution) to transform one sequence to other sequence is called by Edit distance. We have shown by an example to calculate Edit distance matrix.

PQRS_

_QRST

RSTU_

_STUV

Now we can find pair wise alignment of first pair (1,2).

ABCD_

_BCDE

I   D

Here I is for insertion and D is for deletion. Hence two minimum editing operation is needed to convert one sequence to other sequence. Then distance between first pair of sequences is 2.

Similarly, we can find alignment of second pair (1, 3) by using pair wise alignment method.

PQRS__

__RSTU

I I DD

Since in the second pair the minimum number of editing operation to convert one sequence to other sequence is 4. Hence in a similar way we can find Edit distance between all pairs. The minimum number of editing operation in third pair is 6.

PQRS___

___STUV

The minimum number of editing operation in fourth pair is 2.

QRST_

_RSTU

The minimum number of editing operation in fifth pair is 4.

QRST__

__STUV

The minimum number of editing operation in sixth pair is 2.

RSTU_

_STUV

Figure 6 is representing Edit distance matrix.
First matrix:

Now we have chosen one distance matrix in a random manner. Suppose we have chosen Edit distance matrix. After that, we have used UPGMA method to find Guide tree with the help of Edit distance matrix. Distance between first pair is 2.

┌──────────── 1
└──────────── 2

Since according to pair wise alignment the pair (1, 2) is

	1	2	3
2	2		
3	4	2	
4	6	4	2

Fig. 6. Edit distance matrix

PQRS_
_RSTU

Second matrix:

	1,2	3
3	3	
4	5	2

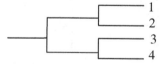

Since according to pair wise alignment the pair (3,4) is

RSTU_
_STUV

Third matrix:

	1,2
3,4	4

Now merge all sequences

Then complete alignment of pair (1, 2) and (3, 4) is

PQRS_
_QRST
RSTU_
_STUV

Now for making a valid solution we have to put a gap in all vacant places.

PQRS_ _ _
QRST _
_ _RSTU_
_ _ _STUV

4 Experimental Analysis

In the experimental analysis we have examined the interpretation of the proposed algorithm.

4.1 Effect of Operators

In this proposed algorithm we have used an improved initial operator and refine mutation operator. This is helpful to performing better than other existing algorithms. We have also designed two sets of experiment one is genetic algorithm with improved operators and other is simple genetic algorithm. For this experiment we have randomly taken 5 datasets (3 from reference set 2 and 2 from reference set 3). We have taken average result after 5 independent runs. We have seen that proposed algorithm performed better in 4 cases out of 5. It proves that advantage of improved initial operator and modified mutation operator. Table 1 is described the results of these experiments in details.

Table 1. Performance test of improve initial generation and simple initial generation

Datasets	Proposed Method	GA with Random initial population
1aboA	**0.825**	0.745
1tvxA	**0.911**	0.815
1ubi	0.721	**0.754**
Kinase	**0.839**	0.811
1ped	**0.804**	0.723
Average Score	**0.82**	0.769

4.2 Performance of Proposed Method

In these experiments we have taken 14 datasets which is explaining in RBT-GA [14]. We have taken also corresponding Bali score of these datasets from [14]. These datasets are outstandingly different in terms of length and number. For examining the interpretation of proposed algorithm, we have compared with well known existence method which is described in RBT-GA [14]. We found 10 dataset out of 14 proposed method performed better than other existence method in reference 2.

Table 2. Experimental results of our proposed method and other existence methods on reference 2 datasets

Name of Datasets	PRRP [19]	SB-PIMA [17]	CLUSTAL X [20]	MULT ALIGN [21]	SAGA [12]	RBT-GA [17]	PROPOSED
1aboA	0.256	0.391	0.65	0.528	0.489	0.812	**0.825**
1idy	0.37	0.000	0.515	0.401	0.548	**0.997**	0.988
1csy	0.35	0.000	0.154	0.154	0.154	0.735	**0.789**
1r69	0.675	0.675	0.675	0.675	0.475	0.9	**0.943**
1tvxA	0.207	0.241	0.552	0.138	0.448	0.891	**0.911**
1tgxA	0.695	0.678	0.727	0.696	0.773	0.835	**0.899**
1ubi	0.056	0.129	0.482	0.000	0.492	**0.795**	0.721
1wit	0.76	0.469	0.557	0.50	0.694	**0.825**	0.794
2trx	0.87	0.85	0.87	0.87	0.87	0.982	**0.988**
1sbp	0.231	0.043	0.217	0.19	0.374	**0.778**	0.748
1havA	0.52	0.259	0.48	0.50	0.448	0.792	**0.810**
1uky	0.351	0.256	0.656	0.585	0.476	0.625	**0.795**
1cpt	0.821	0.884	0.66	0.777	0.776	0.584	**0.894**
1ped	0.881	0.651	0.834	0.741	0.835	0.78	**0.941**
Average Score	0.503	0.394	0.573	0.482	0.560	0.809	**0.856**

We have seen that from Table 2, the proposed algorithm executed better results in 10 test cases out of 14 and the performance of average result is also better than other existing algorithms.

5 Conclusions

In this paper, we have proposed a novel genetic algorithm for solving Multiple Sequence Alignment. We have used Needleman and Wunsch algorithm for generating initial population and we have also used modified mutation operator with the help of Guide tree. To show the efficacy of proposed method we have solved a notable number of experiments. We have also compared the results between genetic algorithm with improved operators and simple genetic algorithms to show the superiority of improved operators. We have taken a significant number of datasets from Bali base 2.0 which is covering approximately all datasets of RBT-GA. In the experimental analysis section we have seen the proposed method is better than most of cases. Since the proposed method is not produce better results in some test cases but at least in these cases results are close to the best solution. We have also seen that average performance of proposed methods is better than other existing methods. Hence we conclude that the proposed method is better than other methods.

References

1. Das, S., Abraham, A., Konar, A.: Swarm intelligence algorithms in bioinformatics. Stud. Comput. Intell. **94**, 113–147 (2008)
2. Wang, L., Jiang, T.: On the complexity of multiple sequence alignment. J. Comput. Biol. **1**, 337–348 (1994)
3. Feng, D.F., Doolittle, R.F.: Progressive sequence alignment as a prerequisite to correct phylogenetic trees. J. Mol. Evolution **25**, 351–360 (1987)
4. Thompson, J.D., Higgins, D.G., Gibson, T.J.: CLUSTALW: improving the sensitivity of progressive multiple sequence alignment through sequence weighting, position-specific gap penalties and weight matrix choice. Nucl. Acids Res. **22**, 4673–4680 (1994)
5. Rabiner, L.R.: A tutorial on hidden Markov models and selected applications in speech recognition. In: Proceedings of the IEEE. vol. 77, pp. 257–285 (1989)
6. Baldi, P., Chauvin, Y., Hunkapiller, T., McClure, M.A.: Hidden Markov Models of biological primary sequence information. Proc. Natl. Acad. Sci. U.S.A. **91**, 1059–1063 (1994)
7. Krogh, A., Brown, M., Mian, I.S., Sjolander, K., Haussler, D.: Hidden Markov models in computational biology: applications to protein modeling. J. Mol. Biol. **235**, 1501–1531 (1994)
8. Eddy, S.R.: Profile hidden Markov models. Bioinformatics **14**, 755–763 (1998)
9. Kim, J., Pramanik, S., Chung, M.J.: Multiple sequence alignment using simulated annealing. Bioinformatics **10**, 419–426 (1994)
10. Lukashin, A.V., Engelbrecht, J., Brunak, S.: Multiple alignment using simulated annealing: branch point definition in human mRNA splicing. Nucl. Acids Res. **20**, 2511–2516 (1992)
11. Chellapilla, K., Fogel, G.B.: Multiple sequence alignment using evolutionary programming. In: Proceedings of the First Congress on Evolution Composition, pp. 445–452 (1999)
12. Notredame, C., Higgins, D.G.: SAGA: sequence alignment by genetic algorithm. Nucl. Acids Res. **24**, 1515–1524 (1996)
13. Thomsen, R.: Evolving the topology of hidden markov models using evolutionary algorithms. In: Guervós, J.J.M., Adamidis, P.A., Beyer, H.G., Fernández-Villacañas, J.L., Schwefel, H.P. (eds.) PPSN 2002. LNCS, vol. 2439, pp. 861–870. Springer, Heidelberg (2002)
14. Taheri, J., Zomaya, A.Y.: RBT-GA: a novel metaheuristic for solving the multiple sequence alignment problem. BMC Genom. **10**, 1–11 (2009)
15. Dayhoff, M.O., Schwartz, R.M., Orcutt, B.C.: A model of evolutionary change in proteins. Atlas Protein Seq. Struct. **5**, 345–351 (1978)
16. Thompson, J.D., Gibson, T.J., Plewniak, F., Jeanmougin, F., Higgins, D.G.: The CLUSTAL − X windows interface: flexible strategies for multiple sequence alignment aided by quality analysis tools. Nucl. Acids Res. **25**, 4876–4882 (1997)
17. Naznin, F., Sarker, R., Essam, D.: Progressive alignment method using genetic algorithm for multiple sequence alignment. IEEE Trans. Evol. Comput. **16**, 615–631 (2012)
18. Yadav, R.K., Banka, H.: Genetic algorithm with improved mutation operator for multiple sequence alignment. In: Mandal, J.K., Satapathy, S.C., Sanyal, M.K., Sarkar, P.P., Mukhopadhyay, A. (eds.) Information Systems Design and Intelligent Applications, pp. 515–524. Springer, New Delhi (2015)

Erratum to: A Hybrid EMD-ANN Model for Stock Price Prediction

Dhanya Jothimani[✉], Ravi Shankar, and Surendra S. Yadav

Department of Management Studies, Indian Institute of Technology Delhi,
New Delhi, India
dhanyajothimani@gmail.com

Erratum to:
Chapter 6 in: B.K. Panigrahi et al. (Eds.)
Swarm, Evolutionary, and Memetic Computing
DOI: 10.1007/978-3-319-48959-9_6

The original version of the chapter starting on p. 60 was revised. The following two references have been added:

11. Jothimani, D., Shankar, R., Yadav, S.S.: Discrete wavelet transform-based prediction of stock index: a study on National Stock Exchange Fifty index. J. Financ. Manage. Anal. **28**(2), 35–49 (2015)
12. Jothimani, D., Shankar, R., Yadav, S.S.: A comparative study of ensemble-based forecasting models for stock index prediction. In: Proceedings of MWAIS 2016, paper 5 (2016). http://aisel.aisnet.org/mwais2016/5

The updated original version of this chapter can be found at DOI: 10.1007/978-3-319-48959-9_6

Author Index

Printed in the United States
By Bookmasters